MW01097433

NEITHER PEACE NOR FREEDOM

Neither Peace nor Freedom

The Cultural Cold War in Latin America

PATRICK IBER

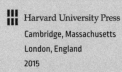 Harvard University Press
Cambridge, Massachusetts
London, England
2015

Copyright © 2015 by the President and Fellows of Harvard College
All rights reserved
Printed in the United States of America

First printing

Library of Congress Cataloging-in-Publication Data

Iber, Patrick, 1981–
    Neither peace nor freedom : the cultural Cold War in Latin America /
Patrick Iber.
        pages cm
    Includes bibliographical references and index.
    ISBN 978-0-674-28604-7 (hardcover : alkaline paper)
    1. Latin America—Politics and government—1948–1980. 2. Cold
War—Political aspects—Latin America. 3. Cold War—Social aspects—
Latin America. 4. Social justice—Latin America. 5. Communism—Latin
America. 6. Democracy—Latin America. 7. Congress for Cultural
Freedom. 8. World Peace Council. 9. Casa de las Américas. I. Title.
F1414.2.I235   2015
303.3'72098—dc23   2015008012

To the memory of my mother
And to Nicole, Isaiah, and Julian,
for the memories to come

Contents

Contents

Introduction

"The intellectuals in Latin America," declared Brazilian sociologist Fernando Henrique Cardoso in 1971, "are the voice of those who cannot speak for themselves." Mexican writer Carlos Fuentes similarly argued, toward the end of the Cold War, that where civil society was repressed, the intellectual had to take on multiple social roles as a "tribune, a member of parliament, a labor leader, a journalist, [and] a redeemer of his society." Both Cardoso and Fuentes were articulating a common understanding of the position of Latin American intellectuals in the second half of the twentieth century. As privileged communicators from a part of the world riven by some of its deepest inequalities, their challenge was not simply to interpret the continent but to change it. Progressive left-wing authors and artists from the region were said to be unusually close to political power. They were appointed to diplomatic posts, they worked to lobby rulers on behalf of an assumed popular voice, they opposed and even assassinated dictators, and they sometimes held high political office themselves.[1]

But the idea that there was in twentieth-century Latin America a cosmopolitan, progressive community of artists and thinkers who could speak for and redeem a region through words and actions was a myth. Not even false, but a myth, for it was an emotive story that obscured a more complex and troubling reality. It was true that the best-known artists from Latin America, with a few notable exceptions, belonged to the political Left. But it was also a divided Left that faced a series of difficult choices. "Every revolutionary," wrote Albert Camus, "ends by becoming either an oppressor or a heretic." Intellectuals' relationships to governments within and outside the region made them both allies and opponents of oppression at the same time. It was not as simple as electing to be an oppressor or a heretic: the choices facing intellectuals from Latin America during the Cold War meant that they were often both simultaneously.[2]

They were not alone, for such were the many dilemmas of the Cold War for intellectuals around the world. The political divisions they debated were heightened by the conflict between the two major world powers: the Soviet Union and the United States. Artists, writers, and other intellectuals on the left, including those in Latin America, tried to pursue justice, peace, and freedom. But, as the historian and antinuclear activist E. P. Thompson wrote, at the onset of the Cold War "the cause of freedom and the cause of peace seemed to break apart"—the idea of freedom being associated with the United States and that of peace with the Soviet Union. In their Cold War struggle, the world's two most powerful states sought dominance in military, economic, scientific, and cultural fields, vying to demonstrate the superiority of capitalist democracy over Communism or vice versa. Education, Stalin explained, is a weapon whose "effectiveness depends on who holds it and against whom it is directed." The Cold War, a U.S. Central Intelligence Agency (CIA) official wrote, was "fought with ideas instead of bombs." The United States and the USSR each assumed that intellectuals would play important roles in influencing public opinion and form the vanguard of social change.[3]

During the Cold War each superpower sponsored organizations whose goals were simultaneously cultural and political, most prominently the World Peace Council (WPC) in the case of the Soviet Union and the CIA-financed Congress for Cultural Freedom (CCF) in that of the United States. Confident in the persuasive weight of "authentic," local voices articulating or reinforcing the messages of Cold War powers, these bodies hoped to attract artists and intellectuals to generate works and ideas that would influence world opinion. The WPC promoted the idea that peace was equal to the interests of the Soviet Union against the warmongering and imperialism inherent in the capitalist West, led by the United States. Although it was headquartered in Europe, the WPC was well represented in Latin America by world-renowned Communist artists: the Mexican painter Diego Rivera, the Brazilian novelist Jorge Amado, and the Chilean poet Pablo Neruda, each of whom devoted his art and years of his life to the cause of peace in the early 1950s and faced persecution for doing so.

The anti-Communist CCF, by contrast, focused on the totalitarian continuities between Nazi Germany and the Soviet Union, insisting that culture could flourish only in the absence of state control and that a just society could not abandon freedom of thought in the way that Communism required. It was brought to Latin America largely by those on the left who had faced political persecution by orthodox Communists during the Spanish Civil War of 1936–1939. These exiled Spaniards shared the anti-Communist priorities of the U.S. government and found local allies in artists and politicians associated with what was known, because of its anti-Communism, as the "Democratic Left." Although its participants spanned the political spectrum, its dominant ethos resembled that of Western European social democracy, with strong anti-Communism attached to moderate social reform in a democratic context. The CCF sponsored conferences, subsidized magazines and book publications, and organized opposition to groups that it viewed as Communist fronts, beginning with the WPC. Established in Europe in 1950 and in Latin America by 1954, it was slowly dismantled after revelations in 1967 that it had largely been financed by the CIA. Like the Communist-aligned organizations it opposed, it too had been a front.

Both the CCF and the WPC were instruments of the propaganda of ideas known as cultural diplomacy: the deliberate exchange of art, music, polemics, students, and scholars for the purpose of shaping international perceptions. But the language of "fronts," inherited from the era, risks reducing the complex dynamics of the Cultural Cold War to a simple story of superpower manipulation. If the independence of intellectuals with respect to the state has been the central issue of the Cultural Cold War, it has sometimes obscured the degree to which the Cultural Cold War was structured not only by state power but also by the intellectual communities of the political Left that came into contact with it. Front groups were indeed instruments of cultural diplomacy, but they were also the work of political and intellectual currents whose existence predated the Cold War, and whose sources lay in what might be described as the international Left's civil war. The arrival of the Cold War meant that the Left's internal conflicts would be inscribed onto superpower competition, and thus that struggles for justice around the world would be refracted through the imperial interests of the United States and the USSR. In Latin America, that would leave the Left with almost no viable options for pursuing its aims without compromising them.

From the point of view of individuals rather than states, the central problem that left-wing intellectuals of the twentieth century tried to solve was how to bring about a humane socialism that would balance social justice and individual freedom. But how that might be achieved in the context of the Cold War was not at all obvious. The debate that unfolded between the midcentury world's two most famous intellectuals illustrates the dilemma most clearly because versions of their argument would play out again and again. Jean-Paul Sartre and Albert Camus shared the vision that intellectuals like themselves should be "engaged"—committed to political participation and responsibility. But at the dawn of the Cold War, they could not agree on whether intellectuals should engage by committing to defend the Communist Party and the Soviet Union as it actually existed. Sartre came to believe that there was no other choice, and that, relatedly, the use of violence to overcome oppression was legitimate and inevitable. Sartre's committed intellectual had to think of himself first as part of a movement, which required self-censorship. "An anti-Communist," he said, "is a dog."[4]

For Camus, the first obligation of the intellectual was to the truth. In his view, the twentieth century had repeatedly justified political crimes with philosophical arguments that could produce plausible abstractions but generated human misery. Soviet partisans, for example, denied elementary truths about their "utopia." "Slave camps under the flag of freedom, massacres justified by philanthropy or by a taste for the superhuman ... cripple judgment," wrote Camus. Camus did not want to countenance murder simply because it was carried out in the name of the oppressed. He was left only with anti-Communism. "The great event of the twentieth century," he announced in the early 1950s, "was the forsaking of the values of freedom by the revolutionary movements."[5]

In the atmosphere of the early Cold War, these views were seemingly incompatible. It was a conflict over politics and personal political conduct, over which of the twentieth century's many models of intellectual life was most morally compelling. Camus's intellectual was a sharpshooter, an exile even in his own land, a denier of dogma—but also an individual, perhaps an individualist. He could not quiet uncomfortable truths about the failures of revolutionary societies. But in Sartre's view, Camus's anti-Communism cut him off from the reality of prosaic violence in the capitalist and imperialist West, and from the only people who truly constituted a movement that could challenge injustice. Sartre's model of intellectual life in the early 1950s was committed to affiliation with a movement whose faults could be only hesitatingly and quietly acknowledged, if at all. Camus's position required the intellectual to be a dissenting voice; Sartre's view—although it would evolve—seemed to make dissent impossible.[6]

The problems Sartre and Camus posed were universal, but different conditions gave them different inflections as they moved throughout the globe. Peruvian writer Mario Vargas Llosa, for example, remembered reading the debates between Sartre and Camus in the 1960s and thinking that Sartre had the better of the argument. The struggle against imperialism and for national self-determination and socialism justified a great deal of discretion. But Vargas Llosa, like many others, would eventually conclude that he had been too quick to dismiss the arguments of Camus. Years of dealing with actual revolutionary governments, from the Soviet Union to Cuba, convinced him that the flaws of revolutionary movements and societies were too great to be passed over in the silence of solidarity and had to be confronted directly. But others, such as the Colombian writer Gabriel García Márquez, remained solidly in the revolutionary camp. García Márquez was Fidel Castro's frequent guest and, in the words of one critic, Castro's "most important instrument of public relations on the international front." The relationship between Vargas Llosa, who grew increasingly right-wing over the course of the 1970s, and the staunchly left-wing García Márquez—perhaps the two most successful Latin American novelists of their generation—deteriorated to such a degree that, as with Sartre and Camus, their friendship could not be maintained. When they met at a theater in Mexico in 1976, Vargas Llosa threw what has been described as the "most famous punch in the history of Latin America," laying out a dazed García Márquez.[7]

But the Cultural Cold War was not simply a matter of literary quarrels. It was the expression in art and ideas of a war that was not fought with weapons but with social systems. It has been studied closely in the North Atlantic world of Europe and the United States, where it is almost always told as a story of the corruption of intellectual life by state power. For those of a liberal cast of mind, the primary sinners were the Communists and their fellow travelers who abetted Stalinist totalitarianism. In the tradition of Julien Benda's influential 1927 work *La trahison des clercs*, which argues that intellectuals should be autonomous and dedicated to universal values rather than responsible for inflaming political passions, many historians have judged that the efforts of Cold War intellectuals to align themselves with the oppressed were morally obtuse failures. The historian Tony Judt, for example, noted that "a disconcerting number of prominent intellectuals on Right and Left alike proved strikingly irresponsible in their insouciant propensity for encouraging violence to others at a safe distance from themselves." Others put it even more strongly, arguing that twentieth-century intellectuals were "philotyrannical": admirers at a distance, or even up close, of murderous and repressive regimes in Nazi Germany and the Soviet Union. "Distinguished professors, gifted poets, and influential journalists," wrote Mark Lilla, "summoned their talents to convince all who would listen that modern tyrants were liberators and that their unconscionable crimes were noble, when seen in the proper perspective." Left-wing revolution was seductive, and since it did not occur in Western Europe or the United States in the twentieth century, intellectuals there could imagine it as a solution to problems they had without confronting the other problems it would create.[8]

But the end of the Cold War was widely understood as a victory for liberal democracy and its economic counterpart, capitalism, which produces no shortage of its own injustices. Another line of scholarship, then, has focused not on the transgressions of the Communists but on those of the anti-Communists, especially those who belonged to the CCF. To this end, the intellectual model usually invoked is not Benda but the Italian Marxist Antonio Gramsci. In contrast to Benda, Gramsci thought that the idea of the autonomous, freethinking intellectual was a convenient fiction. In the early 1930s, writing from a fascist jail, Gramsci warned that intellectuals who considered themselves free of class commitment would in fact organize the defense of society's dominant classes. Gramsci was interested in the "organic" intellectuals produced by class struggle, especially those aligned with the proletariat to undermine the combination of coercion and consent—what he called hegemony—underlying an unjust capitalist social order.[9]

The Cultural Cold War first became a subject of intense political debate in the United States because of revelations in 1966 and 1967 that the CIA, through the CCF and other organizations, had been sponsoring the work of artists, students, and intellectuals at home and abroad. The exposure of the CIA's role meant that a quasi-Gramscian critique was readily available, even if it did not use Gramsci's exact language. An early critical essay by Christopher Lasch, for example, argued that "men who have never been able to conceive of ideas as anything but instruments of national power"—the (North) American intellectuals who had participated in the CCF—"were the sponsors of 'cultural freedom.'" Historians have since debated the merits of Lasch's assertion. Some who sympathized with the antitotalitarian politics of the CCF wrote histories that cast its members as heroic defenders of liberty who dispelled the illusions of Stalinist fellow travelers, and that made the CIA out to be a relatively disinterested and distant sponsor of their work. But subsequent scholarship demolished the notion of the disinterested CIA. Many CCF participants knew of the connection. The CIA's presence, unsurprisingly, shaped the priorities of the organization. In Gramscian terms, CCF members have been likened to the intellectual class produced to articulate the defense of a reformed global capitalism: the "organic intellectuals" of the welfare state. In so doing, it has been argued, liberal Cold War intellectuals and foundations, aligned with the United States, helped establish the basis of U.S. global hegemony, cultural domination, and imperialism. For many scholars who see the Cultural Cold War primarily as an expression of U.S.

government power, the collusion of anti-Communists in the construction of capitalist hegemony is its greatest sin and its lasting legacy.[10]

A careful examination of the documentary record, however, has blurred such sharply drawn images. Without question, the CIA would not have funded the CCF without the intention to advance the interests of the United States. But participation in front organizations did not mean that affiliated intellectuals were reduced to puppets on a string. The CIA did not always get the responses that it sought, even from the organizations it supposedly controlled. Multiple agendas were in play, and anti-Communists, including those on the political Left, had many reasons for their actions and their strategic alliances with the U.S. government.[11]

To be sure, anti-Communists could have seen themselves as independent and uninterested in furthering U.S. hegemony and still have done so through their actions. But the Cultural Cold War needs to be understood on its own terms rather than simply as a history of state institutions and objectives. Although one should not lose sight of the ways in which both Communist and anti-Communist intellectuals could act as accessories of imperial state power, the Cultural Cold War was also a bottom-up phenomenon, not one directed solely from above. It was an integral part of the history of the Left in the twentieth century, and its protagonists included not only spy agencies but also artists, scholars, union leaders, and politicians, who tried to use the conflict as a way of advancing their agendas and visions. Their successes and failures—mostly the latter—in trying to find a path toward a humane socialism helped define and set the limits of the meaning democracy itself would have during the Cold War.[12]

Making democracy meaningful was a particularly acute problem in Latin America, where the challenges of building socially just societies were enormous. In major countries like Brazil and Mexico, only about one in four was considered literate at the beginning of the twentieth century. Caste and race limited opportunities for people of indigenous and African descent, and in some places, labor relations resembling slavery persisted. Sovereignty was constrained by the incursions of foreign empires, especially the rising United States. Electoral democracy was not always part of the Left's agenda. The struggle against injustice sometimes took the form of campaigns to end dictatorship and inaugurate electoral democracy; at other times, movements were democratic in the much wider sense of seeking a more equitable distribution of land, resources, or power in a way that would mollify oppression and undermine established hierarchies. Building politically inclusive and just societies—constructing democracies in more than name alone—proved to be the region's central problem of the twentieth century.[13]

Therefore, if the Cultural Cold War was a universal condition for engaged intellectuals in the second half of the twentieth century, two major factors gave its expression in Latin America unique characteristics. One was the unbalanced and overwhelming power of the United States in the region. The other was the specter of possible social revolution—and the presence of postrevolutionary governments that also made claims on intellectuals' work and authority. Three countries—Mexico in 1920, Cuba in 1959, and Nicaragua in 1979—experienced social revolutions that triumphed in part through force of arms, while Chile elected a Marxist in 1970. Beyond them, imminent revolution seemed a real possibility to many across the region, both those who hoped for it and those who feared it.

The problem that intellectuals from the region would face in their relationships with revolutionary states was therefore an intimate rather than an abstract one. Artists and intellectuals had the capacity to inspire, to strategize, to portray the injustices of the present, and, perhaps above all, to symbolize the struggle for justice. "I arrived at the revolution by way of poetry," wrote the Salvadoran poet Roque Dalton to a friend; "You can arrive . . . at poetry by way of revolution." Many committed important parts of their lives to bring it about. Gabriel García Márquez was undoubtedly exaggerating when he quipped that "in the history of power in Latin America, there are only military dictatorships or intellectuals." But the point that followed was important: "No wonder then . . . that there was so much coddling of the intellectuals by the State. Under these circumstances, one cannot always be completely independent."[14]

Complete independence from the state was not really the norm for intellectual life anywhere, but different social and economic arrangements tied up with state power did lead to different possibilities for sustaining intellectual work in Latin America. The category "Latin America" itself is not especially coherent historically, and the category "Latin American intellectual" is even less so. But the most influential interpretation of secular intellectual life in Latin America has drawn attention to the literate minorities that implemented bureaucracy and law in the colonial empires, creating what Uruguayan critic Ángel Rama described as "lettered cities," islands of symbolic expertise surrounded by seas of illiteracy. Intellectuals had plentiful opportunities for contact with political power; since there were relatively few universities that could give steady employment to them, they were sometimes sustained by diplomatic posts, valued by their governments at home for the aura of cultural achievement that they could convey. At the end of the nineteenth century, the intellectuals who were closest to state power were interested in economic modernization, influenced by local and global trends from positivism and socialism to liberalism and nationalism, and by no means opposed to authoritarian political methods.[15] But when the word "intellectual" came into use in fin de siècle France, describing a person of formal learning who stepped into the public sphere to act as a voice of moral conscience against injustice and as a champion of the oppressed, it was a concept that was immediately intelligible across the Atlantic. The term was in use in Latin America within two years.[16]

In the twentieth century, revolution and the possibility of revolutions carved out new roles for intellectuals to play. Creating meaningful democracy and social inclusion would require making it possible for more people to participate in governing their own lives, and that meant expanding access to education and literacy. Exposure to art—from poetry to cinema—was considered not a luxury but a sign of a more inclusive and just social order. Mexico's postrevolutionary state, for example, sponsored the production of murals on public buildings, and one of the first acts of Cuba's revolutionary government was to establish an institute for cinema that both produced new movies and sent mobile trucks around the country to show films to the poor. Expanding adult literacy came to be seen as an essential precondition of greater social equality, and the enjoyment of culture as a sign of the flourishing of human life freed from oppression.

But if bringing culture to the poor seemed an essential step, basic literacy could not be taught in a vacuum. Citizens had to be shaped into revolutionary subjects; they needed not only education but training, and for that, propaganda was necessary. This propaganda would have to be created or commissioned not by some abstract revolution but by agencies of the governments that claimed to represent the history, the heroes, the legacy, and the future of the nation. Postrevolutionary situations inevitably provoked debates about the responsibility of intellectuals to harmonize with the messages of the state in its efforts to create new forms of consciousness among the people. Training was not just for the poor: both Mexico and Cuba established publishing houses to subsidize the production of books for elite as well as mass audiences. But what could be done if the state grew repressive in the people's name? The true importance of debates about the responsibility of intellectuals did not lie in what they had to say regarding a small group of generally privileged artists and writers. These debates mattered because they were also contests over the rights all people should have in revolutionary times, and in particular, whether they should have the right to object and dissent to the course of political change. When people lost that right, banished, jailed, and silenced intellectuals were some of the most powerful symbols of its absence. Latin America's Cultural Cold War overlapped with and was part of global currents, but it had a special urgency because it involved not just abstract questions of revolutionary solidarity but day-to-day problems of affiliation, support, and dissent.[17]

In the years after its military victory in 1959, the Cuban Revolution thoroughly changed the landscape of Latin America's Cultural Cold War. Many who hoped for revolutionary change found the Soviet Union eclipsed in their minds by the more proximate star of a Latin American country that had defied the United States. Through its international cultural institution known as Casa de las Américas, the Cuban Revolution promoted a more militarized and hard-edged version of Communism than even the Soviet Union had offered. Unlike the rest of the world, Latin America's Cultural Cold War had three international players: the Soviet Union, the United States, and Cuba, which was a small country with the foreign policy ambitions of a much larger one. Many of those who took up arms in the 1960s and 1970s to spread the revolution on the model of the one in Cuba were students and professors who were inspired by the life and death of Che Guevara. "The most sacred thing in the world [is] the title of writer," wrote Che. Trained as a doctor, Guevara disavowed the status of an intellectual for himself but made journeys, even up to his death, with a rucksack full of books and ammunition. To his many admirers, he represented the unity of thought and action, but even among those skeptical of his methods it was a widely shared assumption of Latin America's 1960s that studying society could contribute to changing it.[18]

The other major difference between the Cultural Cold War of the North Atlantic and that of Latin America was the overwhelming power of the United States in the region. Western Europe, which was understood as the first battleground of the Cultural Cold War, also lived under U.S. hegemony in the era after World War II. But if Western Europe was part of a U.S. empire, U.S. imperialism there took a milder form that preserved a good measure of national sovereignty and allowed European states to construct stronger welfare institutions even than those of the United States. Latin America, by contract, contended with a harsher form of U.S. empire. Latin America, it has been argued, has frequently served as a kind of laboratory for the United States to experiment with forms of power that it later deployed elsewhere. When the United States defeated Spain in 1898, taking possession of Puerto Rico and the Philippines and de facto control of Cuba, it was a rising power but not yet a world empire. But it was in Latin America that various imperial strategies would be tried. Especially in the Caribbean (as well as the Philippines), the United States used military intervention and occupation to ensure that debts were paid and that its political and security interests were met. Often these interventions were carried out in the name of democracy and with the logic of a developmentalist liberalism, undergirded by the assumption that the path to modernity for all nations would resemble that of the United States: a market economy and a capitalist democracy. Yet however committed to democracy U.S. occupations were in the abstract, they generally left dictatorships friendly to U.S. business interests in their wake. After he retired, the marine major general who oversaw or participated in many of the occupations of the first decades of the twentieth century confessed, "I was a racketeer for capitalism."[19]

Among the techniques that the United States pioneered in Latin America was cultural diplomacy. As early as the 1920s, the United States began the long process of institutionalizing the work of missionaries and foundations that operated in the region. Rhetorically, the United States employed the idea of Pan-Americanism: the idea that the nations of the Western Hemisphere had a common history and rejected "foreign" doctrines. But the imperial role that the United States played in the region was the very fact that Nazi propaganda came to emphasize as Germany sought to extend its influence in Latin America in the 1930s. Thus, as in many imperial ventures, a light commitment by the United States was pushed ever deeper by the encroachment of a rival. In response to the growing threat of Nazi propaganda, the United States created increasingly formal peacetime programs of cultural diplomacy. The "diplomacy of ideas" coincided with the administration of Franklin Roosevelt and his Good Neighbor Policy toward Latin America that promised an end to military occupations; in that context, increased efforts at cultural diplomacy were part of a strategy for pursuing mutually beneficial exchange without incurring the costs of formal empire.[20]

At the end of World War II, the terms of the conflict changed. With atomic weapons, the destructive potential of open conflict proved too great for either the United States or the USSR to bear. Instead, the Cold War would be a conflict suffered most directly by people living outside the nations of its superpower antagonists as Cold War politics grew like strangling vines through the world's existing political vegetation. Covert action, including that of the CIA, created in 1947, often tried to substitute for open conflict, but that did not make it peaceful. And wartime propaganda was transformed by covert action into "psychological warfare," never again to be dismantled simply because the United States was not technically at war. Through participation in foreign exhibitions, the public efforts of the United States Information Agency, and covert CIA funding of unions, presses, newspapers, radio, films, and intellectuals, the United States tried to present a vision of itself as the global leader in the defense of freedom and democracy.[21]

Although Latin America had been a testing ground for U.S. government cultural diplomacy, it was not an area of high priority in the early years of the Cold War. The region had served its purpose as a supplier of vital materials to the U.S. war machine during World War II, and the United States expected it to remain firmly in its Cold War column. The Soviet Union lacked detailed information about the region, but it could certainly read a map, and it expected the same. Instead of the economic aid from the United States that Latin American nations had hoped would follow the end of the war, they got security agreements and a treaty of hemispheric mutual defense. The United States began relying on frequently repressive secret police forces throughout the region to provide it with information about Communist threats. The nonintervention promise of the Good Neighbor Policy, for what it had been worth, fell away; intervention became the norm, most dramatically in the CIA's simultaneously bumbling and sinister effort to oust the left-wing nationalist government of Jacobo Arbenz in Guatemala in 1954. There were some "cultural" efforts as well: the United States Information Agency ran a semisecret book-publishing program and tried to produce newsreels slanted favorably to the United States. The CIA did parallel work, supporting favored newspapers and organizations like the CCF with a growing presence in the region.[22]

U.S. policy toward Latin America during the Cold War aimed to stamp out Communism in the region and to maintain the prerogatives of empire. Multiple policy strands coexisted and overlapped: some sought more liberal allies to develop the region, while others thought that dictatorships would make the best partners. As formulated by President Kennedy, the dictum was "There are three possibilities in descending order of preference: a decent democratic regime, a continuation of [dictatorship] or a [leftist] Castro regime. We ought to aim at the first, but we really can't renounce the second until we are sure that we can avoid the third." But even when U.S. policies were nominally committed to producing liberal outcomes and political democracy, their outcomes could still be illiberal. For that reason, the history of Latin America has often played an important role as a corrective to more triumphal accounts of U.S. victory in the Cold War, where it can serve either as a reminder of the mournfully high cost of a just victory or as evidence to support the argument that, as dreadful as the politics of the Soviet Union were, justice was not the point of the struggle at all. The historian John Coatsworth has calculated that between 1960 and 1990 anti-Communist Latin America was more repressive than the Soviet bloc when measured by the numbers of political prisoners, victims of torture, and executions of political dissenters. Although U.S. policies were not always the proximate cause of this violence, and the Latin American Right had its own reasons for the actions it took to suppress political opponents, the United States both aided dictatorships and helped bring them about, and the climate of paranoid anti-Communism that the United States encouraged was a significant factor in the darkness of Latin America's Cold War years.[23]

And so the struggle for national sovereignty and anti-imperialism would almost always be a struggle with the United States, with significant consequences for the Cultural Cold War. It was not that the United States was universally disliked or unwelcome; there were many who admired its industry, its democracy, or its level of development. But among intellectuals on the left, for whom anti-imperialism was a major concern, it made anti-Communism an unpopular heritage, sometimes disavowed even by those who seemed to belong.[24] It was not especially surprising that the CCF found its first allies in Latin America among the communities of Spanish exiles, for whom anti-Communism did not seem quite so tainted with imperial interests. Latin America's Cold War was unusual because, with the United States as the imperial power, liberation and anti-Communism were often in tension, if not total conflict.

With that background, the general shape of the Cultural Cold War in Latin America can come into relief. Like its European counterpart, it was based on the debates and practices of the political Left. At the intersection of world and regional history, Mexico City became a key node in the global debate. The combination of the Mexican Revolution, the experiences of the European Popular Front of the 1930s, and the Spanish Civil War provided the foundational experiences that produced the conditions of the Cultural Cold War, with the participation of figures ranging from the Mexican painters Diego Rivera and David Álfaro Siqueiros to European exiles like Victor Serge, Julián Gorkin, and Leon Trotsky. In the 1930s and early 1940s these figures and the groups associated with them debated the relationship of the intellectual to revolution, and especially to Communism, in ways that established the fundamental cleavage of the Cultural Cold War: the identification of anti-Communism with artistic independence from state and party.

Naturally, the emergence of the diplomatic Cold War after World War II did have a considerable impact on the way in which the Cultural Cold

War was conducted: it would give both foundation and furnishings to a prefabricated structure. The Soviet-aligned WPC held symposia and conferences, organized signature drives, published books and magazines, and inspired artistic production, all with the goal of depicting the United States as the great threat to peace and the Soviet Union as the paladin of justice and the defender of national sovereignty. Before Stalin's death in 1953, the Soviet Union had made efforts to reintroduce artistic control in the form of the official doctrine of socialist realism, and Communist artists and those who sympathized with its causes—such as Pablo Picasso, whose doves popularized the bird as a secular symbol of peace—tried to adapt to those standards to inspire support for peace-as-Communism. The Latin American artists who volunteered for the WPC, such as Pablo Neruda, Jorge Amado, and Diego Rivera, all tried to produce art that conformed to official Soviet socialist realism, as well as to organize support for the Soviet position.

For former Communists, Trotskyists, social democrats, liberals, and—perhaps most important—the U.S. government, Soviet-aligned WPC activism provoked a counterreaction. Generally led by former Communists and dissident Trotskyists, campaigns to counter WPC propaganda emerged everywhere. Across Latin America and elsewhere, people volunteered for the cause, and they often did so by offering their services to the most powerful anti-Soviet ally they could imagine: the government of the United States. These relationships were eventually knit together by the CIA into the CCF. Its first meeting was held in 1950, and if it was not a mirror image of the WPC, it was at least a fun-house reflection. Both groups sought to mobilize cultural production alongside political propaganda—imbuing the former with the spirit of the latter—as part of larger political projects that concealed the interests of the states that made them possible.

In response to the radicalization of the Cuban Revolution in the early 1960s, the CCF sought to reorganize. Rather than present a desiccated and transplanted European anti-Communism, it sought to remake itself for the 1960s on the basis of a sophisticated, cosmopolitan, and scholarly foundation. In Europe the CCF is considered to have been effective in the 1950s and out-of-touch by the 1960s; in Latin America the opposite was true. It reshaped itself from a kind of anti-WPC into an anti–Casa de las Américas. Latin America became the largest area program of the CCF, and it would be only a slight exaggeration to say that the CCF began life as an organization for combating Communism in Europe and ended it as one for combating the appeal of Castro in Latin America. After struggling to eliminate reactionary personnel from its national offices, it launched the magazine *Mundo Nuevo* in 1966, which aimed for engaged dialogue on

Cuba and featured a list of authors in its early issues that would define the boom in Latin American letters then under way. Its move toward brokering a cultural peace was met with hostility by an increasingly radical *Casa de las Américas*. *Mundo Nuevo*'s attempt at outreach was seen by *Casa* intellectuals as a sophisticated maneuver of U.S. cultural imperialism. In one way, this proved prescient because it was soon revealed publicly that the CCF and, by extension, *Mundo Nuevo,* would never have existed without CIA support. This only bolstered the Cuban posture, already hostile to dialogue and criticism, of further justifying political repression within Cuba by associating dissent with U.S. imperial interests.

Many studies of the Cultural Cold War in Latin America begin with the Cuban Revolution of 1959, at least ten if not forty years too late. They focus on the phenomenon of the Latin American 1960s and especially the writers of the boom generation. Particular attention has been given to the rivalry between *Casa de las Américas* and *Mundo Nuevo*. *Casa* was proudly affiliated with the Cuban government, of course, but scholars have debated, in parallel to other conversations about the Cultural Cold War, to what degree *Mundo Nuevo* was an instrument of U.S. propaganda. Some have focused on the ways in which *Mundo Nuevo* promoted theories and ideas that were useful to the United States, while others have noted its criticism of U.S. policies and have seen in it and in related ventures some potential for projects that were counterhegemonic.[25]

But a narrow focus on writers has often made it impossible for the Cultural Cold War to be situated within the political currents that make it intelligible. The evidence from the archives and public records of the institutions of Latin America's Cultural Cold War make clear that its course was influenced by debate within the Left as well as its Cold War context. Two apparently contradictory things are simultaneously true. On the one hand, many intellectuals from Latin America sought ways out of Cold War binaries. On the other, they were also responsible for inviting the Cold War in, hoping to use it to advance their interests. That none found great success illuminates the tragedy of the Left in Latin America's Cold War.

In much of Europe the Cold War saw the expansion of social democratic governments with robust welfare states, political freedom, and electoral democracy. Similar projects were much less successful in Latin America despite (or perhaps because of) its deeply unequal societies. Why did social democracy not flourish in Latin America? Why did the effort to define and build a humane socialism in the region fail? Three major arguments have been offered in explanation. One posits that Latin American democracy experienced relatively few gains because of a decision by the Left in the wake of the Cuban Revolution to abandon democracy in favor of Marxist fantasies and the mythology of revolutionary change carried out by small groups of soldiers. A rival explanation imagines democracy as a moderate position and explains that oscillation between "two devils," the extreme Right and the extreme Left, made gradual progress impossible. Alternatively, many argue that the Left's democratic visions, including those of grassroots Marxists, were simply crushed by reactionary alliances of Latin American conservatives with U.S. backing.[26]

The history of the region's intellectuals during the Cold War suggests a different framing of the problem of Latin America's missing social democracy altogether: it shows that each of the Left's currents made important contributions to building and outlining a more just society, but each was also blind in important ways to the destructive elements of its own strategy and vision. In an environment that was partly their own creation and partly imposed on them, artists and intellectuals formed transnational communities that sought to bring a humane socialism to Latin America, but they repeatedly found that their attempts to formulate solutions were tangled up in the interests of empires. They sought independence but could not avoid having the problems of their sponsors—whether the CIA, the Soviet Union, or revolutionary Cuba—become their own.

Cold War debate tended to reduce front groups to the interests of their sponsors, casting each participant in them as nothing more than a warrior in the service of a foreign empire. Such legends deny that multiple logics operate wherever collective action is taken. Although inevitably partial, that reasoning captured enough truth to serve as justification for the suppression of dissent supposedly made illegitimate by its foreign nature. This dynamic recurred throughout the Cold War—and after—where accusations of foreign entanglement served as proxies to delegitimize one's political opponents. If it is true that responses to war should be proportionate to the threat, it has always been the case that responses to the Cultural Cold War have far exceeded the potential of its works to cause harm. The Soviet-sponsored peace movement was suppressed across the "West"; the CCF sometimes defended regimes inimical to "cultural freedom" simply because they were anti-Communist; and, later, revolutionary Cuba exaggerated the importance of the CCF to justify the suppression of internal critics. But the projects of cultural hegemony, even those of the United States, were porous rather than solid. They regularly failed to meet their objectives and sometimes acted in a way that was seemingly indifferent to the interests of empire. Occasionally their most serious consequences proved unintentionally inimical to their patron's plans.

Mundo Nuevo and *Casa de las Américas* became great rivals, for example, and are generally seen as opposites. But the CCF and its personnel had actually played important roles in campaigns to depose Fidel Castro's dictatorial predecessor, Fulgencio Batista, and even participated in Casa de las Américas events in the early years of the Cuban Revolution. Communist fronts could take surprising directions as well: the WPC aligned itself with a significant left-wing social movement in Mexico in the early 1960s known as the Movimiento de Liberación Nacional (MLN). The MLN overtook the peace agenda and defended civil liberties in Mexico. Supporters of Cuba and the Soviet Union, when faced with authoritarian anti-Communism, sometimes defied expectations by becoming some of democracy's best defenders.

By the early 1970s the major front groups of Latin America's Cultural Cold War had been exhausted. The WPC had been repressed and was discredited by its Stalinist associations; the CCF, for its connection to the United States; and Casa de las Américas because of the Cuban government's jailing of a prominent poet in 1971, who was then forced to perform a public self-criticism that reminded many of Stalinist practices. But if the high tide of the Cultural Cold War had receded by the mid-1970s, its watermark remained. The fact that the CCF, the WPC, and Casa were fronts had certainly imposed limitations on their actions. Members of these groups framed issues in ways that made it close to impossible to see their patrons in a negative light. Partisans of the Soviet-sponsored WPC had defended as pacific attempts by the Soviet Union to attain its own security, even through violence, but had defined as warmongering similar actions by the United States. Members of the CIA-sponsored CCF generally criticized the United States only for its "errors" in deviating from an ideal, imagined anti-Communist liberalism and had no coherent plan to help the United States support the region's anti-Communist Left. The commitment of Casa-affiliated intellectuals to anti-imperialism and defense of the revolution made criticism of the Cuban government and its widespread violation of human rights next to impossible. All the fronts unquestionably also provided cover for spies or for the collection of intelligence and could not have existed without the financial backing of their patrons.

Latin America's Cultural Cold War was farce and tragedy not in sequence but simultaneously. For intellectuals engaged in politics, and for the political movements that they supported, there were only troubling options. Communists were repressed, so although their utopias eschewed the traditional freedoms of liberal societies, in the Latin American context, they could sometimes act as the defenders of civil liberties. But the Sartrean position, followed by many intellectuals in Latin America, that the everyday violence of society justified retributive violence was plausible and even correct—except that the violence that it inspired rarely solved the problems it intended to and created others besides. Those who opted for a Camus-like route would find that their moderate socialism could come only via a crooked alliance with the United States, and their reforms would have to be timid, halting, inadequate to the task, and easily appropriated by the Right. Each camp would accuse the others of corruption and of operating in the service of foreign empire. But it was not so much an issue of corruption as of the inscription of intellectuals' preexisting campaigns onto the Cold War. The evidence from Latin America suggests that the Cultural Cold War is best understood within a framework of "ironic Gramscianism"—the pursuit of cultural hegemony through a combination of coercion and consent, incorporating many agendas. But the consequences were so varied that cultural fronts produced nearly as many ironies as they did movements in the direction that their patrons hoped. State sponsorship was accepted and mobilized, but it bore unexpected costs. Compromise—perhaps sometimes even corruption—was not an exception; it was the natural condition of the engaged intellectual. And the experience of Latin America's Left during the Cold War was less a betrayal of democracy than a true paucity of options. The failures of each front group show how difficult it would be to build a more democratic politics in the environment of the Cold War. Social democracy during Latin America's Cold War did not fail because the wrong path was chosen, but because all the paths that could be imagined were so tangled.

CHAPTER ONE

Exile and Dissent in the Making
of the Cultural Cold War

"Nothing of us has a heart condition or the slightest intention to commit suicide," they wrote in a letter addressed to the president of Mexico in January 1942, but still they feared for their lives. The writers were Victor Serge, a Belgian-born Russian novelist, the French socialist Marceau Pivert, and the Spaniard Julián Gorkin, secretary general of a small dissident Spanish Marxist party persecuted by Communist authorities during the Spanish Civil War. All three were weathering World War II in Mexico City, seemingly a world away from a European continent engulfed in war. Yet they remained in the middle of the struggle, and although they were all, in the language of the day, "men of the Left," the immediate danger they faced came not from the fascist Axis but from Soviet-aligned Communists.[1]

Serge, Gorkin, and Pivert had all been sympathizers, if not followers, of the Communist alternative represented by Leon Trotsky, murdered in the study of his Mexico City home two years earlier by a Spanish Soviet agent with an ice ax. By 1942, when they wrote their letter, the Soviet Union and the United States were allies in the war effort against Nazi Germany and the Axis powers, and Mexico would soon officially join the Allied cause. The three men insisted that this wartime alliance should not make criticism of the Soviet Union impermissible and, as a result of their outspokenness, found their Mexico City homes conspicuously and threateningly monitored by orthodox Communist political opponents. If they were found dead, they wanted it publicly known that no one should accept that the end of their lives had arrived by accident.

Peril seemed to mount. The men were accused of heading a Nazi fifth column in Mexico, and a coordinated campaign of slander flowed from the pen of Otto Katz, a Czech journalist who had been part of the Comintern's cultural propaganda apparatus for more than a decade. Writing as

Reproduction of a Communist political cartoon that links Nazism to Trotskyism. The tree growing from the skull of Trotsky is inscribed with swastikas and the names of Victor Serge, Julián Gorkin, Marceau Pivert, Gustav Regler, and one actual Trotskyist, the Spaniard Grandizo Munis. When Regler, Gorkin, Serge, and Pivert reproduced the cartoon in a pamphlet produced to defend themselves, they added a caption that reads "Stalinism openly preaches murder. After felling Trotsky, it announces our liquidation." Image courtesy Archivo General de la Nación, "Marceau Pivert Aujard y Otros," July 1944, Dirección General de Investigaciones Políticas y Sociales (DGIPS), box 121, folder 46.

André Simone, Katz enjoyed the protection of the labor newspaper *El Popular,* whose pro-Soviet patron loathed anything redolent of Trotskyism. News of other deaths arrived in the months that followed: Two Jewish trade unionists from Poland, Henryk Erlich and Victor Alter, were executed in the Soviet Union for advocating more democratic versions of socialism. Carlo Tresca, an Italian antifascist and anti-Communist, was gunned down in the streets of New York. Gorkin had received a letter from Tresca a few weeks before his death stating that he had been having a violent debate with the Italian Communist Vittorio Vidali, and Gorkin suspected that Vidali was responsible for the murder. Although Gorkin was likely wrong—the available evidence points to a Mafia assassin—Gorkin and his associates believed that advocacy of a more democratic socialism than what Stalin offered was becoming a deadly risk.[2]

Serge, Gorkin, and Pivert planned a memorial for Erlich, Alter, and Tresca for the night of 1 April 1943. As they convened in the hall of the Centro Cultural Ibero-Mexicano, a menacing crowd gathered outside. Dozens of men, many of them members of pro-Communist unions, held revolvers, knives, and pieces of broken furniture. Pushing their way into the hall, they yelled "You are Germans! Enemies of Mexico!" A thrown knife struck a Spanish exile who was shielding Serge's daughter, bathing her in his blood. Another blow dented Gorkin's skull. And still the police were nowhere to be seen.[3]

Traditionally, the Cultural Cold War has been seen as part of a clash of empires: an extended argument in poetry and prose, sponsored by the United States and the Soviet Union, to claim the moral high ground and the superiority of capitalism over socialism or vice versa. But in 1942 and 1943 Serge, Pivert, and Gorkin—political writers all—were at risk not precisely because of superpower antagonism but because of a struggle for political and ideological supremacy within the international Left. If their memorial had taken place a few years later, it might have been seen as one of the key moments of the early Cultural Cold War. But the year was 1943, and instead it is evidence both of the porousness of the boundaries of the Cold War and that the foundations of the Cultural Cold War lay in the fractured history of the global Left.

The Cold War, and even more so its cultural counterpart, has no agreed-on beginning. Even given the traditional dating to the late 1940s, it seemed to arrive at different places at different moments. If it came to a clear end with the fall of the Soviet Union in 1991, this too is only in retrospect: the Cold War was repeatedly declared over while it continued to take place. Focusing on ideological competition, some historians have made the Cold War a phenomenon of most of the "short twentieth century," from the Russian Revolution to the fall of the Soviet Union. Seen in this light, the Cold War was a competition over the best way of organizing a just and modern society. It was also global, a kind of international civil war, because of the way in which it elevated political struggle within nations to civilizational heights, justifying repression to defend one system of arranging human affairs over another. Certainly for the world outside Europe, including Latin America, cycles of anti-Communist repression and foreign intervention predated the official years of the Cold War.[4]

Similarly, the particularly Cultural Cold War was built on what could be described as an international civil war within the global Left to define the ideas and practices that would guide political change. The divisions were evident at least from the time the Russian Revolution created an existing form of Communism and, in the Communist International (Comintern), a vehicle for its global dissemination. State interests—essential though they were when U.S.-Soviet diplomatic tensions settled into place over the course of the late 1940s—in many ways only hitched themselves to these existing conflicts. Superpower rivalry came to guarantee that the Cultural Cold War would be relatively well financed, but it began in the Left's internal conflicts and its troubled relationship with dissenters.

Because Mexico City became a haven for left-wing exiles, including Trotsky, Serge, Pivert, and Gorkin, it was one of the key nodes in the global struggle. There, the key events of the Cultural Cold War had little to do with the United States or its government; instead, they originated in the intersection of the legacies of the Mexican Revolution, dissent from Stalinism, and the turmoil of the Spanish Civil War of 1936–1939. The ideological conflict persisted even in the period of formal alliance between the rival powers created by World War II. Mexico City in the 1940s was simultaneously a Mexican, a Latin American, and a global city, and each layer contributed to laying the foundations of the Cultural Cold War to come.

Many of the European exiles who arrived in Mexico in the late 1930s and early 1940s knew almost nothing about the country that was granting them the right to refuge: Trotsky's personal secretary remembers hastily reading an old encyclopedia article about Mexico on the day before boarding the boat that bore him across the Atlantic. But their ignorance was no obstacle, for Mexico granted asylum to left-wing political refugees with more generosity than any other state in the world, making it a haven for tens of thousands. It was an unexpected lifeline and, for some, like Trotsky, an equally unexpected graveyard.[5]

Even if some Europeans knew little about the country that took them in, a certain cosmopolitanism was nothing new to Mexico City. From at least the beginning of the twentieth century, Mexico and the United States maintained a healthy exchange of ideas and thinkers in fields such as sociology and education, making the city and its environs a laboratory for thinking through social problems. But what created the Mexico where Trotsky would live and die was the Mexican Revolution that began in 1910. The first mass popular revolution of the century featured revolutionaries on horseback and armies of peasants, and it made Mexico a locus of international left-wing politics. Even though its most romantic and popular figures, Emiliano Zapata and Pancho Villa, lost out in the armed struggle and were eventually assassinated, Mexico City still became a magnet for revolutionaries from other parts of the world, acquiring a southern polarity to attract northern radicals. Socialist journalist John Reed, for example, profiled Villa in Mexico years before he witnessed the "ten days that shook the world" of the Russian Revolution. By the end of the decade, as the armed phase of the conflict came to a close, Mexico had become an important haven for socialists, pacifists, and draft evaders from the United States who objected to U.S. participation in World War I or who sought to avoid the consequences of antiradical government raids. By 1919 the city was, in the words of historian Mauricio Tenorio, "both a refuge for the world's radicals and a battlefield for world radicalism."[6]

For foreigners from the United States, Mexico's revolution created an opportunity to perform an accessible act of political pilgrimage. If the political culture of the United States seemed intolerant of their views and its society obsessed with material gain and dehumanizing industrialization, Mexico offered an intoxicating brew of poverty, violence, and an easily romanticized indigenous peasantry. Many radicals from the United States would have agreed with the Uruguayan writer José Enrique Rodó, who, in the essay *Ariel*, published in 1900, had argued that the commercial and technological United States lacked achievements in the "interests of the soul," where Latin America supposedly excelled.[7]

Meanwhile, the revolution in Mexico had brought new men to power and had given workers and peasants who had fought some limited claims to social rights. The constitution of 1917, on paper among the world's most progressive, promised good working conditions and access to land and made clear that Mexico, not foreign companies, owned the country's natural resources. But these were aspirations, and a chasm separated them from the day-to-day reality of most Mexicans. Aware of the contradictions, postrevolutionary presidents generally greeted foreign radicals warmly. But they were also cautious and took steps to manage their presence, acting to ensure that friendliness toward the Mexican government remained in their best interest. Subsidies to radicals were not endorsements in Mexico's political system; they were public relations and risk management. Linn Gale, who published an English-language magazine in Mexico City, received a stipend from the government of Venustiano Carranza, who served as constitutional president from 1917 to 1920. When the managing editor of the left-wing magazine *The Nation* arrived, Carranza's successor, Álvaro Obregón, sent him to Yucatán, a state with a self-described socialist governor, where he would see political developments that most pleased him. English classes taught at government colleges were a valuable source of income for other resident radicals from the United States.[8]

Although the gap between paper and practice in the constitution of 1917 was enormous, the revolution did cause considerable cultural change. State bureaucracies for public education were created and expanded during the 1920s, both for the high arts and to begin the long process of expanding schooling to impoverished and isolated regions of the country. Prerevolutionary cultural elites in Mexico had frequently sought to emulate European styles; after the revolution a new set of artists and writers would look to the national, prenational, and even precolonial past for inspiration. The most dramatic manifestation of the change was in the visual arts, where the idiom of choice was the mural.

José Vasconcelos, the philosopher at the head of the Ministry of Public Education from 1921 to 1924, wanted state-sponsored murals to express a new nationalism. His single most potent instrument was the painter Diego Rivera, who returned from a period of European study in 1921. Rivera's political and amorous lives were hopelessly tangled, but he was a hardworking painter and a gifted self-promoter who would become one of the best-known artists in the world by the 1930s. His earliest mural for Vasconcelos resembled the art of the Italian Renaissance, but gradually the movement of mural painting in Mexico, of which he was only the most prominent member, tried to rework European trends for the Mexican setting. Like the foreign radicals drawn into his bohemian circle, Rivera drew inspiration from indigenous art traditions and a romantic idea of Mesoamerican life before the arrival of Europeans. All this was compatible with the two major goals of President Obregón for the murals: to replace the international reputation of instability left by the revolution with one of cultural depth and sophistication, and to aid in the project of integrating the peasantry into the story of the nation, creating a cross-class nationalism.[9]

But the painters, including Rivera, were inspired by more radical and internationalist visions than was Obregón. Rivera and his contemporary and rival David Álfaro Siqueiros were keenly attuned to international politics and were cheered by the Bolshevik Revolution of 1917 and the promise of global transformation that it seemed to represent. In 1922 they formed the Union of Technical Workers, Painters, and Sculptors, committed to the narrow interest of preserving fair working conditions for themselves and their assistants and to the more grandiose projects of anticapitalism and anti-imperialism. *El Machete,* the biweekly organ of the union, eventually became the newspaper of Mexico's Communist Party (Partido Comunista Mexicano, PCM), which had been founded in 1919.[10]

The union's artistic manifesto called for the creation of a revolutionary avant-garde that united the artistic, the social, and the political. It repudiated easel painting as aristocratic and glorified monumental art because it could be a public possession. "Since this social moment is one of transition between a decrepit order and a new one," it declared, "the creators of beauty must put forth their utmost efforts to make their production of ideological value to the people." But the muralists' ambitions outstripped their capacities. Early murals were commissioned for government buildings and were seen more by bureaucrats than by workers or peasants. And Mexico's government wanted social peace, not class conflict. At the end of Obregón's term in office, he halted all mural projects. His successor, Plutarco Elías Calles, took office in 1924 and did not reverse the decision; Rivera was practically the only painter allowed to stay active on state work. Revolutionary nationalism ceased, for a time, to be an artistic movement supported by the federal bureaucracy.[11]

Communist politics, however, beckoned. The PCM was still tolerated, and artists from around the world remained in Mexico City's bohemian circles. "Everyone is a communist, a 'red,' " wrote one visiting art student. "It is evident that one must take sides in Mexico, and the side that the painters are on is red, so I have decided to be a red, too." It was a common-enough experience for foreign visitors. Tina Modotti, for example, an Italian-born actress, had arrived in Mexico in 1922, and she soon apprenticed herself to the photographer Edward Weston, then enjoying his own Mexican sojourn. He returned to the United States in 1923, but Modotti stayed and developed into an accomplished photographer in her own right, crafting elegant still-life images and depicting the lives of Mexico's poor women and workers. One of her best-known photographs gazes down on a group of laborers sharing a single copy of *El Machete.* Her contributions to Communist politics were not only artistic. When Modotti became the lover of Xavier Guerrero, a painter and leading figure in the PCM, the Central Committee of the party began meeting in the living room of her apartment. In 1925, working with Bertram and Ella Wolfe, a Communist family in semivoluntary exile from Boston, Modotti began managing the activities of Comintern organizations in Mexico. These early fronts included the Anti-imperialist League of the Americas and International Red Aid, a kind of Communist Red Cross that took on the considerable task of palliating the sufferings of the victims of what it called "bourgeois injustice."[12]

The scene could not last. Although Calles still helmed a rickety ship of state, he was busy cladding it with iron, and there was an evident trend toward conservative and bureaucratic politics. When Obregón was re-elected in 1928 but was assassinated before he could take office, Calles set about constructing a party that could make peaceful transitions of power possible. In that, he succeeded wildly: his Partido Nacional Revolucionario (PNR), through two name changes, would hold the presidency for seventy-one years. As Calles was assembling a party to match his vision of a united Mexico, the country ceased to be a locus of international radical politics.

If a moment of rupture is needed, then the shots that killed Julio Antonio Mella are as good as any. Mella was a Cuban Communist and student leader living in Mexican exile, writing in *El Machete,* and planning to overthrow the dictator, Gerardo Machado, who had forced him out. Against the wishes of the Comintern, whose policies were tuned to the needs of the Soviet Union, Mella secretly prepared an armed revolutionary mission to the island. He did so at an inauspicious time in Communist history: Stalin, gathering power after the death of Lenin in 1924, had over the previous few years moved toward greater persecution of the internal opposition, particularly the "Left Opposition" of Trotsky, who became a figure of official vilification. Expelled from the Communist Party in late 1927, Trotsky had been forced out of the Soviet Union in February 1929. The same factional divisions were being imposed on Communist parties the world over, and individuals who were considered sympathetic to Trotsky—the most obvious hallmark being an excessive commitment to extending revolution in a time of consolidation in the USSR—found themselves in trouble with local parties. Mella fell well inside that category. Among the international agents who helped guide the PCM was Vittorio Vidali, sent by Moscow to align unreliable Mexican Communists with international norms. Vidali returned from a Comintern meeting in Havana in 1928 with an order for Mella to "subordinate [himself] to the C[entral] C[ommittee] of the Mexican Communist Party." Mella was expelled from

The funeral march of Julio Antonio Mella's body through the streets of Mexico City, January 1929. Diego Rivera walks just behind the floral sickle. Photo courtesy Archivo General de la Nación, Collection Enrique Díaz, envelope 30/1.

the party and then readmitted shortly before he was shot on the street on 10 January 1929.[13]

Years later, during the Cold War, it would become an anti-Communist trope that Vidali was a globe-trotting Communist assassin, and some charged that Mella's murder was the result of yet another sectarian purge. Mella, as he lay dying, blamed Cuban assassins sent by Machado, and the best available historical information corroborates that account. In the wake of the murder, however, a nasty swarm of press sensationalism and official hostility surrounded Mella's lover, Tina Modotti, who had been at his side when he was shot. Diego Rivera, still the PCM's most famous member, shielded Modotti from the press and the prosecutors as best he could. For its part, the party forgot Mella's heterodox views and turned his funeral into a defiant parade. Rivera led much of the procession that enshrined Mella as a martyr of Latin American Communism.[14]

Although it was almost certainly the Cuban dictator who was responsible for the murder, the Mexican government used the resulting scandal as the rationale to repress foreign Communists in Mexico. When some leaders of the PCM endorsed an armed uprising in the state of Veracruz early in 1929, the Mexican government took further action. Police raided the offices of *El Machete* and the PCM in June and again in August, the second time destroying the printing equipment of the newspaper. The paper and the party entered a period of semiclandestine operation that would last until 1935. Modotti was deported later in 1929 even as the PCM, under pressure from Moscow, entered an ultrasectarian period, conducting its own internal purges: most notably, it expelled Diego Rivera for his Trotskyist sympathies and for having failed to endorse the revolt in Veracruz. The next year, the Mexican government raided party headquarters and arrested Communists throughout the country.[15]

The first idyll of bohemian radicalism in Mexico had lasted approximately a decade, from 1919 to 1929. A second wave of revolutionaries would arrive a decade later, coming in large numbers in 1939. But it was the European decade in between that laid the foundations for their Cultural Cold War. Anti-Trotskyist expulsions in Mexico were only the local manifestation of a global phenomenon; many of those leaving or being forced out of the Communist Party had been trained in the favored organizational techniques of the Comintern, including the use of front groups. Some would use the same techniques to defend themselves and tear away for decades to come at Stalin's claim to command the world's revolutionary movement.

Trotsky was still alive and thus the most potent symbol of an alternative revolutionary politics to what actually existed in the Soviet Union. His was a sharp and rigid mind, and by the 1930s he was a powerfully attractive figure to a small camp of followers, especially intellectuals. Two things gave Trotskyism some purchase as a movement. One was that it became an all-purpose term of abuse in orthodox Communist circles. The fabrications of Soviet show trials in the 1930s held Trotsky and his supposed followers responsible for absurd conspiracies; Trotskyist sabotage was blamed for everything from bad weather to industrial breakdown. Trotsky's example made it possible for former Communists, convinced of the sickness of Stalin's leadership, to believe that the problem with actually existing Communism was Stalin's personal betrayal of revolutionary principles, not systemic failure. Trotsky's acid pen etched a critique of Stalinism, and this critique was the one thing that almost none of his followers abandoned, even if they eventually distanced themselves from the man himself. In *The Revolution Betrayed,* published in 1936, Trotsky wrote that the Soviet bureaucracy dominated the masses rather than yielding to them. He argued that the Stalinist system sought to control ideas and history through official texts and by pressuring artists and writers to conform to the interpretations of the will of leaders. This "totalitarian" intention—Trotsky uses the word mainly in this cultural context in *The Revolution Betrayed*—analytically united Communism under Stalin and fascism under Hitler.[16]

The second quality of Trotskyism that made it attractive to intellectuals was its reputation for defending a more pluralistic revolution. Trotsky imagined a different relationship between intellectuals and the state under Communism in ways that were profoundly attractive for dissident thinkers excised from a movement that demanded orthodoxy. In his pamphlet *Literature and Revolution,* published in 1924, he argued that the state should not choose styles or eliminate critical traditions within the revolutionary camp. There were limits, however, for Trotsky was no liberal: he policed the thinking of his followers rather imperiously and believed in the censorship of antirevolutionary art. *Literature and Revolution* made a general defense of critical traditions, but it also contained an attack on the Russian avant-garde that led to affiliated artists being fired and the formalist movement's eventual suppression.[17]

Soviet policies had approximated Trotsky's views in the early 1920s, a period of considerable artistic dynamism, but gradually more and more cultural controls were introduced. Culture was taken seriously as part of social transformation. In 1932, at a meeting with writers at the home of Maxim Gorky, Stalin declared them the "engineer[s] of the human soul." But that gathering also established the principles of official socialist realism, a state doctrine that required artists to express support for revolutionary values with techniques prescribed by party officials. Socialist realist style was heroic and teleological and lacked irony. Above all, it had to be comprehensible to the masses—experimental and nonfigurative works were considered degenerate and unacceptable. But in a pattern that would be repeated, just as the Soviet Union began to insist on artistic conformity at home, it reached out with sophisticated campaigns to secure the sympathy of prominent intellectuals of the Western European Left.[18]

Its campaigns were remarkably successful. The apex of unity was achieved at the International Writers' Congress for the Defense of Culture, held in the sweltering Parisian heat of June 1935. The main goal of the congress was to establish the principle that the defense of "culture" was substantively equivalent to an attack on fascism. It was part of a new conjuncture in Communist politics, a step into the Popular Front era of alliance with bourgeois and non-Communist Left parties in the interest of shared antifascism. The substantive claim that fascism was the opposite of culture was not exactly correct: European fascism had inspired significant artistic movements, and many intellectuals counted themselves among its admirers. But the thesis was appealing, and events like massive Nazi book burnings helped sustain its general plausibility. But in spite of the commitment to the Popular Front, Soviet cultural work abroad always served to draw lines of inclusion in and exclusion from the revolutionary family. Surrealists, for instance, who had been part of a radical cultural vanguard allied with Communists in the 1920s, were now viewed as lazy pederasts, fixated on dreams, indulgent of fantasy, and focused on psychosexual revolution when art should inspire the proletariat. Surrealist leader André Breton was prohibited from appearing at the Paris congress in 1935; a speech he had written, pleading for freedom of expression within the antifascist front, was met with a rejoinder by the Communist poet Louis Aragon, who insinuated that freedom of expression led to fascism.[19]

If times were difficult for surrealists, they grew impossible for Trotsky-ists. In an apparent irony, the era of left-wing unity of the Popular Front made things even more difficult for Trotsky because states menaced by fascism did not wish to anger a potential Soviet ally by granting him safe harbor. Deported from the Soviet Union in 1929, Trotsky had lived first in Turkey, then in France, and finally in Norway. By 1937 he was no longer welcome there either. Only one country offered him a new home: Mexico, a distant haven from dangerous times.[20]

Others with similar histories would join him. Julián Gorkin and Victor Serge were the first translators of *The Revolution Betrayed* into Spanish and French, respectively. Gorkin had founded the Communist Party of Valencia and had trained with the Comintern in Moscow in the mid-1920s. Born Julián Gómez in 1901, he chose his nom de guerre, Gorkin, as the concatenation of the names of Lenin and the writer Gorky. But Gorkin broke with the Comintern in 1929, apparently because of disillusionment with the Stalinization of the state apparatus. He made his way to Mexico after escaping Communist persecution during the Spanish Civil War.[21]

Gorkin's friend Victor Serge had been born in Belgium to anticzarist Russian parents. Serge had been an anarchist, then a Bolshevik, a Comintern organizer, and then a sympathizer with Trotsky driven into internal exile within the Soviet Union. Well known in Western Europe for his novels written in French, Serge became the centerpiece of an international campaign to secure his freedom; its success made Serge one of the few survivors of the Soviet purges of the 1930s and set a pattern by which the right to dissent from political orthodoxy was defended internationally by taking up the case of a single exemplary figure. After years in Belgium and France, Serge made his way across the Atlantic in 1941. Like Trotsky and others who came, Serge took his diminished hopes for a better world with him to Mexico. In some places the antifascist culture of the Popular Front era had proved dynamic and powerful and was deeply rooted in local social movements. But those on the left that it rejected found that their Cultural Cold War was under way and was already a contest between the disenchanted and the faithful.[22]

The period of the Popular Front largely coincided, in Mexico, with the presidency of Lázaro Cárdenas, whose acts of solidarity again made Mexico City a haven for a generation of the world's leftist political refugees. After a period of short Mexican presidencies that depended on the party infrastructure of the newly formed PNR to govern, Cárdenas assumed the office in December 1934. Although he was well known as an enthusiastic advocate of thorough agrarian reform and therefore on the left of the PNR, he was a close disciple of Calles, and his first cabinet suggested continuity with previous administrations. The PCM greeted his ascent with a pledge to be with "neither Calles nor Cárdenas." But difficult economic conditions in the context of the Great Depression led to a break between new and old regimes. Strikes had begun to increase dramatically in frequency in 1934, and their numbers continued to rise in the first months of Cárdenas's presidency. In April 1935 ex-president Calles publicly declared that the strikes were unjustified and leading the nation to social chaos; Cárdenas, by contrast, asserted that labor's claims were legitimate. An embittered Calles was sent into exile in the United States, and Cárdenas began an independent presidency, beloved by a wide swath of Mexico's nationalist Left. Many saw him as the man who fulfilled the historic task of the Mexican Revolution: implementing agrarian reform, siding with labor, and initiating an ambitious program of socialist education in the countryside. He ended persecution of the PCM, and by 1937 it had revised its slogan to "Unity at all costs" with Cárdenas. Although Mexico's government was not a parliamentary coalition and thus not a popular front in fact, it came to resemble one in spirit.[23]

Cárdenas's vision of a Mexican popular front was nonsectarian, a movement that would work with many varieties of leftist thinkers to mobilize a populace for the construction of social justice. Remaking Mexico's labor movement was among the highest priorities. After the Mexican Revolution the majority of Mexico's labor movement had sought benefits in close relations with the state, and this relationship soon devolved into clientelistic and corrupt dependence. To rebuild the labor movement, Cárdenas partnered with Vicente Lombardo Toledano, a Marxist intellectual who had broken from the official unions in the early 1930s and counseled a turn "to the left." At a meeting in February 1936, Lombardo Toledano re-formed his small union federation as the Confederación de Trabajadores de México (CTM). With the Marxist slogan "For a classless society," the CTM quickly became the most important labor federation in the country. Lombardo Toledano said that he wanted independence from the Mexican government, but financial troubles soon made the CTM financially dependent on the state and forced it to abide by the desired policies of the government in all but symbolic disputes. For his part, Cárdenas saw the organization of workers as a necessary step in the construction of democracy: "Democracy in capitalist states," he wrote in his diary in December 1935, "will always be theoretical . . . Political democracy cannot exist without the establishment of economic democracy." For Cárdenas, the organization of the CTM helped workers become educated, improve their wages, and become more equal partners in society. When Cárdenas reorganized the official governing party, renaming it the Partido de la Revolución Mexicana (PRM) in early 1938, the CTM was integrated as the principal representative of the labor movement.[24]

Cárdenas and Lombardo Toledano mobilized workers not only for domestic purposes but also for an international agenda. Appearing at the First Congress of the CTM in February 1938, Cárdenas called for the creation of an anti-imperialist international labor federation. By September it had become reality: representatives of labor centrals from around the continent met in Mexico City to inaugurate the Confederación de Trabajadores de América Latina (CTAL) and elect Lombardo Toledano to head its central committee. For Cárdenas, the CTAL was a means to project the influence of the Mexican Revolution and the goals he had for it: anti-imperialist solidarity and the defense of national sovereignty. In the days after the creation of the CTAL, again at the suggestion of Cárdenas, Lombardo Toledano sponsored the International Congress against War and Fascism, scheduled so that the same workers and international visitors could attend. Cárdenas told the assembly that it would have an important role to play in stopping the outbreak of imperialist wars that were motivated by the view that war contributed to the good health of a country's internal economy. Cárdenas worried that if Mexico did not visibly confront fascism, this inaction could lead to military intervention in Mexico by the United States. His government's support for the CTAL was an expression of his commitment to antifascist diplomacy.[25]

Cárdenas's interpretation of an antifascist popular front and Lombardo Toledano's were compatible in most respects but not identical, for Lombardo Toledano, although he never joined a Communist party, had been recruited by the Soviet Union in 1935. He traveled there just as the Popular Front strategy was being put in place and returned to Mexico with glowing reports on Soviet progress, calling the USSR the "country of the future." From then on, he became resolutely pro-Soviet in international politics. In a private letter from 1937, Lombardo wrote that he considered it his duty not to comment on negative aspects of the Soviet government, just as he would not speak ill of the Mexican Revolution outside Mexico, because, he said, "the proletariat must have faith in its cause and labor leaders should never give to the bourgeoisie a pretext to exploit our confessions about internal errors and defects of the revolutionary movement, sowing confusion among the workers, who in the main remain uneducated." He held to those commitments throughout his life.[26]

The intellectual expression of the Popular Front in Mexico came to be the Liga de Escritores y Artistas Revolucionarios (LEAR), founded in 1933 as the Mexican cousin of the better-known French Association des Écrivains et Artistes Révolutionnaires, created a year earlier by André Gide, Henri Barbusse, and André Malraux. With close but nonexclusive ties to the PCM, the LEAR worked to place Marxist criteria at the center of intellectual self-definition, insisting that Marxism was the correct way to assess the validity of art and literature. The LEAR argued that the proper role for the intellectual was active political militancy, and, after it decided to align with the Cárdenas government, it channeled that militancy into the preferred causes of the Popular Front. Under Cárdenas, the LEAR enjoyed government support, and in turn it assisted Cardenista projects for socialist education, antifascism, and aid for the Spanish Republic. Even as individual muralists, like Rivera and Siqueiros, quarreled publicly over the politics of art—with Siqueiros insisting on pro-Soviet militant orthodoxy and Rivera on an ersatz Trotskyism that allowed him to act as he pleased—the Mexican muralist tradition was recognized the world over as an original contribution to the world scene, resulting in the spread of works of public art in socialist realist style. Even as the LEAR faltered in 1937 and 1938, affiliated artists created the Taller de Gráfica Popular, an artistic community that produced woodcuts and prints in support of left-wing causes for decades to come.[27]

No cause was dearer to the global Left of the Popular Front era than the fate of the Republic in the Spanish Civil War. France, England, and the United States remained neutral in the conflict between the elected government of the Spanish Republic and the nationalist insurgency of Francisco Franco that erupted in 1936. The Western democracies feared that engaging militarily with Franco's forces and his fascist supporters in Germany and Italy would lead to wider European conflict. This left the Soviet

Union as the Republic's only powerful international ally, giving Communists considerable power within the Republican camp and creating in Spain a kind of kindergarten for the Soviet Union's future intelligence operations. It was there, for example, that the grounds for the assassination of Trotsky were laid.[28]

Apart from Stalin, who extracted a high price for his support, Lázaro Cárdenas was the only world leader to provide consistent moral and material aid to the Republic. Mexico sent arms and ammunition to the Spanish Republicans, though far less than the Soviet Union could provide. Additionally, a few hundred Mexicans—most of them recruited by the Communist Party, including the painter Siqueiros—journeyed to Spain to fight for the Republic. Mexican diplomats represented Spanish interests to other countries in Latin America that had sided with Franco. In 1937 Mexico welcomed a group of war orphans; when the war was lost, some 25,000 Spaniards came to Mexico to live in what became for many a permanent exile.[29]

In spite of its symbolic importance in the minds of sympathizers as a heroic stand of a united Left against fascism, the Spanish Civil War became almost as well known for conflict within the Republican ranks. The anarchists, bourgeois democrats, socialists, Communists, and independent Marxist groups who made up the Republican side had forged a volatile alliance. Libertarian anarchists had little philosophical affinity with the Communists, but the greatest animosity existed between the Communists and the small, anti-Stalinist Marxist party known as the Partido Obrero de Unificación Marxista (POUM). The anarchists and the POUM believed that the war could not be won without pushing forward revolutionary reorganization within Republican territory; Communists believed that the war had to be the first priority. In May 1937 the Catalan government and Communists on the one side and anarchists and the POUM on the other erected barricades and engaged in street warfare in Barcelona, resulting in hundreds of deaths. The POUM claimed that the fighting erupted as the result of deliberate Communist provocation; what is certain is that tensions on all sides were high, and open violence was nearly inevitable. The POUM, whose role in the events was marginal, but which had been fiercely opposed to Popular Front alliances that included Communists, was blamed and pursued. The offices of the POUM's principal newspaper, Barcelona's *La Batalla*—edited by Julián Gorkin, the future refugee in Mexico—were raided. POUM founder Andreu Nin was detained and killed on orders from the Soviet secret police. Gorkin and other POUM leaders were tried and sentenced to fifteen years in prison for the roles they had played in the May Days, although they were absolved of charges of desertion and espionage on behalf of fascism. They were evacuated from prison some months later when Barcelona was set to fall to the Nationalists, and the fortunate, including Gorkin, were able to cross into France.[30]

With few governments willing to offer aid, the Spanish Republic courted the favor of the world's intellectuals. Working to portray itself as the cultured and enlightened side in the civil war, the embattled Republic partially sponsored a major conference that was held as the successor to the Paris writers' meeting of 1935. It relied for organization on the Communist-controlled Association of Writers for the Defense of Culture that had been established in Paris. Chilean poet Pablo Neruda, then living in France and not yet officially a member of the Communist Party but considering himself one in practice, received a large sum of money from the Spanish Republican government to aid in the organization of the conference.[31]

Convening primarily in Valencia and Madrid during July 1937, the Second International Congress of Writers for the Defense of Culture generated significant sympathy for the Republican cause. It attracted notable figures—Vicente Huidobro from Chile, Stephen Spender and W. H. Auden from the United Kingdom, César Vallejo from Peru, Nicolás Guillén from Cuba, André Malraux and Julien Benda from France, and Ilya Ehrenburg from the Soviet Union (via France)—who reiterated their support for the Republic and their opposition to fascism in the name of culture. The fate of Victor Serge and the exclusion of the surrealists had been the fault lines at the Paris congress of 1935; the great controversy that occupied the Spanish proceedings was how to treat André Gide. Gide had presided over the 1935 predecessor congress and had been considered one of the most important Communist sympathizers among the world's intellectuals until he returned from a tour of the Soviet Union in 1936 with a critical portrait of official conformity, cultural repression, and a cult of personality surrounding Stalin. "Those who do not applaud him [Stalin] considers his enemies," Gide wrote. "The U.S.S.R. is not what we had hoped it would be, what it promised to be, what it still strives to appear. It has betrayed all our hopes." Gide was effectively excised from the Left for publishing such sentiments at such a vulnerable time for the Spanish Republic and was derided during the congress as a sympathizer of Hitler for criticizing the Soviet Union at a time of active combat with fascism.[32]

Evident in reactions to the Valencia congress are habits of mind and political commitments that endured into the Cold War. For Pablo Neruda, the Spanish Civil War was part of a process of political awakening that drew him closer to official support for Communism. Neruda's close friend, the Spanish poet Federico García Lorca, was executed by Nationalists in

August 1936: the physical and very personal representation of the fascism-as-death-of-culture thesis. For the rest of his life, Neruda's Communist convictions would be linked to the days of Spain's heroic resistance. It was a choice, Neruda thought, between "darkness and hope."[33]

Others saw darkness on the Republican side as well. Mexico's young poet Octavio Paz went to Spain for the Valencia congress and was eventually joined by a large contingent from the Mexican LEAR. Paz, who at that time in his life viewed Communism with sympathy, was troubled by the attacks that made Gide "anti-Spain" because he had been critical of the Soviet Union. In private meetings Paz spoke about the "forbidden" subjects—like the treatment of Gide and the disappearance of Andreu Nin—and he left Spain uneasy about the role that Communists were playing in culture and politics. Although he broke with no left-wing commitments when he returned from Spain, his experiences there established the basis for his future anti-Stalinism. Once they arrived in Mexico, after the end of the civil war, the anti-Stalinists Victor Serge and Julián Gorkin became important political tutors of Paz.[34]

The Spanish Civil War was a foundational experience for many left-wing intellectuals, whose future politics hinged on whether they believed, or came to believe, that Communists had played a noble or malign role in the conflict. In 1939 Franco's forces defeated what remained of the divided Republic, but the intra-Left rivalries continued to burn. Republican survivors and supporters were left believing that betrayals by enemies among their supposed allies had allowed fascism to triumph. Regardless of their views of the matter, Mexico welcomed them, and exiles arrived there not as representatives of a unified Spain but as a divided Spanish Left still at war with itself via separate mutual aid organizations to support the immigration and transition of pro- and anti-Communist refugees. Adding greatly to these tensions was the presence in Mexico of the greatest threat to unity in the Communist world and, at least in theory, to Communist hegemony: Leon Trotsky himself.

Lobbied by Diego Rivera, President Cárdenas granted asylum to Trotsky in December 1936. Trotsky arrived with his wife and grandson in January 1937, taking up residence with Rivera and his wife, Frida Kahlo. Although he had crossed an ocean, Trotsky remained at the center of a campaign by the Comintern against his life and reputation. In 1936 he had been tried in absentia in the Soviet Union for espionage, sabotage, and counterrevolutionary crimes that supposedly dated back to the early days of the Russian Revolution. Those who were put on trial as his coconspira-

From left to right: Antonio Hidalgo, a liaison between Trotsky and the government of Cárdenas; Trotsky himself; Trotsky's wife, Natalia Sedova; and Diego Rivera. Photo courtesy Archivo General de la Nación, Collection Enrique Díaz, envelope 61/21.

tors confessed to elaborate plots and were executed, marking the beginning of a three-year period in which nearly all the old Bolshevik elite was eliminated and hundreds of thousands were killed.

Many in the Western Left did not believe that such confessions could be forced from people, nor that the Soviet government would invent such an apparently elaborate rationale for mass execution. However, some anti-Stalinists in the United States, mostly members of liberal and social democratic groups, came to Trotsky's defense. Combative philosopher Sidney Hook had been one of the first to introduce Marxist thought to the United States but came to hate Stalin's version of it. He might have been a Trotskyist, but he was a poor follower and quarreled with Trotsky in correspondence. Still, he saw Trotsky's show trial as an opportunity to expose the nature of Soviet totalitarianism and organized a countertrial, with the tacit support of President Cárdenas, that would give Trotsky a chance to address the charges made against him in Moscow. Hook persuaded his mentor, the liberal philosopher John Dewey, to head the Committee in Defense of Leon Trotsky, which met in Mexico City to hear Trotsky's testimony and examine the documents he presented. The proceedings produced the expected result: a verdict of not guilty.[35]

During his countertrial Trotsky described himself as a defender of democracy, but what he meant by that term and the way in which his largely liberal judges would have understood it were quite different. Trotsky became an advocate of intraparty democracy after losing an undemocratic struggle for power, not before, and considered a government democratic if it implemented policies on behalf of the proletariat, not because it arrived at its laws with the input of the public. At the end of the presentation of evidence at Trotsky's trial, Dewey had told him, "If all Marxists were like you, Mr. Trotsky, I would be a Marxist," and Trotsky had replied, "If all liberals were like you, Dr. Dewey, I would be a liberal." Subsequent disagreements made it clear that these words were mostly pleasantries, but they did prefigure the kind of "liberal Trotskyism" that some of Trotsky's former followers would advocate during the Cold War.[36]

So it was also with Trotsky's theories of art. Trotsky argued that his Left opposition stood for greater democracy within the revolution, and in the realm of art that implied less power for cultural officials to dictate the acceptable limits for artistic production. This made Trotskyism seem an appealing avocation for those who wanted to maintain revolutionary commitments but found their ideas unacceptable to socialist realist orthodoxy. In New York the group of Trotskyists and near-Trotskyists clustered around the magazine *Partisan Review* considered themselves culturally avant-garde, and official Communist taste in art vulgar. When the surrealist leader André Breton visited Mexico in 1938 on commission from the French government, he and Trotsky coauthored an artistic manifesto calling for art's complete freedom from political or business control, and for the free choice of themes and forms of expression: an independent revolutionary art.[37]

Trotsky and Breton were quick to clarify that their manifesto did not endorse political indifference in art, and that they objected to any attempt to revive any "pure" art that, they argued, "generally serves the extremely impure ends of reaction." The purpose of the artist, they wrote, was to bear witness to the revolution in a time of the death of both capitalism and fascism while rejecting the Stalinist "reactionary police-patrol" spirit. Breton was taken with what he considered the native surrealism of Frida Kahlo, and Rivera, still in his Trotskyist phase, made a few efforts at surrealistic easel paintings and woodcuts. But the most important consequence of Breton's visit was his collaboration with Trotsky, in which the contours of a Cold War politics that linked anti-Stalinism with the right to "cultural freedom" began to take shape.

In May 1939, for example, Sidney Hook formed the Committee for Cultural Freedom in the United States to press the case against government control of artistic and scientific activity in totalitarian states. Although it opposed both fascism and Communism, it was the latter stance that defined the group, since practically anyone who cared about manifestos was already an antifascist. Countermanifestos proliferated. A group sympathetic to the Soviet Union argued in an open letter that there was a sound basis for cooperation between the United States and the USSR for world peace and freedom, and that "fascists and their allies" were determined to sow suspicion between the Soviet Union and other countries. More orthodox Trotskyists responded to Hook by forming the competing League for Cultural Freedom and Socialism, arguing in the spirit of the Trotsky-Breton manifesto that "the liberation of culture is inseparable from the liberation of the working classes and all of humanity." Both organizations were relatively short-lived, but the ideas that undergirded Hook's work would be resurrected during the Cold War. By then, there would be less distance between the liberal and Trotskyist versions of anti-Stalinism.[38]

Meanwhile, the Comintern's position was about to change again, perhaps as dramatically as it ever would. In August 1939 the foreign ministers of Nazi Germany and the Soviet Union signed a pact of nonaggression. For the Soviet Union, this was justified as self-defense, but it put the world's Communist parties in a bizarre position. Communists whirled to defend the action after years of positioning themselves as fascism's greatest enemies, now arguing that what would become World War II was a conflict between rival Western imperialisms. Vicente Lombardo Toledano, for example, decided that his newspaper *El Popular* would begin printing submissions from the German state news agency to provide a more "balanced" view of international affairs.[39]

With the threat of war, the United States was greatly concerned about the presence of fascist influence and propaganda in Latin America. The U.S. government had formalized the use of peacetime cultural propaganda in Latin America beginning in the late 1930s, when it tried to counter Axis-aligned messages. The great fear was of a fifth column: a group committed to internal subversion that could act at any moment, potentially toppling the governments of Latin America and creating a fascist bridgehead in the Americas. President Roosevelt needed the governments of the Americas to support the United States in case of war and preached, through his Good Neighbor Policy, nonintervention and respect for national sovereignty. Those policies were welcomed by democrats and dictators alike; aiding the U.S. war effort against Nazism was the quickest way for an autocrat to burnish "democratic" credentials on the global stage. But the desire for inter-American peace did create some opportunities to duck the heavy-handed U.S. intervention that the region had experienced in prior decades. When President Cárdenas carried out a key aspect of his program and nationalized foreign oil companies in 1938, U.S. companies protested, but Roosevelt's government sought a face-saving solution that compensated the companies but accepted the nationalization.[40]

In an unexpected way, the oil nationalization intersected with the ongoing campaign against Trotsky. Because foreign oil companies had momentarily become the great popular enemies in Mexico, Communists accused him of collaborating with North American oil barons. But there was a stickier charge against him that was partially true: Trotsky, it was said, was collaborating with fascism because of his attempt to testify before the House Un-American Activities Committee in the United States (known as the Dies Committee after its chairman, Martin Dies of Texas). The Dies Committee used its investigations of Communist subversion to target the workers in the unions of the Congress of Industrial Organizations, the programs of President Roosevelt's New Deal, and members of Roosevelt's administration. A forerunner to his more famous postwar fellow traveler in anti-Communist demagoguery, Joseph McCarthy, Dies used the power of subpoena and citations of contempt to punish those who refused to cooperate with his investigations. The committee was a vehicle for Dies—a racist, a nativist, and a Red-baiter—to persecute the program of the U.S. Left, although it claimed some success in uncovering Soviet spies, including ones within the Roosevelt administration.[41]

Thinking of the Dies Committee's potential to disrupt networks of Soviet agents, Trotsky agreed to travel to Texas to testify before it. He planned to deliver a speech that exposed the Soviet secret police's use of murder as a political weapon while simultaneously calling on workers to rise up in revolution. Trotsky was dissuaded from his plan by some of his American followers. Informed of his intention to call for revolution in his testimony, the Dies Committee reconsidered its decision to invite him, and he was denied a visa to travel to the United States. Still, on May Day of 1940, thousands of Communists marched through the streets of Mexico City and accused Trotsky of "intriguing with Dies and the oil companies against the Mexican people." On 24 May, Siqueiros, by this time a veteran of the Spanish Civil War, led a sloppy attack in which a gang armed with machine guns and pistols stormed Trotsky's compound. Siqueiros described the attack—quite wrongly—as revenge for Trotsky masterminding the May Day conflicts in Barcelona during the war in Spain. The attackers got past the gate and fired several shots into Trotsky's bedroom but failed to check that he had been hit—and he had not, for he and his wife had huddled under the bed. The Mexican government stepped up its protection of Trotsky's home, and Siqueiros, once located, was jailed for his role in the attack. Siqueiros jumped bail to leave for Chile under an arrangement made by Pablo Neruda, who had recently arrived in Mexico City to serve as Chilean consul.[42]

If even an abortive effort to use the Dies Committee seemed an ugly bargain for a man of the Left to have made, Trotsky was not alone in judging that the congressional investigation provided him with a reasonable weapon to use against his Communist enemies. Although Diego Rivera had personally broken with Trotsky in 1938, he also sought to use the Dies Committee to disrupt Mexican Communism at the time of the pact between Hitler and Stalin. Similarly denied entry to the United States because of his Communist past, Rivera became an informant for the U.S. State Department in 1940, passing his contact there mostly derivative information about the ongoing work of Mexican Communists whom he considered a danger to Mexico. In 1941 Julián Gorkin too sought to testify before the Dies Committee and was denied entry to the United States for the same reason. These seemingly curious relationships prefigure the alliances that members of the Left, including Gorkin, would make with sections of the U.S. government during the Cold War, each believing that the other could be used to further an anti-Communist agenda.[43]

In the end, neither Trotsky nor Rivera (nor Gorkin) testified before the Dies Committee, and on 20 August 1940, Trotsky was assassinated when a Spanish Soviet agent who had earned the family's confidence pierced Trotsky's skull with a blow of an ice ax. Fearing for his own life after the Siqueiros assault, Rivera had fled the country, gaining entry to the United States by leveraging his contacts in the State Department to obtain a visa. Eventually he reached San Francisco, where Frida Kahlo joined him; Rivera's 1940 mural for San Francisco's Golden Gate International Exhibition, *Pan American Unity*, depicts the heroes of Mexican and U.S. independence together, while Hitler, Stalin, and Mussolini are painted as ghostly and menacing leaders appearing to rise from a corpse. The words "Gestapo" and "G.P.U." (referring to the Soviet secret police) intertwine below a blood-tipped ice ax held in Stalin's hand, correctly identifying Stalin as the intellectual author of Trotsky's murder.[44]

In June 1941, when Nazi Germany attacked the Soviet Union, the United States, which feared possible German domination but not that of the Soviet Union, made an ally of a government that was broadly disliked in U.S. government circles. The world's Communist parties entered a new period of extreme Popular Frontism, suddenly interpreting the United States and its businesses as progressive, for they were aiding the war effort against the fascist foe. Likewise, in the United States, although anti-Communism remained a powerful social and political force, the Soviet Union was the subject of little officially supported criticism: Stalin was often portrayed as the sympathetic "Uncle Joe." In both the United States and Mexico, there was little good will for Trotskyists, who remained critical of the Soviet Union during wartime. Even before the attack on Pearl Harbor brought the United States into the war, the United States arrested members of the Trotskyist Fourth International in Minneapolis and charged them with seditious conspiracy to overthrow the government simply on the basis of their expressed beliefs. Even dedicated anti-Communists, while not changing their opinions, found relatively little traction for their views. Sidney Hook's Committee for Cultural Freedom, for example, fell into inactivity when it found that it could no longer raise funds to sustain its anti-Soviet program.[45]

Latin America's pro-Soviet Left threw itself into the war effort with enthusiasm. Vicente Lombardo Toledano immediately announced that there were now only two sides in the war: fascists and antifascists. Through the CTM in Mexico and the CTAL internationally, he urged Mexican support for the Allied cause and condemned any Axis presence in Latin America. Somewhat inaccurately, he attacked Mexico's nationalist extreme Right as fascist and—extremely inaccurately—called anti-Stalinist refugees such as Victor Serge and Julián Gorkin a "Fifth Column." Instead of a clash of European imperialisms in which Mexico had no part to play, he now presented World War II as a struggle for democracy and for the liberty of peoples, with the Soviet Union as the center of world democracy. Lombardo Toledano became one of the most ardent defenders of the war effort; when the sinking of Mexican ships by German submarines finally made possible a real declaration of war against the Axis in 1942, the CTAL called for it immediately. Lombardo Toledano became one of the most effective supporters of the Allied cause, undertaking extensive tours of Latin America under the auspices of the CTAL. He reached leftist labor audiences who might have been unsympathetic to having the United States as an ally, telling workers that it was necessary to draw distinctions between "Yankee imperialism" and the "great people of the United States." The CTAL pledged to speed production of strategic materials and supported the drive for unconditional surrender by the fascist states, showing that labor did not pose a threat to the wartime interests of the Allies, who depended on the delivery of raw materials from Latin American countries.[46]

Other aspects of Lombardo Toledano's behavior, however, illustrate the conditional nature of his support for the U.S. war effort. He used his visits to the United States to meet with members of the Communist Party to facilitate both legal and illegal political activity. He was formally recruited as an asset of Soviet intelligence, and as the war made Mexico City one of the most important world centers for Soviet espionage, Lombardo Toledano offered his help. He processed papers that other agents could use, assisted in regularizing the immigration status of Spanish Communist refugees whom Moscow wanted to use in other intelligence operations, and helped other agents travel between the United States and Mexico. As the Cold War settled in during the second half of the 1940s, Lombardo Toledano's CTAL, the product of both Mexican and Soviet planning, was ready to transform its antifascism into anti-imperialism directed at the foreign policy of the United States.[47]

Under pressure from the United States at a time of emphasis on inter-American solidarity, Mexico declared war on Germany and Japan in 1942. Mexican politics too were changing. The war brought opportunities for rapprochement with the United States and industrial development: the beginning of a long redefinition of "revolution" to mean material progress rather than redistribution. President Manuel Ávila Camacho, in office from 1940 to 1946, saw himself as a moderator between Left and Right factions within the official party and was less inclined to take risks to defend dissident sectors of the Left than Cárdenas had been at the beginning of his term. Mexico City, in spite of a substantial concentration of anti-Stalinist radicals, became a less and less hospitable place for them. But there continued to be no other place for many to go.[48]

Gorkin, who arrived in Mexico in 1940, lobbied successfully for his friend Victor Serge to be granted asylum. By the time they arrived, neither considered himself a Trotskyist any longer. Gorkin falsely claimed never to have been so. Serge, en route to Mexico, called himself a "Socialist Democrat" and said that Trotskyism had died with the man. (Serge shared a boat with the escaping André Breton and the anthropologist Claude Lévi-Strauss; Lévi-Strauss wrote that Serge reminded him of a "maiden lady of high principles.") But although they possessed quite different personalities—Serge's writing is incomparably more compassionate than Gorkin's—the two men were close friends and collaborators during their time in Mexico. With support from anti-Communist activists in the American Federation of Labor, they formed a small political group for "Socialism and Liberty," which brought out some short-lived magazines under Gorkin's direction.[49]

Times were lean, and the two men could do little but try to publish. Gorkin worked with another exile, Bartolomeu Costa Amic, to establish a publishing house. (Costa Amic had been sent to Mexico in 1936 by the

POUM to lobby for aid to the Spanish Republic.) The product of their collaboration, Ediciones Quetzal, published Serge's *Hitler contra Stalin,* explaining the reasons for Hitler's attack on Stalin and making potentially scandalous claims, such as suggesting that peasants mistreated in the Soviet Union might be grateful to German occupying troops who provided them with food. (This might have been true had it come to pass, but in fact millions of Soviet citizens, most of them prisoners of war, were starved to death under Nazi policies that prioritized food for war needs and the German people.) Quetzal also brought out Gorkin's account of his time in Spain, *Caníbales políticos,* which argued that Hitler and Stalin had both been counterrevolutionary actors in the Spanish Civil War. Serge and Gorkin's arguments had no audience under existing conditions of war, and, short of funds, Quetzal folded shortly after publishing Serge's book.[50]

But if they struggled for influence, Serge and Gorkin were the targets of a formidable campaign of defamation. In early January 1942 Lombardo Toledano's *El Popular* accused Serge and Gorkin of forming a Nazi-fascist "Fifth Column." Responding to the newspaper in a statement addressed to the Mexican public as well as government officials, Serge and Gorkin noted that their perspective was one of opposition to totalitarianism of all kinds. But that was hardly the point: their ongoing criticism of Soviet political terror was dangerous because, at least in theory, it threatened to undermine Allied cooperation. Given Trotsky's fate, Serge and Gorkin believed that such a charge put their lives in danger. It was at this time that they wrote to President Ávila Camacho, declaring that they had no heart ailments or intention of killing themselves.

The campaign of defamation seemed designed to ensure that neither the Mexican government nor the United States would support or defend Serge and Gorkin. In contrast to the troublesome critics of the Soviet Union, Communists were playing valuable roles in the war effort; even the United States was pleased with their messages of unity and their negotiation of no-strike pledges. Exploiting that perception, one Communist newspaper in the United States published an article saying that Serge and Gorkin were giving the orders behind a series of "Trotskyite" wildcat railway strikes that were intended to disrupt shipments of vital war materials to the United States. In reality, the isolated voices of the anti-Stalinists were not a serious threat to wartime unity. On the question of defeating fascism, there was broad agreement to postpone and even accommodate ideological differences. In a pamphlet they published in their defense, Serge and Gorkin stated very clearly that their position was to celebrate the victories of the Soviet Red Army over Nazi forces. What they did not want to see was the use of these victories to justify Stalin's past crimes. "Within democracy under threat," they wrote, "within socialism and the workers movement we defend, essentially, freedom of opinion, the dignity of the militant, the rights of minorities, the critical spirit . . . We are profoundly convinced that it is not possible to defeat Nazi-fascism by accepting another totalitarian servitude, even if this should have a different basis." Serge wrote about GPU tactics in foreign publications, and he and Gorkin argued that this was one reason Communists wanted them eliminated or kicked out of Mexico, from which they would be sent to another country and shot.[51]

The international attention that they received afforded them some protection, but Serge and Gorkin's shared apartment was monitored threateningly. Serge's widow, the archaeologist Laurette Séjourné, recalls that Serge was often followed; his son, Vlady Kibalchich, who became a major painter in Mexico, remembers a drive-by shooting during which his father threw him behind a tree to protect him. In February 1942 a signature campaign from the United States—with support from more than 170 prominent intellectuals, including Roger Baldwin, Daniel Bell, James Burnham, John Dewey, Sidney Hook, Dwight Macdonald, Mary McCarthy, and Reinhold Niebuhr—asked that Serge and Gorkin be protected and that the smear campaign against them come to an end. The signatories— especially when added to labor leaders whose signatures arrived later and were sent as an addendum—made up a who's who of those who would directly engage the Soviet Union in the phase of the U.S.-supported Cultural Cold War that began in the late 1940s. The case of Victor Serge did not bring them together for the first time; they were mostly drawn from the anti-Stalinist circles of "New York intellectuals," of varying Trotskyist, anarchist, socialist, and left-liberal political views, who felt deeply that purging the political Left of Communist influence was a vital task in the United States and around the world. But the case of Serge and Gorkin shows the dense connections that linked these U.S.-based anti-Stalinists and their allies in Latin America. They read and wrote for each other as well: Serge wrote for magazines in the United States and the United Kingdom, and it was also in this period that Octavio Paz joined Serge's circle of friends, learning more about the POUM's experience during the war and being introduced to the cornerstones of the anti-Stalinist left in the English-speaking world, *Partisan Review* and the books of George Orwell, who had fought with the POUM in Barcelona.[52]

But instead of finding safety in the support of their U.S. allies, Serge and Gorkin saw their danger escalate. In April 1943 they suffered a real attack at the Erlich-Alter-Tresca memorial. Many details of the violence that erupted that night remain obscure. *El Popular,* the newspaper of the CTM controlled by Vicente Lombardo Toledano, in which coverage of international events coincided with the Soviet perspective, reported that the speakers' words were met with "unanimous objection that gave rise to violent incidents and scattered clubbing . . . [The act] had to be suspended." That much was true: the event was suspended by the police, who eventually arrived to interrupt the brawl. *El Popular* omitted, however, any indication that the fight was incited by ninety-odd armed men recruited to break up the meeting. Serge wrote that the mob was led by Communist Party militants. Although the police arrived in time to prevent any deaths, several were injured in the attack, including Gorkin, who acquired a prominent indentation in his forehead that remained for the rest of his life.[53]

Some of the attackers were arrested at the scene. According to Serge, all offered a coordinated response to police questioning, giving a false account that they had broken up a fascist meeting, spontaneously enraged when they heard shouts of "long live" Hitler, Franco, and Mussolini. There were members of CTM unions among those taken into custody, and affiliated unions immediately undertook a campaign of letter writing to the president of Mexico. Claiming that their members had been arrested unjustly while acting to defend Mexico from fascists and "Jewish Trotskyists," the letters accused Serge and Gorkin of being Gestapo agents and requested that they be placed in concentration camps or expelled from the country.[54]

Two days after the assault, in the pages of the anti-Communist establishment newspaper *Excélsior*, Gorkin accused Vittorio Vidali and three other foreign Communists of having masterminded it. Five days later he went to the authorities with the same complaint. Gorkin and Vidali had exchanged accusations for some time: Vidali held Gorkin responsible for his arrest and solitary confinement two years earlier. (He had been pardoned directly by the president after the personal intervention of Siqueiros, who had fought with Vidali during the Spanish Civil War and was at the time jailed for his involvement in the first, failed attack on Trotsky's compound.) It is likely that both Gorkin and Vidali exaggerated the influence of the other, cloaking political resentment in fantasies of sinister power.[55]

Rather than protecting them as it had Trotsky, the Mexican government viewed the presence of Serge and Gorkin as inconvenient. One Mexican weekly that brought on Gorkin as an editor and Serge as a contributor fired them under pressure from the Soviet embassy after a failed attempt to force them out by Minister of the Interior (and future president) Miguel Alemán, who was, in turn, pressured by the Soviet and British ambassadors to deny Serge and Gorkin a public platform. When an article appeared in *Excélsior* in 1944, likely based on a forged document, alleging that foreign agents were preparing the Sovietization of Mexico, the authorities interrogated Serge, Gorkin, and their friend Marceau Pivert, worried that they might have been involved in the article's preparation. They seized anti-Stalinist writings from Serge and Gorkin's home.[56]

Although his work could not be published, Serge continued writing, penning his memoirs and two novels, including his masterpiece, *The Case of Comrade Tulayev,* a sophisticated modernist novel of the Soviet purges of the late 1930s. The end of the war thawed Serge's isolation, and there were offers for some of his works in 1946. But he died nearly penniless, of heart failure, in November 1947, before some of the same political forces that had made his life so difficult created a generous bounty of opportunities for others on the anti-Stalinist Left. Proof of the importance of the change in political climate at the start of the Cold War comes from the publisher Bartolomeu Costa Amic's trajectory: a failure with Ediciones Quetzal, he returned to printing with an imprint bearing his own name and became the house publisher of the anti-Stalinist Left in Mexico. What was ruinous during World War II would become a tidy, if modest, business during the Cold War. Gorkin, too, would take advantage of the many opportunities that the Cold War granted to professionalize his anti-Communist activities, working closely with the CIA on multiple projects for many years, on the same grounds established by the anti-Stalinist Left in its long years of exile.[57]

But with respect to the Cultural Cold War, the continuities from earlier decades are more striking than the discontinuities introduced by U.S. government involvement. The Communist movement had spun off dissidents since the 1920s and created more with each passing year. Whatever the circumstances, Soviet propaganda made the USSR out to be the paladin of progressive politics, and its critics the knights of reaction. Anti-Stalinists who tried to make a space for different socialist visions had to call for respecting diversity of thought and art; their experience of the Soviet Union (and that of many others) was totalitarian, so they asked for freedom. With the threat of fascism largely removed by World War II, antitotalitarians were left primarily with anti-Communism, which is what would make them attractive partners for the United States, even though the forms of anti-Communist social democracy most had by then adopted were well to the left of mainstream politics in that country.

Long before the Cultural Cold War of the late 1940s came to be, then, this sometimes bloody international civil war among left-wing intellectuals had already taken shape. The early Cultural Cold War featured organized and often dishonest campaigns by Communists to silence, marginalize, and eliminate their critics. At the same time, professional anti-Communists like

Gorkin pinned any evil on Communists on the basis of thin evidence and general principle. While Communists had their own newspapers to advance their claims, the anti-Communists often did so via publishers whose interest did not lie in a socialist critique of Communism gone awry, but who worked on behalf of more conservative interests, eventually including the U.S. government. More generally, the Cultural Cold War's blurring of the lines between the work of artists and agents, writers and trade unionists, and intellectuals and propagandists was already on full display in these earlier decades. But if some elements of the Cultural Cold War predated the "official" Cold War of the late 1940s, when it did arrive, new state support poured, and then gushed, into the conflict. The USSR and the United States made it possible for the internecine struggles of the Left and its intellectuals to be inscribed in a much grander tale than they would have otherwise managed, while at the same time making words like "peace" and "freedom" simultaneously noble ideas and cheap state propaganda.

CHAPTER TWO

Making Peace with Repression, Making Repression with Peace

The year was 1949, and, contrary to expectations, Pablo Neruda was still alive. Few had seen him for months, and rumors swirled. His home country of Chile, one of the most established democracies in Latin America, had taken a repressive turn. Its president, Gabriel González Videla, had been elected in 1946 in a Popular Front–style coalition that included members of the Chilean Communist Party. In power, however, he turned against that alliance, in part because he needed international loans and had to satisfy a U.S. government that disapproved of coalitions that included Communists. He pushed the Communist Party out of his cabinet and used the occasion of a coal miners' strike to arrest party leaders and close down their newspaper. His government began to hold hundreds of political prisoners at a concentration-camp town in Chile's far northern desert.[1]

Neruda, a party member, might have been among them, but his fame as a poet and his legislative immunity as a senator afforded some protection. In January 1948, on the floor of the Senate chamber, he read out the names of political prisoners and accused the president of betrayal and tyranny. "I am a persecuted man," Neruda said, "and justly so. A tyranny must begin by persecuting those who defend liberty." Neruda fled underground, where he spent more than a year hiding from the police in the homes of sympathizers. In September the Chilean Senate and Chamber of Deputies passed—with broad support, including many members of the Socialist Party—the Law for the Permanent Defense of Democracy, unofficially known as the "accursed law" *(ley maldita)*, barring members of the Communist Party from participating in political activity. In mid-1949 Neruda escaped from Chile to Argentina, making the treacherous journey across the Andes on foot and horseback. Eventually he reached Buenos Aires. Crossing illegally to Uruguay, he sailed for Paris, where his friend

Pablo Picasso had made arrangements for his arrival. The world learned that Pablo Neruda was alive when he revealed his identity to the astonished and ecstatic crowd meeting at an event known as the World Congress of Partisans for Peace.[2]

Neruda's choice of venue was a carefully calculated political act. Pablo Neruda, the great poet of love and passion, persecuted by distant tyrants, appeared in Paris to tell the youth of Europe that peace would vanquish warmongers and imperialists. He was received rapturously. Picasso, who had also joined the Communist Party, had painted a dove for the occasion; the poster was plastered on walls throughout the city, and the success of his image made the dove a secular icon of peace from that moment on. The symbolism of the dove and the poet aligned well. Those who sought war would be defeated: Pablo Neruda survived to show that it was so. The conference established the Permanent Committee of Partisans of Peace—re-formed as the World Peace Council (WPC) in November 1950— a body constituted to work for peace and condemn a nuclear first strike. Neruda and other luminaries joined the committee, showing that the world's great minds were taking responsibility to ensure a more peaceful future for a world shattered by war.[3]

That, at least, was how its supporters saw it. But the WPC was not simply the spontaneous response of frightened citizens to the specter of war. It was also the first great front group of the Cold War, sponsored, supported, and guided by the Soviet Union. Its understanding of peace corresponded to the needs of Soviet foreign policy, which were assumed by definition to be peaceful. At the beginning of the Cold War, it mobilized mass signature drives and inspired the work of famous artists from around the world. Yet in spite of its importance to the history of the Cultural Cold War, the WPC has received relatively little direct attention from historians. Some simply dismiss it as a fundamentally unserious instrument of Soviet propaganda, and plenty of Communists and participants agreed. Fernando Claudin, the dissident Spanish Communist and historian, called it a "chameleon disguise for the Communist movement and its offshoots." Picasso, in spite of his participation, was not unaware of its ironies. Privately, he noted that his painting of a "dove" was an appropriated pigeon, and pigeons are quarrelsome birds. Other disgruntled participants called WPC supporters "pigeons" too, holding them in contempt for flocking to see carefully orchestrated tours of socialist states. To them, the WPC served as a kind of intellectual Potemkin village, its noble rhetoric masking the role it played in shrouding both quotidian suffering and aggressive behavior by the Soviet bloc.[4]

Historians have observed that the WPC created problems for peace and antinuclear activism that fell outside the Communist orbit. Independent activists in the United States and Western Europe and within the Soviet Union itself grew wary of an organization that associated all aggression with the West. This literature makes clear that in spite of Moscow's predominance, Communists outside the Soviet Union and even non-Communist groups developed WPC campaigns for their own ends. Yet the WPC, seen as a Communist front, made all peace activities seem potentially subversive, and that was a notion that hostile governments were only too pleased to encourage.[5]

In Latin America, as elsewhere, WPC activity was largely confined to Communist circles and was best represented by prominent Communist artists such as Neruda, the Brazilian novelist Jorge Amado, Mexico's Diego Rivera, and the Argentine writer María Rosa Oliver. But the evidence from the region does show the situational meaning of WPC work and the way in which it created two types of victims. On the one hand, to the Soviet Union, the WPC campaigns were part of broader efforts to rearm and to create sympathetic buffer states, and also part of strategies of intellectual and cultural repression at home. Through the WPC, the Soviet antifascist campaigns of the 1930s were redirected in the early years of the Cold War as antibourgeois, anti-imperialist criticism of the United States and its presence around the world in the postwar order. It articulated a critique of what it called "cosmopolitanism" that served, among other things, as a platform for criticizing the influence of popular culture from the United States. Artists associated with the peace cause tried to craft, either voluntarily or because they were forced to do so, a socialist realism based on the defense of national and folk art traditions.[6]

Outside the Soviet bloc, supporters of the WPC found in it a vehicle for expressing discontent with imperialism, the growing influence of the United States, and the fear of renewed war. "Independence" was not a virtue within the Communist movement, and they did not seek it, choosing instead to conceal uncomfortable truths about the Soviet Union. But they were also on their own in important ways (including financially), trying to inject creativity into a bureaucratic ideology. To its detractors, however, the WPC movement also became understood as part of the threatening logic of Soviet treachery, masking aggression behind noble rhetoric. Politics in places aligned with the United States, including Western Europe but especially Latin America, were increasingly redefined to exclude Communism from legitimate participation in the democratic process. Thus meetings associated with the WPC were shut down, conferees were denied visas to travel, and anti-Communist organizing sought to unmask the pro-Soviet nature of WPC events. The anti-Communist side's major theme of the Cold War would be the defense of cultural freedom, but anti-Communists sought to deny it to Soviet-aligned WPC activists. Within the Soviet bloc, the WPC was an accessory to repression; in the zones allied with the United States, it became an excuse for the same. For Latin America, its suppression was a signal of the new Cold War order, in which "democracy" was reconstructed to include the rejection of Communism, even at the price of curtailing political and cultural liberties. In Latin America, Communist-inspired art acquired a dual character: it was simultaneously an unconscionable apology for terror and a symbol of resistance to injustice.

The polarization of culture and politics in the Cold War era rent a shared idea of social democracy developed over the course of World War II. As the war drew to a close, international political organizations remade themselves with an unprecedented degree of unity. Since the war had pushed Communism within the boundaries of acceptable partners, many organizations that had been divided on ideological lines re-formed themselves with Communist participation but without Communist dominance. The Women's International Democratic Federation, for example, met in Paris in late 1945 to establish a progressive women's organization with significant Communist involvement; the World Federation of Trade Unions (WFTU) did the same to create, for the first time, a global labor federation that included both Communist and non-Communist centrals, like the Congress of Industrial Organizations of the United States and the Confederación de Trabajadores de México (CTM) of Mexico, as well as major British, French, and Soviet centrals. One worker who saw its creation described it as "the supreme achievement of all trade-union history."[7]

For the countries of Latin America, the end of the war brought new force to movements for democratic change. A "Latin American spring" saw the fall of entrenched leaders and the loosening of repression of the Left. In Brazil, Getúlio Vargas, in power since 1930, was forced to step down to allow elections in 1945. In Guatemala in 1944, protests led to the fall of a brutal fourteen-year dictatorship and the eventual election of a teacher, Juan José Arévalo, to the presidency. Arévalo talked about democracy and social justice and began to expand civil, political, and economic rights to a broader swath of Guatemalans. Latin America's new leaders were not Communists; indeed, Arévalo thought that Communism was "contrary to human nature," but there was a real sense that dictatorships that protected the interests of the privileged had to fall and would be substituted by a "social" democracy of expanded rights and justice. Chile continued to elect the Popular Front government it had had since the 1930s, including members of the Socialist, Communist, and Radical Parties. A military coup in Venezuela in 1945 put in place a progressive junta led by Rómulo Betancourt, who made suffrage universal and increased the share of oil revenue that foreign companies had to keep in Venezuela. Two years later, in 1947, Betancourt's former teacher, the novelist Rómulo Gallegos, was elected president in a free and fair election. Even some states that organized power in authoritarian ways, like Juan Perón's Argentina, offered the poor new avenues for political participation through mobilized labor movements and an expanded welfare state. Most of the countries in the region were making tangible progress toward more politically inclusive societies; internationally, too, diplomats and lawyers from Latin America helped craft the new multilateral institutions that intended to safeguard the peace. The Chilean socialist Hernán Santa Cruz, for example, played a major role in writing the UN's Universal Declaration of Human Rights.[8]

Hopes for the extension of wartime unity into the postwar period animated much of the effort to remake the world's institutions, but they did not last. There were signs of mistrust: changes in tone from Communists and anti-Communists as early as 1944 suggested that they would revert to old patterns of hostility when the opportunity arose. In late 1945 George Orwell wrote of the possibility of a permanent state of atomic "cold war." Although neither the United States nor the Soviet Union sought new conflict with the other power, they did not trust each other and had incompatible interests in Europe. Stalin hoped to avoid provoking his former allies, urging caution on his subordinate partners in the Communist world. But he also believed that he needed sympathetic Eastern European buffer states to ensure Soviet safety. Policy makers in the Truman administration, by contrast, thought that they needed a non-Communist Western Europe in order to maintain traditional American freedoms, including access to markets on which those freedoms were thought to depend. Thus the pas de deux that produced the Cold War began in earnest: each speech, memorandum, and decision seemed only to increase tensions. In 1947 Truman and Secretary of State George C. Marshall formulated plans to contain Communist expansion in Western Europe, Greece, and Turkey through economic and military aid. Stalin viewed these actions as an American attempt to control Western Europe and revive the German economy, and intensified the USSR's consolidation of its control over Eastern Europe. In September the USSR reanimated the defunct Comintern, now calling it the Communist Information Bureau (Cominform). In the minds of the leaders of the two great powers, the world was now divided into two blocs. The Soviets saw themselves as socialist and their opponents as imperialist; the Americans saw themselves as democratic and their opponents as totalitarian.[9]

For the United States, preventing Communist gains among friendly states was considered a priority of national security. The CIA, also created in 1947, began working to influence the outcomes of elections throughout the world. Money was sent to Italy's Christian Democrats during the elections of 1948, which the United States feared would be won by Communists. In 1949 the CIA partnered with established anti-Communists in the U.S. labor movement like Jay Lovestone, who had been the leader of the Communist Party of the United States in the 1920s but had grown into a dedicated anti-Communist. Lovestone, who had operated the anti-Communist Free Trade Union Committee (FTUC) since 1936, saw it incorporated into the official foreign policy establishment of the American Federation of Labor (AFL) in 1944. Lovestone and his compatriot, the bruising Europe-based organizer Irving Brown, ran the FTUC as a kind of anti-Communist labor international. In early 1949 money began to flow from the CIA through the FTUC to anti-Communist labor unions in Europe. Although Lovestone and Brown resented the CIA's influence—they described the CIA as "Fizzland" and its employees as jejune and insubstantial "Fizz Kids," the money was useful. In their correspondence they described the funds as stereotypical national products: the Italians received "spaghetti"—so much spaghetti that Lovestone once noted that "our Italian friends have been overfed . . . If they keep on with their present high caloric diet they will get acute indigestion." The French received "perfume," the Finns "lumber," the Germans "sausages," and the Turks "halavah."[10]

Hardly more than half a decade after the end of World War II, the Cold War was firmly established, and the terrain had become nearly unrecognizable. Social democratic but anti-Communist unions across Europe and Latin America split from their Communist counterparts. They joined together in 1949 to form the International Confederation of Free Trade Unions (ICFTU), in which the AFL participated. The WFTU was left with the Communist rump and became the Soviet-supported and Communist-dominated organization that it had not been at its creation.

These transformations took place all across the world, not simply in Western Europe. Indeed, Latin America was, as it often would be, a kind of laboratory for the creation of institutional arrangements dominated by the influence of the United States. The United States saw an anti-Communist

Latin America as essential to its security, just as an antifascist one had been a few years earlier. Within U.S. diplomatic circles there were different views about how to achieve those ends: some liberals favored supporting like-minded democracies, others any kind of strong anti-Communist government, regardless of its democratic credentials. Most often, both strategies were pursued simultaneously. In any case, mutual security agreements in 1947 and 1948 placed Latin America securely within the United States' geopolitical backyard. The Soviet Union was distant and uninterested in challenging the United States on such unfavorable ground. The CIA formed relationships with security apparatuses to share information about Communist activities throughout the hemisphere, making the United States strategically dependent on what were frequently among the most repressive elements of national governments. The postwar democratic spring in the region soon withered under conditions of the Cold War. In Colombia a popular, antioligarchic leader was assassinated in 1948, an act that led to riots and intensified civil violence that would last for years. In Venezuela the novelist Gallegos was overthrown in 1948, beginning a decade of dictatorship. Even among states that did not suffer military coups, like Mexico, Chile, and Brazil, there were moves to curtail the civil and political rights of Communists specifically and the Left more broadly.[11]

The unions split apart just as surely as they had elsewhere. The anti-Communist unions, with some support from the AFL and the United States, formed their own federation in 1948. "Above all," wrote Serafino Romualdi, the AFL's primary organizer for Latin America, "[I fought] to assist in the development of a new type of Latin American labor leader who would reject the stale concept of class struggle in favor of constructive labor-management relations in a democratic, pluralistic society." The organization he helped foster took Organización Regional Interamericana de Trabajadores (ORIT) as its permanent name and became the Latin American affiliate of the global ICFTU. Vicente Lombardo Toledano's CTAL became the WFTU's Latin American affiliate, to rival ORIT there as the ICFTU rivaled the WFTU around the world. Because the CTAL's support from the then-conservative government of Mexico had been curtailed, it was funded largely through the WFTU and, through it, by the Soviet Union. Lombardo Toledano was expelled from the CTM, the Mexican union federation, in 1948, and the central was dominated by the anti-Communist leadership known as the "five little wolves." Mexico's CTM left the CTAL and joined the ICFTU in 1953. Over the next decades the CTM would be suffused with corruption and support the most authoritarian aspects of Mexico's government; it had indeed abandoned the idea of class struggle, but not in favor of democracy or pluralism. The

dominant idea of democracy in Latin America was, by 1948, less capacious and had less social content than the one so many had hoped for just
a few years earlier.[12]

The euphoria of victory over the Axis powers had been replaced in a few
short years by the uneasy quasi-peace of the Cold War. But that the idea
of "peace" became associated with the politics of the Soviet Union in the
West was a logical outcome of its position at the end of the war. The United
States had the world's only atomic weapons and had used them against
civilians in Japan. Pro-Soviet groups in the West immediately took up the
cause of peace, understanding that if a new conflict were to occur, it would
pit against each other the countries that emerged from World War II as
the strongest states in the world. For the Soviet Union, the peace cause
was a way to transfer the moral authority of antifascism into the postwar
period, in which it stood at a military disadvantage against the United
States. As in the 1930s, the campaign brought together outreach to progressive intellectuals in the West and ferocious repression at home.

   In the years after World War II, Stalin realized that his authority within
the Soviet Union could not be based indefinitely on war mobilization.
Ironically, that realization called for a repressive turn, including one in the
world of culture. Even before the Soviet Union sought political control
of the Communist world through the Cominform, Stalin had sought to
increase state power over cultural production. He empowered Andrei
Zhdanov to enact a cultural program that celebrated Russian nationalism
and eschewed experimental, "formalist" art. The war had been a time of
relative freedom for artists—once-forbidden darker themes, for example,
although not as optimistic as socialist realism would normally demand,
could be engaged since their inspiration could at least be blamed on
Nazis. But after the war Stalin and Zhdanov again decreed that works of
art must display only the "best aspirations of Soviet man." Socialist realism
returned, printers and libraries were brought to heel, and artists who
failed to conform to the new consensus invited both artistic and physical
punishment.[13]

   At almost the same time, Stalin and Zhdanov launched a campaign
against what they called "cosmopolitanism" to deal with the potential
danger of those whose experiences in wartime had given them the opportunity to see parts of the world outside Soviet control. The critique
of cosmopolitanism excoriated those who had been contaminated by
"Western" values and the contagion of capitalist greed, including even sol-

diers returning from the front and those who had been imprisoned by the Nazis. It condemned rootless, anational capitalism and fell especially hard on Soviet Jews, viewed in anti-Semitic frames as lacking connection to Soviet soil. When the Jewish name of a prominent figure was placed in brackets next to his Russian pseudonym in the press, he was marked for replacement; Jewish cultural organizations that had been mobilized during the war were repressed. Anti-Semitism, traditionally widespread among the Russian peasantry and alternately criticized and exploited by the Soviet leadership, was stoked by state action until the time of Stalin's death in 1953.[14]

But although anticosmopolitanism in the Soviet Union targeted Jews, the term was adaptable. Internationally it was taken up by European Communists to express opposition to the growing influence of American material culture that accompanied the reconstruction of Western Europe. In their words, cosmopolitanism became the "predatory weapon of U.S. imperialism," embedded in an American culture dominated by violent comics, films, and pornography. Americans, obsessed with standardization, accepted cultural barbarism in material life, for example, clothes, cars, and refrigerators that undermined traditional ways of living, and in mental cultures, for example, "best sellers" and "idiotic" films that failed in a multitude of ways to uplift the masses. As the writer Ilya Ehrenburg put it, America was not a society; it was a "herd of milling millions." Inverting the traditional critique of totalitarianism, Ehrenburg argued that although Americans complained that Communism destroyed the individual, it was the United States that dazzled its citizens out of their individuality, in cluding their ability to produce works of art.[15]

The second aspect of the European Communists' critique of "cosmopolitanism" indicted it for attempting to spread its bourgeois, American values to other countries. The ideology of bourgeois cosmopolitanism, it was argued, denied the very existence of national sovereignty, including in the field of culture. "The ideology of cosmopolitanism," wrote one French Communist in the official Cominform newspaper, "declares the concept of national sovereignty to be obsolete, preaches complete indifference to the tale of one's own homeland, national nihilism, and declares the very concept of nation and State independence to be a fiction. Cosmopolitanism denies the patriotism of the masses of the people, patriotism which is a bar to the realization of the predatory plans of the imperialists." By contrast, ran the argument, those who opposed this barbarous cosmopolitanism affirmed the values of patriotism, cultural sovereignty, and defense of the nation against imperialism. In this manner, fears of domestic unrest, internal subversion, and the possible outbreak of another war brought into existence Soviet campaigns for peace and anticosmopolitanism at nearly the same time.[16]

The first major postwar congress of international intellectuals, where both trends converged, was held in Wrocław, Poland, from 25 to 28 August 1948 and is usually seen as the opening salvo of the Cominform's Cultural Cold War. Public organizational responsibility for the World Congress of Intellectuals in Defense of Peace was held by Polish and French Communists, and, in a bid for wide influence, they sought not just Communist participation but a broadly representative section of the world's left-wing intellectuals. Nevertheless, out of deference to the Soviet delegation, the Russian writer Alexander Fadeyev was allowed to speak early, and his heated rhetoric evaporated any hope for consensus or cooperation. Fadeyev began by paying homage to the city of Wrocław as a symbol of reconstruction after the catastrophic war with fascism but then pivoted to the United States, the head, in his words, of the "anti-democratic, reactionary, imperialist camp" of nations. From the United States issued only new warlike propaganda, in "cosmopolitan" garb, which he faulted for championing racism and failing to produce any progressive literature. "Numerous American writers belong to this variegated literary agency of imperialistic reaction," he said, "[Eugene] O'Neill, the playwright; [Henry] Miller, author of pornographic novels; [John] Dos Passos, the renegade. The inspiration to this spiritual demoralization comes from a 'newly revealed' philosophy of the Sartre type, that makes an animal out of man ... If jackals knew how to typewrite, and hyenas could write with fountain pens, their work would surely be the same as those of Miller, Eliot, Malraux and Sartre." The culture of imperialism, Fadeyev continued, smelled of decay, like a corpse.[17]

If its Polish organizers had hoped to use the meeting as a way of maintaining their traditional contacts with both the West and Russia, they were bitterly disappointed. Their interests, in a pattern that would be frequently repeated in the history of the WPC, proved subordinate to the desires of the Soviet delegation. "They've screwed up my congress," fumed Jerzy Borejsza, a Jewish Polish intellectual whose idea had led to the conference. "They warned me that 'We have to say difficult things ... to not be conciliatory' ... but [Fadeyev's speech]? No one expected that." Two years later, Borejsza was charged with being "pro-Western" and was stripped of all political responsibilities.[18]

Some of the European Communists rolled their eyes at Russian dogmatism. After Fadeyev's speech, the Polish organizers tried to get new orders from Moscow, and some moderation in tone followed, but it did little to calm those who had hoped for a peace based more on mutual understanding than on the extinction of bourgeois culture. Liberals and socialist colleagues were less forgiving. Bryn Hovde, a U.S. delegate who had been chief of the Division of Cultural Cooperation in the U.S. Department of State from 1944 to 1945, expressed dismay that Fadeyev's approach seemed to presume the impossibility of peace between the Soviet Union and the United States. If the United States could be faulted for racial and religious prejudice, inequality, and civil rights violations, he argued, then the USSR suffered morally for its attempts to control opinion and expression, placing science and art under one ideology, for the power of its secret police, and for the existence of labor camps for political prisoners. "If made by a responsible member of a government," Hovde said, "[Fadeyev's] was the kind of speech that would be made to give propaganda-justification to a premeditated military attack." Julian Huxley, the director general of UNESCO, the UN organization tasked with fostering peace and mutual understanding through science and culture, was so upset by the Russian's performance that he called for the abandonment of recriminations. When he requested that Russian artists and scientists be allowed to join international professional societies, another Russian delegate assured him that "all artistic questions were talked out to the mutual satisfaction of Russian artists and the Russian people" so that no other opinion was necessary. "Let it be so in all lands," the Russian said, "so that national cultures may flourish without the influence of alien ways." Huxley, deeply disappointed, departed the congress quietly.[19]

Few Latin American delegates could have attended the Wrocław Congress, but there were contingents from Brazil (including the novelist Jorge Amado and the architect Oscar Niemeyer, both members of Brazil's Communist Party), as well as a smaller group traveling from Mexico that consisted mostly of Spanish Republicans in exile. Amado's speech invoked his identity as a symbol of Latin American nations wounded by anti-Communist violence. He showed how the rhetoric of cosmopolitanism would be adapted in the context of the Americas, connecting the defense of Brazil's cultural sovereignty to an attack on U.S. imperialism. "Along with the liquidation of our economy, of our industry and of our freedom," he said in his speech, "imperialism aspires to accomplish the liquidation of Brazil's burgeoning young culture which traditionally is [pacifist]. And this culture is still further threatened by the cosmopolite propaganda of the United States because this cosmopolitism prepares ideologically for war."[20] Like the Western Europeans who used the language of cosmopolitanism to express anxieties about American dominance, Amado situated Brazilian anticosmopolitanism in a cultural anti-imperialism that had deep resonance in the thinking of much of both the Left and the Right: he was practicing Communist cultural criticism as a combination of Latin American nationalism, indigenism, and a kind of proto–Third Worldism. Amado also put the persecution of Communists at the center of the struggle for peace by denouncing the persecution of the "conscience and voice of the Chilean people," Pablo Neruda, then still in hiding. Pablo Picasso, who had joined the French Communist Party in 1944, flew in an airplane for the first time in his life to attend the Wrocław congress and articulated the same point, helping make the absent Neruda's case a cause célèbre and the subject of one of the congress's concluding resolutions.[21]

Amado's remarks might serve as a platform from which to observe the widening gulf between the Cominform's emphasis on national cultural sovereignty and the proletarian internationalism of Marx and Engels. But the defense of national cultures was hardly a new phenomenon. Left-wing culture had often looked to folk traditions, which it considered the music and the language of the oppressed, for inspiration and revival. It was also the logical extension of long-standing internal Soviet cultural policy to the rest of the world. In the late 1930s the world of Soviet arts and letters had insisted on conformity, but not conformity to Communism so much as to the old non-Communist cultural intelligentsia and the classics of Russian artistic achievement. Soviet cultural policies served nationalist needs before those of internationalism. It was the "low" culture of the United States—"bourgeois barbarism"—that, in seeking new markets, was more likely to embrace its international character in this period. But the "two cultural camps" message of the Wrocław congress had defined the struggle for peace as anti-imperialist and anti-American, not as conciliation. The artists affiliated with the WPC would wield defense of national culture as a political weapon and would criticize U.S. "cultural imperialism" long before that phrase gained widespread currency.[22]

After the Wrocław congress, organizing continued. In the United States, progressive groups who rejected the bipartisan politics of anti-Communism convened the Cultural and Scientific Congress for World Peace, which met on 25–27 March 1949 at the Waldorf-Astoria Hotel in New York City. The U.S. State Department worried about the propaganda effect of letting the Waldorf conference take place as planned, but it also worried that denying visas to foreign delegates would be perceived as opposition to freedom and peace and settled on a compromise that pleased no one. It denied visas to nearly all the foreign delegations except those from the Soviet bloc (the Latin American delegates, for example, were rejected). This decision made composer Dmitri Shostakovich one of the most prominent foreign figures allowed to attend, and his case serves to illustrate the ugly position of those drafted unwillingly into the Cultural Cold War.[23]

In the 1930s Shostakovich had been subjected to withering official criticism of his "formalism" and had seen his compositions prohibited. For a time he wrote simpler, folkloric and heroic themes compatible with socialist realism, which found acceptance during the war. But in February 1948, as Zhdanov once again gathered power in the state's cultural apparatus, Shostakovich was rebranded a formalist and a cosmopolitan, and many of his works were again banned. In Western Europe and the United States, Shostakovich remained a well-known and well-regarded figure. Out of favor in the Soviet Union, he was nonetheless called on by Stalin himself to go to New York to defend the very policies of which he was a victim. His speech was a dreary exercise in official conformity, written for him by handlers and delivered in a nervous voice, finished only by his translator. He spoke of "formalism" as antidemocratic, pessimistic, degenerate, cosmopolitan, and lacking a national and popular base. He cited Igor Stravinsky (then living in the United States) as a once-promising but now "reactionary" musician who discounted the masses. He insincerely credited party criticism for helping him avoid "los[ing] contact with the people" and helping his music embody "human progressive life-giving ideas."[24]

The Waldorf conference also saw the beginning of an organized counterattack against Soviet cultural policy. Sidney Hook, the New York University philosopher who had arranged for Trotsky's hearings in Mexico and had formed the Committee for Cultural Freedom in 1939, set about arranging a counterconference to the Waldorf gathering. In touch with as many figures from his long-defunct committee as he could reach, Hook formed the Ad Hoc Committee for Intellectual Freedom, holding counterdemonstrations, sending members to challenge the speakers at the Waldorf conference, issuing press releases objecting to the false premises under which the Waldorf conference was being convened, and trying to get non-Communists who had pledged to attend to either back out or pressure the sponsors to include views critical of the Soviet Union.

The composer Nicholas Nabokov, a member of Hook's group, confronted Shostakovich at the end of his speech, asking whether he agreed with *Pravda*'s attacks on Stravinsky and other "formalist" composers. Shostakovich had to lie, stating his full agreement with *Pravda*. Nabokov had what he wanted: an affirmation of Shostakovich's lack of freedom and an indictment of the character of Communism's approach to art and ideology. That it came at the expense of Shostakovich's difficult position was of little consequence. Only one of the two men was in any danger for what he said, and that, perhaps, was the point. Years later, at a press conference in Edinburgh in 1962, a journalist asked Shostakovich whether the Communist Party's criticisms had always helped him, and he again answered in the affirmative. He then turned to a companion and said: "Son of a bitch! Doesn't he know he shouldn't ask me such questions— what can I possibly say?" Shostakovich did what he had to do to exist within the system in which he lived, and that meant cooperating with many more peace activities. He held in contempt those artists who volunteered their time and prestige on behalf of peace campaigns in the West. He called Pablo Picasso a "viper." In a private conversation Shostakovich said, "You understand that I'm in a prison and that I fear for my children and myself, but [Picasso]—he's free, he doesn't have to lie!"[25]

Several branches of the U.S. government, including the CIA, judged Hook's efforts a successful form of "citizen" action against Communism. Since the World Congress of Partisans for Peace was gathering the next month in Paris, the CIA sponsored a counterdemonstration on Hook's model organized by the French socialist David Rousset. (That November, Rousset called for an investigation into Soviet slave labor camps; when the Communist Pierre Daix accused him of falsifying documents, he sued for libel, creating a trial that roiled the French intellectual scene and put the honesty of French Communists on trial. Rousset was awarded damages in 1951.) Hook himself was flown in for the occasion but found the anti-American exhortations of many of the delegates to the counterdemonstration excessive. Frank Wisner, the head of the covert-action arm of the CIA, subsequently worried that a permanent organization to counterbalance the peace movement would degenerate "into a nuts folly of miscellaneous goats and monkeys whose antics would completely discredit the work and statements of the serious and responsible liberals." But CIA sponsorship made possible the convocation of a rival gathering, the Congress for Cultural Freedom, in West Berlin in 1950, and its subsequent transformation into the U.S.'s own instrument in the Cultural Cold War, an antitotalitarian rival to the WPC.[26]

The Paris meeting of the Partisans of Peace elected a permanent committee consisting principally of French Communists, who met regularly with representatives from Moscow, which provided the bulk of the financing for the organization. Fadeyev himself was responsible for communication between the committee and the Communist Party of the Soviet Union, and he kept Stalin informed and listened to his suggestions for new directions for the organization. In November 1949 the Cominform declared the struggle for peace and against imperialist aggression the most important task of the Communist movement worldwide. Stalin himself decided to name the newspaper of the Cominform *For a Lasting Peace, for a People's Democracy,* hoping to make the Western press use that phrase every time it cited the paper. The atomic scientist and Communist Frédéric Joliot-Curie became the head of the World Peace Council, the body created in 1950 as the lasting institutional embodiment of the peace movement. In 1949 Joliot-Curie had traveled to the Soviet Union to coordinate new plans for the WPC, leading to its most famous effort, the mass-signature campaign known as the Stockholm Appeal.[27]

The Stockholm Appeal called for placing atomic weapons under international control, declared the first use of nuclear weapons a "crime against humanity," and called on "all men and women of good will [throughout] the world to sign." (It also called for the recognition of the Soviet Union's right to Eastern Europe as its legitimate sphere of influence.) Signatures were collected around the world, although campaigns to expose the appeal as a "Communist trick" limited its numbers largely to those living in Communist countries (the number of signatures submitted from Bulgaria was said to have exceeded the country's population) and members of Communist organizations in the West. Although the Stockholm Appeal called for placing atomic weapons under international control at the moment when the United States held a significant nuclear advantage, the WPC's campaigns were not for "peace" understood as the absence of conflict. The name "Partisans of Peace," a phrase that was used frequently to describe sympathizers and members of the WPC, evoked the Communist-led resistance movements—many of them irregular, guerrilla forces—to Nazi occupation of Europe. The WPC explicitly rejected "bourgeois" or "passive pacifism," which it saw as the failed legacy of earlier antiwar movements that had been unable to stop two world conflagrations. The French Resistance could hardly be faulted for opposing the Nazis with violence; and so too, struggles for national liberation against imperialism and colonialism would be celebrated by the WPC as progressive actions to—in its oft-repeated words—"impose peace" on behalf of the people.[28]

Nor was the WPC antiwar: it opposed "wars of oppression," defined as wars against Communist interests. It celebrated the victory of Communist forces in China and the struggle of Greek Communists in that country's civil war. It proved not to be antinuclear either; it feted the Soviet bomb as beneficial to mankind, as opposed to the warlike bombs of the United States. (In the United States, anti-Communist thinkers like James Burnham made the same argument, but with the countries reversed.) Although not all the members of the WPC were Communists, to deny that the Soviet Union was playing a "progressive" role in world politics was the single step that it took to be labeled a warmonger; when Marshall Tito of Yugoslavia split with the Soviet Union, Soviet predominance assured that Yugoslavia was quickly labeled an "enemy of peace" and expelled. In countries with Communist governments, the theme of "fighting to defend peace" became central to daily life and the subject of campaigns aimed at workers and children. In 1950 Hungary, for instance, began to require workers to commit part of their yearly salary to the purchase of state-issued "peace bonds," revenue from which was substantially used for rearmament in preparation for war with imperialism and Yugoslavia.[29]

That same year the WPC blamed the outbreak of the Korean War on the United States, and during the war the international apparatus and press of the WPC were instrumental in spreading the allegation that the United States had engaged in bacteriological warfare in North Korea. In 1956, when the Soviet army crushed the Hungarian revolution, national peace councils were divided and could not issue a clear statement of this as a violation of peaceful principles, a situation that led to some defections but an institutional victory for the Soviet position. This failure to confront the events of the Hungarian revolution eventually discredited the WPC in the minds of many of its Western European supporters, particularly those associated with Christian peace groups.[30]

The partiality of the rhetoric of the Partisans of Peace helped convince Western governments that the WPC could not be trusted as a legitimate participant in public debate. If it is true that the Soviet-aligned peace movement marked the start of the official Cultural Cold War, its campaigns provoked repression in two distinct ways. Within the Soviet bloc, the campaign for peace justified repression in the name of anti-imperialism and anticosmopolitanism. In the West, efforts to suppress peace propaganda were justified in the name of anti-Communism. In both settings the WPC and its connection to the Soviet Union helped consolidate new limits on permissible opinion; its decreasing appeal as the 1950s went on made it clear that nothing like a popular front among intellectuals would be created in the atmosphere of the Cold War.

In Latin America, as in the rest of the world, the Partisans of Peace campaigns were limited in scope to the sympathies of the Communist parties and those who objected to the consequences of those parties' demonization and marginalization: the anti-anti-Communists. For artists who aligned themselves with the WPC, like Neruda, Amado, and Diego Rivera, producing works of art that accorded with the needs of pro-Soviet and anticosmopolitan campaigns became imperative. Although it is tempting to see these artists as ceding power over their craft to party officials and commissars, the moral calculus they faced was different from that of those who lived in the Soviet Union. In the Americas there was no threat that Communists would monopolize government power, and the great issue was the strength of "reaction" in their countries, which would use potential self-criticism from "progressive" intellectuals as justification for further repression of the Communist movement. If, for Shostakovich in the Soviet Union, artistic restrictions really did metaphorically resemble a straitjacket, then the sartorial reference for those who accepted such rules voluntarily was, instead, a uniform. A uniform serves both to identify its wearer's role and to fix for the wearer a set of responsibilities to authority and the institution he or she represents. The uniform of the Partisans of Peace conferred a beguiling sense of righteousness and responsibility. A commitment to social change made the idea of intellectual independence a luxury. Men and women aligned themselves with the WPC as an expression of dissatisfaction with the results of capitalism and imperialism. The Soviet Union, even when they had traveled to it and had knowledge of it, remained more important as a symbol than as a concrete reality, which meant that they would have to deny knowledge of its crimes.

If the cases of Neruda, Amado, and Rivera most clearly show the dilemmas of the artist engaged with the WPC, it is the Argentine writer María Rosa Oliver, one of the most prominent Latin American participants in the WPC, whose history best illustrates how the issue of peace strained the wartime Popular Front to its breaking point. Born in 1898 in Buenos Aires, Oliver was known as a writer, a diarist, and an advocate for the rights of women and the disabled (she used a wheelchair after contracting polio at age ten). In 1931 she joined the editorial board of Victoria Ocampo's innovative and highbrow literary magazine *Sur*, which gathered a group of Southern Cone intellectuals interested in political and cultural interaction with the rest of the world. Ocampo, cosmopolitan in her interests and her education (she was always more comfortable writing in French than in Spanish), translated the works of writers such as Rabindranath Tagore and Graham Greene for a Spanish reading audience and published for the first time much of the recondite work of her Argentine contemporary Jorge Luis Borges. *Sur* found its voice as an antifascist magazine and is generally described as liberal because of its advocacy of political freedoms. In the Cold War its antifascism easily became antitotalitarianism: it published, for example, Octavio Paz's 1951 essay about the trials of Rousset in France and concentration camps in the Soviet

Union. *Sur* was an isolated isle of liberalism in Latin American continental intellectual circles; Paz said that he published his essay there because no one in Mexico would consider it.[31]

But some of those who had worked with the magazine, including Oliver, did not share the anti-Communist politics of its director. Oliver had briefly joined the Argentine Communist Party in 1930 but struggled with bourgeois guilt. During the era of the Spanish Civil War, there had been little cause for conflict: both Ocampo and Oliver knew that the Republic must be supported. (Ocampo used the proceeds of the publication of a work of her friend, the Chilean poet Gabriela Mistral, to benefit child refugees from the conflict.) Nor did Oliver face a great dilemma about what to do during World War II. She traveled to Washington, D.C., to work in Nelson Rockefeller's Office of the Coordinator of Inter-American Affairs, where Rockefeller welcomed her as a valued and effective speaker to audiences in the United States and across Latin America. Although Oliver respected Rockefeller, she sometimes chafed at the commercial logic of his bureaucracy, such as the marketing-inflected notion of "sell[ing] this idea," which she wrote reminded her of the "glass beads that the conquistadors bartered for gold and seemed as scandalous to me as *In God We Trust* written on dollar bills." Returning to Argentina after the war, she observed with displeasure the increasing bellicosity of the relationship between the United States and the Soviet Union and became one of Latin America's leading activists on behalf of the peace movement. "My dear Nelson," she wrote to Rockefeller in 1952, "I went to Washington with the belief that once the war was over and Hitler defeated, the victorious countries, united in peace as they had been in war, would bequeath to humanity a better world . . . not in defense of any particular political or economic system . . . I am [now] in complete disagreement with the international policy of the U.S. State Department and for that matter if something has changed it is not my moral line nor conduct but the moral line and conduct of U.S. foreign policy." In a way, she was absolutely correct: by 1952 "progressive" sympathies with Communism were beyond the pale in both the United States and abroad, and the U.S. government was playing a crucial role in frustrating the aims of the peace movement across Latin America.[32]

But Oliver's position strained her friendships with the *Sur* group and Ocampo, whose political ideology was a kind of antipopulist aristocratic liberalism inflected by an admiration for Gandhian nonviolent resistance. Ocampo had grown impatient with Oliver's activities on behalf of the peace movement, writing in 1951: "[My hatred of totalitarianism] has cost me some very bitter arguments with María Rosa, who each day is more sold on Communism and, to my way of thinking, more blind, confused, and on her high horse in this mistake." In addition to organizing, Oliver traveled frequently—"(Oh mystery!), with ease" sneered Ocampo—to Europe, Asia, and the Soviet Union to meet artists, politicians, and, in later years, cosmonauts. In 1954 Ocampo wrote, "I regret that I don't have a sufficient amount of meekness and Christian charity to not get angry when [Oliver] brings up, with a religious tone, her preferred topic: the marvels of the Communist system and how maligned the party's leaders are, since they're really incapable of cruelty." Oliver offered to resign from *Sur*'s editorial committee in 1958 after a note in the magazine, announcing Oliver's receipt of the International Lenin Prize for Strengthening Peace among Peoples—a kind of alternative Nobel awarded largely for work with the WPC—parenthetically mentioned that the award had until recently been known as the Stalin Prize. "I would have been honored to receive the prize even when it was called [the] Stalin [Prize]," wrote Oliver, arguing that it responded to a "foolish, desperate desire for peace by a people that have never launched a war of invasion . . . [and] now needs to see itself free of danger in order to dedicate the efforts and money that go to armaments to the moral and material welfare of the people."[33]

The divisions between Oliver and Ocampo illustrate the broader alignment of the intellectual community into progressive and antitotalitarian camps. Each had changed. The antitotalitarians had gone from a persecuted minority to the center of mainstream opinion, with access to powerful allies. The progressive group, modeled on the Popular Fronts of the 1930s, was much reduced in both number and diversity, relying more on Communist support and on the party's narratives than it had a decade and a half earlier. For a few activists like Oliver, the issue of peace and its relationship to Communism became a life's work.

It was difficult to find a middle ground between Cold War positions. "I'm for peace," one of Oliver's friends told her, "but I don't say so, so that I'm not taken for a Communist." Chile's Gabriela Mistral—at the time Latin America's only Nobel laureate in literature—wrote in 1950 of peace as the "accursed word" *(la palabra maldita),* likening it to the "accursed law" that forbade Communist participation in politics in Chile. Writing in favor of peace carried its own dangers, even if it was done from the point of view of an independent pacifism, as in Mistral's case, where her lifelong attraction to a kind of folk Catholicism, among other things, prevented great sympathy for Communism. Nevertheless, she argued, Latin America was paying a cost in intimidation and self-censorship. But she complained when, a couple of years later, Communists took to printing and distributing thousands of copies of her essay on the "accursed word" as if it had been written specifically in support of the Soviet-aligned peace movement rather than as an argument against its suppression.[34]

As Oliver wrote in her 1952 letter to Nelson Rockefeller, "Persecution [of the peace movement] . . . respond[s] to the same thing: the determination of a minority to maintain a *status quo* that favors only itself." She described the poor residents of Rio de Janeiro, without basic services or hygiene, living cheek by jowl with its luxurious beaches and wondered how long such a situation could last. "Will [the residents of the favelas] go to die for 'democracy' or 'freedom'?" she asked. "The cold war that in the name of those two words is making already precarious conditions of life get worse day by day, makes of democracy a tyranny and leaves freedoms only [as promises] on paper."[35] There were, then, two kinds of repression associated with peace campaigning. On the one hand, its supporters repressed any critical views, and sometimes even their critical faculties, in thinking about the Soviet Union. The defense of peace also implied that fraternal allies must be defended in propagandistic art and language. Any perceived deficiencies within the movement were shared only with other members so as not to succor the bourgeoisie. On the other hand, peace activism was deemed by anti-Communist governments (as well as many labor leaders and intellectuals) to be subversion. Many governments treated political opinion such as Oliver's as a problem of security and subjected it to a broad range of hostile policies: the second face of repression associated with peace campaigns.

Anti-Communist governments moved to block peace organizing as soon as it appeared in Latin America, and the first that did so was Brazil. Leaders of Brazil's Communist Party (Partido Comunista do Brasil, PCB) were released from jail in 1945, having spent the better part of a decade imprisoned for their participation in an ill-fated revolutionary uprising in 1935 against the government of Getúlio Vargas, which they considered fascist. In subsequent elections the PCB achieved a peak of 9 percent national support, sending deputies to Congress and making gains in the labor movement. But Brazil's Superior Electoral Tribunal soon canceled the party's registration, and the government again undertook a campaign of anti-Communist repression and also moved to restrict the actions of leftist labor unions, whether or not they included Communists. Hundreds of labor leaders were removed, and in September 1947 Brazil's Congress voted to rescind the mandates of elected Communists, removing them from office.[36]

For Brazilian Communists, peace campaigning became a way of undertaking political action when electoral politics and labor organizing were

A poster reading "Lute pela paz" (Fight for peace) stands outside the bookstore of the Editora Brasiliense in São Paulo, 1949, advertising the Congresso Paulista pela Paz. The Brasiliense publishing house was founded by the Marxist historian Caio Prado Júnior, one of the elected delegates from the Brazilian Communist Party who was removed from office by the Supreme Electoral Court in 1948. *Source*: National Archives and Records Administration, attachments to Record Group 59, Decimal File 1945–1949, 800.00B/4–1849.

highly constrained. From 3 to 5 April 1949 the São Paulo State Congress for Peace met with the goal of establishing the peace movement in Brazil and the intent to organize a larger conference in Rio de Janeiro. Delegates sounded nationalist and anti-imperialist themes. Marxist historian Caio Prado Júnior, one of the São Paulo politicians removed from office, spoke against the North Atlantic Treaty, arguing that the United Nations already existed to keep the peace and that the treaty would pull Brazil into a capitalist war. But future activities were blocked: a police investigation concluded that peace campaigns were Communist fronts, and authorities in Rio announced that they would prohibit any attempt to meet there. There were campaigns to pressure Brazil not to send troops to the war in Korea, and criticism of the inaugural São Paulo Fine Arts Biennial in 1951 for its abstract, formalist, bourgeois art. When Getúlio Vargas returned to the presidency in 1951 by winning a fair election, Brazilian peace groups scheduled a major conference in Rio for 1952. But after first giving the impression that it might be permitted, Vargas prohibited that conference as well.[37]

The struggle was repeated in other countries in the region with similar outcomes. Argentina's Communist Party could count on less popular support than Brazil's and had less prestigious leadership. It had also been less than enthusiastic about the directives from Zhdanov to draw from national cultural traditions because the majority of Argentina's Communist intellectuals were oriented toward European culture and uninterested in the literature of the rural cowboy-like *gauchos* associated with the national folklore. Challenged by an essay in *Sur* to defend socialist realism and anticosmopolitanism, their publications initially let reprints from Europeans Communists do their arguing for them because they neither wanted to deviate from the imposed line nor defend in their own words that with which they did not necessarily agree. In 1951 the official Communist publication *Cuadernos de Cultura Democrática y Popular* featured essays by Zhdanov and others laying out the logic of formal socialist realism. The reprint of an essay by German Communist Alfred Oelssner laid out the general interpretation that the peace movement held in the early 1950s, arguing that cosmopolitanism was the principal enemy of the national culture of all people but that "growing national consciousness and national pride is today an extraordinary obstacle to the plans for world domination of imperialism—which is today the imperialism of the United States, the continuation of German fascism." But the publication also printed a more ambiguous essay by Argentine folk singer Atahualpa Yupanqui, who wrote that while, of course, socially conscious artists "must be entirely with the people," much popular music as it was actually practiced could be "nativist" and yet still serve reactionary ends.[38]

An Argentine Pro-Peace Council was formed in March 1949, aiming to hold a National Congress for Peace in the city of La Plata that August. But the theater where it was supposed to be held was closed, and instead of being welcomed delegates were met by police with dogs. According to the Communist newspaper in Argentina, one police officer told them, "You cannot ask for peace!" and called for his dogs to be released. More than two hundred of the twelve hundred in attendance were detained. As in Brazil, harassment in Argentina was sustained and the organizing that followed had to be carried out mostly in private. Public meetings were shut down, propaganda was seized, and prominent pro-peace activists were arrested. Alfredo Varela, for example, a Communist writer whose 1943 novel describing the conditions of plantation workers in northeastern Argentina, *El río oscuro,* is considered the only socialist realist novel produced in the country, was detained in 1951 and imprisoned for nearly a year.[39]

In March 1952 peace activists tried to hold another international conference in neighboring Uruguay. Although Uruguay possessed a comparatively robust welfare-state democracy and laws favoring political tolerance, on the day before the start of the planned march, Montevideo's chief of police similarly refused to allow the conference to convene. Since many of the delegates from neighboring countries had already arrived, they held an impromptu outdoor assembly on 15 March, bringing together about a thousand people in front of a makeshift stage. Although they placed a large banner bearing a white dove behind them, the speakers defensively argued that their gathering was but a simple street meeting to which no one could object. The nearly three hundred delegates felt that they had triumphed over censorship, at least in a small way, although they were ignored by all but the far-left press. But the prohibition on the conference sparked a debate in the Uruguayan government and in the media, questioning whether the cause of free speech could be served by prohibiting speech. Many in Uruguay argued that although they did not support the peace conference, they thought that prohibiting the gathering was a dangerous abridgement of democratic freedoms.[40]

In Mexico, however, the peace movement did succeed in breaking out of elite circles and achieved a limited level of popular mobilization. Mexico was experiencing a trend toward conservative and authoritarian politics similar to that of most of the rest of the region, but its ruling party took a different approach toward managing its left flank, and that difference proved helpful to peace organizers. Although they were products of the same party, a great ideological distance had been traveled between the presidency of Lázaro Cárdenas (1934–1940) and that of Miguel Alemán (1946–1952), who was charting a path of capitalist growth marked by widespread official corruption. Alemán renamed the official party the Partido Revolucionario Institucional (PRI) while retaining the idea of the single party as the embodiment of the Mexican Revolution. In his time, Cárdenas had created organizations to ensure that his constituents, including laborers and peasants, shared in political power. But Cárdenas had placed those organizations within the framework of the state, and that made it relatively easy for Alemán to tame them while retaining the ability to use them to mobilize people on behalf of state priorities.

Alemán incorporated anti-Communism into the official discourse of the PRI, and Communists with dual affiliations were expelled from the official party in 1950. With U.S. support, the Mexican government also created a new state security service that monitored and harassed the Left. But the Mexican government also relied to a great degree on co-optation to defang challenges to its rule. Vicente Lombardo Toledano, for example, the pro-Soviet labor leader who would be one of the principal peace activists in the country, sided with the government at key moments and was thus allowed to continue organizing without significant obstacles. In 1948 he founded an independent socialist party known as the Partido Popular (PP). Unlike the traditional Mexican Communist Party, which had adopted a critical stance toward the PRI, the PP supported the Soviet Union internationally and the Mexican Revolution domestically. Lombardo Toledano's approach was either pragmatic or opportunistic—or both. In either case, the PP's role as the loyal opposition in a one-party democracy, free to say what it liked about Lenin or Stalin but leaving President Alemán well enough alone, seems to have been a satisfying arrangement for the PRI, which continued to provide Lombardo Toledano with subsidies that protected the president from serious criticism.[41]

Therefore, when Lombardo Toledano announced his intention to hold a major international meeting of the peace movement in Mexico City, his action did not seem threatening. Where other governments prohibited peace gatherings entirely, Alemán telegraphed his displeasure by blocking the use of public buildings but allowed the meeting to go forward. Private theaters quoted the organizers excessive rental fees, virtually forcing them into the Arena México, a dilapidated sports arena that usually held boxing matches, basketball games, and labor rallies. Banners were created to cover the advertising, and papier-mâché doves hung from the ceiling, drooping a bit more with each day and looking, in the words of one hostile visitor from the U.S. embassy, "more like buzzards than doves."[42]

Nonetheless, the Continental Congress for Peace was held from 5 to 12 September 1949 and enjoyed the support of Mexican Marxists ranging from Diego Rivera and David Álfaro Siqueiros to Vicente Lombardo Toledano. Artists from the Taller de Gráfica Popular produced woodcuts on the theme of peace, including for posters and pamphlets that advertised WPC events. Lázaro Cárdenas, the former president (and not a Marxist) refrained from active participation but sent a message of approval, and honorary presidents included artists with whom the peace movement wanted to be associated, from Gabriela Mistral to Charlie Chaplain, and foreign leaders who had cooperated with Communists, including Chile's Carlos Ibáñez del Campo, Cuba's Fulgencio Batista, and Henry Wallace of the United States.[43]

Vicente Lombardo Toledano gave the keynote address, making an indirect attack on the United States' nuclear monopoly by arguing that scientific progress was the patrimony of all humanity and belonged to no single nation. He criticized U.S.-based companies operating as monopolies in Latin America and stated that a new war would turn Latin America's countries into mere colonies of the United States. He denied that the Soviet Union had anything to do with the conference or that it was of Communist origin, although he quickly added that the Soviet Union had profoundly pacifist ends, and that those who "stoke the horrible bonfires" of war were nothing more than the lackeys of U.S. monopolies. At the closing session on 12 September, before an audience of approximately four thousand, Lombardo Toledano spoke again, calling on the people of the Americas, as supporters of peace, to act as a dike against Yankee imperialism.[44]

Most of the political speeches over the many days of the conference implicated the United States in warmongering. They defined violence not simply as open war but as imperialism. Juan Marinello, the president of the Cuban Communist Party, who, along with Lombardo Toledano, was one of those most responsible for organizing the 1949 event, spoke against American imperialism trampling the sovereignty of Latin American countries. A few delegates criticized both Cold War powers from a "nonaligned" position: O. John Rogge said that the excesses of capitalism were parallel to those of Communism, and that "if the United States and the Soviet Union must compete, let it be for the honor of being the champion of the oppressed." But in general, neither criticism of the Soviet Union, nor—befitting the way in which Mexico managed its Left—of the Mexican government had any part in the congress proceedings.[45]

Pablo Neruda, who had been crossing the world on behalf of the peace movement since his appearance in Paris, delivered a fiery speech that evoked the sectarianism of Fadeyev at Wrocław. "Dying capitalism fills the chalice of human creation with a bitter brew," he said; "When Fadeyev expressed in his speech at Wrocław that if hyenas used pens or typewriters they would write like the poet T. S. Eliot or the novelist Sartre, it seems to me that he offended the animal kingdom." Neruda, however, did more than just endorse the cultural politics of the peace movement: he tried to enact them. He directed an evening of performance that was a logical extension of the cultural project in which he had been engaged for more than a decade. Traveling across the Americas, Neruda had been penning an epic poem of continental history, his *Canto general,* cataloging in verse his views of the heroes and villains of the Latin American past and present and binding the history of a noble, naturalistic, and pan-Latin American past to its Communist future. Neruda had been deeply influenced by the Mexican artistic scene he had encountered while working in the Chilean embassy in Mexico in the early 1940s, and he gathered many of his old friends again for his performance at the Mexico City conference of 1949. Of the many phases Neruda passed through as a poet, this

one—the phase of *Canto general* (published in Mexico in 1950 with il-
lustrations by Rivera and Siqueiros) and *Las uvas y el viento* (published
in 1954)—hews closest to socialist realism. As he traveled through the Soviet bloc, he pledged to reedit his old surrealist poetry, which many of his
fellow writers most admired, because it employed forms that the bourgeoisie used to separate itself from the people artistically. In his speech at
the 1949 Continental Congress for Peace, Neruda spoke of rejecting his
early poetic works as inadequate and inappropriate when they were presented for Russian translation, and of his own process of drawing closer
to socialist realism.[46]

In its nationalist and anticolonial implications, Neruda's form of Communist artistic nationalism was a kind of "indigenist" socialist realism. His
evening performance at the 1949 peace conference placed at its center a
madrigal choir featuring songs in indigenous languages from Peru, Ecuador,
and Mexico. At the end Neruda himself performed a section from his *Canto
general*, "Que despierte el leñador" (Let the woodcutter awake). Dancers
directed by Waldeen, simultaneously the most innovative ballerina in
Mexican dance and a practitioner of heroic movement in indigenous dress,
interpreted the poem. It took the form of a song and a plea to the United
States for a return of the spirit of Abraham Lincoln, who could put an end
to the blight of racism, warmongering, and hatred that Neruda saw as typi-
fying the United States of the late 1940s. "Let Abraham come, . . . and let
him heft his people's ax / against the new slavers, / against the slave's whip,
/ against the poison press, / against the bloody merchandise / that they want
to sell." He imagined a smiling, multiracial uprising against the "manufac-
turer of hatred." It was epic poetry and a pure distillation of the politics of
the peace movement adapted to the Latin American setting.[47]

If North America's hero, Lincoln, lay dormant and absent, "Que despierte el leñador" offered a parallel figure who was the very picture of present
vigilance: Joseph Stalin. ("His bedroom light is turned off late. / The
world and his country allow him no rest.") The Soviet Union's struggle
was portrayed as the world's struggle, and its acts of construction
made possible a new dawn for all countries. The poem ends with hopes of
peace for all of the Americas, but it also contains a warning. Neruda enu-
merated Latin America's hostility to U.S. intervention by invoking a
whole pantheon of revolutionary heroes (Tupac Amaru, anachronisti-
cally; Augusto César Sandino, appropriately; Emiliano Zapata, much less
so) inspiring a people who would rise from the earth itself to destroy any
invasion: "But if you arm your hordes, North America, . . . we'll pound
like a Colombian fist, / we'll rise to deny you bread and water, / we'll rise
to burn you in hell."[48]

The Continental Congress for Peace in Mexico City, September 1949. The background mural features a proletarian worker carrying the flags of many nations confronting a skeletal warmonger. Photo courtesy Archivo General de la Nación, collection Hermanos Mayo, envelope 7851.

The great irony of "Que despierte el leñador" was that Neruda's *Canto general* owed much to the example of Walt Whitman, whom Neruda greatly admired but who never would have been allowed to write under Soviet conditions. Whitman and Lincoln had also been admired by artists of the Popular Front period, especially in the United States, and Whitman was, in some ways, an excellent choice for a distant poetic hero of the peace movement. He believed in an egalitarian democratic community (of men, at any rate) and was known for sounding the drums of war in support of the Union cause during the U.S. Civil War—like the Partisans of Peace, more a believer in justice than in peace. Still, during the war he visited the bedsides of the war wounded of both the Union and the Confederacy and saw them both with sympathy. His poems also drew for their subjects from ordinary objects and experiences, as called for by the directives of socialist realism. On the other hand, Whitman was initially disliked by many critics in his day and largely rejected by the poetry-reading masses. His poems were precisely the sort of erotic and degenerate mess that abandoned structure for free verse; they would have been utterly out of bounds in the peace movement and certainly would never have been allowed to develop under the Communist cultural politics of that period. Still, Whitman's work was reproduced from time to time in peace movement propaganda, and in 1950 the WPC awarded Neruda its International Peace Prize in recognition of "Que despierte el leñador."[49]

In the years after the Mexican conference, Neruda lived in exile in Europe as a guest of the WPC. He spent a great deal of his time in the Soviet Union, China, and the Eastern bloc and was designated as the WPC's representative to the United Nations. He participated in every major European reunion of the WPC. After a meeting in Vienna, held in December 1952, he sought to organize his own conference in Santiago, which would prove to be the last major peace-like gathering held in Latin America in the 1950s. After another trip to the Soviet Union, he returned to Chile in January 1953; by then, Neruda's bête noire, Gabriel González Videla, had been replaced as president by Carlos Ibáñez del Campo, Chile's former dictator who had been strategically made into one of the honorary presidents of the Mexico City gathering of 1949, and who now promised to repeal the anti-Communist *ley maldita*. Still, the mayor of Santiago was opposed to allowing the gathering to meet in the municipal theater, and Neruda had to call on a friend, who pressed President Ibáñez to persuade the mayor to allow the event to proceed in light of the important guests who would be attending. Even so, the visas for the Soviet and Chinese delegations were granted only at the last minute, which made it impossible for the Soviet delegates to attend. According to the CIA, Neruda, who had privately expressed the view in 1950 that the "[peace] campaign in Latin America had been a complete failure," also failed to find funds for his congress while he was in European exile. But even without outside funding, Neruda's Continental Cultural Congress (CCC) was held in Santiago from 26 April to 3 May 1953, opening less than a month after the death of Stalin.[50]

But harassment continued. After the second day of the CCC, a judge ordered *El Siglo,* the newspaper of the still-illegal Communist Party, closed for ten days, citing its campaign of "permanent conspiracy." The bourgeois and government press declined to report on the event, creating a kind of news blackout during the days of the actual meeting. Responding to the climate of suppression, Neruda promised that the CCC would offer culture and not politics. Still, echoes of the language of earlier peace congresses were unmistakable, and the Santiago conference was a final exercise in cultural Stalinism. "I know and admire the Soviet people," Neruda said at the congress, "and its leaders for their extraordinary deeds, indelible in human history. But what I most admire in that land is its dedication to culture. Perhaps above all else, this is the most fundamental and impressive feature of Soviet life, with the full flowering of the individual, as never before achieved in history." The Chilean writer Fernando Santiván spoke in favor of cultural exchange among the American republics but wondered whether the nations of Latin America were allowed an independent economic and spiritual existence, or whether U.S. power was so strong that it stopped them from developing according to their rightful national characteristics. The two congress participants who reported on the proceedings for the Cominform's newspaper, Brazil's Jorge Amado and the Chilean Communist writer Volodia Teitelboim, explicitly connected Santiván's speech to the still-germane rhetoric of cosmopolitanism: "An analysis of the content of the national peculiarities of our cultures led the [Continental Cultural] Congress resolutely to reject all forms of cosmopolitanism . . . Fernando Santiván called on the delegates resolutely to counteract the flow of 'publications' from the U.S., permeated with the venom of cosmopolitanism, and to use on a broad scale, in literature and art, the many-sided richness of our folklore and our national cultural legacy." Within the Soviet Union itself, however, the post-Stalin leadership soon backed away from the paranoid anti-Semitism of the "cosmopolitan" idea.[51]

It would take a few years for Jorge Amado to catch up. Amado had joined the Communist Party in the early 1930s, and his early novels were, at least in broad terms, "Communist novels," populated by malign landowners and noble rural "proletarians." The "indigenous" elements of these works drew not on autochthonous Brazilians but on the traditions and practices of Afro-Brazilians in the country's northeast. When the Communist Party was outlawed in 1948, Amado left for self-imposed exile, traveling on behalf of the Partisans of Peace. For the greater part of two years, he lived in a castle at the invitation of the Czechoslovakian Union of Writers. (Amado named his Czechoslovakian-born daughter, Paloma, after Picasso's dove.) He published an account of his travels through the Soviet Union in 1951, titled O mundo da paz, making the moral case for the Soviet approach to literature and the arts: "In the Soviet Union, literature actually became a weapon of the people in building the future, in the fight against the remnants of the influence of capitalist society, against the remnants of a past full of prejudices from which it is necessary to free man in the same way as [the Soviet Union] did away with social injustices."[52]

O mundo da paz was deemed subversive in Brazil, and Amado was charged with violating national security laws when he returned there in

1952. (The trial concluded without a verdict.) Traveling between Europe and Brazil, Amado finished the major novel he had begun in Czechoslovakia: a three-volume epic of the Brazilian people's struggle to overcome the tyranny of the government of Getúlio Vargas during the 1930s, *Os subterrâneos da liberdade*. As with Neruda's work from this period, it was the most didactic of his career, and one that he himself later agreed deserved criticism for its adherence to Zhdanovite socialist realism.[53]

Neruda's and Amado's artistic participation in the peace movement was primarily driven by moral considerations, but there were material benefits as well. Travel junkets were a not-inconsiderable compensation, particularly for the less famous, allowing beneficiaries to travel at virtually no cost to themselves and enjoy the best luxuries that the hosting societies had to offer. Especially favored authors who were selected by the Soviet government for translation and distribution (like Amado and Neruda) could accumulate significant wealth that could be accessed only on trips to the Eastern bloc because of inconvertible currency. Whether work selected for translation was simply pirated or whether its author would receive royalties was similarly a political decision used to reward favored authors.

At the same time, participants in the peace movement were not bathed in "Moscow gold" and were expected to bear some of the costs of implementing its programs. There is no doubt that, at the widest level of generality, the Soviet Union, and to some extent other Communist countries, provided the great bulk of the financing for the WPC. However, local initiatives were often self-financed, and the best available evidence suggests that the Latin American gatherings generally had few of their costs defrayed. The Mexican Pro-Peace Committee had some of its expenses covered by the WPC but raised most of its money via gifts and loans from its wealthiest supporters and from raffles, book signings, and auctioning off works of art donated by sympathetic painters.[54]

In the waning moments of the Continental Congress for Peace in Mexico in 1949, David Álfaro Siqueiros reminded everyone present that the congress had run a deficit, and he solicited contributions from the audience. The man in charge of peace campaigning for the Mexican Communist Party frequently remarked on the need for local fund-raising, given the absence of support from the WPC. For the conference in Santiago organized by Neruda in 1953, U.S. government documentation reports that Neruda never succeeded in his goal of obtaining funds from international sources. He raised money for the conference by holding a "kermesse" at one of his houses, counting on the support of wealthy Communists and sympathizers to pay a significant portion of the bill. Although all delegates to that meeting except Diego Rivera and Cuban poet Nicolás Guillén paid their own travel and hotel expenses, the congress still closed with a deficit of half a million pesos. The peace movement in Latin America obtained a bit of "Moscow bronze," but Moscow gold was elusive, and in fact, Latin American Communists probably subsidized Moscow's priorities more than the other way around.[55]

Some of the costs could be offset, for the major benefactors if not for the rank and file, by later awarding prizes to wealthy patrons in recognition of their sacrifices. The International Stalin Prize for Strengthening Peace among Peoples (usually known simply as the Stalin Peace Prize) was first awarded in 1950 by the Soviet Union and was given out largely, at least in its first years, in return for work on behalf of the peace movement. (The WPC awarded its own International Peace Prize, which typically went to a rather similar list of people.) The Stalin Prize conferred a medal and a cash award equivalent to about $25,000. In 1956, after Nikita Khrushchev's condemnation of Stalin's crimes, the name of the prize was changed to the Lenin Peace Prize, and previous winners were asked to return and exchange their medals, although some chose not to do so. Recipients of the Stalin Prize also received diplomatic status equivalent to that of a party official while they were in the Soviet Union, and that gave them some power to protect one another. Since prizewinners had to be approved at very high levels, a recipient would be seen as capable of representing the best of art. When the playwright Bertolt Brecht was being harassed for his "formalism" by the East German Communist Party in 1954, Jorge Amado acted behind the scenes to help Brecht win the prize, superseding local pressures with an official stamp of approval and restoring some artistic flexibility for Brecht.[56]

The cost of receiving these benefits was silence on the less appealing facts to which these writers, however shielded the experiences they had in the Soviet bloc, were certainly privy. Ideas of the functioning of the Soviet Union were based on a kind of evolved political fantasy of social justice that had to exist to contrast with the wretched state of affairs that existed in the Americas or Europe. "How can you, as a writer, admire and love the Soviet Union?" a Brazilian official once asked Amado, and he replied with the surprising explanation that as a writer, he loved the Soviet Union because of the full freedom of printing, criticism, and self-criticism that existed there. Amado explained that there was no need for an opposition press when the publishing responsibilities lay with the state, the authentic representation of the people. If one takes the "independent critic" as the ideal model for intellectuals, this was a serious capitulation to power and a reminder that a "committed" intellectual was a compromised one. Amado writes in his memoirs of his deep sadness at learning of the

Diego Rivera, *Pesadilla de guerra, sueño de paz*, 1952. Reproduced by permission. © 2015 Banco de México Diego Rivera Frida Kahlo Museums Trust, México, D.F. / Artists Rights Society (ARS), New York.

existence of official Soviet anti-Semitism—and thus the falsity of his beliefs about the achievement of Soviet ethnic and racial harmony. But this had not stopped him from using the anti-Semitic language of cosmopolitanism in peace propaganda. Under Stalin, Amado later reflected, "It was not easy [being] a Communist." But to stop remained, at least for a time, unthinkable.[57]

Yet it did not remain unthinkable forever. Amado's WPC-supported trilogy also marked his exhaustion with such writing. Settling in Salvador in northern Brazil, Amado distanced himself from Communist political militancy in 1955 and began to write lightly comic works that still engaged issues of social inequality and won him wider audiences. He recovered an ironic sensibility that would have been impermissible during his socialist realist phase. Neruda remained in the Communist Party until his death but toned down the epic scale of his poetry in the second half of the 1950s and dropped the references to Stalin. His most Stalinophile work, *Las uvas y el viento,* is the only one of his works that is almost never anthologized in volumes of his collected poetry.[58]

One artist, however, carried unmodified convictions to the grave. Diego Rivera had been a Communist, a Trotskyist, and a hapless "spy" for the United States. By the late 1940s he was petitioning to rejoin Mexico's Communist Party and was being consistently rebuffed. He broke with Lombardo Toledano's Partido Popular over its accommodations to the PRI in 1949 and tried to use peace movement militancy to earn his way back into the Mexican Communist Party. In 1952 he made an artistic bid for readmittance that nearly succeeded.

Part of Anahuacalli, a building designed by Diego Rivera and Juan O'Gorman to house Rivera's extensive collection of pre-Columbian art. Original mosaics, implemented by O'Gorman on the basis of sketches by Rivera, decorate the interior hallways and display Mesoamerican imagery mixed with symbols of the Communist and peace movements.

Photo by author; reproduced by permission. © Artists Rights Society (ARS), New York / SOMAPP, Mexico City © Banco de México Diego Rivera Frida Kahlo Museums Trust, México, D.F. / Artists Rights Society (ARS), New York.

In some ways, Rivera had to do little to adapt his painting to the precepts of socialist realism. Some Marxist art critics considered Rivera's sprawling murals the epitome of visual socialist realism, even if his rounded human figures lacked the muscled forearms and rosy faces of the era's Soviet painting. Nor was Rivera known for his subtlety. Still, he had rarely put to canvas a political message quite as directly as the one he painted in 1952's *Pesadilla de guerra, sueño de paz*. The quickly executed mural, considered by almost all critics one of his worst, shows the benevolent figures of Stalin and Mao standing with a peace petition, offering a pen to figures representing the United Kingdom, France, and a gun-and-Bible-toting Uncle Sam. The mural, which was intended for an exhibition in Paris, was rejected by the Mexican government as a provocation to its allies but was celebrated in a showing by the Communist Party and the Mexican Peace Committee.[59]

Rivera, although he never again painted anything as didactic as *Pesadilla de guerra, sueño de paz,* did not stop painting pro-peace messages. In spite of this, he was not readmitted to the party until 1954, when he draped his partner Frida Kahlo's funeral coffin with a red flag displaying the hammer and sickle. Sick with cancer in 1956, he was treated in Moscow, where he believed that atomic technology of the benevolent Soviet cobalt bomb would cure him, and where he painted an elegant and colorful scene of a pro-peace march. The treatments, however, failed, and Rivera passed away the following year. The mausoleum-gallery Anahuacalli, constructed during the last years of his life, is a lasting monument to his obsessions both with the civilizations of pre-Columbian "Mexico" and with the campaign for peace. It is perhaps a fitting object to be the largest physical embodiment of the cultural dimensions of peace campaigns in the Americas: a tomb of occasional beauty but one that, at its core, admits little light. To be a Communist intellectual in Latin America's early 1950s was to be the victim of repression, not its perpetrator. It was to incarnate the very real injustices of capitalism and imperialism while silencing the problems of one's own distant empire and trying to spin horror into virtue.[60]

CHAPTER THREE

The Congress for Cultural Freedom and the Imperialism of Liberty

Valentín "El Campesino" González made his name as a Communist general in the Spanish Civil War, famous both for his innovative use of guerrilla tactics and for his brutality. But in the early 1950s the FBI was looking for him—not for his crimes, but so that he might testify before a congressional subcommittee investigating international Communism. When the Spanish Civil War had been lost, El Campesino had escaped to the Soviet Union, had grown disillusioned, had been made to do forced labor digging tunnels for the Moscow subway, and eventually had escaped a Soviet prison camp by traveling on foot to Iran. A valuable convert, he drew the attention of the anti-Communist networks of the early Cold War: anti-Communist unions, social democratic politicians, and U.S. government agencies, including the fledgling CIA. But El Campesino (The peasant) was nearly illiterate and needed a handler. Julián Gorkin became his unlikely partner.

Gorkin too had once been imprisoned: a leader of the quasi-Trotskyist Partido Obrero de Unificación Marxista (POUM), he was accused of treason by Communist authorities during the Spanish Civil War. He served eighteen months in prison and was as lucky to escape Spain as El Campesino would be to escape the Soviet Union, eventually making his way to Mexico via New York with the help of Jay Lovestone's anti-Communist labor network. When Gorkin arrived in Mexico in 1940, Lovestone helped him establish a tiny anti-Communist "international," alongside his small number of friends and allies, like Victor Serge and Marceau Pivert. When Trotsky was murdered, Gorkin used his connections with the Mexican police to expose the responsibility of Stalin's agents. He lived with Serge until Serge's death in 1947; in 1948 Gorkin returned to Paris.[1]

"What a stupendous brute! In the time of the conquistadors he would have been a Pizarro," wrote Gorkin after his first pair of days with El

Campesino. During the Spanish Civil War the Communist El Campesino might have jailed, or even killed, the POUMista Gorkin if he had had the chance. But by 1949 they were both convinced anti-Communists and needed each other. Gorkin shepherded El Campesino through Western Europe. At David Rousset's trial in France, El Campesino testified that the USSR represented nothing more than "fascism with a red flag." Throughout their travels around the world, Gorkin acted as El Campesino's ghost-writer. "Read your article for today in case somebody questions you about it," Gorkin told El Campesino during their trip to Cuba. Eventually they came to Mexico, where they were set up at a CIA safe house in Cuernavaca, kept hidden even from the FBI. There, Gorkin formed El Campesino's life story into an "autobiography" that was quickly published and widely distributed in multiple languages.[2]

"A rumor has been spread by word of mouth that [El Campesino] and I are American agents," Gorkin wrote to a friend around the time when the two were working together in the CIA safe house. "American agents! We who have never received help from the United States for the work we are doing, and who would surely be denied a visa to enter the United States!" As someone who had belonged to the Communist Party, Gorkin had indeed been denied a visa to the United States when he had sought to testify before the Dies Committee in the early 1940s. But the rumor was true enough, and it would not be the last time that Gorkin's path crossed with U.S. intelligence operations.[3]

If Gorkin disliked the thought of being designated as an American agent, perhaps it was because he saw his anti-Communist commitments as prior to those of the U.S. government. Whatever his reasons, he fits the profile of an emerging type of the early Cold War: the "anti-Communist entrepreneur" who sought opportunities, financial and otherwise, to further his anti-Communist career. Like Jay Lovestone, who had helped Gorkin get to Mexico, he may have believed that he was capable of using the CIA as much as it was using him. Lovestone resented it, but his rickety networks, assembled within the American Federation of Labor (AFL) to fight Communist unions internationally, were being fortified with the more solid frames of U.S. government support. Gorkin's friend Victor Serge died penniless in 1947, just a bit too early; Gorkin would not lack for work. U.S. government participation transformed the Cultural Cold War because anti-Communist political priorities now coincided with those of a powerful state. It was not anti-Communism itself that was new, nor were anti-Communist entrepreneurs like Gorkin an invention of the United States. What was different was that, whether they wanted to or not, anti-Communist entrepreneurs could hardly put their ideas into action without becoming entangled with the plans of the U.S. government.[4]

The centerpiece of the U.S. government's Cultural Cold War was the Congress for Cultural Freedom (CCF), secretly supported financially and staffed at the highest levels by the CIA from its creation in 1950. (Many of the initial covert contributions were routed through Lovestone's Free Trade Union Committee before shell foundations were set up to serve as a more permanent and reliable disguise.) The CCF began as a response to the specific provocations of the Soviet-aligned peace movement; to some wits, it was a "Democratic Information Bureau" to stand against the Cominform. Like the World Peace Council that it opposed, it was initially based in Europe and was most concerned with the European scene. The establishing conference was held in West Berlin in 1950, and a permanent headquarters was then created in Paris. At the highest levels, administrative positions were filled by CIA employees or by those who at least knew of the relationship.

But in addition to the CIA, the CCF depended on two other groups to fill out its ranks, and their importance shows why the congress was both an instrument of U.S. hegemony and something more than that. The first group consisted of the anti-Communist entrepreneurs. Around the globe, individuals who had first been working independently to foil peace campaigns sought to extend the CCF's reach, including to Latin America. Soon after his work with El Campesino concluded, for example, Gorkin was tapped to head its Latin American division. (Gorkin also edited the CCF's Spanish-language magazine, *Cuadernos del Congreso por la Libertad de la Cultura*, which was usually known simply as *Cuadernos*.) As the CCF established national headquarters in countries around the world, they were staffed by anti-Communist entrepreneurs who had been involved with antipeace campaigns. These activists were, of course, not confused about the political purpose of the organization to which they belonged—they worked to expand the reach of the CCF precisely because they understood it to be an anti-Communist organization. But they often did not know of the organization's connection to the CIA and brought their own agendas to their work.

The CCF's rank and file, its third group, consisted of intellectuals and politicians who participated in programs but not its day-to-day administration. In Latin America, as elsewhere, this was a diverse group that spanned much of the political spectrum, from Marxists to conservatives. But the dominant ethos of the organization was that of social democratic reformism. Its Latin American members admired the center-left parties of

Western Europe and sometimes Franklin Roosevelt's New Deal, but typically not the domestic politics of the Cold War United States. Their participation raised the central problem that the CCF faced in Latin America during the 1950s. "Antitotalitarianism" in politics and the arts was the CCF's logical justification; "anti-Communism" was the priority of the U.S. government that ensured its funding and its existence. But as the repression of the WPC throughout Latin America showed, in the 1950s Communism in Latin America was in no position to challenge the hegemony of the United States in the region. The CCF's political allies struggled against dictatorships that generally had friendly relationships with the Eisenhower administration. But the management of the CCF in Latin America, including Spaniards like Gorkin, looked at Latin America with European eyes and continued to see Communism as the greatest threat to cultural freedom. Its Latin American allies, anti-Communist though they were, understood things differently. In their view, the defense of cultural freedom in Latin America was not primarily a matter of disabling the Communist threat; it was a matter of removing dictators from power and establishing political democracy.

In 1954, when the CCF held its first international meeting in Latin America, Uruguayan poet Roberto Ibáñez offered a toast: "To the only form of imperialism that I recognize: liberty." He was surely aware of the inversion of assumptions—did imperialism not negate liberty?—that was the source of what wit there was in his remark. But he was almost certainly not aware that the CCF to which he belonged was covertly financed by the U.S. government as a weapon of the Cold War, heightening the contradictions at the heart of the toast. "The imperialism of liberty" would prove a pithy description of the politics of the organization to which he belonged.[5]

In Western Europe in the 1950s, where the CCF's campaigns to shift intellectual opinion away from Communism and toward an Atlanticist position have been viewed as relatively successful, U.S. hegemony proved compatible with the consolidation of social democratic governance. In Latin America, where Gorkin and the leadership of the CCF wanted to bend Latin American social democratic nationalism in the direction of pro-Americanism, the geopolitical background was different. Unlike Europe, the mainstream of U.S. diplomacy was not committed to democracy in Latin America, much less to "socialism." Latin America's social democrats wanted the United States to share their antidictatorial agenda, not merely their anti-Communist one. But the leadership of the CCF prioritized a Latin American Left that would help it undermine Communism's appeal throughout the region. These goals were neither totally incompatible nor completely identical. The conflict between a local politics born of antidictatorial, anti-imperial movements and the CCF leadership's desire to emphasize antitotalitarianism, construed as anti-Communism, meant that multiple agendas coexisted within the CCF. If the Latin American operation of the CCF was unsuccessful in the 1950s, as was the general view of its CIA administrators, it was because of the tensions between the slightly different missions of the three groups that made it up—and, at base, between its anti-Communist priorities and its antidictatorial ones, when anti-Communism was so often a tool of dictatorship in Latin America.[6]

The local leadership of the CCF in Latin America was drawn from the ranks of antipeace campaigners of the late 1940s and early 1950s. Each time the Partisans of Peace had tried to gain a foothold in Latin America, two groups had emerged and ultimately cooperated to try to contain its appeal. U.S. embassies published anonymous material to link peace initiatives with Soviet diplomacy and used their friendships with generally conservative media to ensure that their messages would reach wide audiences. At the same time, local anti-Communist entrepreneurs, generally describing themselves as socialists or ex-Communists, also quietly approached the U.S. government in search of concealed aid.

During preparations for the Mexico City Continental Congress for Peace of 1949, for example, U.S. embassy officials, in the course of regular meetings with journalists from major Mexican periodicals, offered information about the Soviet origins of the peace campaigns. Amplified by a bit of sensationalism, this intelligence was reproduced in the tabloid and mainstream press. But as the conference approached, a man named Rodrigo García Treviño, representing a small organization that he called the Grupos Socialistas de la República Mexicana, approached the embassy. García Treviño, a veteran of the Mexican Revolution and an ex-Communist, was one of the best-read Marxists in Mexico and had engaged in heated polemics with the Communist Party over doctrinal matters for years. He had been a close associate of Trotsky; at the end of the 1940s he worked as a bookseller, a journalist, and an anti-Communist activist. In advance of the peace congress, he asked the U.S. embassy to provide him with information about the Communist affiliations of the soon-to-arrive foreign delegates. Embassy officials were eager to have a left-wing voice join the expected chorus of condemnation from the Right. García Treviño succeeded in distributing his reports widely, farcically attributing the information he had acquired from the embassy to "socialist allies" in other Latin American countries. A few years later, García Treviño would become the head of the Mexican Association for Cultural Freedom, the national affiliate of the CCF in that country.[7]

The 1949 peace conference at the Waldorf-Astoria in New York provided the most direct stimulus for the creation of the CCF. The idea of Sidney Hook's Ad Hoc Committee for Intellectual Freedom, which had organized the counterdemonstration, was further developed, leading to the eponymous Congress for Cultural Freedom, a major meeting held in West Berlin in late June 1950. Although the CIA's role was concealed, U.S. government involvement was widely suspected by those hostile to the congress and even some who participated—it seemed to have been too lavish an affair for anyone else to have footed the bill. CIA money was ubiquitous; it even paid for Hook's substitute teacher at New York University while he was away in Berlin. In his opening address at that meeting, Hook expressed the hope that "the fundamental distinction of our time must be drawn not in terms of [economic or social] programs, about which we may legitimately differ, not in terms of a free market in goods or a closed market but only in terms of a free market in ideas." The German philosopher Karl Jaspers contributed a paper that offered the most concise description of the congress's self-justification: "Propaganda, at first an instrument of ruse used to spread untruths that were seemingly favorable, has now become also an indispensable means for enforcing truth. Just as not only wrong but also right needs a lawyer, . . . so is truth now in need of propaganda." The congress associated itself with a wide swath of anti-Communist thinkers, including a few conservatives. But it sought, above all, to represent the best of anti-Communist thought from leftist and centrist intellectual traditions. Its honorary presidents were Jaspers, Hook's teacher John Dewey, Italian philosopher and historian Benedetto Croce, known in this period as a liberal antifascist, the mercurial libertarian Bertrand Russell, and France's Jacques Maritain, the most important intellectual of European Christian Democracy. It was an eclectic group that suggested the capacious boundaries of antitotalitarian thought. For more than two decades the CCF tried to mitigate the appeal of Communism and to strengthen an antitotalitarian "vital center" of liberal political opinion among the intelligentsia of Europe and the rest of the world while simultaneously receiving the majority of its funding from the CIA.[8]

On the operational side, the CCF placed its headquarters in Paris, organized cultural and political symposia, and began to publish its flagship magazines of politics and culture, including the London-based *Encounter* in English and *Preuves* in French. National committees were operated semi-independently, and eventually some subject committees were set up around special themes, such as science. In the first half of the 1950s the

CCF worked to consolidate intellectual, artistic, and political ties between Europe and the United States. Two CIA officials, Michael Josselson and, when Josselson began to suffer health problems under the strain of management, John Hunt, directed its basic operations. Josselson and Hunt, CIA employees though they were, both impressed their colleagues with their intellectual credentials. Born in Estonia, Josselson spoke several languages and, after retirement, wrote a significant biography of the commander who defended Russia against the armies of Napoleon. Hunt was the author of many novels and had a long history in the political Left. With Josselson and Hunt as the mainstays, other CIA case officers moved in and out of management positions: in the words of one CIA historian, the CCF became the "junior year abroad of American intelligence" for the CIA's liberal-arts-major recruits. Money from the CIA was passed through dummy foundations so as to obscure the CCF's U.S. government connections and deceive even its members; it also received some nongovernment support for its activities, especially from the Ford Foundation, whose personnel shared values and outlooks with the significant liberal contingent within the CIA. In spite of the subterfuge, anyone who worked with the CCF for any period of time at least heard rumors of U.S. government involvement. Although many believed Hunt and Josselson when they denied any such connection, others gained either direct or fragmentary knowledge of the dependence on the CIA.[9]

The only person from Latin America to attend the West Berlin Congress for Cultural Freedom in 1950 was Germán Arciniegas, a Colombian intellectual from his country's Liberal Party who at that time was teaching at Columbia University in New York. The year before, he had witnessed both the closing ceremony of the Waldorf-Astoria peace conference and Hook's counterdemonstration, and it was the latter that impressed him. The peace conference, he wrote to a friend, was "reduced to an attack against the United States . . . without the slightest criticism of the Russian system, which seems to me neither more open nor more free." After attending the meeting in Berlin, Arciniegas hoped to see the activities of the CCF extended to Latin America. "We have responsibilities as writers," wrote Arciniegas to James Burnham, "and we must recall to our companions in all the intellectual, artistic and scientific activities that our main goal now is to survive as free men in a free world. We have to put the word freedom before the word peace."[10]

Burnham had been one of the co-organizers of the Berlin congress, along with Sidney Hook. Although he too had once been close to Trotsky, he had grown increasingly conservative and by 1950 was working as a consultant to the CIA. Burnham tried to involve Arciniegas in planning a

CCF-style meeting in the Western Hemisphere, coordinating with a CIA officer in Mexico City, none other than the future Watergate burglar E. Howard Hunt. But they had a problem. They could find no suitable host country that combined ease of travel with exhibiting the values of "cultural freedom" that they hoped to defend. Early efforts foundered. Burnham and Arciniegas reached out to Mexico's Alfonso Reyes, a classicist, poet, essayist, and humanist intellectual who agreed that it would be a good idea to make a show of free thought against fascist and Communist threats, but who said that it would be impossible to mount a conference close to a Mexican presidential election.[11]

A year and a half later, with the CCF well established in Europe, things remained in the planning stages in Latin America. Gorkin was sent on a continental tour in mid-1952, which convinced him that anti-imperialist rhetoric in the region served as a pretext for Stalinist propaganda. "Nevertheless," he wrote, "the general sentiment of intellectual elements in Latin America is anti-totalitarian, anti-reactionary and profoundly liberal and democratic." Gorkin advised that "the Congress should be based on the liberty and universality of Culture—'Culture has no boundaries'—that it is necessary to defend against all totalitarianisms that threaten it and against all ambition to the management of thought or the submission of it to a political party." He recommended the creation of a magazine in the style of *Preuves* and national committees in Mexico and Chile, as well as taking advantage of the many Spanish refugees working in universities and publishing houses across Latin America to promote the idea of universal culture through writing on Europe.[12]

Gorkin's preference for a European orientation for the CCF may have been partially attributable to his Spanish roots, but it was also strategic. For most of the Latin American intellectuals whom the CCF hoped to attract, Europe, especially France, possessed more cultural prestige than did the United States. And it was Europe, not the United States, that represented, to Gorkin, Latin America's potential modernity. "It is my sincere belief," Gorkin wrote to the CCF after another tour of the region in 1953, "that the intelligentsia and the people of Latin America will understand the problems and realities of North America not through its services of information and education, but through the experience, the necessities, and the language of Europe." Furthermore, in Latin America, U.S. hegemony was too raw. As the CCF leadership was considering expanding to Latin America, a friendly warning came from Serafino Romualdi, the AFL's labor ambassador to Latin America, that "the intellectual elements of Latin America, even those clearly opposed to Communism (and there is still a great deal of confusion on that) are at present outspokenly opposed to the foreign policy of the U.S. Government. Some of them might therefore be reluctant to sponsor a conference in which U.S. elements were prominently interested."[13] An avowedly pro-U.S. organization would have had such limited appeal that the CCF added a step of remove and acted as a pro–Western European one instead.

After years of planning and delays, what finally prodded the CCF to extend its operations to Latin America was Neruda's 1953 Continental Cultural Congress (CCC) in Chile. Not everyone was an unwilling partner of the United States. As it had in Mexico in 1949, the anti-Communist side relied on volunteers to perform key tasks. Before the conference, the composer Juan Orrego-Salas, a non-Communist who had been invited to serve on the planning committee of the CCC, appeared at the office of the U.S. Information Service (USIS) in Santiago to ask what he might do. He was advised to serve as a double agent: to attempt to steer the CCC away from Communist domination, and if he could not, to resign in protest. He eventually followed exactly that course; in the meantime he gave committee proceedings to the USIS, which routed them to sympathetic sources. One of these was Carlos de Baráibar, a Spaniard living in exile in Chile, who was, in the words of the USIS, "a steady and willing 'customer' for [our] materials." During the Spanish Civil War, Baráibar had been co-editor of the newspaper *Claridad*, associated with the left wing of Spanish socialism, but at the time of the CCC he had a powerful perch at *El Mercurio,* Chile's conservative paper of record and a bastion of right-wing anti-Communism. (One editorial cartoon in Chile's Communist paper lampooned *El Mercurio*'s upper-class readership by showing a girl looking up at her father and asking, "Hey, Dad, where can you read something about feudal society?" The father replies, "I suppose in the society pages of *El Mercurio.*") The USIS sent Baráibar's clips to other U.S. government propaganda operations, where they were republished as independent reporting in other newspapers around the continent and on Voice of America stations. The illusion of an independent investigation confirming the Communistic nature of the CCC succeeded in getting delegates from other countries, including Alfonso Reyes and the writer Érico Veríssimo of Brazil, to withdraw their support. Both would later participate in the activities of the CCF.[14]

As Neruda's CCC approached, many non-Communists found evidence of Communist involvement in a cultural gathering unsettling. A group of politically center-left figures, many associated with the Maritain-inspired "social Christian" tradition within Chile's future Christian Democratic Party, publicly sought an accommodation with the CCC while still making known their reservations regarding Communist control. Putting together

a short position paper, they argued that because Communism placed politics above all other spheres of life, it would be naïve to participate in a
"cultural" congress sponsored or organized by Communists. They asked
that the CCC be transformed into a debate on the merits of "directed
culture." Affirming the importance of the "liberty of man's creative spirit,"
they asked for a forum to discuss these important issues and the role of
culture in a conflicted world. The young writer Jorge Edwards thought
the manifesto honest and signed it in spite of his growing friendship with
Neruda. But Neruda called him naïve and snapped, "That manifesto was
only a scheme to destroy our congress." Edwards, Neruda implied, was
too young to recognize that each little manifesto was a token in a much
larger conflict.[15]

The wisdom in Neruda's view became clear when Julián Gorkin arrived
in Santiago a few days before the CCC. Gorkin immediately made a series of radio broadcasts denouncing Communist sponsorship of Neruda's
conference; Gorkin's friend Baráibar helpfully "reported" on his activities
in *El Mercurio*. But in addition to the goal of undermining the CCC,
Gorkin had a constructive agenda as well: he planned to create the first
national chapter of the CCF in a Latin American country. To appeal to
the center-left group that had written the independent manifesto, Gorkin
spoke repeatedly about the CCF as a forum in which issues of culture and
politics could be explored honestly. Before leaving, he put Baráibar in
charge of handpicking the members of the new Chilean committee of the
CCF. Baráibar remained the éminence grise of the Chilean committee for
years. In September the newly formed body celebrated the opening of a
library and conference space at a cocktail party for 150 attendees, inaugurating the first national center of the CCF in Latin America. The committee included prominent Christian Democrats, like future president of
Chile Eduardo Frei, the great intellectual of Chilean Christian Democracy
Jaime Castillo Velasco, the country's most important literary critic, Hernán
Díaz Arrieta, and the humanitarian lawyer Hernán Santa Cruz, who, a
few years earlier, had helped draft the UN Universal Declaration of Human
Rights.[16]

The next year, 1954, the Chilean committee hosted the first international
gathering of the CCF in Latin America. For most of its attendees, it provided an introduction to the CCF and its perspectives and intentions. It
also exhibited the organization's essential schizophrenia. Members of its
committee had only recently criticized Neruda's CCC for hiding political
content in the garb of culture, but they would soon do the same. In the
second issue of the Chilean CCF's local magazine, Jaime Castillo criticized

the use of the theme "culture" to attract people to adhere to a congress that served Communist political ends. Writing in a CIA-sponsored journal, Castillo was—probably without realizing it—doing the same thing in the service of different politics.[17]

Nevertheless, tactical questions remained. Some wanted the committee to take a hard line against Communism, while others recommended a softer approach, sticking to platitudes about "cultural freedom" and, reflecting the strength of Christian Democracy in Chile, the "liberty of man's spirit." Although the administrative secretaries of the national bodies—Baráibar in Chile and García Treviño in Mexico—were the liaisons to the CCF headquarters and held the most power within the national organizations, each was simultaneously too controversial and insufficiently famous to serve as their public face. In Chile, the learned figure chosen as president was Georg Nicolai, a German physician and physiologist best known for his pacifist stance during World War I. Driven out of Germany, Nicolai was an abrasive personality and a gruff humanitarian, but he was an academic celebrity in Chile and Argentina, where he had taught intermittently since leaving Europe and where his reputation was particularly enhanced by his association with Albert Einstein over their shared discontent with the politics of war. Distancing himself from pacifism at the outbreak of World War II, by the early 1950s Nicolai placed great stock in the role that the United States would play in the maintenance of a peaceful future. He wanted the Chilean committee of the CCF to be an avowedly political body and openly supportive of the U.S. government's fight against Communism.[18]

But Nicolai's was the minority view. Even Michael Josselson, the CIA agent who headed the CCF, preferred the softer sell. The anti-imperialist near consensus among intellectuals from the countries of Latin America rendered an avowedly pro-U.S. stance impractical and tactically unsound. When Nicolai wrote to Josselson complaining that the Chilean committee had become "anti-Yankee" under the supposed influence of Baráibar, Josselson rebuffed him, saying that the United States, like all countries, had positive and negative features, and that the latter could be criticized. The task of the committee would be served, he wrote, if it succeeded in contrasting the relative liberty of the democracies with the total slavery of totalitarianism.[19]

During the international forum of 1954, the Communist newspaper *El Siglo* tried to establish the un-Chilean nature of the CCF by accusing it of taking money from a foreign power. *El Siglo* charged, wrongly in fact but perhaps less so in spirit, that the CCF received payments from the U.S.

State Department and from the United Fruit Company, a U.S.-based corporation hated by the Latin American Left for its support of regional dictatorships. Even the CCF's delegates wondered who had paid their travel expenses. The public story, which is likely what Gorkin told the group, was that the CCF received no U.S. government money but was funded by free trade-union organizations and private foundations, including the "Feshman" and the Rockefeller. In truth, the CCF did receive some clean money from the Rockefeller and Ford Foundations, but the delegates would not have known that both the "free trade-union organizations" and the "Feshman" (probably the Farfield Foundation, headed by Julius Fleischmann) were conduits for CIA dollars. Without this knowledge, the Chilean committee of the CCF tried to make its source of funding an asset: in a question-and-answer section of its new national magazine, *Cultura y Libertad,* it argued that receiving money from private U.S. foundations did not make it an instrument of U.S. imperialism. The very existence of private foundations, it held, proved the difference between the directed cultural world of the totalitarian states and one in which private organizations were allowed to operate without government control. But the difference was not as large as was imagined; the obvious irony was that many of those private foundations in the United States, which were supposed to demonstrate the difference between totalitarian and free ones, acted as concealed instruments of the U.S. government.[20]

During the 1950s the CCF slowly expanded throughout Latin America. Friends of the congress formed formal national committees in Uruguay and Mexico in 1954, Argentina in December 1955, Peru in March 1957, and Brazil in April 1958, as well as in Cuba and Colombia. The CCF also operated in other countries on a reduced basis, distributing propaganda even in the absence of organized committees. It sponsored a variety of publications: books, magazines, pamphlets, and articles in newspapers, placed on behalf of the national committees, and the flagship publication in Spanish, the Gorkin-edited vehicle *Cuadernos*. It organized local events, including roundtables, lectures, and showings at art galleries. It sponsored travel to promote dialogue and to stitch together the anti-Communists it deemed respectable into a less patchwork and shabby international community. Whether participants knew of the CIA's involvement with the CCF or not—and most did not—the apparatus of the CCF was filled with precisely the kind of anti-Communist entrepreneurs who saw the United States as an ally in their war against Communism. For them, the Cultural Cold War was a continuation of their anti-Communist war by other means. The remarkable thing was less that the United States was sponsoring their work than that they had managed to inscribe local versions of anti-Communism onto a Cultural Cold War led by the U.S. government.[21]

The CCF was formally a cultural body, committed to the principles of antitotalitarianism and, consequently, cultural freedom. But there were clear and deliberate political implications of its position: it was against Communism, fascism, and dictatorship because they made cultural freedom impossible. It also acknowledged that poverty and illiteracy were incompatible with cultural flourishing, and so its political allies in the region were the reformist parties with social content in their platforms: Christian Democrats in places like Chile where they were strong, some of the region's socialist parties, but most especially the secular nationalist parties that were programmatically committed to anti-Communism and were known by their sympathizers as the "Democratic Left." Along with the CIA and the anti-Communist entrepreneurs like Gorkin, this anti-Communist Left formed the third leg of the CCF stool. But its members brought their own agenda to the enterprise, which sometimes conflicted with the priorities of the CCF's management.

Latin America, like the rest of the world, had non- and anti-Communist Left movements that predated the Cold War. But because Latin America, in comparison with Europe, lacked a substantial industrial proletariat, the parties with "socialist" tendencies were not generally parties of workers but instead drew on multiple sources of support, including the professional and middle classes, peasants, and unionized workers where possible. Peru's Alianza Popular Revolucionaria Americana (APRA), founded by the philosopher Victor Raúl Haya de la Torre in 1924, was an inspiration to many other parties for its anti-imperialism, its nationalism, its emphasis on social justice in the context of political democracy, and its polyclass approach to organizing. It was also highly centralized, opportunistic, and personalistic, and Haya seemed to have flirted with every possible political philosophy, from Communism to fascism, at some point in his career. APRA's most important intellectual, Luis Alberto Sánchez, worked closely with the CCF in the 1950s. Venezuela's Rómulo Betancourt, who had founded his country's Acción Democrática party in 1941 and twice served as his country's president, had a similar trajectory. During a Costa Rican exile in the 1930s he took a leadership position in that country's Communist Party, but by the end of the 1930s he had abandoned Communism and opted for a social democratic agenda, again in the context of a vertically integrated mass party.[22]

In Central America and the Caribbean, where the region's most repressive dictatorships ruled, democratic movements supported one another to try to remove those governments from power, banding together into what was sometimes described as the "Caribbean Legion." Juan José Arévalo, the reformist president of Guatemala from 1945 to 1951, gave military support to invasions of dictatorships that included Cuban and Dominican antidictatorial fighters. The legion aided in one military success, when José Figueres of Costa Rica led a successful armed uprising against a government that had included Communists after an election in which he alleged that fraud had taken place. Although evidence suggests Figueres may not have intervened on behalf of the defrauded candidate, his junta abolished Costa Rica's armed forces, deepened Costa Rica's welfare state, and yielded power to the candidate he thought had been cheated. Figueres was later returned to office democratically, and Costa Rica became Latin America's most successful social democracy in the second half of the twentieth century.[23]

The anti-Communist Left had a complicated set of views about the United States. Haya de la Torre's original formulation for APRA was "democratic inter-Americanism without empire and without imperialism," a vision of affairs that demanded respect for sovereignty but did not entail a complete rejection of the United States. (Haya argued, against Lenin's formulation of imperialism as the last stage of capitalism, that in Latin America imperialism was the first expression of capitalism.) Haya likened foreign investment from the United States to a river: it carried water that was necessary for growing healthy crops, but it had to be channeled and controlled appropriately so that it would not spill over its banks and flood the fields. Most members of the anti-Communist Left came to believe that reaching some kind of understanding with the United States was essential to being allowed to govern—a recognition of the hegemony of the Colossus of the North. Accepting this reality, they sought allies among socialists and liberals in the United States who could help them advance their interests.[24]

However, although Latin America's anti-Communist Left had a few sympathizers in the State Department and the CIA, it was generally too far to the left to be considered as a governing partner in the region by either the Truman or the Eisenhower administrations. The United States pressured the Organization of American States to stop Caribbean Legion activity in 1949 and 1950. There were some alliances to be had with the Democratic Left in the AFL, through people like Jay Lovestone and Serafino Romualdi. The AFL supported the creation of union alternatives to Vicente Lombardo Toledano's Confederación de Trabajadores de América Latina (CTAL) in the late 1940s and the incorporation of the formally anti-Communist federations aligned with the parties of the anti-Communist Left.[25]

For the most part, however, the anti-Communist Left had to be responsible for organizing itself. As early as 1940 the Chilean Socialist Party hosted the Latin American Congress of Leftist Parties—excluding Communists but including socialists from Argentina and Ecuador, as well as Rómulo Betancourt, then living in exile in Chile and observing socialist operations there. A decade later they met again, this time in Havana, where Rómulo Betancourt was living, again in exile, with the financial support of a like-minded Cuban government. They called their 1950 meeting the Inter-American Conference for Democracy and Freedom, assembling about 150 people from many of the same groups of the non-Communist Left that had met in Santiago ten years earlier: Chilean socialists, members of Venezuela's Acción Democrática and Peru's APRA, Uruguay's most important socialist leader, Emilio Frugoni, and social democratic groups from Costa Rica, Cuba, and other countries throughout the region.[26]

Unlike earlier meetings, the Havana conference brought these individuals together with allies from the United States: activists for civil liberties and human rights like Roger Baldwin and Frances Grant; regular members of the anti-Communist Left, including Sidney Hook, Robert Alexander, Archibald MacLeish, Pearl Buck, Max Ascoli, Sol Levitas, Arthur Schlesinger Jr., Bryn Hovde, and Walter White of the National Association for the Advancement of Colored People; officials from both the AFL and the Congress of Industrial Organizations; Norman Thomas of the Socialist Party of the United States; and liberal elected officials from both major parties. Discussion focused not on Latin America per se but on the idea of the Western Hemisphere in the maintenance of peace and the creation of a democratic front against all forms of totalitarianism. The meeting created a New York–based office called the Inter-American Association for Democracy and Freedom (IADF), which became the lobbying arm of Latin America's anti-Communist Left within the United States, with Frances Grant serving as its secretary general.[27]

Grant, the motor force behind the IADF for its more than thirty years of subsequent operation, had been the head of the Latin American Committee of the International League for the Rights of Man and had helped establish the defense of human rights as part of an antitotalitarian agenda in the hemisphere. A pamphlet published shortly after its founding meeting explained that the IADF "was founded in 1950 . . . to stave off the inroads of communism and neo-fascism, both of which are exploiting the unrest of the peoples to their own ends, often in an unholy alliance. It was felt that unless a vital counter-force of democracy was developed to arrest this active and aggressive offensive, we might have a new 'Korea' on our doorstep." Whether this was intended as a serious analysis or a sort of cri de coeur to a U.S. political environment that took the "inroads of communism" far more seriously than those of "neo-fascism" is probably impossible to say. But for better or worse, it was a sign that what constituted Latin American social democracy had, in the last instance, accepted the logic of the Cold War and would fight for its place within the constraints imposed by U.S. hegemony.[28]

On the other hand, the purpose of the IADF was to loosen those constraints and bring the United States around to a more sympathetic politics. Although the IADF was intended to function dually in Uruguay and New York, only the New York office ever operated properly. That office has been described as a kind of "Red Cross" for the Latin American Democratic Left, representing its interests to U.S. audiences, harboring exiles, holding press conferences, cultivating sympathetic journalists, and lobbying the United Nations and the U.S. government. The earliest funding of the IADF came from anti-Communist labor groups based in New York, including small contributions from the Free Trade Union Committee that might have been contaminated by CIA dollars. But its largest and most stable funding source became the Venezuelan governments of Rómulo Betancourt and Raúl Leoni of Acción Democrática, which regularly contributed $1,000 a month to the IADF throughout their terms in office, from early 1959 to 1969. The IADF was not, in other words, yet another CIA front.[29]

Many of the same people who participated in the non-Communist Left conferences of 1940 and 1950 were championed by the CCF in the 1950s. Haya de la Torre and Betancourt, for instance, were published in *Cuadernos*. And the personnel of the CCF shared much with Latin America's Democratic Left: an active rejection of Communist politics and an admiration for Western European democratic socialism. But there was a fissure on the issue of anti-imperialism. For Gorkin, for example, Latin American anti-imperialism was only a distraction from the world's only true imperialism, that of the Soviet Union. But many of Latin America's anti-Communist Left had spent decades in exile, working to restore democracy to countries ruled by U.S.-supported dictatorships. The anti-Communist Left knew that Gorkin's position was weak: if the cause of the Democratic Left in the region was to be advanced, U.S. power would have to change. It would have to be imperialism placed on the side of democracy. The anti-Communist Left, through the CCF and in other more direct contacts with the CIA, would show itself willing to accept covert financial support from the United States, but it also wanted the United

States to actually support its preferred policies, a point on which it would be repeatedly disappointed. Gorkin filled *Cuadernos* with anti-Soviet essays, trying to steer the Latin American department of the CCF toward a European kind of anti-Communism, in which the suffering of Eastern Europe under Soviet rule loomed as the central moral problem with which the world needed to grapple. Given such a perspective, Gorkin failed to recognize that the practice of antitotalitarianism might require a different kind of anti-Communism in Latin America than in Eastern Europe. Thus Gorkin, an important voice within the CCF, would end up arguing—in the name of cultural freedom—in defense of counterrevolutionary violence.

———————

The fissures between the management of the CCF and the anti-Communist Left it sought to influence were exposed most dramatically by events in Guatemala during the mid-1950s. The country's reformist president, Juan José Arévalo, had been a central figure in the Caribbean Legion and, although he tolerated individual Communists, had opposed party organization and supported non-Communist internationalism. His successor, Jacobo Arbenz, who served from 1951 to 1954, took a somewhat different path. At the end of Arévalo's term, Arbenz was elected democratically. But, unlike Arévalo, he cultivated close relationships with Communists, some of whom he appointed to subcabinet posts. They helped craft his signature initiatives, including the far-reaching land reform that angered the country's largest landowner, the United Fruit Company. The reform did not aim to establish Stalinist collectives but rather to diminish the power of large landowners and create a free, property-holding peasantry— it was, one of its Communist coauthors later insisted, a "bourgeois law." But the context frightened the Eisenhower administration. Arbenz sent anti-U.S. Cold War signals by deepening his government's connections with Soviet-aligned groups, including the CTAL and the World Peace Council. (CIA monitoring found teachers passing out peace movement propaganda to students, for example, and said that they were disciplined for not signing peace petitions.) In the United States, Arbenz's government came to be seen as an ally of the Kremlin and a potential danger to U.S. national security and economic interests; the United Fruit Company lobbied the U.S. government to take action to stop him.[30]

Whether its efforts succeeded, or whether, in the words of Guatemala's Communist leader José Manuel Fortuny, "they would have overthrown us even if we had grown no bananas," remains a subject of debate. In spite of Arbenz's close ties to Communist intellectuals, the Soviet Union was not eager to support Guatemalan Communism, which, apart from some participation in Soviet front activity, remained isolated. The United States took a shipment of Czechoslovakian arms as significant evidence of Communist connections, but it was no gift and had been purchased by Arbenz. Still, the CIA, assisted by Anastasio Somoza, the dictator of Nicaragua, propped up the obscure Guatemalan colonel Carlos Castillo Armas as an alternative to Arbenz. The CIA orchestrated a series of propaganda and paramilitary campaigns that led Guatemala's military to remove Arbenz from power in 1954. The coup sparked popular protests throughout Latin America and toppled not just Arbenz but also the teetering notion that something like the Good Neighbor Policy remained in effect. Vice President Nixon appeared on television with Castillo Armas and called his victory "the first time in the history of the world that the [*sic*] Communist government has been overthrown by the people." In power, Castillo Armas undid nearly all of Arbenz's land reforms. The coup in Guatemala was not the beginning of Latin America's Cold War, but it announced a new phase, demonstrating the power of the CIA to undermine even a democratically elected government to pursue reactionary goals. A young Argentine doctor, Ernesto "Che" Guevara, witnessed the events and concluded that Latin America's revolution could not compromise with the United States and would have to strike directly at the sources of its power.[31]

Arbenz's government had long been controversial within the CCF. While the first international meeting of the CCF was taking place in Santiago in 1954, Arbenz had imposed censorship, rounded up government opponents, and attempted to silence opposition media in Guatemala in a failed effort to deal with the threat of a coup. The CCF headquarters in Paris wanted all the delegates to sign a resolution of protest that stated that "even temporary suspension of constitutional guarantees [leads] inevitably to a totalitarian state." When Gorkin tried to gather support for the measure, he encountered substantial resistance. The Mexican delegates did not want to sign anything that did not protest the exploitation of the Guatemalan masses by foreign companies, and others were worried that the passage of a resolution would upset public opinion in their countries. Eventually all agreed on a compromise resolution that condemned Latin American dictators who deprived their peoples of liberty, as well as the suppression of cultural freedom in Guatemala.[32]

Gorkin's hatred of the government of Arbenz surpassed anything that he could muster from the rest of the delegates. Gorkin believed himself to be in possession of a letter between Arbenz's predecessor Arévalo and the Soviet Union's head of trade relations in Mexico, which convinced him of Arévalo's and (a fortiori) Arbenz's subordination to Moscow. The letter promised greater harmonization between the Guatemalan and Soviet governments and credited Soviet spiritual and economic aid with permitting the unification of the Guatemalan masses under Arevalist auspices. Although the letter convinced Gorkin of the presence of the Soviet hand in Guatemalan Communism, it was an obvious forgery, and even cursory knowledge of Arévalo's behavior in office would have sufficed to cure Gorkin of his illusions.[33]

Yet in *Cuadernos* Gorkin wrote that Guatemala's democratic revolution, which should have served popular interests, had instead been twisted by Communists to serve Kremlin strategy. He conceded that Guatemalan Communists had worked for just ends, such as agrarian reform. "But that," he wrote,

> corresponds to the general tactic of Communism in its march toward power . . . Talk of democracy serves as a springboard . . . For them, it has nothing to do with serving people, but in using people for distant ends contrary to their own interests. In general, whether they impose their own dictatorship or provoke the establishment of a reactionary one, the people are sacrificed . . . If the triumph of anti-Communism leads to new *caudillista* dictatorship, to the semifeudal system that existed before [Arévalo], to the predominance of foreign capital and the maintenance of the masses in their condition of misery and ignorance, Communism will be the winner.

Gorkin's labored logic assigned the blame to Communism whether the ill that befell Guatemala was revolutionary or counterrevolutionary. He also argued that reforms carried out by a democrat were progressive, but that the same actions taken by a Communist served the Kremlin. How then to work for justice? He seems to have thought that the sort of work that he was doing was the only way out of that cycle of revolution and counterrevolution. "[So that Communism does not triumph,] it is necessary to develop and apply an authentic politics of liberty in the Latin American setting," he wrote. "Its intellectual 'elites,' its democratic political groups, and its free trade unions should take charge of developing and applying it . . . with the collaboration and the help of whatever democratic and progressive elements exist in the United States, Europe, and Asia. We have a world to defend. But for it to be worth defending, it has to be habitable and decent." Gorkin had decided that Guatemala in 1954 was neither, and he tried to set CCF policy accordingly.[34]

But the fall of Arbenz would not disappear as a source of controversy; instead, it would fester as the global CCF's interest turned more toward Latin America. The CCF held a major international gathering in Milan in

1955 called "The Future of Freedom." Many of the delegates there seemed to think that their European work was largely complete: some synthesis of the European liberal and socialist projects had diminished the intellectual appeal of Communism, showing that there was no inherent contradiction between its understandings of individual freedoms and state participation in the economy to ensure common prosperity. When the Milan conference came to an end, University of Chicago sociologist Edward Shils wrote of "the end of ideology": his sense that Communist ideological extremism had been defeated by the more pragmatic postwar politics of Western Europe and the United States.[35]

Shils was quick to note, however, that whatever liberal-socialist consensus did exist at the Milan conference did not extend to the delegates from Asia, Africa, and the Middle East.[36] According to Shils's generalizations, the Third World delegates defended the importance of nationalism against the European delegates, who generally dismissed it as a dangerous relic of the nineteenth century, and they put greater emphasis than some of the Europeans on the necessity of economic development as a prerequisite to freedom. Ideology may have ended in Europe and the United States, Shils thought, but "we must no longer think only for European or American society. Our theories of liberty, of the relation between religion and progress, tradition and intellectual independence, must be thought out and formulated in such a way that they will do justice to the situations of the new countries of Asia and Africa and South America." The Milan conference marked the CCF's turn toward increasing engagement with the non-European world, and at a private meeting between the U.S. and Latin American delegates, the urgent need for a Western Hemisphere version of the Milan conference was agreed on.[37]

That meeting took more than a year to plan and proved to be the only major international conference that the CCF held in Latin America during the 1950s. There, the issue of Guatemala reemerged, as if to show how difficult it would be for the European fusion of liberalism and socialism to be compatible with U.S. interests in the region. The conference tried to bring together like-minded thinkers from the United States and Latin America, including the venerated literary figures Alfonso Reyes of Mexico and Rómulo Gallegos of Venezuela. In addition to these, the conference was attended by APRA's chief intellectual, Luis Alberto Sánchez, Colombia's Germán Arciniegas, Jaime Castillo Velasco and Carlos de Baráibar from Chile, Jaime Benítez from Puerto Rico, Raúl Roa and Mario Llerena from Cuba, Érico Veríssimo from Brazil, and the historian José Luis Romero from Argentina. The U.S. delegation included writers John

In the main room at the Inter-American Conference for Cultural Freedom, September 1956, in Mexico City. At the table, from left to right, author and playwright Mauricio Magdaleno of Mexico, poet Sara de Ibáñez of Uruguay, Venezuelan author and ex-president Rómulo Gallegos, Mexican politician Pedro de Alba, Spanish diplomat Salvador de Madariaga, Mexico's Alfonso Reyes, and an unidentified man. In the back row, Venezuelan politician Gonzalo Barrios, Socialist Norman Thomas from the United States, and another unidentified man.   Photo courtesy Special Collections Research Center, University of Chicago; IACF, series V, section C, box 204, folder 6.

Dos Passos and Ralph Ellison, founder of the American Civil Liberties Union Roger Baldwin, Norman Thomas, and the historian of Mexico Frank Tannenbaum.[38]

Finally scheduled for 18–26 September 1956 and officially hosted by the Mexican Association for Cultural Freedom, which had been established in 1954, the Inter-American Conference for Cultural Freedom enjoyed enough favor from the Mexican government to obtain something that the peace movement never had: a government-approved room at the Palace of Fine Arts in Mexico City. Just like the peace movement, the CCF never worried about vacant seats at its events, since allies in the labor movement could order workers to sit in empty chairs. Unlike peace movement gatherings, which were never reported by the nonleftist press in Mexico, the CCF event received considerable media attention in print, radio, and television. The government even allocated part of its Sunday radio hour to publicizing the event. Pedro de Alba, a medical doctor and diplomat who had worked in the 1930s as assistant director of the Pan American Union and was, in 1956, a senator from the Partido Revolucionario Institucional (PRI) as well as a member of the Mexican Association for Cultural Freedom, worked to obtain government support for the proceedings. Speaking at the opening session, Senator de Alba emphasized the "constructive" nature of the conference's anti-Communism, noting that it was motivated by a "reformist socialism detested by the Soviets, for it advocates methods to soothe the class struggle and avoid a possible revolution."[39]

Early speeches expressed points of consensus. Luis Alberto Sánchez identified dictatorship as one of the principal impediments to cultural freedom in the Americas. Another delegate made a plea for intellectual independence from the great powers, contrasting "decent intellectuals" with "servile" ones who accepted invitations from either Moscow or the U.S. Department of State. This might have been read as an attack on the conference itself, but the speaker naturally classified all those in attendance as "decent intellectuals" who would accept no form of servility.[40]

But the conference took a sudden turn when Gorkin, in his capacity as conference secretary, read out a telegram of generic support for cultural freedom that Guatemala's Carlos Castillo Armas had sent the conference. Gorkin was engaged in a quixotic effort to defend the so-called liberal nature of Castillo Armas's repressive regime. Most did not agree, and Gorkin confessed surprise that the response of so many Latin American democrats had been almost unanimously in favor of Arbenz. But Castillo Armas had collaborated not just with the CIA to overthrow Arbenz but also with the Nicaraguan dictator, Anastasio Somoza; there was no way to pretend that he was part of the Democratic Left. As much as many of the other conferees shared Gorkin's anti-Communism, their response to his reading of the telegram from Castillo Armas was to censure Gorkin. He put it away and never brought it up again.[41]

Reading about the telegram incident in the newspaper, the Guatemalan author Mario Monteforte Toledo, who had not originally been invited to the conference, appeared the next day to make a speech. Monteforte was no Communist fellow traveler. In time, he would join the Mexican branch of the CCF. He had volunteered to fight in the U.S. Army during World War II. A government official during the Arévalo years—he had been president of the Guatemalan Congress in 1948 and 1949—he resigned in 1950 and departed for Mexico, frustrated in part with what he saw as growing Communist influence over governmental decisions. He held Ar-

Julián Gorkin speaking at the Inter-American Conference for Cultural Freedom. The indentation and scarring on his forehead, the result of a childhood accident coupled with his injury at the Erlich, Alter, and Tresca memorial meeting with Victor Serge in 1943, are visible. Photo courtesy Archivo General de la Nación, Collection Hermanos Mayo, envelope 10,424.

benz in especially low esteem. (In 1957, Monteforte published a novel that he had finished in 1955, *Una manera de morir,* that paints a bleak picture of ideological conformism and in another environment might have been something of a Spanish-language *Darkness at Noon.*) But he liked the coup even less, and after Castillo Armas took power by force in 1954, Monteforte returned to Guatemala, where he published two opposition newspapers critical of the new government and its ties to the United States. Eventually, in 1956, citing a conspiracy on Castillo Armas's life, Guatemalan government officials threw sand in his presses, pulled him from his house, took him to prison, and dumped him at the Honduran border along with other intellectual dissidents. He made his way to Costa Rica, where, with the assistance of President José Figueres, he was able to return to Mexico.[42]

At the Inter-American Conference, Monteforte Toledo told the story of his life. He spoke about his experiences serving in the U.S. Army, the good spirit of many North Americans, and the extraordinary lack of knowledge of most Americans about their own government's actions in Latin America. "North American imperialism is real," he said, and he implored those in the audience with academic jobs in the United States to explain this to the North American public. His speech struck a chord. In a follow-up to Monteforte, while warning that the United States still needed to play an important role in fighting Soviet propaganda in Latin America, even the temperamentally conservative Spaniard Salvador de Madariaga expressed his agreement that the ill-advised policies of the United States were a great threat to culture in the Americas.[43]

From that point onward, the problem of U.S. imperialism dominated discussion. Some of the North American delegates defended the United States against specific charges while acknowledging that U.S. policy toward Latin America merited criticism. Others broadened the discussion. Argentine historian José Luis Romero argued that the problem with imperialism was not the character of the North American people but part of the nature of the capitalist system. Future president of Costa Rica Luis Alberto Monge, then secretary general of the anti-Communist union confederation Organización Regional Interamericana de Trabajadores (ORIT), headquartered in Mexico City, criticized the U.S. government for supporting Latin American dictators and for having intervened in Guatemala. "The politics of the United States," he said, "has taken a belligerent attitude against the Communist threat, but frequently that belligerent attitude has ended up as a hysterical anti-Communism that instead of constituting a true defense of liberty becomes a straitjacket for intellectuals. Because of that hysterical anti-Communism, labor leaders can acquire habits contrary to that very liberty."[44]

Comments like these made their way to officials of the CCF in the United States and Europe, who found them alarming. In response to the proceedings in Mexico, the American Committee for Cultural Freedom in the United States proposed to convene a forum called "The North American Image in Latin American Culture" to think about the so-called problem of anti-Americanism. Norman Thomas wrote to Josselson in Paris that "after a pretty honest facing of the lack of various freedoms in Latin America . . . our Latin American friends turned with enthusiasm to criticism of the United States as somehow responsible for most of their

THE CCF AND THE IMPERIALISM OF LIBERTY   107

ills. This criticism with few exceptions wasn't well documented and was very repetitious . . . It was criticism of the United States which got the real applause from the galleries." Gorkin vigorously defended the conference to Josselson and sent out surveys to each of the participants to ensure that they did not share Thomas's dim estimation of what had occurred. Many supported Gorkin: Roger Baldwin of the American Civil Liberties Union wrote to Josselson: "You need not be disturbed about the expressions of anti-Americanism. They were to be expected from people who experience the effects of policies which we liberals in the U.S. also criticize and seek to change." Gorkin looked to the positive: he was glad that the proceedings had given no opportunities for the Communist press to accuse those gathered of being agents of the State Department. The planned response by the American Committee for Cultural Freedom went nowhere because that group's financial troubles caused it to vote to cease operations in January 1957. Josselson, however, thinking in stereotypes, became convinced that it was difficult to get "Latin-Americans to talk sensibly on specific topics instead of indulging in empty rhetoric and demagogy" and thereafter remained wary of approving any further major work in Latin America.[45]

Although the CCF's major international gathering in the 1950s had made a bad impression on CCF management, local committees worked diligently throughout the decade. The actions of the most active and most successful CCF chapter during the 1950s, the Chilean committee under Carlos de Baráibar, illustrate the techniques that the CCF used to frustrate Communist front activity. Responding to a minor Chilean conference associated with the peace movement in 1955, for example, Baráibar used members of the CCF, ORIT, and allied student organizations to encourage delegates to request that a resolution be included that condemned not just Latin American dictatorships but totalitarianism and dictatorship everywhere. When this was declined, anti-Communist student organizations walked out. Subsequently, when a meeting of the Communist-affiliated youth organization was set to be held in Chile, the CCF published material that persuaded the government to ban the meeting. A few months later the CCF supervised a rival inter-American meeting of youths that included representatives from the U.S.-based National Student Association, which, like the CCF, was secretly backed by the CIA. Baráibar received considerable praise from centrist anti-Communists for his work, including future president Eduardo Frei, who was a member of the committee. The Argentine committee was similarly active; it was established in December

The streets of Santiago, Chile, 1956. A poster at a news kiosk advertises various events of the Congress for Cultural Freedom: a meeting of the youth committee and speeches by Julio César Jobet, a socialist intellectual who argued for a humanist Marxism; Raúl Rettig, a leader of the Radical Party who later served as Salvador Allende's ambassador to Brazil and the lead author of the truth commission's report on crimes committed by the Pinochet regime; José Ignacio Palma Vicuña, a Christian Democratic politician; and Eduardo Moore, a liberal. Photo courtesy Special Collections Research Center, University of Chicago; IACF, series II, box 204, folder 10.

1955, shortly after a military coup deposed the government of Juan Domingo Perón, which was generally understood by CCF affiliates as a manifestation of Latin American totalitarianism. It brought together some of the country's most prominent intellectuals and similarly worked against efforts by Communists to extend their cultural programs to Argentina.[46]

At the continental level, the CIA and the CCF worked together with favored publishers to support the publication of dozens of book titles. In the United States, the CCF's regular partner was Frederick A. Praeger, an Austrian immigrant who frequently worked with the CCF and more directly with the U.S. government and the CIA on other work. Praeger, who was personally and professionally invested in the success of the anti-Communist Left, used U.S. government subsidies and purchases to make otherwise unprofitable works good business. The U.S. government, for its part, got from Praeger an independent imprint that betrayed no immediate sign of state support. For example, the CCF considered it essential that Milovan Djilas's *The New Class*—which argued that contrary to rhe-

toric that made Communism out to be a classless society, it was producing a new class system based on proximity to the state bureaucracy—get
wide distribution. The final pages of the manuscript were smuggled out
of Yugoslavia by a *Time* reporter and eventually supplied to Praeger by a
CIA officer who supervised its translation and distribution. The particular
power of the argument came from Djilas's history as a Communist, so
Josselson was incensed when Praeger's paperback edition failed to include a biographical note. The purpose of publication was not only the
book's content but also its context and the political consequences that
it was expected to generate. Praeger had several offers as he sought to
prepare the Latin American edition of *The New Class,* but Josselson and
Gorkin sought to maximize political influence instead of profits and
insisted that he accept an inferior monetary offer from Argentina's Editorial
Sudamericana, since they believed that it would be in the best position to
distribute the book widely throughout the continent. Praeger balked, but
Josselson insisted, and, threatened with the loss of future business, Praeger
assented.[47]

For publications that were more specific to certain Latin American contexts, the CCF had other publishers with whom it worked closely. One of
the most important of these was Bartolomeu Costa Amic in Mexico, the
publisher living in exile who had once been close to Trotsky and was a
personal friend of Julián Gorkin. Many CCF publications for Mexican
and Latin American audiences rolled off Costa Amic's presses, including
the magazine of the Mexican Association for Cultural Freedom, *Examen.*
Bankrupt in Mexico after bringing out the works of Gorkin and Victor
Serge in the early 1940s, Costa Amic found success in the Cold War era
as the house publisher of the works of the anti-Communist Left. "[It was
the] best deal I ever had," Costa Amic reportedly once said. "The CIA pays
for the printing, and then they buy all the copies!"[48]

The politics of the CCF, so centered on the antitotalitarian idea of the
freedom of the individual artist or writer to produce as he or she pleased,
also involved the sponsorship of original works of art and analysis. The
irony of the matter was that freedom was defined as the absence of state
interference in the production of thought and culture, but then, through
the CCF, the U.S. government was interfering in the production of thought
and culture. The mildly mitigating factor in this hypocrisy was that much
of the interference was not especially effective.

The centerpiece of the CCF's Latin American publishing efforts, for example, the magazine *Cuadernos,* was never a great success. It circulated
many fewer copies than the English-language *Encounter* and fewer even
than the German-language *Der Monat,* despite serving the better part of

two continents plus Spain. Gorkin wanted *Cuadernos* to be at the heart of the CCF's political and cultural project, and, like Josselson, he did not want CCF activity in Latin America to be primarily constructed to bridge the divide between Latin America and the United States. Under Gorkin's editorship, the pages of *Cuadernos* were filled almost entirely with Hispanic poetics, anti-Soviet propaganda, and reports on the culture and politics of Europe and Latin America. Its favored authors were mostly Spanish Republicans. When the Chilean Communist newspaper *El Siglo* described Gorkin's activities as "to subjugate [Latin] American culture to a cosmopolitan and de-nationalizing politics," the description was plainly hostile but really not inaccurate. The idiom of Gorkin's campaign was European, and his model of Latin American cultural identity was cosmopolitan in the sense of being international and urban. In contrast to artists associated with the WPC, Gorkin paid little attention to the contributions of indigenous cultures to national cultural identities in Latin America. His Latin America was, for the most part, one of "universal" elites, esteemed not for speaking to nationally specific concerns but for their ability to achieve renown among European peers. But Gorkin's was an ersatz universalism. *Cuadernos* reprinted prominent pieces from CCF-affiliated magazines such as *Encounter* and *Preuves,* but the editors of *Encounter* were not interested in using articles from the less-prestigious *Cuadernos.*[49]

For all of Gorkin's reputation as a European "universalist," his taste in literature was surprisingly old-fashioned. Gorkin's favorite Latin American writer was Rómulo Gallegos, the novelist and deposed president of Venezuela. As a writer, Gallegos was best known for 1929's *Doña Bárbara,* which by the 1950s was beginning to seem a novel out of a different century. A profoundly creole book that made no obvious concession to European tastes, *Doña Bárbara* employed regional language, evoking Venezuelan Spanish as it was actually spoken. Its central dramatic tension was that of civilization versus barbarism and the necessity for Latin America to build its political and cultural identity around the former. It was a respected work with a liberal message that in the 1950s was particularly championed by intellectuals of the anti-Communist Left—Gallegos had been Rómulo Betancourt's teacher and was a symbol of Acción Democrática. This may have served to put off some of the best young writers in Latin America, who imagined more thoroughgoing social change than its author called for and were branching out from regional literatures to participate instead in international, experimental literary influences. In the 1950s many young writers were not looking for works that would find acceptance in Europe for their universal qualities; they were reading world literature for its most interesting writers (like Franz Kafka and William Faulkner) and trying to participate in those inspirational modern currents. One of those young writers, Gabriel García Márquez, later famous for his decades-long friendship with Fidel Castro, was once asked whether he held Gallegos to be a great novelist, and he replied, "In his novel *Canaima* there's a description of a chicken that's really quite good." A magazine that held out Gallegos as its icon was unlikely to find many followers among the rising generation of writers. But the purpose of a magazine like *Cuadernos* was less to win converts than to consolidate an outlook—a set of ideas about culture and politics that would aid the anti-Communist cause in the Cold War.[50]

Above all, CCF campaigns were directed against what the CCF took to be examples of Communist cultural hegemony: against Neruda in Chile and the muralists Rivera and Siqueiros in Mexico. The anti-Neruda work had a long pedigree and both Chilean and international dimensions. After Khrushchev's "secret speech" in 1956 detailing his predecessor's crimes, the Chilean Committee for Cultural Freedom issued a pamphlet, *Así veían a Stalin,* that contained examples of prominent Chilean Marxists, including Neruda and Salvador Allende, offering fawning praise of Stalin's character and accomplishments rendered absurd by Khrushchev's indictment. For years the CCF tried to advance the career of its own politically centrist poet, Julio Barrenechea, at the expense of Neruda's; indeed, in 1959 its efforts helped get him elected over Neruda to the presidency of the Sociedad de Escritores de Chile. One of Neruda's friends said that the results were the work of "reactionary" agents of the CCF, and although the "reactionary" designation had more to do with entrenched habits of name-calling, the assigning of responsibility was fair. Baráibar had been promoting Barrenechea as an anti-Neruda for some time and planned—without evident success—to use the CCF to raise his profile after his election. In other publications and in *Cuadernos,* the CCF followed the line of the Spanish Nobel laureate Juan Ramón Jiménez that Neruda was a "great poet, [but] a great bad poet." One frequent provider of anti-Neruda materials for the CCF, the ex-leftist Uruguayan poet Ricardo Paseyro, so irritated Neruda that he referred to him as the "revolting little Uruguayan" in private correspondence. The CCF's campaign against Neruda reached a peak in the 1960s when it tried to undermine his candidacy for the Nobel Prize.[51]

The CCF's other major artistic project was directed against the hegemony of the Marxist painters in Mexico. The Mexican government under Miguel Alemán, even as he moved away from the social commitments of Cárdenas, was the first to give consistent state support to the fine arts, finally creating a kind of official muralism. This led to the apparent paradox of a modernizing state looking to the past and a president who repressed the Left domestically supporting Marxist painters to craft its official story, showing heroic revolutionary masses overcoming the revolution's familiar cast of villains. The ironies were not lost on painters coming of age in the 1950s, who had no memories of the Mexican Revolution and few meaningful ones of Cardenismo. They saw a landscape clogged with official reverence for the Big Three (Rivera, Siqueiros, and José Clemente Orozco) but little support for experimentation and a chill on practices that could be construed as critical of the ruling PRI, such as the depiction of contemporary poverty.[52]

The ongoing debate about politically committed art and the Mexican school stretched back years before the creation of the CCF, at least to the 1944 publication of Siqueiros's orthodox manifesto "No hay más ruta que la nuestra" (There is no other path but ours). By the early 1950s it was evident that a new generation of painters, known in Spanish as "La Ruptura" and often translated as the "Breakaway" generation, was defying Siqueiros's pronouncement by modifying both the form and content of their painting. The painters of the Breakaway generation were challenging many of the muralists' assumptions: the importance of depictions of mass actors in history, the interweaving of leftist politics and Mexican nationalism, the disfavor shown to easel painting, and the rejection of abstraction for realism— indeed, the very identification of painting as a form of political action. Some of the artists who embraced different forms of less realist painting identified their works with a specifically anti-Communist project, rejecting the compulsory moralizing of the great living muralists.[53]

Rufino Tamayo, for example, who inspired many of the Breakaway painters, was of the same generation as Rivera and Siqueiros and had been exhibited alongside them in the 1920s and 1930s. But his color-soaked canvases, sometimes featuring oblique references to pre-Columbian art, bore little relationship to the work of Rivera or Siqueiros. Rivera, questioned about Tamayo in 1954, said that his work had some merit, but that "some great artists" avoided revolutionary and anti-imperialist content in their works, preferring not to be combative, engaged artists. That, said Rivera, was "selling silence," and it would be better just to take money to defend imperialism openly, so that everyone could see the relationship for what it was.[54]

The debate between old and new styles manifested itself in part as a conversation about the meaning of "freedom of expression" for the contemporary artist. In 1954 Diego Rivera pointed specifically to the CCF's defense of "freedom of expression" to argue that the idea was in fact a weapon of the U.S. Department of State and other conservative and foreign influences. Rivera was correct to argue that a deliberate attempt had been made to identify certain types of art with freedom. In the aftermath of the war, liberals in the United States sought to exhibit the work of abstract expressionists abroad in a bid to show that the United States was the center of innovative artistic production and freedom itself: this was art, after all, that neither Nazi Germany nor Stalinist Russia would allow. Seen as an identifiably "American" school, the complex and often nonlinear geometries of the abstract expressionists were exhibited around the world by New York's Museum of Modern Art as representing the pinnacle of artistic freedom and a direct challenge to totalitarianism. Although many of the artists who practiced abstract expressionism rejected the label and fully intended their art to be a radical critique of postwar society in the United States, this did not prevent the enlistment of their works in a tug-of-war widely understood to be between liberalism and totalitarianism.[55]

Rivera was also correct in arguing that the CCF was at the center of debates about freedom of expression in the arts in Mexico. In a way, that was proof enough that the embrace of apparently apolitical painting was in no way free of political content. The Mexican Association for Cultural Freedom formed a joint arrangement with the gallery space of the newspaper *Excélsior* to hold meetings, conferences, and showings of art. The *Excélsior* galleries exhibited the work of artists who did not conform to the tradition of socially committed art on a grand scale that had become identified as belonging to the "Mexican school." The poet and art critic Octavio Paz, who had once been tutored by Victor Serge and Julián Gorkin in anti-Communist politics and now eclipsed them both in fame, appeared at the *Excélsior* galleries in his capacity as the great defender of abstract art in Mexico. The CCF took pride in what it saw as breaking the "dictatorship" of the Communist artists on the Mexican arts scene. At a group exhibition of young painters in 1958, some of whom painted in less realist forms, the Mexican Association celebrated them for fulfilling the "first and highest responsibility [of the artist]: the defense of culture, and, therefore, of liberty."[56]

In debates about the artist and society, "abstraction" had replaced "formalism" as a term of abuse in Communist cultural criticism. But a simple dichotomy between realism and abstraction did not capture the complexity of artistic practice in Mexico, where some abstract expressionists were on the left and few of the artists of the Breakaway generation actually painted purely abstract forms. The point was that for the artists of the Breakaway, art had meaning other than its social content. Tamayo, usually classified as a postimpressionist, explained in an interview that art fought to present new visions of reality, and that modern art strove to represent four dimensions on canvas just as the revolution in perspective hundreds of years earlier had introduced three dimensions. Juan Soriano, a painter and sculptor who worked in abstract forms, was younger than Tamayo and more militant in his break with the older traditions. Soriano, a favorite of the CCF, embraced the criticism directed at him by painters like Siqueiros: Soriano did not paint for Mexico, and so what? He did not care about being a "Mexican" painter and sought a worldwide audience. He did not paint to be enjoyed by the masses; the great muralists were bureaucratic, propagandistic, and bait for tourists. He thought that their supposed political rebellion was a form of publicity. The only revolution that interested him, said Soriano, was the revolution in taste.[57]

The CCF did its best to promote the works and views of such artists. In 1957 it arranged for an exposition titled "Art and Liberty" at the city government's gallery that was explicitly conceived as a showcase of anti-Communist artists, featuring Rufino Tamayo most prominently. Rodrigo García Treviño intended to show that, in quality and quantity, the anti-Communists surpassed the Communist painters. But some of the painters in the exhibition quarreled publicly, and author Mauricio Magdaleno, a CCF associate in charge of the city gallery, encountered political pressure not to allow the exposition. The *Excélsior* galleries, though smaller and not officially connected to the government, had to substitute. Tamayo backed out of the project, and the exhibition made no great impression. The following year an exhibition of young painters at the same gallery organized by the Mexican Association of the CCF featured an enthusiastic denunciation of the "Mexican school" in its brochure. In the end, the CCF's contributions to promoting the artists of the Breakaway were modest. José Gómez Sicre, for instance, the Cuban art critic and director of the Visual Arts Section of the Pan American Union, was another determined opponent of social realist art and much more successful in using international exhibitions to elevate artists of the Breakaway generation, such as José Luis Cuevas, to international fame.[58]

The basic ingredients of Gorkin's brand of "liberal universalism"—the fusion of liberalism and socialism, anti-anti-Americanism, universalism in literature, and anti–socialist realism in the arts—were capacious enough to attract a wide variety of writers and thinkers to align themselves with the CCF in the 1950s. They included both those hostile and those sympathetic to indigenism, Catholicism, figurativism, or whatever current might be identified as the primary form of thought within the movement. There was no style that was be the equivalent of socialist realism for anti-Communists, and antitotalitarian action in the arts was largely reduced

to the promotion of artists who explicitly identified their work with political antitotalitarianism. Although it could claim a wider array of allies,
the CCF's method of selecting works and artists that were to be celebrated
or abhorred was little more sophisticated than that of the Communist artists; the politics come first. Both groups worked backward from the
political content of the art and the political engagement of the artist to
approval or disapproval of the work.

If the CCF's contributions to the arts in Latin America were modest
during the 1950s, its very presence inflamed debate. It helped weap-
onize the idea of freedom because critics on the left cited it as powerful
evidence that liberal notions of freedom were a form of imperialist propaganda. "Liberty" was the mantra of the CCF during the 1950s, and it
was pronounced to be synonymous with anti-Communism. But although
its members were right that liberty, as they understood it, required anti-
Communism, they did not all see clearly that anti-Communism was perhaps a necessary but not a sufficient condition for it. Gorkin's endorsement
of Castillo Armas in Guatemala, for example, showed that he identified
liberty with the forceful suppression of a popular political movement.
When the CCF was accused of being right-wing or of acting in the interests
of U.S. empire, Gorkin's behavior would be the sort of thing that would
justify the charges, bringing to mind the Chilean "antipoet" Nicanor Parra's quip: "And that was how they converted him from a useful idiot of the
Left to a useless idiot of the Right." Gorkin's was the logic of the "imperialism of liberty," and it made the term hollow both for those who thought
"liberty" an important value and for those who saw in it only the interests
of empire. Mario Monteforte Toledo, whose presses were destroyed by
Castillo Armas, was fully aware that liberty required more than anti-
Communism. The end of the 1950s soon brought a new opportunity to aid
in a country's political transformation along the lines sought by the anti-
Communist Left. The country was Cuba. It would prove to be the CCF's
greatest success, as well as its greatest failure.[59]

CHAPTER FOUR

The Anti-Communist Left
and the Cuban Revolution

The language of humanism suffused the early months of the Cuban Revolution, a social transformation not in the name of any particular ideology, its supporters insisted, but simply for the benefit of people. "Freedom with bread, bread without terror: that is humanism," Fidel Castro declared while visiting the United States. In 1959 outgoing mail from Cuba to the United States bore a special stamp that read, "In Cuba, we are living happy now with humanism, not Communism." The mark refuted those in the United States who identified independent nationalism with Communism, but in using the word "humanism" to place the Cuban Revolution apart from Communism, Fidel Castro was making an able run to gain the affection of multiple audiences. These included the anti-Communist Left, which had often used "humanism" to indicate a commitment to a balanced course between the Scylla and Charybdis of capitalism and Communism.[1]

Indeed, one of the magazines in which the Democratic Left worked out its agenda was called *Humanismo*. Founded by an intellectual from Peru's Alianza Popular Revolucionaria Americana in 1952 and edited by the Cuban academic Raúl Roa beginning in 1954, *Humanismo* was a noncommercial publication supported by advertising from the Mexican government and based in Mexico City. It was especially important to the members of the anti-Communist Left who made the Mexican capital their home during periods of exile, like the Venezuelans of Acción Democrática during the years of dictatorship between 1948 and 1958. *Humanismo* published many of the same writers and thinkers as the Congress for Cultural Freedom (CCF) and *Cuadernos,* although there was no affiliation between the two, and *Humanismo* focused more consistently on Latin American affairs, in contrast to the European orientation of *Cuadernos*.[2]

Opposed to both Communism and dictatorship, the magazine supported the struggle against the Cuban dictator Fulgencio Batista. A special issue published in early 1958 was dedicated to the people of Cuba and included published correspondence from Fidel Castro and several essays expressing hope in a democratic future for Cuba. A year later, the revolution victorious, *Humanismo* aligned itself with Cuba's new government and began to publish summaries of its new laws. But its tone began to change. Over the course of 1959, *Humanismo* published more Marxist authors, criticism of non-Marxist leftists, and unadorned compendia of the actions of Cuba's revolutionary government. The Mexican advertising disappeared, and by the end of the year the magazine's operation had been transferred to Cuba, where it was supported by the National Bank. It began to publish a large amount of material about and by Che Guevara. His account of killing a howling, potentially disruptive puppy in the Sierra Maestra appeared there as an allegory of necessary sacrifice, even of the innocent. Then, in mid-1960, the self-proclaimed magazine of "democratic orientation" suddenly vanished. Its disappearance could have stood in for the feelings of many of the Cuban Revolution's non-Marxist supporters: like the magazine, the hopes of Latin America's democratic revolution had seemed to move briefly to Cuba, only to be co-opted and then destroyed.[3]

The Cuban Revolution changed everything for the region's Left, lifting spirits and expectations but also creating new axes of division. The revolution began with roots planted firmly in the island's anti-Communist center-left political parties, while the orthodox Communist Partido Socialista Popular (PSP), one of the region's most established, sneered at Castro's military adventuring. The PSP joined Castro's 26th of July Movement only in the final months before victory. As he became the leader of a heterogeneous mixture of antidictatorial groups, Castro took steps to assure that both the moderate anti-Communist wing of his movement and the radical wing, which included the Communists, remained content. But after victory PSP members were given positions of privilege in the armed forces and influence in crafting early revolutionary legislation. As conflict with the United States escalated, Castro turned to the Soviet Union and suppressed expressions of anti-Communism among his supporters. In April 1961, just before the invasion of a CIA-trained exile army at the Bay of Pigs, Castro declared the Cuban Revolution socialist; by the end of the year he was calling it Marxist-Leninist. Cuba's example created a new generation of revolutionaries across the continent and forever changed the parameters of Latin American Communism. Debates about Communism in the 1950s had relied on analyzing the distant European experience; Cuba made that conversation passé. The Cold War in the Americas from that point onward would be less about East-West conflict than about rejection or acceptance of Cuba and its intellectual, political, and military influence.[4]

For the CCF, too, Cuba changed everything. It changed the future of the organization, prompting it to push aside the European focus of the 1950s and displace an entire generation of crusty anti-Communist activists in favor of skeptical socialists who would be able to speak more directly to the appeal of revolutionary Cuba. But the revolution did not simply change the future; it also changed the past. The important role that the explicitly anti-Communist Left had played in supporting the revolution, especially in public relations work that helped Castro gain legitimacy, was erased both by the Cuban government, which saw that group as traitorous, and by the anti-Communists, who felt the same way about Castro. When, in advance of the attack on the Bay of Pigs, *Encounter* and *Cuadernos* published articles by Theodore Draper arguing that Castro had betrayed the revolution and had become a totalitarian ruler, it marked a breach that obscured how much Castro and the anti-Communist Left had once had in common. The Cuban Revolution was the CCF's most important political triumph. For once, CCF personnel played a part in an anti-dictatorial campaign and had a reasonably important role in bringing a new government to power. Yet its victory proved one from which the CCF would never really recover.

———————

Jorge Mañach was an essayist and author with social democratic political views and an early biographer of the poet and martyr of Cuban independence, José Martí. Mañach was entrusted by Castro with editing the speech that made his name, "History Will Absolve Me," during Castro's imprisonment in 1954. After the revolution he initially defended Castro, but by 1960 he left for exile in Puerto Rico and died there in 1961.

Mario Llerena was a journalist and propagandist for Castro's 26th of July Movement in the United States. He broke with Castro in the months before his victory and became a fierce critic, returning to Cuba briefly in 1959 and 1960 before joining the middle-class exodus to Miami, where he remained for decades as a member of the rabidly anti-Castro exile community.

Raúl Roa was a student radical in the 1930s who grew to be a philosophy professor and dean of the School of Social Sciences at the University of Havana. In the mid-1950s he edited *Humanismo,* and after the revolution he became Cuba's representative to the Organization of American States and then its foreign minister. He defended its foreign policy with such distinction that he was nicknamed the "Chancellor of Dignity."

Aureliano Sánchez Arango was an ex-Communist and former minister of education with close ties to the anti-Communist Left. He was involved in many military conspiracies, including international ventures to topple Caribbean dictators, and headed a small group of anti-Batista fighters in the mid-1950s. Forced out of Cuba in 1960, he joined up with CIA efforts to overthrow Castro's government.

Four different paths through the Cuban Revolution—different forms of support and opposition—and one common biographical fact: all four men had been important figures in the Cuban national affiliate of the CCF, the Cuban Association for Cultural Freedom. That four such divergent trajectories could all, for a brief time in the late 1950s, intersect in an anti-Communist cultural organization reveals not confusion and betrayal but the strategic ambiguity of the politics of Cuba's revolution. These ambiguities sprang from the revolution's deep and tangled roots and the failure of Cuba's social democrats to deliver either socialism or democracy.

There is some irony in the fact that it was Cuba that captured the international imagination of what it meant to be "Latin American," for Cuba's history had long diverged in important ways from that of the rest of the region. Along with Puerto Rico, it remained a Spanish colony nearly eighty years longer than the rest of Spanish America. Its independence in 1898, in the wake of the war between the United States and Spain that interrupted Cuba's own anticolonial struggle, came at a moment when voices in the United States were debating the merits of formal empire. Although some in the United States hoped to annex the island and others pledged to support its independence, a compromise emerged that left Cuba formally independent but less than fully sovereign, governed by the Platt Amendment, in which the United States reserved the right to intervene whenever the Cuban government failed to maintain "a government adequate for the protection of life, property, and individual liberty." Military occupations during the Platt Amendment years ensured that many forms of Cuban nationalism would direct anti-imperial ire against the United States, even as geographic proximity made it logical for the two countries to maintain close economic, cultural, and political relationships. As in other countries in Central America and the Caribbean in the early decades of the twentieth century, U.S. intervention in Cuba's domestic affairs was the norm rather than the exception and, as elsewhere, resulted in dictatorships that could maintain good investment climates for U.S. businesses rather than democracy.[5]

The first dictatorship to produce a generation of resisters was that of Gerardo Machado, after 1929. Machado had subverted Cuba's political institutions to take a second term as president and found himself facing multiple opposition groups. The Communist Party of Cuba, which drew supporters from the working and lower-middle class, was among them. But there were many others. In 1931, for instance, a group of upper-middle-class professionals, under the meaningless and inscrutable name ABC, engaged in bombings and propaganda. Jorge Mañach, who in the 1950s would be active in the CCF, was the ABC's principal spokesman, issuing manifestos calling for a new regime of social justice and political liberty, including the nationalization of industries that tended toward monopoly. Students, not the middle-class ABC, bore the brunt of the repression of Machado's state apparatus, including extrajudicial killing. Even exile did not guarantee safety. The Communist Julio Antonio Mella was gunned down on the streets of Mexico City in 1929 while he walked with his lover, Tina Modotti. Students at the University of Havana formed revolutionary groups, issuing manifestos proclaiming liberation from foreign political and economic domination and the domestic tyranny that abetted and enacted that imperialism. One of the groups, the Ala Izquierda Estudiantial, produced a number of significant political leaders: Aureliano Sánchez Arango, Raúl Roa, and Carlos Prío, who all would go on to important roles in subsequent Cuban governments. The Ala advocated agrarian revolution and anti-imperialism, and many of its members, including Sánchez Arango, joined the Communist Party.[6]

When Machado was eventually forced to resign, the resulting political void was filled by a young sergeant named Fulgencio Batista, who staged a military revolt and then stepped back to allow a scholarly medical doctor named Ramón Grau San Martín to become president. Grau refused to swear to the constitution that included the Platt Amendment, ending the years of constitutionally compromised sovereignty. Grau's government frightened many powerful economic interests by quickly implementing a number of left-wing reforms: a minimum wage, the eight-hour workday, guarantees of collective bargaining, women's suffrage, and university autonomy. He also set a minimum requirement for Cuban participation in foreign firms operating in Cuba. But Grau's government fell after a few short months—the United States maneuvered for his removal—and Batista remained the real power in Cuban politics for the remainder of the 1930s. Out of power, Grau formed a new party, the social democratic Partido Revolucionario Cubano-Auténtico. Claiming the "authentic" mantle of the poet-martyr of Cuban independence, José Martí, its members were known as Auténticos.[7]

In 1939, facing considerable political pressure, Batista consented to a constitutional convention. A democratic and reformist consensus prevailed; even Cuba's Communist Party sent delegates to the convention, where they helped craft some of the document's more progressive clauses, including the right to work, strike, and unionize. Jorge Mañach was a member of the constitutional assembly, where he advocated for the inclusion of social services as constitutional rights. In the end, Cuba's constitution of 1940 was social democratic, guaranteeing individual rights but assigning the government the responsibility for seeing to social rights and welfare. Not unlike the Mexican constitution of 1917, it was one of the world's most progressive on paper, although the state had neither the will nor the capacity to fulfill the commitments made there.[8]

In 1940, after six years as the unofficial power behind the Cuban presidency, Batista was legitimately elected to the office. Carrying out a populist program, he made Cuba a close ally of the United States during World War II. Batista's wartime Popular Front government included members of the Cuban Communist Party, which Batista had legalized in 1938, and which Batista placed in charge of constructing a unified labor federation, the Confederación de Trabajadores de Cuba (CTC). In tune with moderating currents during the war, the Cuban Communist Party gave itself the more tranquil name Partido Socialista Popular in 1943. The residual effect of Batista's alliance with the PSP was that he retained a good name among Latin American Communists and, for example, was honored at the peace conference held in Mexico City in 1949.[9]

In elections in 1944, Grau was elected president, and for the next eight years the island was governed by Auténticos during a brief era that had the patina of an electoral democracy. But Cuba's Congress scarcely met, and Grau governed largely by executive decree. While observing formal freedoms, his government permitted high levels of corruption and gangsterism. The University of Havana was notorious for the presence of armed gangs, shielded by Grau's reliance on student support and abusing his commitment to the principle of university autonomy. (Fidel Castro, who began studying at the university in 1945, later said that it was more dangerous there than in the mountains of the Sierra Maestra.) And, like Batista's before him, Grau's ministers used their sinecures to assemble a vast system of spoils and personal benefits.

Internationally, the consequences of Grau's supposedly "social democratic" views were somewhat more visible. He aligned his government with the Central American and Caribbean antidictatorial reformers of the Caribbean Legion. Many political exiles from dictatorships elsewhere in Latin America lived in Havana during the Auténtico years, where the corruption in public finances aided their acquisition of arms. In 1947, with Grau's encouragement, a force to invade the Dominican Republic and depose the dictatorship of Rafael Trujillo was established off the coast of Cuba. A young Fidel Castro joined the approximately one thousand expeditionaries-in-waiting—apparently against the wishes of his mother, who offered him a car and a trip to the United States if he stayed and established his law practice. After the Cuban government laundered $1 million through the Ministry of Education to support the force, the Cuban army decided to shut down the expedition, and its participants were briefly detained. Awaiting arrest on board ship, Castro threw himself into shark-infested waters rather than be apprehended.[10]

Grau's labor minister, Carlos Prío Socarrás, was elected to succeed him in 1948. Prío committed himself to cleaning up corruption and gang-sterism, appointing Aureliano Sánchez Arango, his former companion from their days as student radicals, as minister of education. Sánchez Arango oversaw mass firings in an attempt to curtail some of the illicit activity that had proliferated during Grau's presidency. But although Prío was able to create some of the institutions that would make it possible to implement the constitution of 1940 vigorously, such as a national bank, he too did so while accumulating an enormous bounty of personal wealth and made little progress in reducing the power of armed political gangs.[11]

Although Grau's and Prío's actions in office did much to discredit the idea of democratic reform in Cuba, Prío especially acted as a member of the Latin American anti-Communist Democratic Left. After the coup in Venezuela in 1948 that deposed the novelist Rómulo Gallegos, Gallegos and Acción Democrática party leader Rómulo Betancourt resettled in Havana. In 1950 Prío's government hosted and sponsored the continental conference that brought together the Inter-American Association for Democracy and Freedom (IADF). Prío understood the symbolic politics of the early Cold War very well, arresting a group of Mexicans—including Vicente Lombardo Toledano and David Álfaro Siqueiros—who passed through Havana en route to a peace congress in Europe. Prío also met with Julián Gorkin and El Campesino during their travels to promote the latter's ghostwritten autobiography. Sánchez Arango, Prío's minister of education, was elected to be first vice president of the IADF and was especially active in coordinating conspiracies within the regional anti-Communist Left.[12]

Auténtico anti-Communism had more repressive dimensions as well. Because Batista had ceded labor organizing to Communist organizers, Prío was determined to push aside the leadership of the major union confederation, the CTC. For this, Grau and Prío turned to Eusebio Mujal, an ex- and strong anti-Communist. Beginning in 1946, after a meeting in Miami with the American Federation of Labor's (AFL) Serafino Romualdi, Mujal began to plan the removal of Communists from power in the CTC. In 1947 he engineered a coup within the union federation that forced out the old leadership. In 1949 he placed himself at its head and dominated the organization until 1958. Mujal made a mockery of responsible union leadership: corrupt, venal, and thuggish, he too accumulated a vast personal fortune. He was also one of the most important players in the creation of the "antitotalitarian" Organización Regional Interamericana de Traba-jadores (ORIT) that was supposed to represent the "democratic" alter-native to rival union federations like Vicente Lombardo Toledano's Con-federación de Trabajadores de América Latina; with a subsidy from Prío's government, the CTC was the greatest financial contributor to ORIT other than the U.S. union federations.[13]

Fed up with corruption, some former Auténticos split to form rival par-ties, dividing Cuba's anti-Communist Left. In 1947, a popular and bom-bastic radio broadcaster, Eduardo Chibás, created the Partido Ortodoxo, and some social democrats, like Jorge Mañach, joined. So too did Fidel Castro, becoming a leader in the youth division of the party. Ortodoxo plans fell apart when Chibás accused Aureliano Sánchez Arango of cor-ruption. When the education minister denied the charges and Chibás failed to provide the evidence he had promised, he shot himself on the air, lin-gering for days before passing away. Hundreds of thousands of Cubans filled the streets to mourn Chibás at his funeral, and Castro reportedly contemplated using the crowd to launch a mass insurrection to topple the government of Prío.[14]

Without Chibás, who many had thought would be the next president, the Ortodoxos and Auténticos contested the 1952 election, while another candidate languished far behind: former president Fulgencio Batista. In spite of the problems facing the two established parties, Batista realized that the electoral path to recapture power held no promise for him, and so he engineered another coup. Eusebio Mujal, after briefly approving a general strike, made a bargain with Batista that allowed him to stay in power, maintaining his sinecure at the price of union autonomy. Mujal's actions were strongly criticized by many within ORIT, but the CTC de-feated efforts to label Batista's government a dictatorship and call for the restoration of civil liberties and rights. Throughout the 1950s Mujal sub-ordinated the CTC to Batista's governments and then insisted that Batista deserved support because—unlike totalitarian governments under the Soviet yoke—he allowed workers their "independent" union organiza-tions. A "CTC in exile" drew up a damning bill of particulars showing

government collaboration, including the destruction of unions, intimidation, unlawful firing, murder of antigovernment labor leaders, strike
suppression, and official theft from social security funds. Mujal also used
this "independence" to have his workers disrupt actions during the eventual armed struggle against Batista.[15]

After his return to office, Batista eschewed his earlier populism, focusing
less on enacting reforms that would maintain support and more on en-
riching himself. With CIA assistance he intensified the efforts of Prío's anti-
Communist police force, inaugurating the unguardedly titled Bureau for
the Repression of Communist Activities in 1954 for the specific purpose
of battling Communism in Cuba. Only much later was the CIA willing to
recognize that the bureau would become, under Batista, a tool of repression to squeeze the opposition, Communist or otherwise.[16]

Opposition to dictatorship might have provided an opportunity for the
Auténticos and the Ortodoxos, both ostensibly committed to democracy,
a chance at unity, but that did not occur. Hard-line Ortodoxos, including
Castro, rejected a negotiated pact between the two parties. As in the
Machado years, the opposition to Batista's dictatorship created diverse opposition groups among the political classes, the Communist Party, the
students, and even business elites who tired of Batista's corruption. Although Che Guevara, in an act of deliberate self-mythologizing, later tried
to leave the world an image of the mountain guerrilla uprising that cas-
caded to victory, this was not an accurate rendering of the process of the
Cuban Revolution. Urban warfare was more important in keeping the regime off balance than were the guerrillas throughout most of the 1950s,
and Castro began as just one leader among many. His eventual victory
had much to do with lucky elimination of other claimants to power (urban
warfare proved more dangerous than the guerrilla struggle), his military
success, and skillful media relations that consolidated his hegemony within
the opposition to Batista. But the roots of his eventual differences with
the anti-Communist Left lay deep in the history of Cuba's brief and troubled practice of democracy: anti-imperialist in theory but aligned with the
United States in the Cold War; social democratic in principle but limited
in its ability to deliver either socialism or a satisfactory democracy.[17]

Although Castro and the anti-Communist Left would eventually find
themselves acting as enemies, they had once depended on each other to
advance common interests. The exact moment of Castro's conversion to
Communism may forever remain a matter of myth and mystery, but it is
clear that Cuba's anti-Communist Left once considered him an ally and a

friend. In 1954 Castro languished in the notorious prison on the Isle of Pines, sixty-two miles off the Cuban mainland. On the previous 26 July, in 1953, he had led an assault on the military barracks at Moncada in an attempt to begin a revolution that would bring down the government of Batista. The attack failed, and many of Castro's fighters were killed during or after the attempted raid. Castro was arrested, and, given the chance to make his own defense, the young lawyer made a courtroom speech titled "History Will Absolve Me."

The court did not listen to "History" and sentenced Castro to fifteen years in prison. But he was not idle and was able to smuggle letters out of jail to his sympathizers, who continued to work against Batista from the outside. His supporters had the responsibility of editing and indeed creating "History Will Absolve Me" for publication as a pamphlet—as published, it was a statement longer than he could possibly have delivered in court. It was a lengthy attack on the unconstitutional government of Batista and a defense of Castro's own actions, intended to circulate throughout the country as useful propaganda. A nationalist text, it lacked, save for one reference to the "capitalist class," any sign of Marxist influence. Castro called for the restoration of legitimate power via the constitution of 1940 and a program of land reform, profit sharing, the punishment of ill-gotten gains, and solidarity with the democratic peoples of the continent. Its distribution throughout Cuba made Castro more famous than he ever had been as a free man and created new adherents, including liberals and professionals.

Several sympathizers helped smuggle out "History Will Absolve Me," edit it, and prepare it for public distribution. The most important among them were members of the anti-Communist Left. Castro wanted Jorge Mañach, the distinguished writer and social democrat, to edit the document, and many have since asserted that Mañach was its author. However, Luis Conte Agüero, an Ortodoxo journalist who had known Castro since their student days together at the University of Havana in the 1940s, claims that he protected Mañach by doing the work himself. Whatever the case, both Conte Agüero and Mañach experienced a similar fate when the revolution triumphed. In March 1960, some fifteen months after the victory of the revolution, Conte Agüero made a public criticism of Castro's increasing closeness with the Soviet Union. Accused of betrayal and facing calls for his death, he fled Cuba for exile in Miami. Mañach, too, left his country in 1960, going to Puerto Rico, which took in many Cubans with social democratic political views at that time, and died the following year.[18]

During the anti-Batista struggle Castro was far from the only insurgent leader. Student organizations played an important role in the cities. And although the Auténticos were divided, the official Democratic Left had plenty of experience with clandestine operations and did not give up its attempts to play a role in reclaiming power in Cuba. Carlos Prío left office a wealthy man and, from his exile in the United States, tried to use his fortune to secure himself a place in the post-Batista era. "I stole lots of money from Cuba," Prío reportedly said. "But the money that I stole will return to Cuba. If anyone goes to Cuba and fights against Batista, I consider myself well-paid." While Castro was in prison, Aureliano Sánchez Arango remained free, suspected of being with Prío in Mexico or the United States but in fact back on the island, where he had formed a small political group around himself known as the Triple-A, which probably stood for the Asociación de Amigos de Aureliano. Sánchez Arango also plotted Batista's downfall, but by the end of 1954 he turned himself in to the Uruguayan embassy, asked for asylum, and was granted safe conduct from the country. In his absence the Triple-A ceased to function.[19]

In 1955, hoping to tamp down internal opposition, Batista granted an early release to Castro, who left for exile in Mexico and began a period of military and political training to prepare to return to Cuba. Castro increasingly declared his independence from the Ortodoxos—among whom he still had many supporters—and named his organization in exile the Movimiento 26 de Julio, the 26th of July Movement, commemorating the day of the assault on the Moncada barracks. Still, Castro sought support almost wherever he could get it, including from disgraced former president Carlos Prío and parts of the Cuban bourgeoisie. After the victorious revolution turned against anti-Communism, this period of cooperation would prove embarrassing to both sides. Neither the anti-Communist Left nor the bourgeoisie wanted to admit the role that it had played in bringing Castro to power, and Castro's partisans did not want to admit that his liberal and social democratic supporters had not, in fact, meekly acquiesced to Batista's rule but had had an important part in making opposition to Batista respectable. Both sides settled on narratives of betrayal to explain what had happened.[20]

In fact, Castro depended on the anti-Communist Left to make his victory possible. Even the CCF's Cuban affiliate played a significant role in the defense of Castro. The Cuban Association for Cultural Freedom was formed the same year as Castro's release from prison, in 1955, in the midst of anti-Batista ferment. Made up mostly of the well-educated elites in Havana, the association drew on several distinct currents of thought. Jorge Mañach, the first vice president of the group, represented the first: a well-educated and now middle-aged group that had been, during the 1920s and 1930s, part of the cultural vanguard involved with anti-Machado activities. Although Mañach had briefly been part of the wartime Popular Front government of Batista (he was foreign minister for half of 1944), he did not accept the unconstitutional version of Batista's power. Mañach, during the 1950s, was also involved with a civic group known as the Movimiento de la Nación, which, like the ABC of the early 1930s, of which he had been the spokesman, sought a negotiated end to the dictatorship.[21]

Pastor del Río, by contrast, served as the second vice president of the Cuban Association for Cultural Freedom and represented a Pan-American current of thinking within the group. Del Río had been the editor of the Cuban magazine *América,* the organ of the quasi-governmental Asociación de Escritores y Artistas Americanos (AEAA), since its inception in 1939. *América's* Pan-Americanism was a reflection of the moment of its creation. Optimistic for the future of U.S.–Latin American relations, the first issue featured the text of Lázaro Cárdenas's speech at the International Congress against War alongside one by Cordell Hull of the U.S. State Department. Although it was based in Cuba, the AEAA had a continental presence, with national associations in many countries throughout the Americas. Pan-Americanism, as an ideology of continental unity, had most recently been mobilized in order to combat the threat of Nazism and to win a war against it. But when that war ended, *América* changed very little; it continued to defend the president of the United States unconditionally and reported cheerily on the events of groups hated by cultural nationalists as evangelists for Anglo-U.S. culture, such as the Rotary Club and the Boy Scouts. It was a far more pro-U.S. publication than anything that the CCF ever published.[22]

In the early 1950s the AEAA received an elegant new building in the wealthy Havana neighborhood of El Vedado, adorned with flags of the American republics and featuring a map of the two continents above its entrance. Known as the Casa Continental de la Cultura, this building symbolized Cuban hopes to play a leadership role in international cultural affairs, hosting visiting dignitaries and cultural ambassadors, as well as local events. Despite the differences in their outlooks, there was substantial overlap in membership between the AEAA and the Cuban Association of the CCF. The CCF held a series of conferences at the facility of the Casa Continental and even hoped to use it as a permanent headquarters.[23]

Alongside elite democracy advocates and AEAA-affiliated Pan-Americanists, there was also a more politically radical contingent within the Cuban Association of the CCF. Its most active representative was the journalist Mario Llerena. He too had come of age under Machado and in the mid-1950s worked as a journalist on the staff of the popular Cuban weekly *Carteles,* where he often wrote about the activities of the CCF. Like Mañach, Llerena was a middle-class liberal who wanted a democratic and reformist revolution. He differed from his more august counterpart only in that Llerena did not seek alternatives to Castro's victory, instead working openly on Castro's behalf. He tried to use the Cuban Association of the CCF to form a pro-Castro bulwark. Under his guidance the Cuban Association of the CCF became a gathering point for a young group of Cuban intellectuals who openly began to support the 26th of July Movement in 1956.[24]

Given that he would become Castro's foreign minister after the revolution, it is a considerable irony that Raúl Roa held some of the strongest anti-Castro views among the membership of the CCF. Roa had been a member of Sánchez Arango's clandestine Triple-A. As dean of the social sciences at the University of Havana, he had seen the corrosive effects of violence among student groups and, knowing Castro's past, came to describe him as a "gangster." In Mexico for the Inter-American Conference for Cultural Freedom of September 1956 at the same time when Castro was nearby preparing an invasion of Cuba, Roa refused to meet with him. As the other Cuban delegate to the Inter-American Conference for Cultural Freedom, Llerena made the opposite decision. He carried papers to Castro, who tested the terrified Llerena's revolutionary mettle by driving him speeding around mountain curves in the dead of night. For approximately two years thereafter, Llerena made working for Castro his full-time job. Llerena's position and salary with the Cuban Association of the CCF made his work for Castro possible for part of this time.[25]

The Cuban Revolution, indeed, could not have succeeded without its liberal and social democratic supporters. Although his words and actions suggest that Castro's plans to confront the United States predated his victory, he was careful to maintain a broad coalition to oppose Batista. Batista, at least, understood the threat. Secret police narrowly missed arresting Llerena at his house and at that of a friend in 1957. He ran straight to the Mexican embassy after the second attempt, was granted asylum in Mexico, and from there left for New York with the help of Rodrigo García Treviño and other friends in the CCF. Mañach, host of a popular radio discussion program called *University on the Air,* was beaten by police along with other members of the staff. Batista's customs officials refused to allow into the country a pamphlet written by Julián Gorkin about Marx and the Soviet Union and confiscated the thirtieth number of *Cuadernos,* which contained an article by Mañach that described the violence of the Batista regime and speculated on the prospects for Castro's military victory. The same issue also contained a supplemental manifesto cheekily invoking José Martí and issuing a call for democratic awakening in the Americas. In exile in New York, Llerena was named by Castro as director of public relations for the 26th of July Movement outside Cuba, and he became responsible for representing the movement to a curious U.S. press. When charges appeared that the 26th of July Movement was Communist inspired, Llerena refuted them, assisted by the liberals and socialists at the IADF.[26]

Llerena also played an essential role in the most significant propaganda coup of the battle against Batista: smuggling Herbert Matthews of the *New York Times* into the mountains for a conversation with the rebel leader. Matthews's reporting was demoralizing to Batista, disproving his government's contention that Castro had already been killed. Che Guevara later described Matthews's presence in the Sierra Maestra as "more important for us than a military victory." In his memoirs Batista acknowledged that the interview "was of considerable propaganda value to the rebels." With it, Batista argued, "Castro was to begin his era as a legendary figure" and, in his view, "end as a monster of terror." Matthews's reporting also strengthened Castro's position within the anti-Batista groups, making him the most romantic and appealing figure among the opposition. When official censorship aimed to prevent the *Times* articles from ever reaching Cuba, it was Llerena who, from New York, arranged for thousands of copies to be printed and mailed to prominent members of Cuban society, who could then distribute them further. Later, Llerena arranged for Robert Taber of CBS News to meet secretly with Castro, and Taber portrayed him on television as a democrat and a fighter for social justice.[27]

Nor were the anti-Communist Left's contributions to military success trivial. Castro had forded the Rio Grande to meet with Prío in southern Texas; that trip earned him the money that purchased the famous yacht *Granma*, which he used to return to Cuba. Alberto Bayo, a veteran of the Spanish Civil War who trained Castro and his guerrilla fighters in Mexico, had for years been the military tutor of the anti-Communist Caribbean Legion. When Castro traveled to Costa Rica to seek arms in 1956, President José Figueres decided not to receive him directly, but once Castro returned to Cuba and was fighting in the Sierra Maestra, the anti-Communist Figueres sent him an arms shipment through a Cuban intermediary, Huber Matos, who eventually became the commander of a column of Castro's rebel army. As military victory drew closer throughout the course of 1958, the coalition that supported Castro included parts of the divided anti-Communist Auténticos and Ortodoxos, the Communist PSP, and groups of student radicals. Even the CIA, hedging its bets, seems to have sent some money to the 26th of July Movement in 1957 and 1958. The United States cut off aid to Batista in 1958, and although there was some sympathy for Castro in the CIA and in the State Department, the main lines of U.S. diplomacy hoped to secure a political solution that would proffer an alternative to both Batista and Castro. They could not achieve it.[28]

Batista fled the country on 1 January 1959, and Castro marched into Havana a week later as the uncontested leader of the revolution. Castro's first cabinet was made up of judges, lawyers, and economists—professional and generally liberal men who were part of the politically moderate groups that had supported him. His choice for president, Manuel Urrutia, was a provincial judge who had ruled that armed revolt against Batista's government was legitimate. Urrutia had also appeared in April 1958 alongside Mario Llerena in the offices of the IADF in New York to declare before the U.S. press that the 26th of July Movement would repudiate collaboration with the (Communist) PSP, which had just declared that it would seek to work with the 26th of July Movement. Raúl Roa had experienced another change of heart and, in spite of his earlier criticisms of Castro, became Cuba's ambassador to the Organization of American States in February and was promoted to foreign minister in May. On 13 January 1959 philosophy teacher and CCF member Pedro Vicente Aja wrote to Julián Gorkin from Havana to assure him that the language of the revolution was "democratic and nationalist," without Communist infiltration. Castro declared the revolution "humanist" and neutral with respect to the Cold War.[29]

In the first months of revolutionary victory there was a range of views regarding the future course of the revolution, and many people projected their own hopes, aspirations, and views onto Castro. Pedro Vicente Aja wanted the reorganized and reactivated Cuban Association for Cultural Freedom—which had declared itself unable to operate in late 1957 in the face of repression from Batista—to provide a kind of technical counterweight to Communist influence in Cuba, supporting democratization and helping solve the country's economic problems. He was convinced that Castro would look favorably on this activity. Although some members of the CCF had already soured on Castro, most had not. Llerena had broken with Castro in August 1958 and had written to Gorkin to ask the Spaniard whether the struggles for power that he saw taking place within the guerrilla groups were normal for revolutionaries who had not yet even taken power. In Mexico, concerned by reports of executions in Cuba after the victory of the revolutionary forces, Rodrigo García Treviño sent a cable to Castro in the wake of military victory that was only tepidly congratulatory. But on 20 January the experienced revolutionary Gorkin dismissed the negative reaction of the U.S. and Mexican press to Castro's government. In a letter to Aja, he echoed Castro's own arguments: "The North Americans and the Mexicans seem to have forgotten their own histories; and, what is more, those who never protested against the mountains of cadavers that Batista's regime created are those who now most loudly decry the passionate acts of a people that has suffered so much. You feel, as I do, ever less inclined toward violence and bloody acts. But we understand that one does not escape a situation like [Batista] without breaking some eggs." By April the restructuring of the Cuban Association for Cultural Freedom was complete. Mañach served as president, Aja as secretary general, and Raúl Roa simultaneously as vice president and an official in Cuba's new government.[30]

The victory of the Cuban Revolution made possible the transformation of Cuba's social life and institutions with a speed and dedication that would have been impossible in an ordinary democracy. Life changed quickly in ways that improved conditions for the poor: during 1959 many rents were slashed in half by decree; agrarian reform broke up large estates; and foreign companies were nationalized. But to bridge the divide between cosmopolitan, urban Havana and the many poor people of the countryside would require missionary zeal and, furthermore, new cultural institutions. The most concentrated effort would come in 1961, with a literacy campaign that mobilized hundreds of thousands to teach the illiterate the rudiments of written communication—and how to write a letter of thanks to Fidel, the final assignment that served to mark their status as newly lettered.

But the process of cultural transformation began almost immediately after the victory of the revolution. In March the government created a national press and the Instituto Cubano de Arte e Industria Cinematográfica to support Cuban film and to bring film arts to Cubans with little or no access to the quintessential modern art form. In April Castro's government issued a proclamation to create a new cultural organization, Casa de las Américas, that would serve as a way of coordinating cultural efforts, projecting the influence of the revolution. Casa de las Américas took over the Casa Continental de la Cultura that had belonged to the Pan-American AEAA, replacing the moribund institution with one that had a revolutionary mandate. Haydée Santamaría, a veteran of the assault on the Moncada barracks, was designated to run the new organization. The new Casa de las Américas began publishing its eponymous magazine in

The Casa de las Américas building in 2013 had not changed much since 1959, nor had the cars in front of it. Before 1959 the same building housed the Asociación de Escritores y Artistas Americanos, and the Cuban Association of the Congress for Cultural Freedom held meetings there. Reproduced by Creative Commons Attribution Share-Alike 2.0; © 2013 by Sandra Cohen-Rose and Colin Rose.

1960 and sponsored famous prizes for literary and artistic works. In time, this magazine and institution would come to be seen, as the World Peace Council had once been, as the chief rival to the CCF in Latin America. But in the beginning Casa de las Américas was more like a companion of the CCF than a rival to it. Jorge Mañach himself served on the jury for the first literary contest, which was awarded to a story about agrarian reform.[31]

Cuba's new kind of democracy would be participatory, calling the people out to huge assemblies. It would, Castro announced definitively in mid-1960, not hold elections. And its new institutions began to clash almost immediately with the complex of organizations associated with the anti-Communist Left. Its most illiberal organizations were affected first. Eusebio Mujal, whose unions of the CTC had aided Batista, was working with such an obviously impoverished definition of democracy that he had done much to discredit the concept in Cuba. He was granted asylum by the Argentine embassy; an attempt to fly him out of the country was initially blocked on the runway by an angry crowd of thousands. But with Mujal out, ORIT tried to maintain a good relationship with Castro. Luis Alberto Monge, ORIT's secretary general, had befriended Castro in Mexico and made a trip to Cuba to try and smooth over any differences. For most of 1959 ORIT remained generally enthusiastic about Castro's revolutionary plan, thinking that it would benefit working people and do away with the immorality that had marked the previous governments. But anti-Communist leaders were removed from office in mid-1959 and replaced by members of the Communist PSP; during its Tenth Congress in November 1959, Castro arranged to have the CTC withdraw from ORIT and pledge to lead a new international. Over the following months many prominent anti-Communist labor leaders were imprisoned, and the Communist Lázaro Peña was placed in charge of the CTC again at the beginning of 1961. Anti-Communist labor would go on to complain bitterly about involuntary labor in Cuba and the withering away of an independent labor movement under Castro.[32]

The pattern was similar in other areas. Although Castro had needed the anti-Communist Left in order to win the battle against Batista, he needed more radical allies in order to govern. As relations with the United States deteriorated, the institutions of liberal society that had existed (for some) during the Auténtico years and in opposition under Batista were replaced by those of a one-party state. In April 1959 Castro traveled to the United States. While he was there, he had a secret meeting with CIA officials in which he convinced them that he was a genuine anti-Communist and agreed to receive CIA information on international Communism. But Castro never responded to the first message sent, and in general, his meetings with U.S. officials ended without any pledge of mutual understanding. By summer the Eisenhower administration had decided that it would be impossible to carry on friendly relations with Castro's government and began to fund the internal opposition and seek ways to remove him from office. Although in May Castro was still talking of an "entirely democratic" revolution, the recently reopened University of Havana was purged of those hostile to the regime. When the liberals of Castro's first cabinet resigned because of mounting concern over the course of social change, he replaced them with more radical allies. After President Manuel Urrutia made a public criticism of Communism in late June, Castro publicly upbraided him, saying that attacking Communism interfered with Cuba's pledge to remain neutral in the Cold War. Castro replaced Urrutia with Osvaldo Dorticós, who had been a member of the Communist PSP, an early indication of many to follow that the Cuban Revolution, while not yet a Communist one, intended to be an anti-anti-Communist one.[33]

International relations with the anti-Communist Left soured. Rómulo Betancourt had been elected president of Venezuela in late 1958, and he and Castro made a pact to continue Caribbean Legion–like activities, cosponsoring a failed invasion of the Dominican Republic to overthrow the dictatorship of Rafael Trujillo. But Betancourt wanted his interventionism to be antidictatorial, not anti-U.S., and became a hated enemy; eventually, Cuba would support some of the many leftist insurgent groups that sprang up in Venezuela. For his part, José Figueres, who had been president of Costa Rica until 1958, traveled in March 1959 to Cuba and made a speech advising Castro not to confront the United States; Castro in turn described Figueres as a "bad friend, a bad democrat, and a bad revolutionist."[34]

The most troubling case for liberal supporters of the Cuban Revolution was that of Huber Matos. Matos, who admired the social democratic anti-Communism of Figueres, had been a military commander during the revolution and had helped oversee the confiscation of large estates during the agrarian reform. But he became alarmed at the appearance of Marxist propaganda in the military magazine controlled by Fidel's brother, Raúl. By October 1959, however, it had become impossible to criticize Communist influence within the revolution publicly, since, in the face of U.S. hostility, doing so could be interpreted as an invitation to foreign intervention. Matos tried to be discreet. On 19 October he insisted that he be allowed to resign; two days later he was accused of treason and threatened with execution. Those within the government who sided with him were dismissed. He was convicted in a demonstration trial in December and served a prison sentence that included torture until he was released in 1979. The arrest of Matos sent yet another signal that internal opposition would be sharply constrained.[35]

If the Batista years had been full of censorship and repression, the Auténtico years had, in spite of their other democratic failings, featured a free and freewheeling press. At first, it seemed that the revolution would resemble the latter, with additional revolutionary voices joining the scene. The 26th of July Movement's newspaper, called *Revolución,* was edited by Carlos Franqui, who had been, with Llerena, part of the 26th of July Committee in Exile. *Revolución*'s weekly cultural supplement, *Lunes de Revolución,* which began publishing on 23 March 1959, was directed by the satirist and novelist Guillermo Cabrera Infante. But anti-Communist groups of both the Left and the Right struggled to adapt to the new circumstances. Popular publications, like the pro-Ortodoxo and anti-Batista periodical *Bohemia* and the newspaper *Prensa Libre,* where Mario Llerena was then writing, were sympathetic to the revolution but hostile to Communist participation in it. (The oldest and most conservative paper, *Diario de la Marina,* inveterately hostile to the new order, was widely detested by the new revolutionaries.) During 1959 and early 1960, in spite of worrying signs, many anti-Communists (including Mañach, for example) believed that Castro was using Communists to his advantage without sympathy for their programs, and that his remained a safe path forward. But conflicts emerged between the management of some publications and their workers. By the end of 1959 workers at one paper refused to print articles from international wire services that compared Che Guevara to Hitler. Workers at many papers began to add *coletillas,* little postscripts to the end of articles, that argued against content that they found defamatory or insulting. To some, this seemed a form of censorship; to others, it was the eruption of the voice of the workers into a space formerly controlled by the bourgeoisie. In January 1960 Castro sided with the workers, declaring that news cables should have statements of clarification added at the bottom by the printers' union.[36]

Around the time of the new requirements, Llerena wrote an article for *Prensa Libre* in which he implicitly compared what was taking place in Cuba to what had happened during the Communist takeover of Czechoslovakia. First, he wrote, conservative newspapers were closed on account of having "served the fascists." This was followed by psychological terror, in which a special committee of journalists was formed to "defend the integrity of Czech journalism." Although censorship never took on any explicit form, criticism of Communism or the Soviet Union carried the risk of arrest. Llerena intended to suggest that similar processes were at work in Cuba. He called Czechoslovakia "a gloomy picture that reflects uneasily in the mirror of our times."

The *coletilla* appended to Llerena's article responded: "CLARIFICATION— This article is published voluntarily by this printing house using the freedom of the press that exists in Cuba, by the Union of Journalists and Graphical Workers of this work center . . . Although the author of this article maliciously tries to make it appear so, the situation of the press in Cuba bears no resemblance to what happened in [Czechoslovakia]. Neither the Cuban workers nor the journalists have tried, and therefore the Revolution has not tried, to control the organs of expression or to serve the interests of any particular political party." Llerena responded in print. He wrote that he was proud to have received his first *coletilla* and said that he would be ashamed to have written during this period and not to have been issued one. He then addressed the institution of the *coletilla* itself, declaring that he knew many journalists who disapproved of the content and the process of the clarifications. He hated the anonymous character of the *coletilla* and thought that all those who agreed with it should sign their names. Above all, he believed that a newspaper had to have its own personality, a soul that created the reasons that the public sought it out to buy it. The *coletillas,* as a form of internal censorship, interfered with the editorial process that gave a newspaper its character. Llerena concluded what he called his "pointless" response with an invocation of José Martí: "Words are not for hiding the truth, but for saying it."[37]

The *coletilla* appended to Llenera's critique demonstrates how differently its authors thought of the freedom of the press:

> CLARIFICATION: This article is published voluntarily by this printing house using the freedom of the press that exists in Cuba. The journalists and graphical workers of this work center express, in the legitimate use of that right, that the clarifying postscript is not mere pageantry. Rather, it is a legal institution that revolutionary-minded workers (intellectual and manual) apply simply in order to speed up the right to reply in defense of the Revolution against the barrage of the opposition, without having to wait out the long process of a tribunal. Its purpose is not to hurt or decorate anyone, nor is it to earn merits for those who might sign it (it is not anonymous, it is "solidarinous"). With respect to the idea that in this work center there are journalists who don't share the views of the *coletilla,* that is obviously not the case. This one has not been refuted by any comrade.

As conflicts with the press escalated, the conservative *Diario de la Marina* began publishing a count of the new *coletillas* that appeared in each independent newspaper. In April the Executive Board of the Provincial College of Journalists in Havana defended the *coletilla,* saying: "There is freedom of the press in Cuba. This freedom is no longer simply for the owner or seller of information, but for the journalist, for the manual worker and intellectual to make known his position regarding false, anti-patriotic, and tendentious information by means of postscript or annotation, a procedure that . . . is one of the finest achievements of journalism and freedom of expression." Cuba's revolutionaries saw themselves as overcoming the institutions and limited freedoms of bourgeois society, and the developments in the press merely as one manifestation of that process. The idea of a bourgeois press in the most literal sense—one that was owned by and reflected the interests of the bourgeoisie—was widely seen as discredited. This left open the problem of who would decide what constituted antipatriotic discourse or tendentious information, or, indeed, what political incentives those making the decisions might have to act in ways that suppressed dissent or criticism.[38]

What was clear was that the emerging Cuban state—centralized, revolutionary, and with popular, mass participation—chafed against liberal ideas of social institutions that placed explicit value on pluralistic public space. Llerena's predictions were not far off the mark. In April the offices of the newspapers *El Mundo* and *Avance* were seized. On occasions when newspaper workers refused to insert *coletillas,* they were humiliated by their union bosses and fired. In May *Diario de la Marina* was stormed, and the paper shut down. President Dorticós declared that journalists were "rank-and-file soldiers in this great struggle to diffuse our great revolutionary truth before the world" and said that press freedom meant "the right of journalists to defend the integral interests of the Cuban Revolution." Another *Prensa Libre* columnist warned of the "solid and impenetrable totalitarian unanimity" that would come when the government eliminated all opposition press. Three days later *Prensa Libre* itself was shut down. *Avance* and other papers did in fact become assets of U.S. policy, as they had been accused of being, when the CIA gave them money to publish Miami-based versions in advance of the Bay of Pigs invasion.[39]

By mid-1960 it was clear that there would be no reconcilation between the anti-Communist Left and Castro. In Venezuela, Rómulo Betancourt met resistance from the youth wing of his own party, which was inspired by Castro and disliked Betancourt's attacks on Communism. In April 1960 his government hosted the second international meeting of the IADF, ten years after the first had met in Prío's Cuba, bringing together groups representing his idea of the Democratic Left. The Cubans who attended were mostly Betancourt's friends from the Auténtico party, such as Aureliano Sánchez Arango, who were already plotting to try to remove Castro from power. Although the IADF was not a CIA front, the U.S. intelligence agency used the occasion of the conference to meet with anti-Castro Cubans and to begin to mount a program of covert action to remove Castro from power. The Frente Revolucionario Democrático (FRD), which would be the political front group for the Bay of Pigs invasion, was formed in May 1960 around five politically centrist figures who had formerly supported Castro.[40]

Scarcely more than a year after its enthusiastic return, the Cuban Association for Cultural Freedom once again existed in name only. In February 1960 Castro had signed a trade deal with the Soviet Union and in May declared that his government would not hold elections. Llerena was by then fully convinced of Castro's totalitarian ambitions. He wrote to Gorkin that "Cuba is now the first attempt at totalitarianism in Latin America, and . . . he [Llerena] and others used to believe that [Gorkin] exaggerated about the methods of Stalinism, but now we understand that [Gorkin] stopped short [of the full truth]." When the CCF held a major gathering in West Berlin to celebrate the tenth anniversary of its first meeting, it was decided to close down the Cuban Association for Cultural Freedom. The association's program of conferences scheduled for 1960—including "Liberty and the Processes of Revolution," "The Limits of Freedom," "Freedom of the Press," and "Freedom and Exercise of Professional Activity"—had to be cut short. The association's members, including Llerena, Aja, and Mañach, once again felt the need to flee the country. Another member, the professor of sociology Rosario Rexach, left after a Communist student minder—there was one in every university class—denounced her as a counterrevolutionary because her lectures on the French Revolution credited it with having done much to develop systems of modern education. But she could have easily represented the ways in which intellectual freedom, for some ardent revolutionaries, seemed a proxy for counterrevolutionary privilege: Rexach said that she could have stayed if she had kept her mouth shut, with a good income of $6,000 a year, an air-conditioned house, and three servants.[41]

Some, including Mañach and Aja, resettled in Puerto Rico. Given shelter by the University of Puerto Rico, whose leadership sympathized with the anti-Communist Left, Aja tried to reconvene the Cuban Association for Cultural Freedom in exile. Aja, described by one future representative of the CCF as "rather silly and vaguely ridiculous as an intellectual," suffered from low personal prestige and debilitating mental health problems. His attempt to recreate the Cuban Association for Cultural Freedom made no impression. By the end of 1961 both Mañach and Aja had died, Aja by suicide. Not until after the fall of the Soviet Union decades later could Mañach's writings be openly admired in Cuba.[42]

Llerena, by contrast, joined the large group of mostly privileged Cubans who were making new homes in Miami, where he enjoyed a long career as a journalist among the anti-Castro exiles at the center of the whirlwind of activities, conspiracies, and publications, more often than not connected to the CIA through a spaghetti of absurd relationships. Other members of Cuba's anti-Communist Left who had not had any direct relationship with the CCF began new careers fronting for CIA efforts to damage and unseat Castro, especially through the FRD. The FRD was responsible for propaganda and sabotage operations and intended to display the future leadership of a post-Castro Cuba. (Before his suicide Pedro Vicente Aja had served as the head of the Puerto Rican delegation of the FRD.) Aureliano Sánchez Arango joined its leadership for a time, falsely claiming that his Triple-A commanded thousands of armed men in Cuba and, alongside Mujal, had support among labor. Sánchez Arango began to claim that the Soviet Union had completely taken over the island of Cuba after 1961. One CIA official remembered his Triple-A as just one of many anti-Castro rackets, trying to leverage phantom guerrillas and anti-Communist credentials to secure financial support from the U.S. government. Whatever the case, Sánchez Arango soon broke with the FRD, complicating CIA efforts to keep its favored exile assets together.[43]

Raúl Roa and some of the younger members of the Cuban Association of the CCF, including Roa's son, served the new government with distinction. In 1956, when Roa had refused to meet with Castro in Mexico, he had thrown himself wholeheartedly into the CCF's favorite campaigns: he denounced the "brutal methods of the Soviet army to repress the patriotic rising of the Hungarian people" and "the brain-washing and systematic engrossing of the sensibility [that occurs under] Marxist-Caesaro-papism." His classical education was useful after he became foreign minster under Castro because he defended some of his government's initiatives by pointing out that they could be derived from definitions of justice advanced by Aristotle, not Marx. In 1960 he returned from a visit to Yugoslavia very enthusiastic about a model of an "alternative Communism." The U.S. government sometimes tried to craft campaigns using Roa's anti-Communist words from a previous era against him, but to little effect. By the late 1960s Roa had as little sympathy for his former colleagues as he had once had for Communism; in 1968 he described Sánchez Arango as the greatest fraud of his generation and Carlos Prío as (in loose and inadequate translation) a "piece-of-shit thief."[44]

Roa's son, "Raulito" Roa Kourí, was one of the group that Llerena had helped bring into the 26th of July Movement in 1956 via participation in the CCF; he was eventually named Cuban representative to the United Nations. Llerena, who came to despise the dedication that many of these mostly educated and affluent Cubans showed to Castro, later wrote: "I used to think that my personal influence had played no small part in bringing them into the fold of the 26 of July Movement. I no longer believe that. Those young people had within themselves the habits of leisure, the undigested knowledge, and the spiritual vacuum that ultimately determined their ideological conversion [to Castroism]." That line of reasoning reflected Llerena's subsequent bitterness more than any reality;

others whom he had recruited independently made their own breaks
with Castro.[45]

To most Cubans, the fate of the CCF would have passed entirely without
notice, and the problems of intellectuals and the press would have seemed
like minor disturbances compared with the actions that affected them all:
the agrarian reform, suspension of relations with the United States and
the signing of trade deals with the Soviet Union, and the beginning of the
literacy campaigns. By 1961 Cuba's liberals had mostly returned to exile.
But concentration of power in state hands provided an opportunity for a
second wave of disillusionment, this time among more committed socialist
revolutionaries. This disenchantment with Cuban socialism—not the liberal disappointment that it had become socialism in the first place—was
the one that would reorient the Cultural Cold War in the region.

Lunes de Revolución, edited by Guillermo Cabrera Infante, began publishing in March 1959 as the cultural supplement of the 26th of July
newspaper, Revolución. Its third issue, on 3 April, in a still very open atmosphere, was dedicated to different ideas of revolution from history and
published selections from the writings of Thomas Paine, Peter Kropotkin,
Karl Marx and Friedrich Engels, Vladimir Mayakovsky, Isaak Babel, John
Reed, André Breton, and Leon Trotsky. Throughout its first year it published new and established currents in Cuban writing, including works by
José Lezama Lima, Virgilio Piñera, Heberto Padilla, Severo Sarduy, Alejo
Carpentier, Nicolás Guillén, and Roberto Fernández Retamar. When Jean-
Paul Sartre and Simone de Beauvoir visited Cuba and declared that the
new society was a direct democracy resulting from a spontaneous and
nonideological revolution, they did so after conversations in the offices
of Lunes. On its first anniversary Lunes queried major leaders for their
opinions of what they did and did not like about Lunes: Fidel Castro called
it "a good effort in the need to express three similar things: Revolution,
people, and culture," and Che Guevara replied that Lunes was sometimes
very good, sometimes suffered from "intellectualisms" divorced from
Cuban reality, but in the end was one of the major contributors to Cuban
cultural reality.[46]

But in the next few months Lunes encountered trouble. Perhaps it was
Cabrera Infante's publication of Trotsky's writings as the Cuban government
drew increasingly dependent on the Soviet Union. Or perhaps it was
Cabrera Infante's enthusiasm for a cinema verité film titled P.M., filmed
outside official channels, that showed Havana's nightlife, complete with
debauchery that the revolution had not eliminated. The revolution saw

itself as increasingly under threat as confirmed reports about an exile army, trained mostly in Guatemala by the CIA for an invasion, reached Cuban shores. On 16 April 1961 Castro formally declared the Cuban Revolution to be "socialist." The very next day some 1,400 Cuban exiles, trained and supported by the CIA, landed at the Bay of Pigs. Within three days they had been completely defeated.[47]

The CCF had long since turned against Castro's Cuban Revolution and had sought to undermine Castro's standing among European social democrats by soliciting a piece from Theodore Draper for the March issue of *Encounter,* printed just before the Bay of Pigs invasion. Influenced by Mario Llerena's writings for the 26th of July Movement, Draper warned that "Castro promised one kind of revolution and made another. The revolution Castro promised was unquestionably betrayed." Draper warned of terror ahead and said that Castro had delivered "not a national revolution but an international civil war." (Arthur Schlesinger passed Draper's article on to President Kennedy in advance of his decision to approve the attack, calling it the "best that I have seen on the Cuban Revolution.") After the attack failed, *Encounter,* and then *Cuadernos,* published Draper's oft-repeated critical assessment of the Bay of Pigs: "The ill-fated invasion of Cuba . . . was one of those rare politico-military events—a perfect failure." From the liberal perspective, the invasion had not only left Castro in power but also had provided a developing Cuban Communism with the prestige of having defeated an attack by the United States and the rhetorical ammunition to rally anti-imperialists to its cause. It also made Castro, even more than he had already been, revolutionary royalty: the man who had defeated the Colossus of the North. Che Guevara, on this point at least, agreed with Draper. In a meeting with a U.S. official later in 1961, he thanked him for the invasion that had transformed Cuba from an aggrieved little country into an equal.[48]

Heightened international tensions were not for the ideologically suspect. With the case of the troubled *P.M.* on the minds of many, Castro convened the Conference of Intellectuals for June 1961. On June 30 Castro pledged to clarify his position and assuage the anxieties that some felt. Socioeconomic revolution produced a cultural revolution, Castro stated, but while revolutionary art naturally followed, not all artists had to be committed revolutionaries. Artists should be free to practice as they chose, with the only exception being art that went against the revolution's own "right to exist." Therefore, artists should not be concerned about the absence of freedom, for the revolution would defend freedom; artists could produce unpopular and useless works of art if they chose. They should only be concerned not to be against the revolution, fearing not the executioner of culture but the judgment of posterity. Castro's pithy formulation "Within the revolution, everything; against the revolution, no rights" summarized the position clearly. On the one hand, it was a clear statement that there would be no Cuban equivalent to socialist realism—no officially sanctioned form or artistic content. On the other hand, it created a category of "antirevolutionary" art and made it impossible for an artist to know in advance whether his or her work would be judged to be in that category.[49]

In the end, *P.M.* was banned permanently, and *Lunes* closed a few issues later. By the end of the year all newspapers and magazines were under state control. In August the Unión de Escritores y Artistas de Cuba was created, headed by the stalwart Communist poet Nicolás Guillén, and the state assigned control over literary production to the union. When Sartre and Simone de Beauvoir visited again, Guillén, a veteran of peace campaigns from the Stalin era, told them, in classic antiformalist style, that he judged "all research into technique and form counter-revolutionary." He would later use an anecdote to explain Cuban cultural policy: "During [World War II], a Soviet author sent Stalin a romance that he had written in those dramatic days; an egoistic book of intimacies, hidden passion and unbridled devotion. Cannons thundered on all fronts: the Nazis tightened their bloody siege of Stalingrad; millions of men and women fell, never to get up again. Stalin was asked what he thought of the book and he responded: 'Very interesting, even good. But only two copies should be printed: one for her and one for him.'" With Cuba under siege from enemies from without and from within, he meant to say, the intellectual process had to respect the needs of the people and be responsible for building revolutionary culture.[50]

The situation was perhaps not as constrained as Guillén's reference to Stalin would suggest. Debate was not brought to an end; it merely had to be carried out "within the revolution." And so it was: there were lively print debates between those who favored a more Soviet cultural and political model and those who preferred a more independent and sui generis revolution that had done so much to inspire a radical "New Left" around the world. In its first years, many Cubans experienced the new institutions of the revolution as expansions of freedoms and democratic practice: assemblies and rallies that gave people ways of communicating their desires to their government. But dissent was curbed in ways that represented real loss. "Voluntary" labor for intellectuals in the cane fields turned, in the mid-1960s, into camps for those defined as deviant, such as homosexuals, intellectuals, and political dissidents. On the other hand, there was no ban on abstract art, as in the Soviet Union, and Cuban painters participated fully in international currents, making very effective use of the decade's pop art, for example. Poets emerged from factories and fields, and far more books were printed and read in the new Cuba than in the prerevolutionary years. Casa de las Américas marched on, defending its members from the worst abuses of state interference and growing in prestige.[51]

The most important Latin American writers associated themselves with the Cuban Revolution and—especially if they were not Cuban—wrote with considerable freedom. The urbane and urban Argentine writer Julio Cortázar—whose novel *Rayuela* (1963) is often identified as the beginning of the period of enormous productivity and expansion in the interest in and market for Latin American writers known as the "boom" in Latin American letters—traveled to Cuba from Paris to work with Casa de las Américas and observed: "Except for four or five writers . . . *all* of the intellectuals and the artists are up to their necks with Fidel Castro, working like crazies, teaching literacy, directing theater and going out to the countryside to learn its problems . . . It goes without saying that I feel old, dried up, *French* beside them. If I were twenty years younger . . . I'd stay . . . What incredible people." Cortázar's astonished admiration for what he saw taking place could stand in for the reaction of a generation. The absent liberals were quickly forgotten; Cuba seemed to offer a fresh set of symbols and ideas, a new set of subjects for artists and writers to confront. It helped disseminate the ideas and works of the cultural Left that supported it, and it helped make that work meaningful.[52]

Cortázar's *Rayuela* was set in Argentina and France, can be read in multiple orders, was aesthetically unconventional, and centered on psychological drama. In the wrong era in the Soviet Union, it might have been seen as decadent. Cuba was different. *Rayuela* was greeted with enthusiasm by Latin American leftists because its author was a friend, and revolutionaries embraced it because, in making the chapter order the choice of the reader, it could be understood as inviting the reader to become more active and self-conscious. International interest and enthusiasm for the Cuban Revolution generally made Latin America seem a more interesting and attractive region to those in the United States or Europe who might have ignored it otherwise, and that unquestionably played a part in making the boom possible. So too, did the Casa de las Américas prizes, which helped signal potentially prestigious works to a wider world and would soon be imitated by Catalan literary agents whose work would eventually be most closely associated with the boom. That the boom, with its commercial and marketing overtones, was a phenomenon of the capitalist marketplace, inspired in part by the Cuban Revolution, would be just one of its many ironies. Another was that the cosmopolitan and universalist project that CCF organizers like Julián Gorkin had hoped to create through their works was now being implemented by a revolutionary government that they had helped bring to power, only to find that it created a new kind of future in which they had no part to play. Passing along the way through a dictatorship that offered neither democracy nor socialism and leaving the anti-Communist Left excluded and bitter, Cuba had gone from a flawed democracy without socialism to a flawed socialism without democracy.[53]

Peace and National Liberation in the Mexican 1960s

The Congress for Cultural Freedom (CCF) understood itself to be a defender of democracy and a foe of totalitarianism, but its most consequential political action in Latin America before 1961 had been to help bring to power the government of Fidel Castro, which it soon came to view as representing precisely the kind of totalitarianism that it opposed. When Castro declared the content of the Cuban Revolution to be socialist in 1961, Cuban Communism became the nightmare that haunted the dreams of U.S. policy makers and the region's political Right. The next year, the United States pressured Latin American governments to expel Cuba from the Organization of American States. The CCF spent the next several years trying to mobilize an anti-Castro center-left as it had once tried to mobilize an anti-Soviet center-left.

Just as Cuba transformed the politics of anti-Communism in Latin America, it also remade the region's radicals. Old-fashioned pro-Soviet Communists remained across Latin America, of course, and if they seemed moderate in comparison to the Cubans, it was because they were indeed moderate by comparison. The Soviet Union, for domestic political reasons, needed to avoid conflict with the United States; Cuba, also for domestic political reasons, but with less choice in the matter, needed to maintain a state of conflict with U.S. imperialism. Especially after the withdrawal of Soviet missiles from Cuba in 1963, the Soviet Union became more cautious about sponsoring revolutionary activities abroad. Cuba did not. Prompted by the Cuban example, and sometimes with Cuban support, guerrilla warfare defined the global 1960s and 1970s as small groups sprang up around the world to liberate their countries from imperialism and capitalism by force of small arms. The model never worked. Che Guevara's martyrdom was complete when he was killed in 1967 on a hopeless foray

deep in the Bolivian jungle that had the support neither of the people of
the country nor of the Bolivian Communist Party. But his image and his life
continued to inspire. Guevara wrote that making revolution was largely a
matter of will. One did not wait for the right historical circumstances,
he argued: they could be created with a small band of guerrilla fighters.
Although the notion was not even an accurate history of the Cuban
example on which it appeared to be based, it remained a powerful one.[1]

But if left-wing revolutionary insurgency seemed to define the decade,
it was counterinsurgency and counterrevolution that would change the
landscape of Latin American politics in the 1960s and 1970s. Military
regimes took command over much of Latin America's population: coups
put military governments in power in Brazil in 1964, Bolivia firmly by
1971, Chile and Uruguay in 1973, and Argentina in 1966 and again in
1976. Guerrilla movements were crushed there and in other places, like
Guatemala, where repression was hardly novel. The regimes collaborated
with one another in an era of torture, murder, and disappearances that
went far beyond the destruction of the insurgent Left, targeting civilian
politicians, journalists, and labor activists who were trying to restore democracy. These "dirty wars" of military governments against their own
civilian populations made a new era of darkness for the region's Left.[2]

In at least one major country in the region, however, the story is commonly said to have been different. Mexico maintained diplomatic relations
with Cuba even after other countries were pressured to break them, arguing
that Cuba had the right to self-determination. Castro reciprocated by
brushing off Mexican would-be guerrilla fighters who tried to train in
his country. As a result, revolutionaries in Mexico lacked international
support. There would also be no military government in Mexico, where
the Partido Revolucionario Institucional (PRI) remained firmly in control.
The quiescence of Mexico is more myth than reality—its version of the
dirty war was also brutal and cruel—but it ruined perhaps many hundreds
of lives rather than many thousands. This limited form of Mexican ex-
ceptionalism has traditionally been explained as the result of revolutionary
solidarity with Cuba, a consequence of the distinctive tradition in Mexican
diplomacy that calls for respecting the internal affairs of other nations.
But it also had other sources: a secret deal with the United States to keep
one Latin American embassy open to Cuba and also the fear of the domestic
Left, organized in the 1960s into the Movimiento de Liberación Nacional
(MLN, the Movement for National Liberation).[3]

The MLN was established in 1961 and quickly mobilized hundreds of
thousands of supporters into a broad left-wing front, but it faded quickly.
By 1964 it had broken on the familiar jagged rocks of sectarian division,

onto which it had been enthusiastically thrown by a hostile Mexican government. Although it limped on until the end of the decade, it lost in its first few years many of its most prominent supporters, including Lázaro Cárdenas, who had emerged from political retirement to become its symbolic leader. Within Mexico the MLN called for a return to the democratic values of the Mexican Revolution, associated with the presidency of Cárdenas, and lamented that the present leadership of the PRI tolerated and abetted venality, corruption, and poverty.

But the MLN was not simply a domestic political movement. It was also a product of the global Cultural Cold War. Its politics were aligned with and developed from an interaction with the Soviet-sponsored peace movement. The MLN's foreign policy, which called for the defense of Cuba and of movements of national liberation, echoed the established rhetoric of the World Peace Council (WPC). This was no accident, for Lázaro Cárdenas and many of its other leaders had become active members of the WPC in the years before the establishment of the MLN. In 1962, when the MLN was at the peak of its strength, former president Emilio Portes Gil tried to cast it as illegitimate by calling it dependent on Moscow and directed by the Kremlin. Cárdenas responded by declaring that the MLN was dependent on no foreign power and was dedicated to the postulates of the Mexican Revolution. Cárdenas was correct, largely because he worked assiduously to keep out foreign funds. The germ of truth in Portes Gil's charge lay in the organizational impetus that the WPC gave to the MLN.[4]

The tension between the domestic and the international layers of the MLN was a source of trouble for the movement, and it achieved few of its goals. Yet if its impact was "ephemeral," as one historian has argued, its struggles reveal a great deal about Latin American politics in the context of the global Cold War, demonstrating how difficult it was to create a movement for democracy in the face of domestic opposition and international polarization. The history of the MLN reveals at least three important ironies: one having to do with Mexican domestic politics, one with Cuba, and one with the global Cold War.

Within Mexico the MLN has typically been seen as an expression of Cardenismo in the 1960s. Lázaro Cárdenas was the figurehead of the movement, and it had the sympathies of most of those who had made up his political coalition. (It was also the first major political movement in which his son, Cuauhtémoc, played a major role. Cuauhtémoc's first bid for the presidency in 1988 and the founding of the center-left Partido de la Revolución Democrática the following year would rely on many of the same parties and people and much of the same platform as had the MLN.)

To raise support for the MLN, the elder Cárdenas briefly acted like a president again, campaigning in the countryside. But the irony that the MLN never confronted was the degree to which President Cárdenas was the architect of the state that repressed him in the 1960s. To be sure, the PRI had evolved since Cárdenas's presidency and had changed its name, and the state had grown in scope and capacity. But the centralized union bureaucracies and the state monopoly on public newsprint that vexed the MLN were products of that earlier time, now turned against the Left. If the MLN was indeed an expression of Cardenismo in the 1960s, it also confronted the undemocratic aspects of the legacy of Cardenista democracy of the 1930s and was substantially defeated by them.[5]

The MLN grounded its critique of the Mexican state in the language of democracy, which it understood as essentially populist rather than procedural, in that democratic legitimacy was conferred on governments that acted in ways that benefited "the people" rather than those that held competitive elections. The MLN was inspired by the progressive legacy of the Mexican Revolution and analogized the Mexican experience to the one taking place in Cuba. "Cuban sugar is today what Mexican oil once was," said Lázaro Cárdenas in 1961: it belonged to the nation and its people. The second irony, then, was that decades of revolutionary degeneration in Mexico had provided the MLN with the tools it needed to see through the government's claim to represent an evolved form of direct democracy, but the same skepticism was not applied to Cuba. Fidel Castro too claimed to be a democrat because he acted in the interests of the people. In 1961 his claims seemed to many to be both fresh and plausible. But the MLN missed the ways in which the authoritarian aspects of the Mexican system it disliked—the use of political detention and government control of unions and the press—were being put in place in Cuba in the very years in which they held it out as a model. Mexico's government smoothed its claims to democratic legitimacy with rigged elections and bribed its way to a "free press"; Cuba soon dispensed with both.[6]

Observing the final irony requires seeing the MLN as part of the Cultural Cold War. In that context the MLN followed a Popular Front model, bringing together leftist Cardenistas with Vicente Lombardo Toledano's Partido Popular and small Marxist parties, including the Partido Comunista Mexicano (PCM). It categorically rejected anti-Communism and, through the WPC, was a kind of fellow traveler of the Soviet Union's anti-anti-Communist network. But it was not a Soviet front group. Furthermore, its calls for union autonomy and an independent press inverted traditional Cold War patterns in which these causes were typically associated with anti-Communist groups. The final irony, then, is that the MLN's platform, if enacted, would have made Mexico more democratic in precisely those ways anti-Communists sought across the continent. Its very existence undermines the equation of anti-Communism and an idea of democracy based in civil society institutions independent of the state, the idea that outlets like the CCF tried so hard to establish. Indeed, the CCF's local representative in Mexico, the ex-Communist Rodrigo García Treviño, volunteered for a secret and horrendously undemocratic campaign to repress the MLN. The history of the MLN is another reminder that prodemocracy movements in Latin America, whether of the anti-Communist or the anti-anti-Communist variety, used languages of liberation that were implicated in support for empire somewhere on the globe. Perhaps there was no other way.

Although the MLN was a movement of the 1960s, it inherited an organizational legacy from the Soviet-aligned peace movement of the 1950s. After the major peace conference held in Mexico in September 1949, the Mexican Pro-Peace Committee was established to continue its work. The first important task was signature gathering on behalf of the Stockholm Appeal. The Mexican committee set its sights on 1 million signatures and established prizes and trophies for associates who gathered the most. Much of this activity was undertaken by the PCM, which directed its followers to apply limitless energy to the organization of local peace committees. Members of the national committee of the pro-peace group took to the streets to round up signatures from passers-by; Diego Rivera himself spent a morning in front of the post office in Mexico City, making speeches in favor of peace next to signs reading "Damn the warmongers" and "Down with the atomic bomb." He then spent the afternoon with David Álfaro Siqueiros and Vicente Lombardo Toledano at a little table, collecting more signatures. In spite of its high-profile endorsements, the signature-gathering campaign did not meet its goals in Mexico. When the final tallies were presented, the Mexican committee furnished 300,000 signatures, about one-twentieth of 1 percent of the reported global total and well short of its own goal.[7]

As with its other fellow-traveling organizations, the PCM wanted both to control the actions of the peace campaign and to have membership in those groups represent a broad front. It instructed its supporters not to be "sectarian" in their actions within peace campaigns and as they formed local chapters. These directives did not succeed. The party soon reported

Vicente Lombardo Toledano (standing behind table in dark suit) collecting signatures for the Stockholm Appeal on the streets of Mexico City, 1950. Photo courtesy Archivo General de la Nación, DFS, document 11–71–50, binder 1, page 234.

that "detrimental sectarianism" had caused Communist groups simply to convert their own cells into peace chapters, and this was leading to inactivity and narrow support for their initiatives.[8]

The figurehead of the Pro-Peace Committee incarnated the contradiction. General Heriberto Jara Corona was not a member of the Communist Party but was no less a believer in the goodness of the Soviet Union for that. Still, he had ample biographical reasons for his peace work. He was born in the coastal state of Veracruz, which was relatively developed industrially, was exposed to international political currents because of its port, and had many areas with strong organized labor movements. The son of a middle-class factory owner, Jara worked as a young man doing accounting in textile factories, where he saw the misery and poor treatment of the workers. In the afternoons he worked as a reader to groups of cigar makers (the work was quiet, and the practice of hiring a reader was common), performing books with social content, like Jack London's nightmare of a fascist United States, *The Iron Heel*. Jara became a general during the Mexican Revolution and was ordered by future president Venustiano Carranza, who was then first chief of the Constitutionalist Army, to march on Veracruz to enforce the departure of the North American military from its occupation of that city in 1914. Elected to the Constitutional Assembly in 1917, Jara was a prominent member of its radical wing and was instrumental in crafting the statements of workers' rights in Article 123. "Political freedom," he argued at the Constitutional Assembly, "as beautiful as it is, as well guaranteed as you like, cannot be assured if economic freedom is not guaranteed first. Poverty is the worst kind of tyranny, and if we do not wish to condemn our workers to that tyranny, we must emancipate them by voting in effective laws." Jara was appointed to govern both the federal district of Mexico City and his home state of Veracruz, where he was associated with the causes of the urban working class. Lázaro Cárdenas, while president, made Jara the president of the official party. While president of the Partido de la Revolución Mexicana (PRM), Jara showed a populist rather than a liberal understanding of democracy. He fought with President Cárdenas when Jara advocated nonrecognition of elections in Mexico City that had been won by an anti-Cardenista politician. Jara argued that democracy had to be in accordance with popular will—which plainly meant in favor of Cárdenas—and he thought that that should supersede the results of actual elections.[9]

Jara had participated in many ways in the construction of the Mexican state and was an honored member of the official party during all three incarnations: the Partido Nacional Revolucionario, the PRM, and finally the PRI. He had been a close friend of the cultured and talented Soviet ambassador to Mexico, Constantin Oumansky, during World War II but had never been a member of the Communist Party. But by the 1950s the content of his political experiences made him a passionate defender of the Soviet Union. He was named president of the Mexican Pro-Peace Committee and vice president of the Latin American organization, traveling in that capacity to Europe and Moscow. As one of the seven recipients of the Stalin Peace Prize in its inaugural year, 1950, Jara traveled to the USSR, which awed him both physically and morally. He returned to Mexico with a birch sapling and planted it in his garden, cherishing the symbolism of a tree from the country of socialism growing in Mexico.[10]

In Mexico, Jara took up advocacy of the peace cause. As the United States prepared for war, Jara wrote for a pamphlet published in Mexico, the Soviet Union spent less and less on war and increased the amount it spent on social services. In response to charges of forced labor in the Soviet Union, he quoted a Russian worker he had met who praised the scientific nature of the USSR's five-year plans, and who then adeptly pirouetted to a condemnation of the inhumanity of the Taylorist system of production (associated with speedups and the "rational" exploitation of labor in the United States), which he said left workers too exhausted to

participate in the world of culture. Jara, like the organization he represented, was the very picture of a fellow traveler: not quite embracing
Communism for himself while simultaneously making the case for it for
others. He called anti-Communism "nothing . . . more than the mask for
Yankee imperialism to dominate the world" and wrote, "Now, if the desire for justice, if the longing for freedom, if the urge to rid oneself of
hunger is called communism, then where justice is absent, there will be
communism; where freedom is shackled, there will be communism; where
there is hunger, there will be communism, and it will not be imported from
the Soviet Union; it will be very national, whatever country it is in." Jara
had seen anti-Communism used to bludgeon Mexico's non-Communist
Left and U.S. troops raising the American flag in his home state. His belief in popular government and the right to national self-determination
made him naturally sympathetic to the Soviet Union's situation in the late
1940s, which he understood as that of another "government of the people"
attempting to chart its own path to economic and political liberty, but
menaced by imperialism.[11]

After Stalin's death in 1953, the new Soviet leadership that came to
power sought to de-Stalinize several aspects of Soviet life, including both
culture and foreign affairs, and the idea of peace faded as a cultural force.
To improve domestic conditions, the USSR needed to decrease military
spending and consequently sought reasonably good relations with the
United States. WPC rhetoric shifted from a belligerent anti-imperialism
to antinuclear talk of peaceful coexistence. Although the WPC remained
unquestionably pro-Soviet, Nikita Khrushchev went so far as to suggest
to the WPC leadership that it should act on principle, even if that meant
going against the USSR. At the same time, however, Khrushchev believed
that the Soviet Union was the only major power genuinely interested in
peace, and that decolonizing Asia and Africa would join a great "zone of
peace" that would bring the "Third World" closer to the USSR over time.
The WPC's president, Frédéric Joliot-Curie, died in late 1958 and was
replaced by his close friend and associate J. D. Bernal, an Irish biologist
and Communist. Bernal, in keeping with the times, looked to reach out
to non-Communist leaders who shared the values of the WPC, and he
struck on the idea of inviting Lázaro Cárdenas to join the organization.[12]

The man who had once granted asylum to Trotsky would seem an odd
choice for affiliation with a Soviet-aligned group. But Cárdenas, in spite
of his sympathy and personal respect for Trotsky and his deep frustration
at the time of the Hitler-Stalin pact, had never been anti-Soviet. In the
1940s he had still never traveled outside Mexico, which remained his sole
point of reference. Like his friend Heriberto Jara, he associated anti-

Communism with the politics of the privileged. World events and personal contacts moved him rather naturally toward opinions that aligned with those of the WPC. Shocked by the use of nuclear weapons against Japan at the end of World War II, Cárdenas concluded that President Truman was a war criminal. In 1946 he met with Henry Wallace and wrote that Wallace was "not a Communist as his enemies say," but simply a "progressive democrat, a friend of the working class and an enemy of imperialism." He and Wallace were thinking in similar ways about politics in the early years of the Cold War, defining themselves as progressive "anti-anti-Communists" in opposition to dominant anti-Communist political cultures. "Communism is the bogeyman of the rich and the hope of the poor," Cárdenas wrote in his diary in late 1946. He gave his blessing to the Continental Congress for Peace when it took place in Mexico City in 1949, though without violating his custom of refusing to appear in public in support of political causes.[13]

Cárdenas remained personally close to the small group that maintained the Mexican Pro-Peace Committee. Heriberto Jara was a close family friend. Elena Vázquez Gómez worked as Cárdenas's secretary; she and her partner Teresa Proenza were also close associates of Frida Kahlo and Diego Rivera during the early 1950s, when the painters devoted considerable emotional and physical energy to the peace cause. Proenza and Vázquez Gómez had organized the 1953 Continental Congress for Culture alongside Pablo Neruda. Like Vicente Lombardo Toledano, Vázquez Gómez had been an asset of Soviet intelligence during World War II.[14]

Even so, Cárdenas was not directly involved with the Mexican Pro-Peace Committee in the early 1950s. What remained of the committee was managed rather directly by the PCM. Evidence suggests that during its leanest years the Pro-Peace Committee could carry on its activities only because of operational subsidies from the Soviet Union. Jara's figurehead role obliged him to donate large sums personally, but financial problems were already acute by 1952. The magazine *Paz*, edited by Proenza, was accumulating large debts until Juan Pablo Sainz of the PCM, speaking with some officials at the WPC, was able to arrange for the WPC to provide financial assistance. With the threat of closure still urgent and Jara unwilling to indefinitely give the magazine loans that were unlikely ever to be paid back, the line of credit from the WPC seems to have been extended. The socially committed poet Efraín Huerta, secretary general of the Pro-Peace Committee, arranged for more money to go to the magazine after further conversations with the WPC. Jara rejected attempts by the WPC to pay back loans he had made, writing that his contributions had been given for personal reasons and then adding, "As for what you [the WPC] are giving for the magazine, you know what you are doing, but I don't want to know anything about the movement of funds for it." Jara stopped contributing financially; that the magazine continued publishing for several years would seem to be the result of support from the WPC and, by extension, the Soviet Union.[15]

The necessity of such an external subsidy was a sign of broader weakness in the Mexican Left during the 1950s. Vicente Lombardo Toledano continued to work, but the Confederación de Trabajadores de América Latina (CTAL) had lost ground to the Organización Regional Interamericana de Trabajadores (ORIT) in Latin America. The Confederación de Trabajadores de México, which he and Cárdenas had built, expelled Lombardo in 1948 and, in joining ORIT, aligned itself with the anti-Communist trade-union movement. Lombardo Toledano's crushing defeat in the 1952 presidential elections was a measure of his limited influence: he came in fourth, earning fewer than 100,000 votes. For its part, the PCM was passing through very lean years. Suffering from poor leadership and the consequences of expelling many of its more dynamic workers, it retained fewer than a thousand members. Although the aged president Adolfo Ruiz Cortines, who served from 1952 to 1958, relied on the Cardenista left wing of the PRI to balance the power of the associates of his conservative predecessor, Miguel Alemán, economic growth helped stabilize the regime, and Cardenistas had to fight to retain influence. The PRI's machinery for co-opting and undermining challenges to its rule was improved by the development of a professional intelligence service that infiltrated opposition movements.[16]

Reflecting the increasingly urban demographics of Mexico, student politics became more important to the Left and its program. After the overthrow of the Guatemalan government of Jacobo Arbenz in 1954, for instance, Cuauhtémoc Cárdenas, the son of Lázaro Cárdenas, led a demonstration that laid a floral wreath at the U.S. embassy with a note reading "For the hurt caused by the death of the Good Neighbor Policy." Lázaro Cárdenas broke from his usual pattern of public silence and issued a statement of support for the government of Arbenz, lamenting the damage done to the sovereignty of Guatemala. After the coup the WPC increased its attention to the defense of peace in Latin America in precisely the same terms, defining peace as the defense of national sovereignty against imperialism.[17]

In December 1955 word arrived that Lázaro Cárdenas had been awarded the Stalin Peace Prize. His decision to accept it was controversial. Many of his critics had always wanted to believe that he was a Communist and reasoned that only a Communist would accept an award with the name "Stalin" engraved on it. But not all who objected were his political enemies. The historian Frank Tannenbaum had been his friend and counselor in the 1930s, but the anarchism of his younger days had hardened into liberal anti-Communism by the 1950s, and he wrote Cárdenas to warn of the "diabolically clever" actions of the Communists to "lay claim on you before the world." He continued:

> But you do not belong to them. Your life and work on behalf of the Mexican people lies within the Mexican tradition and is inspired by the democratic philosophy of the Western World. You believe in freedom, in justice, in a free press, free assembly, free speech, in human dignity and in that no man has a right to impose his ideas by force upon another. You do not believe in concentration camps or in liquidating people whose political opinions are different from yours, (as illustrated by the case of Trotsky) and you believe in the freedom and equality of little nations.[18]

Cárdenas did not see the matter in those terms. For him, accepting the Stalin Prize expressed approval of the steps that major powers had made toward peace with each other (talks held in Geneva in mid-1955 had reduced nuclear tensions) and the hope that a thaw in the Cold War would mean the end of interventions. To Tannenbaum, he replied:

> If the world is asking for peace; if the old allies of the past war have returned to meeting to try to find solutions to their differences . . . how can it hurt Mexico or a Mexican to accept the Peace Prize? You refer to the tradition of Mexico and Western democratic philosophy, and go on, "you believe in freedom, in justice, in a free press, freedom of assembly, human dignity, equality of small nations, etc." We really do believe in those things and we desire them for all to whom those liberties have been forbidden. If it is as you express, and there are peoples on other continents that live under oppression, we ought not to turn around and do the same thing by damaging "small nations" and suppressing freedom of expression.

In February 1956 the Soviet film director Grigori Alexandrov conferred the award in a lavish ceremony in Mexico City, referring to Cárdenas as a "paladin of democracy and independence," a defender of justice and of the interests of the Mexican people. Thousands packed the room to witness the event; thousands more waited outside to catch a glimpse of Cárdenas as he left. The multitude that turned out to see him was a sign of how many missed his leadership in a rapidly developing but capitalist Mexico. Cárdenas was famously impassive in public and unwilling to criticize his successors in office directly, and the short speech that he made at the ceremony was oblique. He heralded improvements in relations between the great powers and, without mentioning Guatemala by name, stressed the importance of ending the Cold War because of the damage it had done to the sovereignty of smaller nations. Cárdenas described propaganda against Mexican partisans of peace as tendentious, saying that the aspiration for peace was shared by millions of men and women working for universal peace; it was the supreme ideal of the "people." Cárdenas's distrust of anti-Communism led him to doubt that Tannenbaum's concentration-camps-and-secret-police description of the Soviet Union was accurate. But what he objected to most strongly was the Cold War logic that transformed criticism of the Soviet Union into a justification for oppressive intervention in the Western Hemisphere and beyond.[19]

Heriberto Jara wrote to Lázaro Cárdenas in May 1957, after his prize had been awarded, trying to keep him involved in WPC activity. But Cárdenas, while expressing sympathy, kept to his usual pattern of public silence. International overtures from J. D. Bernal in 1959 were a different matter and did not raise the problem of interfering in Mexican politics. Then, Cárdenas agreed to serve as a member of the WPC on condition that he be allowed to send proxies in his stead to international meetings. Mexican thinkers like Jara and Cárdenas were, for reasons of their own, reworking the message of the WPC through the lens of national liberation, laying the intellectual groundwork for the MLN.[20]

The president who took office in Mexico in December 1958, Adolfo López Mateos, presented a puzzle to the Mexican Left. Compared with his somewhat dour predecessor, he was young, handsome, and seemingly concerned with the plight of common people. In 1960 he characterized his administration as "extreme left within the Constitution." But to those who outflanked him on the left—those he considered outside the constitution— he responded with severe repression. In 1958, at the very beginning of his term, an independent railroad workers' union had issued a series of demands and, toward the end of February of the following year, called for a national strike. López Mateos responded by ordering mass arrests and firings. Leaders of the striking workers were members of the Partido Obrero-Campesino Mexicano (POCM), formed in 1950 by Communists who had been expelled from the PCM. Alleging that the railroad strikes were the consequence of Soviet subversion, the government rounded up other Communists, including leaders of the PCM. (Vicente Lombardo Toledano cannily criticized the leadership of the railroad union, and his Partido Popular ducked persecution.) Charges against the POCM and

PCM leaders included the crime of "social dissolution," created in 1941 by a law that prohibited the dissemination of foreign ideas that could upset public order or affect the sovereignty of the Mexican state. It had been crafted to allow the government to arrest undesirable spies at the dawn of Mexican participation in World War II, but its first use was against the railroad workers in 1959. The POCM and PCM leaders were imprisoned in Mexico City's notorious "preventive prison," the Palacio Negro de Lecumberri.[21]

Outside prison walls the repression of the independent unionists galvanized the Left, which considered the charges of social dissolution illegitimate and unconstitutional. A committee was formed on behalf of the political prisoners, growing out of the activity of a five-year-old Marxist study group known as the Círculo de Estudios Mexicanos, where discussions were being held on the reconstruction of the Left. The geographer Jorge L. Tamayo, a member of the Círculo and a supporter of the peace movement since its earliest days in the country, began paying visits to the jailed railroad workers. Securing their release became a major goal as members of the Círculo undertook to reorganize the committees and the causes of the Left. At nearly the same time, Tamayo, who had traveled to Stockholm for the Tenth World Peace Congress in 1959, also developed a critical view of the Mexican Pro-Peace Committee's inactivity and scanty public presence under the leadership of Jara. After negotiations with younger members, the eighty-year-old Jara retained an honorary position but accepted reorganization, and the following month the Steering Committee for Peace and International Cooperation was formed with the idea of retaking the initiative that the old peace organization had lost. The new committee, in addition to Tamayo, included a number of other young leaders, among whom were Alonso Aguilar Monteverde, Cuauhtémoc Cárdenas, Elí de Gortari, Ignacio García Téllez, Guillermo Montaño, and Janitzio Múgica. These were the future leaders of the MLN, and most of them were also traveling internationally to events sponsored by the WPC in the late 1950s.[22]

Lázaro Cárdenas, accompanied for much of the time by Cuauhtémoc Cárdenas, made his first lengthy trip outside Mexico from October 1958 to February 1959. He traveled to Paris, Moscow, Beijing, Tokyo, and finally the United States. In Moscow he and Cuauhtémoc were greeted by the Soviet Peace Committee and taken to the Bolshoi Theater. In Beijing they were met by Kuo Mo-jo, the most important personality on the Chinese Peace Committee. At the end of his trip Cárdenas traveled from San Francisco to Chicago to Knoxville, Tennessee, where he examined approvingly the work of the Tennessee Valley Authority. In a diary entry he noted: "All the peoples of the world desire peace. The people of Europe, Latin America and the United States itself have serious internal problems, such as a lack of sources of work for their entire populations . . . China with its 600 million inhabitants is solving that problem with an enormous impulse in agriculture while it also develops industry to absorb the excess rural population of each province. Other countries could do this too if the state, and not financiers and industrialists, directed their economies." When he returned to Mexico, the statements that he made to the press set off another convulsion of speculation that he had been won over to Communism. But what fired his imagination was state-driven development, not Communism as such. He had, it was true, accepted the claims of the Soviet government and of China to be fully representative of their people, and he had failed to notice the millions of deaths by starvation that resulted from China's Great Leap Forward, under way during his visit. But he saw other self-denominated revolutionary states in terms of the plans they were making to improve the lives of their populations. In the early 1960s Cárdenas defined the ideological program of the Mexican Revolution as "national sovereignty, economic emancipation, comprehensive agrarian reform, political democracy, union democracy, [and] freedom of worship and of the press," and he read this interpretation of the Mexican Revolution onto other revolutionary states. It was an imprecise analogy: agrarian reforms in the Soviet Union and China (but not Mexico) produced some of the greatest humanitarian catastrophes in all of history. But Cárdenas's agenda was not really to defend the Soviet Union or China, and their situations were not as analogous to Mexico's as was that of the country that he noted in his diary really inspired hope: Cuba.[23]

Castro and Cárdenas had met before. Training for invasion in Mexico after his release from a Cuban prison in 1954, Castro had not been able to count on the automatic sympathy of the Mexican Left. Both Cuban and Mexican Communists thought of him as an "adventurer," and Cárdenas had been on good terms with Fulgencio Batista during the months in 1940 when their presidential terms had overlapped. But Castro's allies reached out to Cárdenas when Castro was threatened with deportation, and Cárdenas wrote on his behalf to President Ruiz Cortines, asking him to honor Mexico's traditional right to asylum. Castro subsequently met with Cárdenas, who described him as a "young intellectual with a vehement temperament and the blood of a fighter." Cárdenas reasoned that if Castro were to be successful in overthrowing Batista, it would be because it was the will of the Cuban people.[24]

When Cuba decreed its agrarian reform, Cárdenas compared the steps with Mexico's own actions and noted that he hoped that Cuba would take

POLITICA

Quince días de México y del Mundo

LAZARO CARDENAS Y FIDEL CASTRO

15 DE SEPTIEMBRE DE 1960   ... *la solidaridad de dos pueblos revolucionarios* ...
VOL. 1, NÚM. 10   (Nuestro Continente, página 28)

$2⁵⁰

A photo of Lázaro Cárdenas's appearance with Fidel Castro at the 26th of July celebrations in Cuba appeared on the 15 September 1960 edition of *Política*. Many of the writers associated with the MLN contributed to the new magazine, which was denied paper by Mexico's government newsprint monopoly.

a socially integrated approach that would avoid the internal convulsions that Mexico had suffered. Invited to Cuba to celebrate the 26th of July—the anniversary of the attack on the Moncada barracks—Cárdenas appeared triumphantly alongside Fidel Castro. Cuba became the symbol of the democratic aspirations that Cárdenas had for Mexico, for a return to the values that he associated with the Mexican Revolution. He had some reservations about the course of the revolution that he kept private: he shocked visiting Cuban president Osvaldo Dorticós and the others in the room by telling him that he found the "climate of the Revolution . . . troubling" in 1960, but he would never have said so publicly.[25]

The Cuban example was inspiring to many on the Mexican left, and its defense was largely posed in the language of democratic reform. In the new newsmagazine *Política,* for which many of those associated with the peace movement and the future MLN wrote, democracy was presented as the goal of the Cuban Revolution. Cuba was described as the most democratic country in the region: in the words of Víctor Flores Olea, "a direct, plebiscitary, *concrete* [democracy] . . . in which people and Government are perfectly identified [with one another]." Fidel Castro himself told the assembled crowds in Cuba on 1 May 1960 that "[Cuba's previous rulers] invented a strange democracy in which you, who are the majority, counted for nothing. Democracy is that in which the majority governs; democracy is that in which the interests of the majority are defended . . . Democracy is the right to bread, to work, to culture, and the right to count within society." That he made that argument in the context of announcing that there was no need to hold elections did not seem a problem to those who believed in the unity of Cuba's government and its people.[26]

To its critics on the left, Mexico's government did not satisfy that sort of definition of democracy because the interests of the people had been abandoned. That argument became even more compelling in August 1960, when the government again used the social dissolution law to arrest and sentence the muralist David Álfaro Siqueiros to eight years in prison. Siqueiros, a member of the PCM, had made comments critical of the government of Mexico on trips to Cuba and Venezuela. The government argued that in advocating for the dictatorship of the proletariat, Siqueiros sought the dissolution not only of the Mexican government but of Mexican society itself. But Siqueiros continued to paint while he was in prison, turning his work into a symbol of the power of freedom of expression over state repression. It was the kind of case that the anti-Communist CCF might have taken up on civil libertarian grounds had Siqueiros not been a Communist. Instead, his sympathizers were intellectuals, like Pablo Neruda, who visited in January 1961 and composed a quick verse: "I have seen your painting jailed / which is like jailing a blaze / . . . Mexico is a prisoner alongside you." For political prisoners like himself, Siqueiros declared gallantly from behind bars, "Jail is the same thing a battlefield [is to a soldier]."[27]

In 1960 discussions began in WPC circles about holding a large peace congress—the first in many years—somewhere in Latin America. The Steering Committee decided on Mexico, and in December Latin American delegates arrived in Mexico to meet with Lázaro Cárdenas to plan the event. In mid-January 1961 Cárdenas and the others issued a call to the Conferencia Latinoamericana por la Soberanía Nacional, la Emancipación Económica y la Paz (the Latin American Conference for National Sovereignty, Economic Emancipation, and Peace). The convocation argued that the people of Latin America, like those around the rest of the world, wanted to enjoy freedom and democratic rights, sovereignty, education and culture, independence, and economic development. The declaration asserted that all these positive qualities were found most clearly in revolutionary Cuba.[28]

Speaking at the inaugural event of the conference on 5 March 1961 to a room full of four thousand people, Cárdenas made explicit an argument that had existed embryonically from the beginning of peace movement campaigning: that there was a distinction between "revolution" and "war." The difference lay in ends, not means. War, argued Cárdenas, threatened to extinguish humanity, and those who brought it about did so intending to profit from it financially. Revolution, by contrast, sought political and economic changes that favored the collectivity of the people who carried it out. Cárdenas was quick to add that respect for the will of the citizenry was the desired mechanism for change, and that that did not necessarily imply that violence was the only means to express it. What gave the Cuban example such an impact in Latin America, he argued, was that its government understood this distinction: the government and people of Cuba were pacifist, but they defended their revolution. Later in the event, the Brazilian delegate Domingo Vellasco called the Cuban government democratic, "of and for the people."[29]

During the conference, commissions were established to write resolutions on four areas of concern: national sovereignty, economic emancipation, peace, and common action. The national sovereignty commission produced recommendations asking for juridical equality among Latin American states, self-determination, nonintervention, anti-imperialism, anticolonialism, defense of the Cuban Revolution, and condemnation of the Rio Treaty, U.S. military missions, and instruments of imperialism like ORIT and the Organization of American States. The economic emancipation group called for economic development, the right to strike, fiscal democracy, agrarian reform, nationalization, and the rights of workers to freedom, autonomy, and union democracy and again denounced ORIT as an instrument to divide and corrupt the workers of Latin America. Other resolutions expressed solidarity with Cuba and with Africa and Asia, advocated economic cooperation and disarmament, and championed individual liberty and the defense of political prisoners. "The defeat of imperialism is the fundamental condition of any development plan for our countries," read the final resolution: "The works of the Cuban Revolution show the way to put an end to foreign domination."[30]

Lázaro Cárdenas undertook to raise awareness of the causes of the Conferencia Latinoamericana in the manner he had used so effectively during his presidency: by traveling out to villages in person. Accompanied by many of the Latin American and Chinese delegates to the conference—as well as novelist Carlos Fuentes in his capacity as sympathetic journalist—Cárdenas traveled to Querétaro, Guanajuato, Jalisco, and Michoacán. In Guanajuato, Fuentes overheard citizens remark about Cárdenas: "Look at him, he is a true democrat." "He knows how to mix among the people." The path forward for Mexico's democratic reconstruction, reflected Fuentes, would be dependent not on one man but on the active expression of popular will. "Comprehensive agrarian reform, union democracy, and political liberty," he wrote, "will not be gifts given to the people, nor will it be a single *caudillo* who obtains them for the people. It will be the people, organized . . . that achieves them."[31]

Organization continued. In May the Provisional Committee for National Sovereignty, Economic Emancipation, and Peace was formed, dedicated to disseminating the messages of the conference, especially freedom for political prisoners and defense of the Cuban Revolution. On 4 and 5 August a national assembly was held that established the Movimiento de Liberación Nacional, dedicated to the same causes as the March conference: national sovereignty, economic emancipation, and peace. It sought to unite all the "democratic and progressive," "popular" interests without regard to party and included former members of the PRI, those who identified with the tradition of Cárdenas but had never belonged to any party, members of Lombardo Toledano's recently renamed Partido Popular Socialista (PPS), and the PCM. The MLN espoused the subversive notions that the results of elections should reflect the outcomes

desired by voters, and that demonstrations and speech should not be curtailed by the use of police violence. The document released to the public,
a call to the Mexican people, emphasized that the movement situated itself as a nationalist rather than a class-based organization, and it called
for the simultaneous pursuit of many objectives: full enforcement of the
constitution, freedom for political prisoners, a democratic, honest, and independent justice system, free expression of ideas, comprehensive agrarian
reform, union and *ejido* (communal farm) democracy and autonomy,
Mexican control over Mexico's natural resources, industrialization without
recourse to foreign loans, just distribution of national wealth, independence, dignity, international cooperation, solidarity with Cuba, trade
with all countries, democracy, honor, well-being, bread and freedom, sovereignty, and peace. Although democracy was not the only possible political
goal for an anti-imperialist movement, in this case, the MLN's nationalism
was also part of a democratic program for Mexico.[32]

Although the movement mobilized, at a minimum, tens of thousands,
its impact was limited. What pressure the MLN could exert on the Mexican government came about mostly because of Lázaro Cárdenas. In the
wake of the Conferencia Latinoamericana in 1961, President López Mateos called a meeting with Cárdenas in which he pressured him not to
travel to Cuba. López Mateos tried generosity. He offered Cárdenas the
opportunity to take charge of the PRI; the former president replied that
he was not up to the job. Soon thereafter, Cárdenas declared that he belonged to "no party," simultaneously denying that he was a Communist
while also suggesting that he did not see himself as part of the ruling party
in Mexico. Although it was obvious that he had not been active within
the machinery of the PRI for some time, such a declaration still came as
a surprise and raised the possibility that Cárdenas, especially if he were
expelled from the PRI, would take large numbers of supporters with him
and create a genuine electoral threat to the stability of the regime. He was
seen as the only person who had the power to split the PRI, even though
his private behavior suggested that he had no desire to do so. At the end
of 1961 he accepted an executive position overseeing the Balsas River
Commission, a regional development project based in his home state of
Michoacán, hoping that in taking the post he might be able to influence
López Mateos to grant clemency to the jailed political prisoners. Repeated
meetings with López Mateos yielded no results, however, and opened him
to charges of co-optation. Cárdenas had helped build the MLN to respond
to problems in Mexico, aided by the transformed infrastructure of the
WPC. Even as the MLN tried to emphasize its Mexican roots, it would

soon come to pay a price for its international connections, however limited they were.[33]

Many of its detractors saw the MLN not as a domestic movement but as part of the Cold War. Rodrigo García Treviño of the Mexican Association for Cultural Freedom, for example, called the 1961 conference a "Russophilic-Cardenista conclave" and imagined that its most important result had been the unmasking of Lázaro Cárdenas as an active agent of Moscow, leading inevitably to his political "liquidation." Others accused Cárdenas of being a foreign agent and a recipient of "Moscow gold."[34]

Both the analysis and the prediction by García Treviño proved inaccurate. It was true that the infrastructure of the peace movement had provided the organizers of the 1961 conference with support and personnel. But Lázaro Cárdenas insisted on maintaining financial and programmatic independence from foreign governments. Vicente Lombardo Toledano had remarked at a meeting of the PPS in December 1960 that individual contributions were needed to pay for the upcoming conference because offers of financial support that had come from the Soviet-bloc countries had been rejected so as to not to invite criticism in Mexico. Clementina Batalla de Bassols, a leader in the Soviet-aligned Women's International Democratic Federation and widow of Marxist former minister of education Narciso Bassols, was made treasurer of the 1961 conference. She recorded each contribution and expenditure on behalf of the Mexican sponsoring committee and made the results available to the public. The conference sought to be seen, as a point both of pride and of political necessity, as a fully national undertaking and not the result of Soviet or Cuban manipulation. Contributions totaled nearly 300,000 pesos, and no single source dominated. Heriberto Jara made one of the largest personal contributions, of 6,000 pesos. Vicente Lombardo Toledano's CTAL did receive money from the Soviet Union to keep it operational and might have been a conduit for support of the conference, but Lombardo Toledano's personal contribution was only 1,000 pesos. The donations of various communal farms dwarfed that amount many times over. If any foreign government managed to contribute to the conference, it did so by circumventing rules in place to prevent it. The Vienna-based International Institute for Peace, the front office for the WPC, made several airline tickets available to Jorge L. Tamayo, but Cárdenas even agreed to pay for those, and the money for the tickets was returned. The need for the work to remain Mexican was well known throughout the movement and stemmed from the wishes of Lázaro Cárdenas himself. At an organizational meeting in

March 1961, after Cárdenas had taken his leave, an Argentine journalist and Communist Party member proposed obtaining 100,000 pesos from Cuba for the printing of pamphlets and offered to do so, but Tamayo told her that Cárdenas would not approve.[35]

Ironically, however, the campaign against the MLN was international. President López Mateos, in negotiating with the United States in 1961, had explained that "Castroism" was a problem of national security for him, and he would take no direct actions to unseat the Cuban leader. But he did offer the CIA cooperation in its efforts to undermine the 1961 conference. Intelligence cooperation with the United States expanded, and Mexico increasingly served as an intermediary for U.S. efforts to monitor events in Cuba. Although the details of the CIA campaign to undermine the 1961 conference are not known, the Mexican government's steps— which may have been assisted in some respects by the CIA—are clear. The Mexican government sought to infiltrate the MLN with secret police, stifle it by denying it press coverage, and mobilize a phony civic group to oppose it. Even as organizing was just beginning, the Mexican government flooded the MLN with agents of the Dirección Federal de Seguridad, Mexico's primary intelligence agency. The MLN became so riddled with agents that some of its members argued against adding a youth section because it would invite further penetration by police agents. In a meeting recorded by those agents, others countered that they were already infiltrated by police and, because they were not engaging in any illegal activity, had nothing to hide. As time went on, the government used the information it gathered on prominent members of the MLN to blackmail them.[36]

The second part of the Mexican government's plan to undermine the MLN hardly needed to be coordinated: the major Mexican press was habituated to ignoring events that presented the government, and especially the president, in a critical light. A complex network of government advertising, direct special payments to journalists, and a government newsprint monopoly underwrote this system. Although members of the press attended the Conferencia Latinoamericana, nothing on it appeared in the papers. (The major newspapers gave front-page coverage that week to the Sociedad Interamericana de Prensa, meeting in Acapulco, during which many earnest statements were issued celebrating the existence of freedom of the press in Mexico.) The absence of press coverage in major newspapers was the main reason that Lázaro Cárdenas undertook to raise awareness for the cause by traveling to villages in person.[37]

News coverage of the MLN had to flow through very narrow channels, which the government dammed and dredged as it saw fit. Vicente Lombardo Toledano's newspaper, *El Popular,* went bankrupt in 1961, and the government passed its equipment (and its subsidies) to a new paper, *El Día,* which it hoped would be the moderating press organ on the left. Although the director of the paper was a member of the MLN, he had also recently rejoined the PRI. *El Día* became popular with left-wing students and professors, but its most significant achievement was to give an outlet for coverage of the Left without allowing it to flow into the mainstream, mass-circulation papers. The paper remained dependent on direct government support for years.[38]

Two magazines, *Siempre!* and *Política,* similarly faced and suffered strains from their involvement with the Left. *Siempre!* was a colorful and relatively popular weekly that featured large photo spreads, a bit of news coverage, witty political cartoons, a racy photo or two toward the back of the magazine, and regular columnists ranging from Vicente Lombardo Toledano on the pro-Soviet left to the anti-Soviet Víctor Alba, a regular contributor to CCF publications. The magazine's director, José Pagés Llergo, had a checkered past that included admiration for fascism and a long history as an opportunistic pen-for-hire: he had been employed by both German and Japanese propaganda operations in Mexico during World War II. *Siempre!,* by contrast with his earlier publications, seemed to tilt to the left, perhaps because its start-up financing came from President Adolfo Ruiz Cortines, who used the magazine to break with his right-wing predecessor. Pagés Llergo's editorials were easy on whoever occupied the office of the presidency, but he developed a reputation as a tolerant editor: "[My journalists] can write whatever they want, as long as they don't touch the President of the Republic or the Virgin of Guadalupe," he once said. However suspect his motivations, *Siempre!* became the rare place in which a variety of left-wing and centrist perspectives could coexist in print, exchanging opinions and letters. *Siempre!* actually benefited from the left-wing revival when it inherited a vibrant cultural supplement, *La Cultura en México,* edited by the MLN sympathizers Fernando Benítez and Carlos Fuentes. The supplement, which frequently published writers including Elena Poniatowska, Carlos Monsiváis, Sergio Pitol, Luis Guillermo Piazza, Luis Cardoza y Aragón, and Gabriel García Márquez, had been expelled from the conservative paper *Novedades* in 1961.[39]

The biweekly newsmagazine *Política: Quince días de México y del mundo,* in contrast to *Siempre!,* was thoroughly a product of the Left. It was created in mid-1960 under the direction of Manuel Marcué Pardiñas. He had trained as an agricultural engineer and for years had been involved in the production of a technical, think-tank-type publication for the resolution of Mexico's agrarian problems, *Problemas Agrícolas e Industriales de México,* which had survived with a government subsidy. *Política,* published under the authority of *Problemas Agrícolas,* focused on current affairs and almost immediately provoked the ire of the government, which refused to sell it paper from the government monopoly importer, Productora e Importadora de Papel, S.A., known as PIPSA.[40]

Política was not, strictly speaking, the organ of the MLN—it was more like the voice of one particular current of the MLN—but it was the most important magazine that shared its goals. Most of *Política*'s staff worked with the MLN, and Manuel Marcué Pardiñas had nearly constant access to its leadership, talking frequently with Jorge L. Tamayo, Cuauhtémoc Cárdenas, Lázaro Cárdenas, and sometimes Clementina Batalla de Bassols. Without access to PIPSA-subsidized paper, it was forced to purchase excess newsprint on the black market from another newspaper at inflated prices. This pushed its cover price up too high to be a mass-circulation periodical, and the Mexican political police claimed that it received Soviet and Cuban support to continue publication.[41]

It is in the problems with PIPSA that the ironies of the MLN as Cardenismo in struggle with itself across time can be seen most clearly, for PIPSA was a creation of Cárdenas's presidential administration. It was established in 1935 by Cardenista progressives who had grown angry with a newspaper that had been too direct in its criticisms of the president. Although the idea for PIPSA had originated in a direct threat to the country's main private paper producer, one of its creators later insisted that during the government of Cárdenas the press enjoyed complete freedom, and it was never necessary for PIPSA to deny paper to any publications. Nevertheless, it drove the country's private paper factory out of business and, because it enjoyed monopoly control over the distribution of newsprint, became a powerful instrument for ensuring that the press did not overstep government-established boundaries. In the colorful phrase of *Política*'s angry staff, PIPSA was "the ignominious guillotine that decapitates freedom of expression." President Cárdenas had hoped for a responsible state-subsidized press, as he had hoped for responsible union coordination with the state to benefit workers, but in time both of these organizations created with "popular" intentions had been transformed from instruments of cooperation into instruments of control. Cárdenas had seen the corporatist structure of the postrevolutionary regime as potentially democratizing; by the 1960s it proved also to be an enormous obstacle to Mexican democracy.[42]

The final method that the López Mateos administration employed to make the path forward difficult for the MLN was to authorize the creation of a citizen counterforce under the apparent leadership of anti-Communist ex-presidents Miguel Alemán and Abelardo Rodríguez. The organization, known as the Frente Cívico Mexicano de Afirmación Revolucionaria (FCMAR), issued a call to the Mexican citizenry warning of the danger of the "infiltration of exotic doctrines . . . [which,] disguised as a false radicalism, aspire to suppress democratic institutions and substitute them with a totalitarian regime that will end our liberties and, destroying country, home, and family, will end forever traditional forms of Mexican life." Rodrigo García Treviño of the Mexican Association for Cultural Freedom, who had longed for a conservative "Alemanista" rejoinder to "Communism" since the late 1940s, signed the manifesto and joined the FCMAR. The group was capable of mobilizing thousands for rallies against the Left and was used by the government for multiple purposes: to co-opt and control anti-Left mobilization by the Catholic Church, to demonstrate seriousness of purpose to the U.S. government, and to provide politically reliable troops when necessary. (When President Kennedy visited Mexico in mid-1962, for example, members of the FCMAR monitored the crowds that surrounded his motorcade for suspected agitators and showered the visiting president with confetti.) For its part, the FCMAR did a bit of social service work, beat up suspected leftists, and mobilized to make sure that the PRI did not select left-wing candidates for major offices. In his diary Lázaro Cárdenas commented on the creation of the FCMAR: "Anti-Communism has been used as an instrument to fight against freedom and democracy in the countries of Latin America and on other continents." Although his comment was perhaps not a universal truth, his personal experiences gave it a kind of firm local plausibility.[43]

Even with all these obstacles, the MLN brought a kind of energy to the Mexican Left that it had not seen in years. Volunteers numbering at least in the tens of thousands fanned out across the country to try to mobilize support for progressive causes. But most of the MLN's specific campaigns proved unsuccessful, undermined by government intervention. Organizing in Baja California Norte around the issue of salinity in the Colorado River, which harmed Mexican farmers, frightened the United States. Cuauhtémoc Cárdenas (seen by U.S. officials as a Communist sympathizer) seemed poised to be named to head the Mexicali Valley Irrigation District, so López Mateos pressured Lázaro Cárdenas to have his son withdraw from contention. López Mateos then sent federal troops to the Mexicali valley and forced a dissident, MLN-aligned leader to quiet down by threatening him with murder. A new peasant organization created in 1963 by MLN leaders, the Central Campesina Independiente, was supposed to be independent of the ruling party but was captured by it in little more than a year.[44]

Lázaro Cárdenas speaks at the closing session of the First National Conference of the Movimiento de Liberación Nacional on 6 October 1963. The background portraits of José María Morelos and Emiliano Zapata serve to situate the movement as part of a national, rather than international, political movement. From left to right, seated at the table, appear Ramón Danzós Palomino, Manuel Terrazas Guerrero, Marta Borquez, Manuel Marcué Pardiñas, Enrique González Pedrero, Víctor Flores Olea, Lázaro Cárdenas (standing), Alonso Aguilar Monteverde, Ignacio García Téllez, and Guillermo Montaño. Photo courtesy Archivo General de la Nación, Collection Hermanos Mayo, envelope 18,421.

The MLN, bringing together as it did several left-wing groups, inevitably suffered from internal tensions. Heriberto Jara, for example, thought that its young leaders had been seized by extremism and gave no credit for the good things that the PRI did. But its real threats to internal cohesion came from party leaders. Conflict with Vicente Lombardo Toledano arose almost immediately. He was apparently disappointed to learn that the Cuban embassy had given its delegates instructions to deal with Alonso Aguilar Monteverde on the recommendation of Lázaro Cárdenas, ignoring members of his own PPS, and began to complain publicly about the MLN. Lombardo Toledano was seen by many of the MLN's young activists as politically compromised and opportunistic, and so tensions increased throughout 1962. In June the Mexican Pro-Peace Committee—whose work had been merged into the "peace" division within the MLN—called for a national congress of the MLN. Stating that he thought that the peace movement and the MLN should be separate undertakings, Lombardo Toledano took the PPS out of the MLN at midyear. The remaining leadership of the MLN described the departure of the PPS as an act directed against the "representative sectors of the Mexican Left"—placing Vicente Lombardo Toledano's organization outside that category.[45]

In 1963 further conflicts arose regarding the 1964 presidential election. Some, especially in the PCM, wanted to use the MLN to launch a presidential candidate, but the internal line had always been that the organization was multiparty and that members would work within their own parties to have them adopt the principles for which the MLN advocated. Nonetheless, the PCM created the Frente Electoral del Pueblo and offered as a presidential candidate Ramón Danzós Palomino, a member of both the PCM and the MLN. While insisting that it did not want to damage the unity of the MLN, the PCM tried to recruit other members of the MLN to support the Frente Electoral, creating distrust and resentment. Some disillusioned members, such as Cuauhtémoc Cárdenas, distanced themselves from the MLN, and the elections of 1964 proved to be the beginning of a long decline because the organization ceased to be able to motivate the kind of unity and organizational drive that it had had for the eighteen months or so after its creation in late 1961. It had one concrete victory in 1964 when Siqueiros was released early from prison, freed by presidential decree on 13 July, but even that had to wait until nearly the end of López Mateos's term in office, when it became clear that his successor, Gustavo Díaz Ordaz (1964–1970), would take the action if he did not do it himself.[46]

If Lázaro Cárdenas had hoped that the existence of the MLN would pressure the PRI to put forward left-wing candidates, Díaz Ordaz would prove what a failure it had been. Díaz Ordaz clashed with students throughout his term in office and held paranoid views of leftists and the young. The 1968 massacre of students at Tlatelolco by government troops made the MLN's critique of the lack of democratic legitimacy of the PRI all the more powerful, but it was no longer around to make it (although some of the same people were, unsurprisingly, also involved in the student movement that was being repressed). The cells of the Palacio de Lecumberri once again filled with political prisoners. Díaz Ordaz's successor, Luis Echeverría, president from 1970 to 1976, had been his minister of the interior and surely shared much of the blame for the massacre at Tlatelolco, but he took a different approach, adopting much of the Third Worldist language of the MLN and securing the cooperation of many of the cultural figures associated with it, such as Carlos Fuentes. Echeverría's style aside, the changes to Mexico's political system that did occur during his administration proved more cosmetic than substantial. Mexico's Left was still trapped in the Cardenista paradox: dependent on centralized power to enact democratization.

If the MLN left a limited domestic legacy within Mexico, it contributed to one major action outside its borders. Few saw Latin America as part of the Third World at the end of the 1950s. Decolonization that was fresh and ongoing in Asia and Africa was nearly a century and a half old in the region, and the nonaligned stance between the two superpowers that characterized much of Third World politics could hardly be applied to most of Latin America, which clearly belonged to the U.S. side of the global ledger. But the potential was there to build an idea of the "Third World" on the basis of a common history of imperial exploitation and subsequent underdevelopment. One expression of that idea was the Tricontinental Conference, held in 1966 with the intention of uniting the representatives of Asia, Africa, and Latin America.

Although Che Guevara had imagined Cuba as an inspiration to Asia and Africa as early as 1959, the idea to hold the Tricontinental Conference was not originally Cuban. Rather, it was broached at the Conferencia Latinoamericana in Mexico in 1961, and Latin American delegates continued to discuss it among themselves while attending WPC events in the early 1960s. Lázaro Cárdenas wanted it to be convoked by the national liberation movements—such as the MLN—of different countries. In late 1962 Brazilian delegate Valério Kondcr and Argentine delegate Alberto T. Casella convinced the WPC to sponsor the Tricontinental Conference along lines that had been drawn up in a memorandum by Lázaro Cárdenas. Cuba was especially interested and offered to host the conference. But a major international meeting in Brazil, similar to the Conferencia Latinoamericana and billed as the Continental Congress of Solidarity with Cuba, encountered trouble in 1963 when visas were denied to foreign delegations and the justice minister raided the building where planning was taking place. Lázaro Cárdenas remained the most forceful advocate for the Tricontinental Conference from 1961 through 1963.[47]

Within the WPC the Soviet delegation had become the moderate one, far outstripped in its belief in the possibility of rapid social change by the Chinese and the Cubans. The Chinese saw Khrushchev's efforts to sign agreements that decreased tensions with the United States as "collaboration with U.S. imperialism" and a violation of the principles of national liberation. In 1962 the Chinese peace committee issued a decree that the Soviet delegation's 1956 decision to replace the Stalin Peace Prize with the Lenin Prize had been taken unilaterally and without consultation within the international peace movement, thus besmirching the great name of Stalin. The Chinese committee retaliated by issuing its own International Stalin Peace Prizes. For his part, Lázaro Cárdenas saw Sino-Soviet differences as debilitating to the unity of peoples in the fight against imperialism and tried to gather information to understand the tensions between the two countries. But there was nothing he could do, and he became progressively less involved with the WPC as a result of his frustration with its divisions.[48]

When the Tricontinental Conference of African, Asian, and Latin American Peoples finally did meet in January 1966, it did so under Cuban auspices and against the backdrop of continued Sino-Soviet tension. The WPC was the most important participating organization and had hosted the discussion that had led to its convocation. The Mexican delegation came from the MLN. But the most significant figure of the Tricontinental Conference was the absent Che Guevara, whom Castro invoked as a symbol of the fight against imperialism. Castro denounced China at the event and made the worst villains of his closing speech "Trotskyists," a signal of cooperation with the Soviet Union. But it was the Chinese position of anti-imperialist insurgency that was reflected in the solidarity organizations that were created there. The Cubans used the conference to recruit guerrilla fighters, unnerving Moscow. That April, at a smaller tricontinental meeting held in Cuba, the delegates heard a message from Guevara from the Bolivian jungle, looking for the bright future that the world could enjoy with the creation of "two, three, or many Vietnams." National liberation, to be achieved by armed revolution, had supplanted the cause of peace. Both Mexico's Conferencia Latinoamericana of 1961 and Cuba's Tricontinental Conference of 1966 had their origins in discussions and planning supported by the WPC, but under very different leadership they created very different movements that in neither case acted precisely in the interests of Moscow. In spite of the vertical nature of power within global Communism, the MLN showed that connections to a Communist front organization did not necessarily imply the abandonment either of independence or democracy.[49]

But if the MLN left relatively few signposts to mark its work, it trailed little ironies like so many breadcrumbs. In domestic politics, Cardenismo in the 1960s confronted the legacy of the 1930s, especially in the form of union centralization and PIPSA, and lost. The MLN looked to Cuba as its democratic model at the very moment when that country was building similarly repressive institutions. At the level of the global Cold War, it made a Stalinist like Siquerios a symbol of free expression and advocated a more democratic Mexico in precisely the "civil society" terms that were usually the province of anti-Communism. In the midst of the Cultural Cold War, it showed both how a prodemocracy movement could result from involvement with a Soviet front group and that it was difficult but possible to construct a financially and programmatically independent national political movement even amid such connections.

But there remains one further irony, having to do not with the MLN's failures but with its success in pressuring the Mexican government to maintain relations with Cuba. In the end, that proved to be a decision that benefited everyone. The Mexican government could cling to a tatter of revolutionary solidarity while giving Cuba a reason to direct its support for insurgency elsewhere; Mexican presidents were placed on the CIA payroll at the same time at which the head of the Mexican intelligence service was a personal friend of Fidel Castro. The United States, meanwhile, came to rely on Mexico's continued relationship with Cuba to gather intelligence about developments there and in the rest of the Caribbean and Central America. As with the CCF, some of the most powerful effects of the MLN's actions were those that it did not intend.[50]

CHAPTER SIX

Modernizing Cultural Freedom

Twin transformations were under way in the structure of intellectual life during the 1960s in Latin America. One was the rise of the internationally famous writer-intellectual who would achieve a global audience and platform as a result of the boom in Latin American letters. At the same time, there was a shift toward the value of specific expertise, especially in the social sciences, where "experts" who studied human affairs would to some degree displace the generalist "intellectual." The Congress for Cultural Freedom (CCF) simultaneously tried to play a part in establishing both trends and to take advantage of them as it remade itself in response to the radicalization of the Cuban Revolution, for just as the Cuban Revolution had reinvigorated and reoriented the peace movement in Latin America, it did the same to the CCF. Within the CCF the 1950s had belonged to the right-wing socialists, many from Europe. One of the Spanish affiliates of the CCF, Carlos Carranza, who lived in Argentina and worked to distribute *Cuadernos,* returned from a trip to other countries of Latin America in 1961 disgusted and alarmed by the "infection of Castro-ite demagoguery." "Intelligent and brave action is needed urgently," Carranza warned, "if we do not wish to be consumed by totalitarianism . . . We are going to have to mobilize to defend democratic positions." But the mobilization that was undertaken did not resemble the one that Carranza expected, and the CCF soon forced him into retirement.

Responding to a new, more fashionable and local form of Communism, in the early 1960s the CCF began a shift toward openness to the Left. Instead of anti-Soviet essays, it moved to try to offer something new that it considered "productive." It engaged more directly with "Latin American" issues and with writers and thinkers who identified with the Left. It sought to become more scholarly so as to assist in an analysis of the situation in Latin America and how conditions there might be improved. "We have begun a new type of work," one of the architects of the change announced in 1963. "It has less to do with defending cultural freedom and more with practicing it."[1]

Anti-Communism, of course, still remained central to the self-conception of the organization, and it shared that priority with the U.S. government. The trajectory of the CCF in the region was in some ways parallel to U.S. policy toward the region. When John F. Kennedy assumed the U.S. presidency in 1961, he announced the Alliance for Progress, promising to use the power of the United States to push for social reform and economic development in Latin America. The new approach was supposed to differ from previous policies that had used allies of convenience and had left most U.S. involvement in Latin American development to private corporations. The ideas of the Alliance for Progress were not exactly new; at its end, even the Eisenhower administration had begun to rework its inter-American diplomacy toward a more statist approach. But many of the ideas of the Alliance for Progress resembled requests for assistance made by democratic allies in the region, including those associated with the CCF. Kennedy's closest ally in Latin America, for example, was Rómulo Betancourt of Venezuela. The anti-Communist Democratic Left had always promised the United States that it was its best partner in the fight against Communism on the grounds that only it, and not conservative administrations, could remove the conditions of poverty and inequality that supposedly made Communist ideas thrive.[2]

Indeed, many of those who had long been active in the CCF were part of the Kennedy administration. The framework that both the CCF and the Kennedy administration used to look at Latin America was principally that of modernization theory. At its core, modernization theory expressed the idea that societies passed through linear stages of growth that would end in a modernity that resembled the United States: a political democracy and a capitalist market economy. Although some saw it as an anti-ideological, neutral form of scholarship, modernization theory was explicitly conceived as a kind of Marxist antivenom. Walt Rostow, the economic historian who served as a policy adviser to Presidents Kennedy and Johnson, made the connection between antirevolutionary politics and modernization explicit when he subtitled his book on stages of economic growth *A Non-Communist Manifesto*. Arthur Schlesinger Jr., a Kennedy aide who was also a participant in many CCF events, called modernization theory "a very American effort to persuade the developing countries to base their revolutions on Locke rather than Marx."[3]

And so, while those on the center-left welcomed the Alliance for Progress, its left-wing critics saw it as a means to forestall the revolutionary change that would truly deliver justice in the region. Instead, much of Latin America's radical Left worked in the 1960s from a framework of dependency theory, arguing that Latin American underdevelopment resulted from the structures of domination that the North Atlantic capitalist core imposed on developing countries. Latin America's problems, they reasoned, lay not in an absence of capitalism but in its presence. The meaningful distinction, argued Cuban poet Roberto Fernández Retamar, was not between underdeveloped and developed countries, but between underdeveloped and "underdeveloper" countries, whose exploitative capitalism created poverty in the periphery. There were moderate dependency theorists who thought that the principal remedy was political reform—among them Raúl Prebisch, who was published by the CCF, and Fernando Henrique Cardoso, the sociologist who in the 1990s would enact a neoliberal program of privatization of state assets as president of Brazil. But in the 1970s even Cardoso was writing that capitalism could not solve the basic problems of the region's poor, and that the task ahead was to "construct paths toward socialism." The most radical dependency theorists saw the solution not in political reform but in armed insurrection followed by autarky—economic separation from the capitalist world—as the only possible means of breaking from dependency.[4]

The dependency idea was an argument about the past and future of Latin America's political economy, but it was also a worldview. Not only would Latin America have to cut itself off from capitalist markets to break its dependency, but it would also have to purge itself of the contagion of capitalist culture. The United States was the regional hegemon, the most powerful nation on earth in both military and economic terms, and its power was everywhere: in the CIA's actions to overthrow governments of the Left and its attempts to assassinate Fidel Castro, in U.S. military training of counterinsurgent forces, and even in the efforts of U.S. foundations and universities to study Latin America. In 1964, for example, the U.S. Department of Defense had sponsored Project Camelot, which aimed to study the conditions that would lead to revolution in Latin America, state actions that might prevent it, and the potential use of U.S. military force in response. The project had been in the planning stages when it was exposed by one of its participants and canceled. Those involved with the project had seen it as a scholarly way to contribute to the prevention of a catastrophic revolution and did not feel that they were in any way spying for the United States.[5]

But to those who not only thought that revolution would not be catastrophic but also believed that it was absolutely necessary, the project became known as Plan Camelot and was seen as a means of preparing the ground for U.S. intervention. The social scientists contracted to carry it out were portrayed as spies and puppets of Yankee imperialism. Although it never began, the project created an atmosphere of doubt about U.S.-backed social scientific research and the ways in which it might be put in the service of U.S. imperialism. Major U.S.-based foundations and the CIA-sponsored research programs that supported the United States' antirevolutionary empire were seen as part of a coordinated project to suppress the Latin American Left. The existence of the CCF was part of the evidence that supported this claim, and there was some truth in it.

The CCF did not quite seek to destroy the Left, but it did seek to strengthen its moderates at the expense of its radicals. In the early 1960s it tried to reach out to the Left in ways in which it had not during the 1950s, hoping to convince leftists to break taboos on criticizing Cuba. It also sponsored scholarship, generally within the framework of modernization theory, which it saw as undermining the appeal of radical dependency theory. But insofar as it formed one piece of a massive U.S.-led reactionary campaign, it was a poorly coordinated and messy piece. There were even moments when the ideas and actions that the CCF undertook, including those of the CIA agents directing it, departed in important ways from mainstream U.S. policy. But whether the CCF's participants wanted to defend U.S. interests or not, they could not escape the consequences of their affiliation. At the end of the period of reform within the CCF, in 1966 and 1967, it was publicly revealed that the organization had long been the recipient of CIA funding. The result of those revelations was that what the CCF had understood to be "open-minded" analysis and the moderate socialist politics that typically accompanied it, rather than the explicit and direct anti-Communism of the 1950s, were most discredited.

The CCF sought to professionalize its Latin American project beginning in 1961, as the Cuban Revolution became more radical. If its ethos, an anti-Communist and antidictatorial program, had been a kind of Alliance for Progress *avant la lettre,* its active personnel had long passed their sell-by dates. Whatever leftist credentials they may have once had, the CCF's professional anti-Communists (like Julián Gorkin, who edited *Cuadernos,* and Rodrigo García Treviño, who led the Mexican Association for Cultural Freedom) had spent the better part of a decade focused solely on attacking Communism without playing a role in a constructive program for the Left. Their agenda might have been greeted as liberatory in parts of Eastern Europe or in Spain, but because an anti-Communist agenda in the Americas was so frequently the province of the most illiberal and undemocratic elements of state and society, their preoccupation with this cause was hard to square even with the limited goal of "cultural freedom." Gorkin and García Treviño may still have considered themselves men of the Left, but few others did so any longer. The Cuban Revolution had brought attention to the desires of a younger generation and its politics, and the top leadership of the CCF came to believe that its current coterie of aging liberals and bitter ex-Marxists could not hope to rouse any significant support in the 1960s.

In Latin America, one CIA case officer, John Hunt, and three relatively unwitting employees of the CCF, Luis Mercier Vega, Keith Botsford, and Emir Rodríguez Monegal, had the responsibility of remaking the CCF operation. Hunt, an Oklahoma-born novelist, was a Harvard graduate and Marine Corps veteran who had been recruited as a CIA case officer and officially joined the CCF in February 1956. Hunt arrived a few months after Michael Josselson suffered his first work-related heart attack and took over a great deal of operational work from his ailing superior.[6]

The second reformer was Luis Mercier Vega, an improbably buttoned-down anarchist born Charles Cortvrint in Brussels in 1914 to a French father and a Chilean mother. He had fought as a member of the famous anarchist Durruti column during the Spanish Civil War and later with the Free French Forces in Africa and Lebanon during World War II. After the war he worked as a journalist and organizer for France's anarchist trade unions and for both the French and Latin American branches of the CCF. Disciplined and organized, Mercier Vega was disdainful of literary quarrels and preferred the world of social science. He was a "walking card-file," according to a colleague, and one of his major projects with the CCF was to build a reference library on social movements in Latin America. He took over responsibility for the Latin American department of the CCF from Gorkin on 16 October 1961, marking the end of the generation of the 1950s within the organization.[7]

When Mercier Vega inherited the Latin American department of the CCF, he became the head of an organization that, as he later acknowledged, had become known as an "anti-Communist center without other intellectual content." In Argentina, for example, when Mercier tried to organize working groups on social and cultural problems, he encountered opposition both from meritorious intellectuals who wanted nothing to do with the CCF and from active CCF members who preferred polemics to analysis. Mercier expanded the role of scholarship in CCF activity and was drawn to technical subjects: education and the university in society, the structure of political parties, the social role of the military, and even demography. Traveling with Gorkin through Latin America in 1953, Mercier had concluded that an intellectual "crossroads" was desperately needed to put an end to isolation of individual scholars and to allow them to enter into a "permanent exchange of ideas, works and men between Latin America and other continents." He tried to make the CCF in Latin America into such a forum.[8]

In some places the CCF achieved the kind of openness that it sought. In 1962 Mercier Vega established an office in Montevideo, where he remained for about a year. There he formed an especially close alliance with Benito Milla, another anarchist in exile who had fought with him in the Durruti column and who had since founded Editorial Alfa, one of Uruguay's major publishing houses. In Uruguay the members of the most influential group of left-wing intellectuals—especially among students and professionals—were known as the *terceristas,* who declared themselves neutral in the Cold War between the United States and the Soviet Union. Most aligned themselves, at least in the last instance, with Cuba. Milla published the works of the *terceristas,* as well as of their critics. This reputation for evenhandedness helped Milla when he decided to take charge of the Uruguayan national committee of the CCF and to publish a cultural bimonthly affiliated with the CCF known as *Temas.* The Uruguayan office, including *Temas,* was as intellectually open to writers of different parts of the political Left as any that the CCF had ever created in Latin America.[9]

But in other countries, achieving a more open CCF required the direct dismissal of older affiliates. In Argentina, Carlos Carranza seemed to have given up on his job and was retired and replaced with the younger and more dynamic Héctor Murena, the director of *Sur.* (The staff of *Sur* had long worked with the Argentine Association for Cultural Freedom, and its existence obviated the need for a local magazine in that country.) In Chile, even Carlos de Baráibar, who had overseen what was probably the most active national center of the 1950s, was offered a book contract as severance and given false assurances that he was not being fired.[10]

With Mercier Vega's operations covering most of South America and focusing on social science, John Hunt recruited Keith Botsford in late 1961 to help with literary figures and to catalyze reform in the major countries of Brazil and Mexico. Botsford, a North American novelist, editor, and critic, had met Hunt at the Writers' Workshop of the University of Iowa in 1950. In 1959 Botsford was made assistant dean of the University of Puerto Rico and in 1960 became assistant to Chancellor Jaime Benítez, a close associate of Luis Muñoz Marín, Puerto Rico's first democratically elected governor and an important broker between the U.S. government and Latin America's anti-Communist Left. In 1961 Botsford had watched the Cuban Association for Cultural Freedom flounder during its exile in Puerto Rico. Although he was convinced of the importance of combating what he considered fuzzy-headed Latin American radicalism, Botsford confessed to unease with much of U.S. government policy toward Cuba and thought that any moderating influence that the CCF would have on the Latin American cultural Left would have to be on the basis of dialogue, not hectoring.[11]

Botsford was a mercurial presence; charismatic and multilingual, he seemed to know everyone who mattered. He was once told that the CIA had considered recruiting him but thought him unreliable—"a badge of honor," he later wrote. Still, as an American going about the continent on a mission to meet and charm as many Latin American artists as he could, he seemed to enjoy the inevitable speculation that he was some sort of intelligence official. Saul Bellow, a friend with whom he had once started a magazine, based the character of Thaxter in *Humboldt's Gift* on him, writing that "Thaxter wanted people to believe that he was once a CIA agent. It was a wonderful rumor and he did everything to encourage it. It greatly added to his mysteriousness, and mystery was one of his little rackets." Four months into his work with the CCF, Botsford reported that he had "rarely had work more congenial to me, or [that] offers me more scope for my possibly foolish messianism." In spite of his reputation, Botsford was never let into the circle of those who knew details of the CIA's relationship to the CCF; his friend Hunt, who did know, lied to him for years.[12]

Botsford first traveled to Brazil, where the reforms that the CCF thought its operations required were not achieved with ease or grace. Since its inception in 1958, the Brazilian Association for Cultural Freedom's secretary general had been Stefan Baciu, a Romanian poet and diplomat who had left his country after Communists came to power there in 1948. He was also editor of *Cadernos Brasileiros,* the independently operated Portuguese-language affiliate of *Cuadernos,* which began publishing in April 1959. The most important intellectual who worked with the CCF in Brazil was Gilberto Freyre, a sociologist most famous for 1933's *Casa-grande e senzala (The Masters and the Slaves),* an argument for locating Brazilian identity in its slaveholding past that inverted views of European racial superiority by making a virtue of cultural diversity and racial mixing. Freyre considered himself part of the Democratic Left in the 1940s but was seen as growing increasingly conservative over the course of the 1950s. In Brazilian intellectual circles Freyre straddled the line between fame and infamy; many considered him a reactionary nationalist for his celebration of the particularities of Portuguese colonialism.[13]

The CCF's other prominent intellectual associate in Brazil was the literary critic Afrânio Coutinho, who had been the editor of *Seleções do "Reader's Digest"* from 1942 to 1947, the widely distributed Portuguese edition of the conservative *Reader's Digest*. During that time he lived in New York, and there he learned the close reading techniques of New Criticism. The success of New Criticism in the early decades of the Cold War has sometimes been attributed to its standing as a quintessentially anti-Communist mode of literary analysis; it offered an apparently apolitical reading of texts, taking objects of study on their own terms and divorced from historical context. Coutinho's work to spread it to Brazil supports the idea that New Criticism was seen as a way of depoliticizing cultural criticism—in a way that was necessarily political. Like Coutinho, another of the major practitioners and proponents of New Criticism was John Crowe Ransom, who was much admired in the CCF, and many of whose pupils were recruited for CIA work.[14]

Cadernos Brasileiros and the entire Brazilian operation had acquired a reputation for reactionary anti-Communism, and the CCF sent Botsford and the composer Nicolas Nabokov to try to create a fresh start. Baciu grumbled that Nabokov acted like a "fellow traveler" for not maintaining a constant posture of explicit anti-Communism. But Nabokov chided Baciu for misunderstanding the new climate: they wanted "a firm position with respect to some various aspects of totalitarianism," to be sure, but in a way that made it possible to "win friends, and to win them in what is now called in Italy 'the opening to the left.' " Nabokov reminded Baciu of the problem that many organizations—not all of them Communist—believed that the CCF was a right-wing American organization specifically designed to fight Communism. This was not the reputation that it wanted, and Baciu resigned not long after receiving Nabokov's letter, complaining to Mercier Vega that he felt "intrigues and police-like tone adding up to political pressure to work with Communists like [the economist] Celso Furtado."[15]

Baciu's version of anti-Communism, illustrated by his attitude toward Furtado (who was not a Communist) was widespread among Brazilian conservatives, who reacted with panic to the left-wing administration of João Goulart, president from 1961 to 1964. Furtado, a young economist, had in 1959 become the first director of a government planning body (the Superintendency for the Development of the Northeast, SUDENE) to deal with extreme poverty in Brazil's arid northeast region. It aimed to use state power to spur industrialization—officials frequently compared it to the Tennessee Valley Authority of the U.S. New Deal. At first, the U.S. government considered SUDENE an important program in the Alliance for

Progress, recognizing it as a nationalist project motivated by reformist goals of both political and economic modernization. But hated as it was by Brazil's Right, SUDENE had to draw on support from a wide spectrum of left-wing technocrats, including Communists. From Furtado's point of view, imposing an ideological test for employment would have undermined the delicate political coalition that supported the agency in the face of conservative opposition. But Communist participation eventually turned the United States against the project. For the Brazilian Right, which opposed SUDENE from its inception, Furtado's supposed Communism became a trope that it used to undermine the legitimacy of President Goulart.[16]

Keith Botsford arrived in Brazil in early 1962 and immediately overhauled the layout and content of *Cadernos Brasileiros*. The magazine began to rely less on the regular stable of anti-Communist CCF writers and more on Brazilian authors. But in the year and a half he remained in Brazil, Botsford made only limited progress within the Brazilian Association. Although he tried to sponsor talks and speakers, the most important foreign guest whom the Latin American department ever hosted provided him with a harrowing experience. The North American poet Robert Lowell came to Brazil in June 1962 under Botsford's supervision. He was, Botsford later reflected, brought in to be "an outstanding American to counteract . . . Communist people like Neruda—[Lowell was] our side's emissary." But Lowell, who had been a rather conservative Catholic in the 1930s, a conscientious objector in the 1940s, close to the Kennedys in the early 1960s, and an antiwar campaigner later in the decade, was not exactly politically reliable. Lowell spoke before mostly small audiences, and his trip down the coast of Brazil passed without major incident. When he and Botsford crossed into Argentina in September, however, things unraveled. Lowell, who suffered from periodic attacks of manic depression, was drinking excessively and buying expensive food and clothing, expecting the CCF to pick up the tab. He insisted on being taken around to the equestrian statues of Buenos Aires; disrobing and mounting one statue after another, he declared himself the "Caesar of Argentina." Botsford felt powerless to control Lowell's mania, his spending habits, or his public disquisitions on the character of the American imperium and returned to Rio. But Lowell, who had stopped taking his medication, could not be left behind. Returning to Argentina to fetch him, Botsford found himself at a party watching Lowell wrestling on the floor with the exiled Spanish Communist poet Rafael Alberti. Botsford tried to get the other guests to help him restrain Lowell, insisting that he was sick and needed to be taken back to the United States for treatment. The other partygoers were stunned by what they saw as an attempt by the CIA to kidnap him. In the end, Botsford had to spend days with Lowell restrained and sedated in a clinic before he could be flown back to the United States. The disastrous Lowell trip was probably given the most positive spin possible by Botsford when he wrote his CCF superiors that "[Lowell] is sort of a blowtorch thaw, and terribly useful. It is impossible for these [leftist] people to hold on to their rigid positions with [him] around."[17]

Botsford left Brazil in 1963 as the situation in the country grew tenser. President Goulart, in an attempt to deal with the destructive inflation that plagued Brazil's economy, had brought Celso Furtado into his cabinet and charged him with developing a plan to fight it. Representing the consensus ideas of the moderate Left, Furtado's three-year plan sought to maintain economic growth while reducing the rate of inflation, which required a devaluation of the currency and an immediate increase in the cost of living. Much of Goulart's restive union base disliked the plan, and he abandoned it after six months, replacing Furtado within his cabinet and turning to the Left for political support. Accused of being unable to govern by the military, Goulart was toppled in a coup on 1 April 1964, and replaced by Humberto Castelo Branco as the first head of the military regime that, with changes in leadership, lasted until 1985. At the time, however, many thought that the military would soon yield to democratic elections. The Brazilian Association for Cultural Freedom, unconcerned, opened an art gallery in Rio de Janeiro to showcase abstract art the very week of the coup.[18]

Brazil's coup proved to be the beginning of a wave of military uprisings in South America. The military governments conducted brutal counter-insurgencies against the Left in their home countries and even abroad, suppressing both electoral democracy and, relatedly, cultural freedoms. Although he was a moderate among the military rulers, Castelo Branco was still empowered by a series of so-called institutional acts to suspend constitutional guarantees, leading to repression at the universities and exile for many potential opponents of the military government. Castelo Branco also used his powers to cancel the political rights of many opponents, including Furtado. The coup itself was not something that the CCF was in a position to do anything about: the U.S. government, though not one of the major actors in the coup, had communicated its willingness to see Goulart removed from office and had provided covert support to coup plotters.[19]

The CCF, however, whether following CIA guidance or acting on its own, hoped for a quick return to political normalcy and disapproved of

Castelo Branco's persecution of the moderate Left. A few weeks after the coup, John Hunt wrote to Afrânio Coutinho asking *Cadernos Brasileiros* and the Brazilian Association to "play a constructive role in the new intellectual and political environment in Brazil." Hunt said that he welcomed the end of "political and economic chaos" and the "threat to freedom" represented by Goulart, but he wanted it made clear that the CCF should be opposed to persecution of liberals or the Left and specifically mentioned Furtado, who he had heard had been imprisoned. "Your record is such that no one can accuse you or the Congress of being pro-communist," he wrote Coutinho, "and, at the same time, this gives us a chance to show unmistakably our liberal standpoint. In short, being anti-Goulart is not a sufficient reason for excesses committed against democratic procedures, and I think we should be courageous enough to say so."[20]

Coutinho rejected Hunt's facts and his reasoning. He believed that the military had the support of the Brazilian people and had put an end to Communist infiltration, thus normalizing the constitution. He insisted that leftists, including moderates, had been attempting to install a leftist totalitarian regime. He described a military that had just removed a government from power by force as belonging to the "democratic center." Furtado, he allowed, was not a Communist, but he had been allied with them; besides, Coutinho added, Furtado had not been arrested, he had only had his political rights suspended for ten years, being stripped of his right to vote or hold office. Coutinho wanted nothing to do with any campaign to restore Furtado's political rights or in any other way upset the military government.[21]

Hunt, however, continued to press his case, stating that the defense of Furtado should be taken up out of general respect for intellectual freedom. But sensing that he would get no cooperation, Hunt tried to outmaneuver Coutinho by using other parts of the CCF apparatus, including the Science and Freedom Committee—which was not part of the Latin American operation—to carry out an investigation of the state of educational freedom in Brazil. Its report on the situation in Brazilian universities documented 42 cases of professors leaving the country or about to leave, 20 living outside the country who were thinking of not returning, 25 deprived of political rights, 31 dismissed or placed on retirement lists, and 129 intellectuals who were imprisoned. The report also documented books confiscated (from an encyclical of Pope John XXIII to Graham Greene's spy farce *Our Man in Havana*) and an atmosphere in which meetings of students, intellectuals, and workers were considered subversive. Hunt tried to bolster the authority of the report by obtaining the supporting signature of Robert Oppenheimer Jr. and pressed the members of the Brazilian

Association to get a response from the government. One member was able to meet directly with Brazil's military leadership, but the government declared the CCF's report naïve, saying that it gave the impression that the government came to destroy the universities. It could not be doing so, it argued tautologically, because "we never had Universities in Brazil." True, the military government acknowledged, some professors had been replaced. But, it was said, "The new ones are as good and serious as the others; the freedom of teaching is respected." Although the government's response was almost self-refuting, Coutinho had effectively outflanked Hunt; the Brazilian Association for Cultural Freedom took no action to defend the rights of critics of the military government. The government, instead, ordered its cultural attachés to declare the CCF report a misinformation campaign. Over a period of about two years, contributors to *Cadernos Brasileiros* gradually moved into the opposition as the military government it had initially greeted with relief showed that it would not relinquish power quickly. But Hunt, the CIA case officer, had been unable to bring Coutinho, the local representative, around to a more liberal plan of action. In this instance, when the CIA tried to call the tune, the piper packed up his flute and left.[22]

Botsford left Brazil in mid-1963 for Mexico to try his hand at similar reforms there. As in Brazil, the Mexican Association for Cultural Freedom had earned a reputation for vitriolic anti-Communism. Like *Cadernos Brasileiros,* the Mexican national magazine, *Examen,* had a poor reputation, having become, in Botsford's words, "no more than a virulent and reactionary platform for the small section of the Mexican anti-Communist Right." In 1961 the CCF requested that *Examen* cease calling itself the organ of the Mexican Association for Cultural Freedom and then that it stop carrying the affiliation at all. Even other professional anti-Communists thought that Rodrigo García Treviño, in charge of both the Mexican Association and the magazine, had gone a bit wild.[23]

García Treviño, like Baciu in Brazil, actively resisted the new "open" tendencies within the CCF. García Treviño could not understand what was wrong with his behavior: was not the point of the CCF, he asked, to defend political liberties and help politicians with "democratic" inclinations? Luis Mercier Vega wrote a reply rich in ironies:

> The Congress for Cultural Freedom is not, and cannot be, a contra-Cominform. Whether for good or for ill, that is how it is. To imagine a contra-Cominform would be to suppose the existence of a worldwide force, a group

of powers, a state totally committed to a worldwide strategy opposing the Soviet strategy, not only on military grounds, but also in the domains of politics and society. That does not exist. That will probably never exist. And, for my part, I am not convinced that the democracies could safeguard their claim to superiority if they adopted totalitarian methods in order to use them against totalitarianism. On the other hand, by favoring argument, improving information, and stressing their responsibilities, the Congress can, and intends to, immunize intellectuals against totalitarian gangrene and stimulate them to think for themselves. It has to do only with one sector [of the population], but it is an essential sector. And on that terrain we must wage our battles, as others wage theirs in other sectors.

García Treviño was pushed out of the CCF and engaged it in bitter polemics, as he had once done with Communists.[24]

When Botsford arrived in Mexico, he was greeted with a suggestion from García Treviño that he was some kind of secret Communist. Once he began his more routine activities, however, the far more common question from the Mexican intellectuals he approached was whether he was an agent of the CIA. "You will both be pleased to hear," he wrote jokingly to Hunt and Josselson in October 1963, "that the current Mexico City rumor is that there's some American in [the neighborhood of] San Angel [where Botsford settled], trying to buy Mexican intellectuals. Thus, from being a CP agent I've passed to the more eminent status of imperialist." Botsford concluded that discretion was the only possible path forward for the CCF in Mexico, where he encountered suspicion of foreign meddling in cultural matters. Attempts that had been made in 1962 to recover support for CCF activities by forming groups called the Friends of *Cuadernos* had not been successful because, as Botsford observed drily, "*Cuadernos* had relatively few friends."[25]

Many of the paths Botsford started down in Mexico proved to be dead ends; he did make friends but did not build institutions. He tried to produce an anthology of Latin American poetry together with Robert Lowell, Octavio Paz, and other editors, but it was never published. A semiacademic quarterly review of Latin American social science also fell apart. The CCF briefly sought to forge a relationship with the writers' center known as the Centro Mexicano de Escritores (CME), a fifteen-year-old initiative of the North American writer Margaret Shedd that had largely been funded with money from the Rockefeller Foundation. It provided yearlong grants for writers to allow them to devote themselves full-time to a project, and it had a remarkable track record in the 1950s of selecting talent. In its first years the CME was an extraordinary success: the most important writers of the generation—those who came to define

Mexican literature of the 1950s and 1960s—wrote some of their early works while they were under grants from it. Juan Rulfo wrote both *Pedro Páramo* and *El llano en llamas* there, and Carlos Fuentes finished his early novel *La región más transparente* on a grant from the CME. Shedd was already getting money from the Farfield Foundation, which she would have had no way of knowing was one of the CIA front groups that existed primarily to fund the CCF. Contacts with the Farfield Foundation may have also provided opportunities for the CME's favored writers to benefit from other CCF operations; some of Shedd's stories appeared in *Encounter,* as did one of Rulfo's from *El llano en llamas.*[26]

John Hunt had written Keith Botsford about the possibility of contacting the CME while the latter was still working in Brazil in 1962. The CME was one of the few cultural institutions in Mexico in which the state did not exercise a predominant influence, and Botsford saw his central task as constructing a viable alternative to the centralized power of the Mexican government in the arts. In contrast to the 1950s, when many foreign observers thought of Mexico's PRI as among the most democratic of Latin America's governments, its limitations from the liberal perspective were by then much clearer. The innovative young writers and artists who were clustered around the cultural supplement of *Siempre!,* for example, were generally critical of the PRI. In response to Botsford's inquiries, Shedd asked the CCF to finance a salary for Rulfo to bring him onto the CME's staff to work with its younger writers. But other than paying Rulfo's salary for a couple of years, the CCF ultimately did nothing further with the CME. But although it went totally undetected, even by its recipient, additional money from the CIA did go to Rulfo. Because he was seen as a brilliant but temperamental author who had given up producing new works, at the end of the 1960s the Farfield Foundation helped him purchase a plot of land in the countryside to try to give him the space he needed to resume writing. He adored his country home but never published a complete work again. At least in this case, Farfield and CCF money did not succeed in buying anything of political value.[27]

A few of Botsford's friendships did pay off. Everyone acknowledged that Carlos Fuentes, an ambitious and cosmopolitan young writer, was one of Mexico's most important literary talents. In the 1950s he had coedited a literary magazine, the *Revista Mexicana de Literatura,* that sought a middle ground politically between the directed cultural world of the Soviet Union and what he described as literary McCarthyism in the United States. He looked warily at the Neruda of *Las uvas y el viento,* rejecting both "socialist realism" and the "capitalist realism" of U.S. popular fiction. But the older writers of the Mexican Association for Cultural

Freedom of the 1950s had worked to alienate Fuentes; an official review in *Examen* declared that his ambitious debut novel "did not interest them as a literary work." Yet when Botsford discovered that he and Fuentes lived close to each other, he reached out. Fuentes, still shuttling between Cuba and Mexico on behalf of the Movimiento de Liberación Nacional, had recently visited the United States and had been pleasantly surprised by the attitudes of his interlocutors there. He and Botsford discussed the possibility of his engaging in a kind of trilateral diplomacy to bring together some kind of debate about Cuban cultural politics with critical members of the U.S. intelligentsia. In one conversation Botsford put it to Fuentes that it was hard to understand why "such obviously intelligent people as himself support regimes in which he would find himself quite uncomfortable, unable to speak with even the relative freedom he enjoys in Mexico, and so on . . . He [Fuentes] said he understood the argument perfectly well, but thought that a good number of intellectuals, from pride, through rationalization, for nationalistic reasons, or even to 'work from inside' and not to abandon the field totally to their opponents, would stay, even granting that the situation was far from ideal." Botsford thought this a significant admission and began to treat Fuentes as a convert. When Hunt planned a visit to Mexico, Botsford described Fuentes, perhaps aspirationally, as "a good man and on our side." The next year, when Botsford played an organizational role in a meeting of International PEN, the human rights organization for poets, essayists, and novelists, the CCF arranged to pay Fuentes's travel expenses. None of this indicated that Fuentes had ceased to be a left-wing intellectual, but it did show that the CCF could notch some successes with its more open approach.[28]

But for literary impact, there was no one more affected by the presence of the CCF than the satirist Jorge Ibargüengoitia, who become Botsford's closest friend during his time in Mexico. Ibargüengoitia was a graduate of the CME and, in the early 1960s, a struggling playwright. He later remembered Botsford's time in Mexico as slightly ridiculous. Botsford lived in an enormous and opulent house that was absurdly grandiose by the standards of all but the most successful Mexican writers. His attempts to entertain there ran up against insuperable cultural obstacles. Several guests walked out when Botsford put on a performance of modern music that included a deck of shuffling cards as a percussion instrument. Although Botsford was frequently irritated that his guests arrived late, taking it as a sign of their lack of seriousness, Ibargüengoitia remembered that Botsford kept giving out the name of his street incorrectly. Still, Ibargüengoitia valued his friendship with Botsford. First, he gave fine career advice: Ibargüengoitia, looking back, said that it was Botsford who had encouraged him to leave drama for novel writing; he helped him publish chapters of his work-in-progress farce of postrevolutionary Mexico, *Los relámpagos de agosto,* in *Cadernos Brasileiros* and gave him the idea that later became the novel *Las muertas.*[29]

Still, it was Cuba's Casa de las Américas, not the CCF, that in 1964 recognized *Los relámpagos de agosto* as a masterful short novel. Ibargüengoitia also drew on his relationship with Botsford to satirize 1960s Mexico's atmosphere of literary suspicion combined with financial neediness. In "Conversaciones con Bloomsbury," a story that features Bloomsbury as a lightly fictionalized Botsford, the stand-in for Ibargüenogitia writes of his surprise at discovering that *Cuadernos* is a real magazine: he had thought "Bloomsbury" a complete impostor when he had first met him. And he wrote that "*Cuadernos,* which I had never read, [had] a decidedly anti-Communist air; but on studying it carefully, I began to suspect that it was just the opposite; that is, an apparently anti-Communist magazine, made by the Communists, to discredit the anti-Communists."[30]

Botsford left Mexico in 1965, frustrated and wondering how he had managed to fail so spectacularly. "All travelers are liars and carry their own countries about with them, like great weights," he wrote. He had not been able to avoid showing his impatience with what he considered petty nationalism; he had hobnobbed with elites but had failed to meet common people; he remained, in their minds and his, a Yankee, a gringo. "The air grew so oppressive in Mexico," he wrote retrospectively, "the sinister totem-Stalinism of that most subtly totalitarian of states so intolerable, that instead of the easy drive North I had promised myself, I did twenty hours flat out to Laredo, and practically kissed the chiliburger-littered macadam of the Customs shed." He continued to work with Hunt, however, and, through CCF and CIA connections in International PEN, was put in charge of assembling the roundtable discussions at its 1965 meeting in Bled, Yugoslavia. Through the Farfield Foundation and the CCF, many writers who were friendly to the CCF (or at least not unfriendly, like Carlos Fuentes) had their travel expenses covered, helping ensure that Arthur Miller was elected head of International PEN instead of Guatemala's Miguel Ángel Asturias, considered by many too much a fellow traveler.[31]

Whatever Botsford's failings as a cultural ambassador, he at least saw clearly the problems of *Cuadernos,* which everywhere proved an obstacle to his labors. Luis Mercier Vega and Botsford agreed that the magazine was the CCF's most important asset in Latin America and were frustrated that it seemed so inert. In 1963 they wrote that the magazine needed a "more open attitude, politically and culturally, [in order to create a] place for intelligent debate and the presentation of diverse points-of-view."

Botsford pleaded with Germán Arciniegas, who had replaced Gorkin as editor in chief, to consider publishing more exciting up-and-coming writers, even Cuban writers, regardless of whether they were politically too far to the left for his comfort. Botsford even compared *Cuadernos* unfavorably with *Casa de las Américas,* which published a more diverse array of writers before 1965 (including Botsford himself). Trying to cut the cultural Left out of the conversation, he said, would be like "cutting out from US literature all artistic movements to the left of the *New Yorker.*" But Arciniegas refused.[32]

Trashing *Cuadernos* became a sort of sport among the younger CCF affiliates. Horacio Daniel Rodríguez, an Argentine journalist with social democratic political opinions who was brought into the CCF as part of Mercier's new generation, wrote in 1963: "Did you get number 76—September—of *Cuadernos?* You couldn't ask for anything better: an essay by Borges that's approximately 15 years old and that has been published to death in Argentina; a story by the ultra-McCarthyist Manuel Peyrou; a reproduction of [Héctor] Murena's article published in *La Nación* last June 23rd, but slightly modified so as not to be recognized right away . . . In sum, whatever." Murena, who worked for *Sur* and directed the fine-arts program for the Argentine Association, was similarly dismissive of the magazine. On one occasion, when he received a submission that did not fit into *Sur*'s plans, he offered to send it to *Cuadernos* instead. Its author declined, saying that "that magazine is too [politically] committed." "Committed to what?" Murena asked Mercier privately. "Nonsense?"[33]

But Arciniegas remained oblivious to the small niche that his magazine occupied and opposed to any opening to the Left. The other supporter of maintaining *Cuadernos* as it existed was Michael Josselson, the principal CIA agent responsible for the CCF, who bristled when Botsford sent in field reports indicating problems. But Josselson's deputy John Hunt came to agree with the views of Mercier and Botsford and began to search for a new editor to launch a new magazine. Arciniegas was told that *Cuadernos* would be discontinued because of irresolvable financial problems in June 1965, and the debut of its replacement, *Mundo Nuevo,* was slated for July 1966. Arciniegas, however, liked his work and wanted to continue it. He traveled to the United States, unaware that the death of his magazine was widely considered a strategic necessity, to ask for funds directly from the philanthropic foundations that had contributed to the CCF. Arciniegas arranged to meet with a friend of his who worked for the Ford Foundation. Before his interview Alberto Lleras Camargo, former president of Colombia and the Organization of American States, warned

Arciniegas that the person he was going to meet "doesn't give a cent without the prior approval of the CIA." Indeed, Arciniegas was out of luck: the Ford Foundation denied his request for funding. Embittered by his experience, he asked to be removed as a member of the CCF.[34]

But if its impact on Latin American literature had been limited, the CCF did play a role in increasing the international renown of its favored writers. In 1963 the CCF received notice that Pablo Neruda was on the short list for the Nobel Prize in Literature and might win. Over decades of poetic production, Neruda had surely written enough transcendent poetry to deserve the prize as much as anyone—and enough purple propaganda to disqualify him for life, depending on how one chose to judge the oeuvre. Gorkin and John Hunt worked to make sure that the history of Neruda's engagement with Stalinism was well known in Sweden, publishing pamphlets in French and English and articles in Swedish journals. They reproduced the works from the height of Neruda's cultural Stalinism, especially the portions of Las uvas y el viento dedicated to Stalin. They tried to show the importance of political engagement to Neruda's poetry while arguing for the "low quality" of that engagement, supposedly unbending even as the Soviet Union liberalized. They were also keen to remind the conservative Swedish academy of Neruda's role in arranging for David Álfaro Siqueiros's transfer to Chile from Mexico after his release on bail for the attempted murder of Trotsky.[35]

As alternatives, the CCF pushed the candidacies of the pro-Western socialist president of Senegal, Leopold Senghor, an accomplished poet and essayist, and the Argentine metaphysical obscurantist Jorge Luis Borges, whose short stories and essays were often difficult to distinguish from one another and who was best known in politics as one of the liberal, anti-Peronist members of Victoria Ocampo's Sur group. (Borges was a member of the Argentine Association for Cultural Freedom.) The CCF's London-based magazine, Encounter, had published Borges's work, and the CCF also supported his trips to Europe with the goal of raising his profile in Scandinavia. Hunt had hoped to get Borges to Sweden in 1963, at the same time at which it was preparing files to damage Neruda's Nobel candidacy, but Borges was unable to travel to Stockholm until the following year.[36]

The CCF's whispering campaign against Neruda was perfectly consistent with the understanding of literature as combat possessed by the cultural institutions of the Cold War. The Chilean Communist press tried to discredit the anti-Neruda campaign by attributing it to the CCF; "Almost a tribute to the influence of the Congress," wrote one of its employees. If the campaign had any effect, it certainly did not elevate any of the CCF's

Keith Botsford (left), the roving fixer for the Congress for Cultural Freedom in Latin America during the 1960s, with Jorge Luis Borges in West Berlin in 1965. In the 1960s the CCF tried to promote Borges in Europe as a Nobel Prize candidate to rival Pablo Neruda, but Borges never won. Photo courtesy Keith Botsford.

preferred candidates: the prize that year went to Jean-Paul Sartre, who declined it. In any case, the CCF was hardly the only politically minded lobby on the scene. Neruda's defender and translator in Sweden, the poet Artur Lundkvist, counterbalanced the negative campaign from the CCF and was hardly a Cold War neutral. He was Neruda's friend, was a member of the World Peace Council, and had received the Lenin Peace Prize in 1958. A decade later Lundkvist was selected for a seat on the eighteen-member Swedish Academy that awards the Nobel Prize in Literature, and Neruda was awarded the prize in 1971. Lundkvist never forgave Borges, whose deep anti-Peronism had led him to a dark place politically, for his endorsements of the Argentine and Chilean military dictatorships of the 1970s. Borges, famously, never won.[37]

In addition to its work with writers, the CCF in the early 1960s sought greater engagement with social scientists. There, its most intellectually prestigious collaborator was the Italo-Argentine sociologist Gino Germani. Germani had been born in Italy in 1911 and had been imprisoned as a young man for distributing antifascist literature. He described his dislike of Mussolini's fascism as stemming from its "uniformity of ideas and . . . fear of freedom" and took his liberal preferences with him across the Atlantic to Argentina in 1931. But trouble seemed to follow. When Juan Domingo Perón came to power in 1946, many of his critics compared him to Mussolini. Germani, having lived under both leaders, noted the different composition of their social bases and did not equate the two, but the suppression of the anti-Peronist opposition and of intellectual and cultural life in general nevertheless left him scrambling for work.[38]

After Perón was overthrown by the military in 1955, Germani became the director of the Institute of Sociology at the University of Buenos Aires and worked to modernize social scientific training in Argentina. To that end, he traveled to the United States, visiting major universities and speaking with scholars working in the modernization tradition. To build his program and sponsor research, he took grants from the Ford Foundation and UNESCO, among other international organizations. Most of the first generation of students in his sociology programs were socialists, and the study of society—Germani was interested in class structure and social stratification, among other things—was politically appealing to them. But Germani's analysis in his classic work *Política y sociedad en una época de transición,* first published in 1962, described Argentine modernization as having been distorted by Perón. Like other scholars in the modernization tradition, he wanted the rational study of society to be used to ease conflict and guide the political process toward better outcomes, reflecting his hopes that non-Peronist social integration could occur in a free, democratic context.

Modernization theorists like Germani hoped that social justice could be achieved by liberal democracy. University of Chicago sociologist Edward Shils, for example, another affiliate of the CCF, wrote in 1959 that the modern world would resemble a fully articulated welfare state. It would display concern for the condition of the poorest and feature democracy, advanced industry, and scientific progress. "No country could be modern without being economically advanced or progressive," Shils argued. "To be advanced economically means to have an economy based on modern technology, to be industrialized and to have a high standard of living. All this requires planning and the employment of economists and statisticians . . . It is the model of the West detached in some way from its geographical origins and locus." His hopes resembled, not by accident, a kind of utopian global New Deal. Planning required technocrats and scientists; those elites required training that the United States could provide. The CCF had produced the "end of ideology" thesis, the idea that welfare-state democracy was the endpoint of political struggle, having undermined the extreme ideologies of fascism and Communism. Modernization theory worked as a kind of "end of ideology" thesis in action and became the primary ideology that justified the U.S. effort to remake the world in its non-Communist image during the Cold War, not only in Latin America but also through the war in Vietnam. But it also reflected the hopes and anxieties of what liberals thought the United States and other countries had yet to achieve: more equal societies, economic growth, and political democracy existing together in ways that were supposed to be mutually reinforcing.[39]

One of the analytical vulnerabilities of modernization theory was its fear of the crowd: social justice was supposed to be planned calmly and technocratically, not fought for in the streets. The rational transformation of society would avoid the perils of mob rule; economic development would take place through state-guided market economies, and so modernization theory objected to populist "distortions." In the Argentine context, this manifested in Germani's anti-Peronism. But Germani found that his work received a chilly reception from multiple audiences. His equation of modernization with secularization placed him under attack from the Catholic Right, which saw his studies as dissolving traditional values. At the same time, his collaboration with North American foundations and the methods he modified from abroad caused the empirical study of society to be associated with anti-Peronist critique, and many young students, who were both left-wing and pro-Perón, saw in him a tool of Yankee cultural penetration.[40]

It was perfectly true that the frameworks used by modernization scholars held that social problems grew out of institutional failures—especially by universities and bureaucracies—to meet the needs of a modern world. Marxism as a tool of analysis was ignored, and blame for social problems was not directed abroad at foreign imperialism. The key task for the engaged modernization scholars was to see that a middle-class elite got proper training and then took responsibility for national problems. "The non-Communist literate elites in . . . transitional societies bear a heavy responsibility for the future of their peoples," wrote Walt Rostow in *The Stages of Economic Growth*. "It is they who must focus their minds on the tasks of development . . . as they complete the preconditions and launch themselves into self-sustained growth." The alternative was frustration, stagnation, and insurgency. The elitist and technocratic aspects of modernization theory assigned important roles to the social scientists and technicians who could help the state achieve modernity, and this focus on growth by an educated and elite middle class—certainly not via a revolution from below—also conformed to the expectations and the mission of the CCF. In this, modernization theory was a kind of truncated Leninism: social change was to be delivered by an intellectual vanguard, but with a capitalist welfare state, not socialism, as the desired end product of history.[41]

Working in that vein, in 1965 the CCF cosponsored its largest international gathering in Latin America since Mexico City's troubled reunion of 1956. Held in Uruguay, the conference "The Formation of Elites in Latin America" was cosponsored by Aldo Solari, a sociologist and socialist working at the University of Montevideo, and Seymour Martin Lipset of Berkeley's Institute for International Studies, a sociologist working in the modernization tradition. In contrast to the anti-Communist manifestos of earlier gatherings, the meeting offered scholarship that embodied the activist promise of an engaged anti-Communism. Germani was one of the prominent contributors. The theme of the Montevideo conference, the formation of Latin American elites, was conceptualized in a developmentalist rather than explicitly anti-Communist framework. "We are interested in elites," the organizers of the conference wrote in their introduction to its compiled papers, "because of our larger concern with social, economic, and political development. And while there are many factors which affect the propensity of a nation to develop, it is clear that regardless of differences in social systems, one of the requisites for development is a competent elite, motivated to modernize their society." The idea that the elites would change Latin American societies and bring them closer to a modernity modeled on Europe and the United States was fully intended to contrast with concepts of transformation that assigned the agency for change to popular action.[42]

This was not lost on thinkers to the left of the CCF. Uruguayan critic Ángel Rama observed with trepidation the expanding interest in Latin American affairs in the United States and the growing number of sponsored conferences and workshops for workers, businesspeople, and educators. As the CCF's conference approached, Rama wondered whether the United States was truly interested in a dialogue on "education" or whether it was instead preparing the "training" of Latin American political elites. If not the latter, he wondered, then why allow the conference to be cosponsored by the CCF, an organization "whose political militancy is more than well-known"? Rama was convinced (correctly) that the CIA had financed the CCF and wondered whether the conference on the formation of Latin American elites was, like Project Camelot, another example of "scholarship" behind which lurked the interests of empire.[43]

Solari, as one of the conference's sponsors, objected to the notion that it might have been put in the service of imperialism, saying that if the CCF were financed by the CIA (which he doubted), he would stop collaborating with it. But, he countered, "The systematic campaign to represent sociologists as spies and potential spies of imperialism tends to increase the difficulty that sociology encounters in every under- or semideveloped country. Its surest effect is to impede research, because everything which is asked in a survey, for example, could be argued to serve imperialism . . . [The effect of such an attitude] is to help maintain the status quo."[44] Solari and Rama were engaged in a debate about who was the real scholarly defender of present injustice; Rama responded that attempts to stimulate disinterested and objective sociology sought to purge values from scholarship, leading to conservative thought and the maintenance of the status quo. The doctrine of the "end of ideologies," which argued that future problems would be solved through the growth of prosperity within a mixed capitalist economy, promised that future conflicts would be technocratic, not ideological. This was the sort of scholarship that the CCF was trying to promote, and in this context, he wrote, it did not matter whether the CIA paid for the CCF, for "one way or another, the [conference] will serve its ends." It was the achievement of the Latin American department of the CCF to have politicized its own depoliticization, Rama argued. "The ideal of 'neutralization,' " responded Rama, "is the new form of imperialistic action in the cultural front." Rama's views show how the CCF, in its efforts to reform itself, had succeeded mostly in tying a position it understood as neutral scholarship to the politics of empire. As if to reinforce the point, in 1966 Germani himself had been given control over a special issue of the CCF's new magazine, *Mundo Nuevo,* which was to be dedicated to an empirical analysis of the Latin American Left. When it was in production, the *New York Times* published articles showing that the CCF had been a recipient of CIA funds.[45]

At the time those articles appeared in 1966, the CCF and the CIA had for a couple of years been endeavoring to sever their financial relationship. Those efforts began with urgency in 1964, when a congressional investigation into the tax-exempt status of U.S. foundations exposed the CIA's relationship with the J. M. Kaplan Fund of New York, which was being used to fund training institutes for the anti-Communist Left in Latin America, though not the CCF. Although the investigators were persuaded to keep the operation secret after meeting with officials from the Internal Revenue Service and the CIA, Michael Josselson became more determined to spin off the CCF's best assets to inoculate them as much as possible from harm done by any future revelation of CIA support of the CCF. In mid-1966 the CCF's leaders sought to preserve their organization by negotiating an agreement with the Ford Foundation that provided $6 million over six years on the condition that financial ties with the CIA were broken.[46]

On 1 January 1966 the Latin American department split off from the CCF to form an independent affiliate called the Instituto Latinoamericano de Relaciones Internacionales (ILARI), still under Mercier Vega's direction. ILARI was an obfuscation; little changed other than the name. It kept the same Paris office and maintained its relationship with other parts of the CCF family. Still, it was an opportunity to start fresh and secure some new names for an advisory committee that would be displayed on ILARI letterhead. Octavio Paz, among others, declined an invitation to be involved, but one big name did accept: Mexico's preeminent liberal historian, Daniel Cosío Villegas. At the end of that year, Cosío Villegas was flown to Paris to participate in a discussion and advise the International Secretariat about problems and prospects in its Latin American work, and he became an important consultant on ILARI's initiatives and magazines. Incorporated in Geneva, ILARI presented itself and its mission as a more cosmopolitan version of the old CCF, "to organize and utilize the intellectual resources of Latin America in such a way as to secure their full participation in the sphere of international cultural exchanges." Culturally, it presented itself as a more fashionable version of its old self, noting that it had sponsored the first concert of electronic music in Argentina and had introduced Uruguay and Peru to the 1960s art event known as the "happening." It maintained a close relationship with the Instituto di Tella in Buenos Aires, the leading institution for the promulgation of modern and experimental art in the Argentine 1960s.[47]

ILARI strengthened its efforts to facilitate Latin American sociological research. Mercier Vega saw ILARI, somewhat simplistically, as the vital center of a consciousness-raising project between two antithetical extremes in Latin American society. The first pole adhered rigidly to the status quo and feared any change, while the second was convinced that a violent revolution was the only path to development. In between lay the "no-man's land" of "concrete economic and sociological processes that [constitute] the terrain for which both sides are contending, but which neither side appears willing to investigate objectively." He had ILARI sponsor work groups at major Latin American universities in order to fill this perceived gap, addressing his sociological concerns: the social composition of political parties, the social composition and civic role of the armed forces, the university and society, censorship in Latin America, and problems of the Latin American novel. At the end of 1966 he launched a journal called *Aportes* to publish scholarly papers.[48]

But the most important journal linked to the CCF in Latin America was the literary magazine *Mundo Nuevo*. "It was," wrote the Chilean novelist José Donoso, "the voice of Latin American literature of its time." The first issue, in July 1966, featured a long interview by its editor, Emir Rodríguez Monegal, of Carlos Fuentes. In the second, Rodríguez Monegal included an excerpt from Gabriel García Márquez's as-yet-unpublished *One Hundred Years of Solitude,* which, when finished, would make its author the most famous of all the novelists of the boom. *Mundo Nuevo* published early pieces of Donoso's *El obsceno pájaro de la noche;* it helped launch the careers of Cuban exiles like Severo Sarduy; and it raised the profile of Guillermo Cabrera Infante, formerly of the suppressed *Lunes de Revolución.* In the words of John King, the magazine offered Latin American intellectuals of the 1960s a "revolution in style." It was surely one of the finest magazines that the CIA ever had a hand in creating, a diamond in the murk of most of the CCF's work in the region.[49]

Mundo Nuevo was the successor to the much-unloved *Cuadernos.* Its motive force was Emir Rodríguez Monegal, a biographer of Borges and a widely respected critic and editor. Born in Uruguay, he knew nearly everyone who was or would become famous on the Latin American literary scene. In the 1940s he had been the editor of the literary pages of the left-wing Montevidean weekly *Marcha* and later the editor of a small magazine called *Número.* In the mid-1960s Rodríguez Monegal had an idea for another magazine. *Marcha,* his former employer, was the voice of Uruguayan *tercerismo*—a form of New Left third way between the Cold War powers of the United States and the Soviet Union—that had fallen hard for the Cuban Revolution. Rodríguez Monegal described himself as a socialist who drew cautionary lessons about Communism from the history of the Spanish Civil War. By the late 1960s he was not so sure that Cuba deserved uncritical support, and he imagined a magazine that would publish dialogue among different political views, including those of Cubans. He planned to call the magazine *Diálogos,* but a Mexican magazine was already using that name, so Rodríguez Monegal's project was christened *Mundo Nuevo.*[50]

Because the Ford Foundation financed *Mundo Nuevo* for most of its existence, Rodríguez Monegal—defensive about his involvement with the CCF—would later say that the Ford Foundation had wanted a new magazine and selected him to edit it. (Even though he had never driven a car, he joked, he thought this one of Ford's "better ideas.") But this was a fiction: he was selected not by the Ford Foundation but by the CIA's John Hunt, who had for years been casting about for someone who could direct a suitable replacement for *Cuadernos*. Benito Milla, the Uruguayan publisher, had recommended Rodríguez Monegal, and he had been Hunt's top candidate to lead a new magazine as early as 1964, well within the CIA era of the CCF. As he prepared to publish the magazine, Rodríguez Monegal would soon find himself repeating endlessly that *Mundo Nuevo* was "linked to the Congress but not dependent on it." When the first issue of *Mundo Nuevo* was released in July 1966, the CCF was still financed primarily with CIA money; the Ford Foundation took over completely only that November. From that point forward, Rodríguez Monegal negotiated a separate line of funding from the Ford Foundation for *Mundo Nuevo* and always had full editorial control over the magazine.[51]

As he prepared to launch the review, Rodríguez Monegal was attempting to engineer a kind of thaw in the Cold War in Latin American letters. In June 1966 International PEN met in New York City for its first major gathering since the 1965 meeting in Yugoslavia where CCF efforts had helped elect Arthur Miller to head the organization. Like Rodríguez Monegal, Miller also wanted to establish a calming tone, ratcheting back the rhetoric of writers' responsibility to political commitment. Preconference work ensured that Communist writers, like Pablo Neruda and even some Soviet authors, had no visa troubles in applying to come to the United States and were able to attend and participate in a generally cordial exchange of views. Miller insisted that none of the writers need be an apologist for the culture or political system in which he or she worked; the point, he said when conversation got heated, was to restore "diversity" within PEN.[52]

Rodríguez Monegal did analogous work with the Latin American writers, chairing a panel at the meeting to discuss the specific problems of the writer in that region. The intellectual diversity of the panel was more important than anything that was said: it included Pablo Neruda, Mario Vargas Llosa, Carlos Fuentes, Nicanor Parra, and Victoria Ocampo. Miller and Rodríguez Monegal both saw the conference as a means of combating "literary McCarthyism" and hoped that it would lead to the end of the Cold War in culture. Fuentes, writing about the event, called Rodríguez Monegal a "cultural U Thant," referring to the secretary general of the United Nations, for his diplomatic efforts. It proved to be a moment of visibility and solidarity for the Latin American writers who attended, establishing important networks that defined the emerging boom in Latin American literature.[53]

Inge Morath, Arthur Miller, and Pablo Neruda at a bookstore in New York City during Neruda's visit to the PEN Conference in 1966. Miller and Emir Rodríguez Monegal sought to engineer a thaw in the Cold War in Latin American letters at the conference, but Cuban writers criticized Neruda for his participation. Photo courtesy Fundación Pablo Neruda.

But if Rodríguez Monegal wanted a magazine of dialogue, he had the past and present of his sponsoring organization to contend with. In mid-1966 the CIA-CCF relationship was not yet widely known, but the CCF's dependence on the U.S. government was widely suspected. Other episodes that had nothing to do with the CCF, like Project Camelot, signaled that interests of state had dangerously compromised intellectual efforts. For radical critics, *Mundo Nuevo* was simply another part of a broader "Yankee cultural offensive."

The group that had the most to lose from the potential success of *Mundo Nuevo* was Casa de las Américas. In 1964 Haydée Santamaría, the head of Casa de las Américas, was hearing complaints about the relatively apolitical nature of the editors of the literary review that bore its name. *Casa*, which everyone understood operated proudly with a subsidy from the Cuban government, had on two occasions published politically inopportune content and had been punished for it. The last offense came in 1965, when the review invited beat poet Allen Ginsberg to be part of its prize jury and published a homoerotic poem that seemed to challenge the government's official persecution of homosexuality during that period. (Ginsberg, who had been a member of the Fair Play for Cuba Committee in the United States, was forced to leave Cuba after describing over the radio an erotic dream he had about Che Guevara.) *Casa*'s old editors were dismissed and were replaced by Roberto Fernández Retamar, a poet who transformed *Casa* into a vibrant brief for the unity of Cuban nationalism, intellectual responsibility, and the world revolution. In the new era, the five-pointed star of the Cuban flag became a recurring graphic motif. Representing revolutionary thought and practice was the goal of the new *Casa de las Américas,* and the proper metaphor for understanding culture, in Fernández Retamar's mind, was that of revolutionary struggle.[54]

At the moment at which one iteration of *Casa de las Américas* ended, to be replaced by a more hermetically sealed one, the CCF was closing down its limited *Cuadernos* and launching the more expansive *Mundo Nuevo*. Rodríguez Monegal was well to the left of any of the editors of *Cuadernos;* he was critical of Cuban Communism but not rabidly anti-Castro. His view of the responsibility of the intellectual, however, leaned not toward the political commitment of Sartre but rather toward the perpetual rebellion of Camus. "A writer's actions are words," Fuentes and Rodríguez Monegal agreed in the interview that established *Mundo Nuevo*'s tone. "The essential function of the writer," Rodríguez Monegal argued, "is to call into question the world [as it exists] through the use of words . . . For that reason McCarthyists of the Right and Left want to stop us from talking." For Rodríguez Monegal and Fuentes, the writer's commitment was revolutionary because it called into question existing relations of power, not because it submitted to revolutionary discipline. The writer's freedom consisted, in Fuentes's words, in "maintaining some room for heresy."[55]

The problem raised by that position was, inevitably, that of the writer's relationship to the government in Cuba: given its punitive treatment of hostile intellectuals and political opponents, did it count among the "McCarthyists of the Left"? Since the victory of the Cuban Revolution, a friendly attitude toward it had practically defined the responsibility of the left-wing Latin American writer-intellectual. But within Cuba, cultural policy shaded into anti-intellectualism as intellectuals were seen as potentially counterrevolutionary, bourgeois, and producers of unnecessary luxuries. If Cuba's government were cast as McCarthyist, Rodríguez Monegal would have successfully redefined what it meant to be a left-wing writer. But Fuentes, in his observation, did not yet mean to signal any break with revolutionary commitment to the Cuban cause. His permanent insurrection was still conceived as directed primarily against bourgeois society.[56]

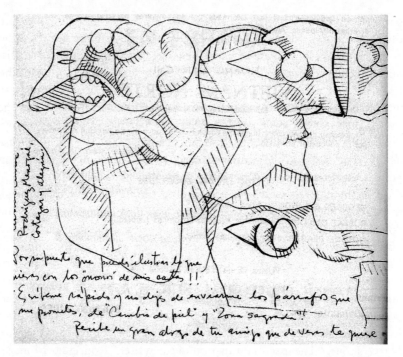

Mundo Nuevo strove to present fashionable and contemporary art and writing, portraying its artists as thoughtful, independent dissenters. Its first issue included sketches by the internationally known Mexican artist José Luis Cuevas, of the Breakaway generation. His grotesque figures were understood both as a critique of the PRI and of the socially committed painting of Mexico's Marxist muralists. The sketches were clipped from letters Cuevas sent to Emir Rodríguez Monegal and Carlos Fuentes. Reproduced by permission. © 2015 Artists Rights Society (ARS), New York / SOMAAP, Mexico City.

But the potential for the idea of the McCarthyism of the Left to be used against Cuba was latent (and indeed, Fuentes would distance himself from the Cuban government in 1971 on essentially those grounds). Cuban officials understood that any definition of the intellectual that pointed away from revolutionary commitment could undermine an important form of international support for them, and they tried to mete out discipline that would keep the Left in line. Cuban writers had refused to participate in the 1966 PEN meeting and had condemned Pablo Neruda for his visit to the heart of the empire. Before the appearance of *Mundo Nuevo*, Roberto Fernández Retamar announced that Cuban writers from his circle would "boycott" the magazine. Soon the exchange of letters between the two rival editors was given wide circulation in left-wing political magazines across the continent. In his letter to Rodríguez Monegal, Fernández Retamar argued that "because it is financed by the United States, [the CCF]'s only mission is the defense of U.S. imperial interests, not the defense of 'cultural freedom.' To achieve those ends, it gets collaboration from intellectuals of different shades, some of which are not necessarily hostile to our [Cuba's] causes." *Cuadernos,* Fernández Retamar asserted, had been a crudely executed work of propaganda. Other CCF magazines, such as *Encounter,* were superior in quality but aspired to the same ends. Since the orientation of CCF-affiliated magazines was clearly opposed to Cuban interests, he declared, Cuban intellectuals would neither contribute to *Mundo Nuevo* nor collaborate with it. Although this might appear to deny Cuban writers the chance to defend their perspectives in the short term, he thought it the right policy for the long term:

> It is possible (it is almost certain) that in the first numbers, with the goal of attracting high-quality collaborators, you will achieve the "freedom of choice and orientation" that you write to me about . . . but it is equally certain that ultimately, the orientation will escape from your hands, following the example of *Cuadernos.* And the magazine will end up adopting (no doubt more skillfully and less negatively) positions contrary to the interests of our peoples. Or should we believe that U.S. imperialism . . . had suddenly entered into disinterested patronage of the purest work of the mind . . . and that they will send you to Paris to give to Latin America the magazine that its literature requires? No one could seriously propose that these fantasies be taken for reality.

In the judgment of many, Rodríguez Monegal did wrangle the magazine that Latin American literature "required," for a time, from the complex circumstances that gave him his opportunity. But as a description of what would happen to *Mundo Nuevo,* Fernández Retamar's predictions proved almost perfectly prescient.[57]

In his reply, Rodríguez Monegal foregrounded the details over which Fernández Retamar had blundered. The U.S. State Department did not finance the CCF, as Fernández Retamar had alleged, and in any case, Rodríguez Monegal argued, the lessons of *Cuadernos* had been learned. The crude anti-Communism found in its pages was no longer necessary. He insisted that those who had contributed to the CCF had always been independent of the politics of the United States. Recently, for example, CCF affiliates had criticized the military occupation of the Dominican Republic that had taken place that spring:

> When the [U.S. military] intervention in Santo Domingo occurred [in 1965], the Congress demonstrated publicly against the State Department. Don Sal-

vador de Madariaga published an open letter in the *New York Times* in which
he protested the intervention; Luis Mercier, who was then in charge of Latin
American affairs, wrote an article against it; and even the departed *Cuadernos* published a pamphlet by Theodore Draper that contains some of the
most virulent criticism of the intervention that I have ever read . . . I ask myself if this is how an organization that depends on the State Department
would behave.

This much was true—the U.S. invasion blocked the return to power of a
member of the anti-Communist Left and was therefore deplored by the
social democrats in the CCF and similar organizations. But Fernández
Retamar maintained that writers like Madariaga and Draper were "against
our revolution [in Cuba]." Rodríguez Monegal protested in turn that "I
will not accept the role that is being eagerly designed for me as the enemy
of Cuba and of Cuban writers. I will continue to believe in the virtues of
dialogue." Yet in the same issue as Rodríguez Monegal's final letter, in
late April 1966, *Marcha* published the translation of a *New York Times*
investigation of the CIA that named *Encounter* and the CCF as "anti-
Communist but liberal organizations of intellectuals" that the CIA had
sponsored. Probably few *Marcha* readers would have concluded that Rodríguez Monegal understood the organization for which he worked better
than Fernández Retamar did.[58]

After the *New York Times* published its exposé, people associated with
the CCF wrote in to protest that their organization had been intellectually independent, but no one disputed the charge that it had received
funding sourced to the CIA. These nondenial denials prompted concern
among some who had worked with the CCF in the past that there might
be truth in what the *Times* had reported. Mercier Vega responded to such
worries by declaring that neither he nor they had anything to hide. He
realized, however, that the issue was not whether he felt himself to be independent, but whether he could convince others that the CCF was. Because the *Times* article was being widely translated and republished by
Latin American newspapers and magazines, the scandal was unlikely to
burn out quickly.

At the end of May, Héctor Murena in Argentina wrote to Mercier that
"all of the leftist individuals that I was getting have gone away as if by
magic . . . I confess to you that I spent a few days very worried, because
of the possibility that all of us, as innocents (including you and Hunt) had
been serving the CIA, something that isn't very pleasant in spite of all the
rationales one can use to gild the pill. Now I'm inclined to think that
everything has been one big joke. Nevertheless, a thorough clarification

from the foundations whose funds we use would be welcome." In the press, CCF representatives emphasized that no one was saying that the CIA had exercised any control over what anyone had said or done. If such responses did not satisfy ILARI's critics, they seem at least to have satisfied its allies, and within a few months most of the affiliates noted no decline in participation in their activities.[59]

Mundo Nuevo, too, survived the first round of revelations. Rodríguez Monegal had substantial personal credibility, and many of his friends and acquaintances found it difficult to decide whether to participate in the new magazine. This was especially true for the many Latin American writers then residing in Paris, where *Mundo Nuevo* was to be edited. Jean Franco has described the way in which *Cuadernos* differed from *Mundo Nuevo* as the difference between the ethos of "universality" of the former and the "cosmopolitanism" of the latter. *Mundo Nuevo* was, in its first era, a participant in a cultural vanguard in a way that *Cuadernos* never was. Affiliated writers like Borges, Cabrera Infante, and Fuentes all had aesthetic projects that were far more innovative than the writers associated with the Latin American branch of the CCF in the 1950s. But the difference also registered in the way its writers were living. If "universality" had meant that Latin American writers hoped to be recognized alongside their European peers, *Mundo Nuevo*'s "cosmopolitanism" offered the appealing possibility that Latin American writers would actually live in Europe. As many took up residence in Paris or Barcelona, Rodríguez Monegal slyly boasted that Paris had become the cultural capital of Latin America. He used the *Mundo Nuevo* expense account to host events and dinners, trying to act as the coordinator of the new cultural energy.[60]

But the claim advanced at the PEN meeting in New York—that the Cultural Cold War was at its end—was mistaken. The Cold War's awesome capacity to politicize every aspect of life instead turned precisely that claim into yet another battle in the Cultural Cold War. Pablo Neruda, who was the subject of considerable press attention and public adulation during his visit to New York for the conference, not least because of his criticism of the U.S. war in Vietnam, soon found himself the target of a campaign by Cuban writers. In a complaint drafted by Roberto Fernández Retamar and other members of the *Casa* group, Neruda was condemned for his visit to the United States and for accepting an award from the president of Peru. "We must proclaim an alert on this imperialist penetration into the field of culture," said the letter, "against the publications financed by [the] CIA, against the conversation of our writers into trained parlour monkeys and Yankee sycophants." Some signatures were added to the complaint without the alleged signers' knowledge; others, worried about the political implications of having their names omitted, rushed to add them. Neruda was deeply hurt by the Cuban attack, which he interpreted as a concealed attack by Castro on his Chilean Communist Party's preference for an electoral approach to politics rather than the Cuban insurrectionary route. He never forgave Fernández Retamar and would never again travel to the island.[61]

When *Mundo Nuevo*'s first issue appeared, Neruda's friend Jorge Edwards wrote to him from Paris to say that it had been released to neither "shame nor glory, with the necessary dose of anti-Communism to justify the collaboration of North American foundations, and, according to rumor, the CIA." This was not so much a problem for Neruda, who had seen the controversy and still sent Rodríguez Monegal poems for one of the first issues of the new review, but the Cuban letter wounded him, and he began to become concerned that appearing in *Mundo Nuevo* would seem to confirm him as an outsider on the literary left. He wrote to Edwards in Paris, asking him to rush to Rodríguez Monegal and retrieve the verses he had provided for publication. But, he added, "The [attacks] are part of the result of the Cult [of Fidel]." Like an out-of-favor writer in the Stalinist system he had once defended, Neruda found that his attempt at engagement was being treated as heresy and so tried to withdraw. A few of his poems, however, appeared in the fourth issue of *Mundo Nuevo*. Neruda could never have participated in *Cuadernos;* only a few years earlier the CCF had been trying to undermine his candidacy for the Nobel Prize.[62]

In the face of the "Yankee cultural offensive" of *Mundo Nuevo*, Fernández Retamar sent around an appeal to writers throughout the world to fill out a survey. "There is no lack of new *collaborationists* [with the Yankee offensive]," he wrote, "and these people must be unmasked." Fernández Retamar's only question was, "What do you think that the attitude of Latin American intellectuals should be in view of the growing campaign of penetration and division that, in the cultural domain as well, the United States is carrying out in our continent?" Even María Rosa Oliver worried that the letter implied an attempt by Cuba to set up a "cultural Vatican" that would have the power to determine who and what counted as a member of the authentic and appropriate Left.[63]

In spite of the controversy that surrounded its origins, *Mundo Nuevo* was in many ways an unassailable success. The introductory note in the first issue explained that "the quality of the Latin American artist and writer has not been recognized to the degree that it deserves. For that reason it seems today not only opportune, but necessary, to undertake to recognize, in a truly international journal, the most creative work that Latin America has to give to the world." Within a few short years the boom in Latin American literature was a recognized phenomenon; writers signed important international book contracts and began to sell hundreds of thousands of copies of their works around the globe. Scarcely fifteen years earlier, even the continent's best writers rarely did better than to sell a few hundred copies of their works, sometimes passed around among small circles of friends. In very short order, the goals of *Mundo Nuevo*, were, remarkably, achieved.[64]

Although the boom was under way by the time *Mundo Nuevo* published its first issue, the magazine supported the phenomenon. Many of the magazine's featured writers—none of whom would have contributed to a magazine like *Cuadernos*—became the great successes of their generation. And *Mundo Nuevo* helped ensure that the boom would be remembered for its stylistic and aesthetic inventiveness as well as its leftist political commitment. (Some authors of the boom, like Gabriel García Márquez and Julio Cortázar, intended to be both leftist and aesthetically inventive.) But although *Mundo Nuevo*'s most remarkable features were literary, it did run some political essays, such as a critical assessment of intellectuals involved in the war in Vietnam that appeared in its second number. Rodríguez Monegal wrote to a friend that "the political commentary about Vietnam, to be completely frank with you, reflects a necessarily critical attitude in a magazine that has been accused of maintaining connections with the CIA." The response of Max Aub, a Spanish writer who maintained an independent position in the Cold War and thought that minimizing the issues of Cuba and Vietnam meant that *Mundo Nuevo* should rename itself *The Ostrich,* suggests that Rodríguez Monegal had a point.[65]

But privately, Rodríguez Monegal cared less about CIA involvement than he might have. Initially, he responded to the revelations by arguing that they showed only that money had been passed through dummy foundations to the CCF; he did not think that this meant that the CCF had ever known that it was receiving money from the CIA. He wrongly thought that all the money that had funded *Mundo Nuevo* came from the Ford Foundation, and he insisted that the articles critical of U.S. policy that appeared in *Mundo Nuevo* demonstrated its independence. "We have no interest in defending the Congress publicly or privately," he wrote to a friend, "much less the CIA whose intentions are very difficult to champion." But in a bit of private bravado, he later wrote: "My position is that if the CIA is surreptitiously paying for *Mundo Nuevo,* blessed be the CIA because this magazine does not play their game: it reflects an authentically Latin American position . . . I don't see why we, who are making a truly independent magazine, have to carry around the skeletons of our inglorious ancestors." But he understood that others would have to be convinced that what he thought was "ancient history" actually had little or no bearing on the present.[66]

In fact, the history of the CCF could not be avoided. In March 1967 a San Francisco–based journal of the New Left titled *Ramparts* published an account of the CIA's covert relationship with the National Student Association. Its reporter added a level of detail that the articles in the *New York Times* the previous year had never revealed. Through foundation records, *Ramparts* traced contributions to their proxy foundations (such as the Farfield Foundation) and finally to their intended recipients, including the CCF. The "*Ramparts* flap" was, in the words of one intelligence historian, "one of the worst operational catastrophes in CIA history." Dozens of programs had to be dismantled almost immediately. President Johnson appointed a committee that recommended that covert funding to private groups be eliminated; if such organizations still wanted government funding, it should be given to them openly. Cord Meyer, who had been responsible for liaison and support of the "non-Communist Left" programs since 1954, later wrote that the CIA carried out this "dismantling" with considerable regret, aware that powerful Communist-controlled fronts still operated, and that they had no such restrictions on their behavior. Tom Braden, who had overseen the programs before 1954, published an article in May titled "I'm Glad the CIA Is 'Immoral,' " defending the CIA's actions as a necessary part of the Cold War and stating that more licit funding had been impossible because, he wrote, "the idea that [the U.S.] Congress would have approved many of our projects was almost as likely as the John Birch Society's approving Medicare." Although his provocative remarks probably did little to convince skeptics, they did at least put to rest any notion that the journalists might have had the basics of the story wrong.[67]

The Ford-financed CCF had made Latin America its major priority. At the beginning of the 1950s CCF activity in the region was minimal. In 1966 the Latin American budget made up the single largest institutional cost to the CCF, receiving about 40 percent of its overall budget allocation. The CCF had remade itself over the course of the 1960s. It had worked to engage both writers and social scientists with a common and related logic. To the social scientists, it had tried to create an environment in which social problems could be studied within a framework that it considered rational. To the writers, it had tried to send the message that, in the words of Emir Rodríguez Monegal at PEN, it is "difficult for writers to be independent spirits," but that there was no other choice.[68]

Having been taken in, Rodríguez Monegal was in a difficult position and tried to twist the scandal to bolster his reputation. "As hurtful as they are," he wrote, "these [CIA] revelations do nothing except confirm something obvious: the difficulty of winning and keeping freedom. The condition of the independent intellectual in the modern world is a condition of risk and poverty . . . The CIA, or other corruptors from other factions, can pay independent intellectuals without them knowing. What they cannot do is buy them." He had proved by his own example his thesis that maintaining one's status as an independent critic and an outside thinker was difficult work. But he was not convinced that the very idea of the intellectual as an "independent critic" was useful to the United States in the Cold War context, because adopting it transformed the stance of the politically committed radical intellectual from one of responsibility to one of irresponsibility.[69]

Privately, however, he decided to work to end his affiliation with ILARI. "In the present context of literary life in Latin America (a context which continues to deteriorate owing to guerrillas more or less encouraged by Cuba, military dictators congenial to the Pentagon, the big stick of Mr. Johnson in the Caribbean, and the war in Vietnam)," he wrote, "it is quite impossible to envision the continuation of a revue that is at the same time 'independent' and published under the patronage, even indirect, of the International Association for Cultural Freedom." *Marcha* covered the controversy, securing exclusive rights to the Spanish translation of the articles in *Ramparts* that definitively established the CIA-CCF relationship. It published, as did other major publications, an account by Mario Vargas Llosa of the history of the CCF and its downfall: "The 'cultural empire' [the CCF] built with such painstaking cleverness, at such expense, has collapsed like a house of cards, and the pity is that, among its smoking ruins lie, broken, dirtied, guilty and innocent, those who acted in good faith and those who did so in bad faith, those who believed that they were there to fight for freedom and those who solely were interested in picking up their pay." Vargas Llosa was concerned that the CIA's intervention might have distorted the literary world in which he moved. He now wondered whether, for example, the support that the CCF's Melvin Lasky had offered Soviet dissident author Aleksandr Solzhenitsyn had been earned on the basis of literary merit or for the political gain that the United States might get from promoting his work. In his assessment Vargas Llosa wrote almost exclusively of the scandal in the European context—he too lived in Paris—making just a single mention of *Cuadernos,* and then only to note how little it had accomplished.[70]

The consequence of the CIA revelations, then, was to undermine the entire project that the CCF had been engaged in over the 1960s. Its attempts at outreach and engagement were, inescapably, a part of empire. The CCF had worked to become more liberal in the 1960s and had in some ways succeeded. It demonstrated the manner in which sets of ideas, from modernization theory to the definition of the intellectual as an independent critic, were intended to play their roles in the Cold War. But its lasting legacy, through its connection to the CIA, had less to do with any particular programmatic success than with making anti-imperialist discourse credible. Revelations of CIA involvement in a variety of cultural and civil society organizations combined to give the intelligence agency a reputation for sinister efficacy, but they also showed that the agency could not control its public reputation or keep its programs secret. The experience of the CCF reveals the limits of CIA power even within its organization: as elsewhere, it was neither helpless nor powerful enough to alter fundamental trends. Anti-Communism had its own, often local, logic. John Hunt's attempt to liberalize the CCF in Brazil after the coup failed. Mexican intellectuals wanted different things from the CCF than what it offered, and Keith Botsford's most lasting legacies there were to deliver a few years' salary for Juan Rulfo and to inspire, both intentionally and by accident, some of Jorge Ibargüengoitia's finest writing. Its best candidate, Jorge Luis Borges, never won the Nobel Prize. Meanwhile it published a magazine, *Cuadernos,* that lost friends and failed to influence people. *Mundo Nuevo* arrived in 1966 and finally achieved the openness that the CCF had been seeking, just in time to be the most discredited by the CIA revelations. The CCF was far more complex than a simple puppet of U.S. empire, but it could not escape the consequences of affiliation with its secret patron. The CCF remained for years a symbol of the strength and power of U.S. cultural imperialism. If the facts surrounding it had been shrouded in less secrecy, they might also have pointed toward its weaknesses and contradictions.

CHAPTER SEVEN

Disenchantment and the End of the Cultural Cold War

In 1967 the Peruvian novelist Mario Vargas Llosa was awarded the Rómulo Gallegos Literary Prize, given by the Venezuelan government, in recognition of his novel *The Green House*. At the time, Vargas Llosa was a radical socialist and a member of the board of directors of Casa de las Américas, convinced of the hopeless corruption of Latin American politics outside Cuba. Venezuela's head of state, meanwhile, was a member of the center-left Acción Democrática party, which had good relations with the United States. Venezuela's government had been fighting a leftist guerrilla insurgency supported by Cuba and had suspended constitutional guarantees. Within Vargas Llosa's radical circles, the country was considered a murderous puppet of North American imperialism. Casa's Haydée Santamaría wrote that its president represented "murder, repression, [and] treason to our people." Notified of his award and unsure whether he should accept, Vargas Llosa asked the board of Casa for guidance. It recommended that he accept the prize but publicly donate the prize money to Che Guevara.[1]

"Literature is fire," Vargas Llosa declared in his acceptance speech, "it means nonconformism and rebellion . . . The raison d'être of the writer is protest, contradiction, and criticism." The work of the writer, he said, was a form of "permanent insurrection." Capitalist society was beyond redemption; only by following the Cuban model, Vargas Llosa announced, could Latin America free itself from its current oppressors. He made his speech on 2 October; seven days later Che Guevara was killed by the Bolivian army with the assistance of the CIA, ending his doomed effort to foment continental revolution.[2]

This moment epitomized the Cultural Cold War in Latin America at its height in the late 1960s. The period was marked by an unprecedented degree of polarization, in which nearly all ideas were understood relative to their position in the war of ideologies. "The atmosphere of guerrilla warfare . . . will not be limited to the jungles and mountains of Latin America but is now being extended to include literary life," lamented Emir Rodríguez Monegal after he was assaulted by some Far Left students during a trip to Chile. But Vargas Llosa spoke for the many radicalized writers and intellectuals of that decade who were inspired by Cuba and disgusted with liberal reform. The moment of the 1960s produced the boom in Latin American literature, and thus the new style of "Latin American intellectual," of which Vargas Llosa was an archetypal example—a man (and almost all were men) who wrote a literature that revealed the corruption of local politics and of capitalism, were lauded with international prizes, and lived as easily in Europe as in the Americas.[3]

If one thing can be said to characterize the intellectual moment of the 1960s, it is perhaps how close many felt to realizing their utopian visions. Literature professor Diana Sorensen argues that the era featured an intensity of belief and feeling, "framed by the twin rhythms of euphoria and despair." Those who wanted to replicate Cuba and create many Vietnams across the region had their version of utopia. But although the moderates who opposed them thought of themselves as antiutopian, in a way their own utopia—in which the United States acted in good faith as a friend to regional democracy, and in which technocratic leadership would improve living conditions without requiring popular mobilization—was just as implausible. The great hope of the left-wing intellectual in the twentieth century had been the construction of a humane socialism. As the institutions of the Cultural Cold War fell, one by one, they represented the loss of possibility and pathways to it. Even moments of triumph contained warnings of the fragility of the utopias they meant to construct. When Vargas Llosa had queried the board of Casa about how to respond to the offer of the Gallegos prize, he had been assured that if he donated the prize money to Che Guevara, he would be secretly reimbursed by the Cuban government. It was an offer he declined, but one he would later point to as a key moment in his eventual disillusionment with the Left. Max Weber had written of the "disenchantment of the world" that came when modern science displaced religious feeling as an explanation for natural phenomena. As the utopias of the 1960s fell away in the 1970s and beyond, the Cultural Cold War underwent a disenchantment of the word. Intellectuals lost faith in the states that had inspired them. And states would never consider intellectuals so powerful, or so valuable, again.[4]

Given the shock of the CIA revelations, the subsequent decline of the Congress for Cultural Freedom (CCF) was surprisingly gradual. Perhaps unexpectedly, given that he was widely considered to be among the CCF employees most likely to be CIA agents, Keith Botsford was among the most offended. In the initial wake of the disclosures, many CCF affiliates argued that the CIA had not interfered with CCF activity and had only financed it at a distance. Even when it was acknowledged that Michael Josselson had been a CIA agent from the beginning, private debate continued among its members about the degree to which the CCF had operated independently. In May 1967, for example, Daniel Bell wrote to Keith Botsford, arguing that he had of course heard about government financial involvement for years but had not pried, trusting his friends' integrity and that measures would be taken to reduce any secret dependency over time.[5]

But the CIA's influence had not been insignificant. Botsford countered Bell with a long letter, outlining his personal anguish over whether he should go public with evidence that suggested the CIA had in fact played the CCF to conform to the needs of the intelligence agency and to the U.S. national interest more broadly. He admitted that it was difficult to draw distinctions between Josselson's private behavior and his behavior in his capacity as a CIA employee. But he cited his work with PEN and his disagreements with Josselson over *Cuadernos* as evidence that, at the very least, Josselson's CIA affiliation had shaped the CCF's work more than was being conceded publicly:

> Take the parlous case of *Cuadernos*, against whose direction I fought for three arduous years. Arciniegas was a fink. That much was clear. His magazine would do nothing in |Latin America|, that much was also clear. No one read it, that was clear. It was a pile of shit, that was clear. I am sure that John [Hunt] agreed—so John is let out. Most of the Congress agreed. I sat in a meeting at which everyone condemned the poor bloody mag outright . . . It lasted because Mike [Josselson] insisted that it would last. I have that on paper. Now, what were the alternatives? Let it die? Have another? Open up *Cuadernos* to new contributors? Well, the last was covered because Mike had put in Arciniegas, and Arciniegas wanted no one but his own kind of Latin American. Let it die? That would have implied failure of an operation—unthinkable to Mike. (Let me be clear: that CUADERNOS was not ENCOUNTER or MONAT: it was a fink magazine, admittedly. Its distributors in [Latin America] were Cuban exiles; its correspondents belonged to the paralytic wing of the "Liberal" reaction.) Start a new one? There were grave risks involved. If *you* handled the CIA's money, which would be used to start it, what would you do?

Botsford said that he could think of countless examples of phone calls in which Josselson played a role in shaping the content of *Encounter*. That Botsford had "won" most of his disputes with Josselson over a period of years, he argued, did not prove that pressure had not existed. "Ideas freely arrived at are fine things," he wrote, but he pointed out that Josselson's influence came from his constant, diligent work behind the scenes: "In short, there is no substitute for administrative efficiency." Botsford was torn but could not forgive Josselson his years of lies. In another letter to a colleague, he wrote: "It is simply not true that each member of the Congress acted in total freedom. Josselson disposed of us all." What Botsford could not countenance was the thought that John Hunt, whom he had known for some seventeen years—and who opposed Josselson on many questions of strategy—was capable of, as he put it, "lying to me with such cold consistency." On that matter he was mistaken.[6]

When the *Ramparts* story broke, Luis Mercier Vega wrote to his colleagues that the information appeared to be "serious and well founded." He assured his friends that what had been organized and published in Latin America had nothing to do with U.S. foreign policy or the CIA, and that he would do all he could to save the Instituto Latinoamericano de Relaciones Internacionales (ILARI). Horacio Daniel Rodríguez in Buenos Aires wrote to Mercier Vega to explain the uproar and confusion that the news had created. More than forty people were pressing him for a "clarification," and one contributor to a CCF magazine of sociology asked that his submission be postponed until the nature of ILARI could be clarified. Others requested detailed financial information from Mercier, who in turn pressed Hunt to explain (accurate) media reports that the CIA was passing money through the Hoblitzelle Foundation. Hunt, as one of the CIA men inside the CCF, told Mercier less than he knew; he explained that he would have to "go back into our records" and that "at no time did the Hoblitzelle Foundation do anything other than simply respond affirmatively or negatively as the case might be to our request for funds." In spite of his work in Paris, the fact that Hunt answered him evasively suggests that Mercier Vega may have been among those who worked for the CCF without direct knowledge of its relationship to the CIA. The clearest expression of Mercier Vega's views comes in a letter he wrote to Horacio Daniel Rodríguez at the beginning of March:

> I find myself in a delicate position. On the one hand, the information published in the United States seems this time to correspond to some kind of reality. Departments of the CIA have supplied foundations, who in turn subsidized activities that were liberal, democratic, and sometimes directed against the politics of the United States. That's why we see [Barry] Goldwater attacking those methods and Robert Kennedy defending them . . . We are entering there a complex, contradictory world unknown to me. On the other

hand, I remain convinced that what we did, what we are doing and what we plan to do has nothing to do, directly or indirectly, with the—or one of the— policies of the CIA. In other words I can't stake my life on the origin of each dollar we've spent in Latin America, but I can on that each dollar was spent for activities determined according to the needs of Latin America.

Mercier apparently continued to believe that the CCF had unknowingly received money from the CIA, and that there was no need to apologize for its work.[7]

But the scandal was tearing the CCF apart. In Uruguay, Benito Milla reported that although people still wanted to display their art in the CCF's gallery space, no one wanted to be the first to do so after the scandal. In Chile, the Communist paper *El Siglo* launched a campaign against the personalities at the head of the CCF operation there, and a professor leading one of the work groups worried that the news would negatively affect his work among the university community. In Mexico, Rodrigo García Treviño, showing why he had been let go some years earlier, wrote that "to fight against red totalitarianism, I would accept the help of Satan himself." In Colombia and Venezuela, Germán Arciniegas made public his experience trying to obtain future funding for *Cuadernos,* creating another unsettling round of questions.[8]

Over the summer Michael Josselson was forced to admit that the CCF had received money from the CIA, and that he had been responsible for maintaining that relationship. Josselson resigned his position, and Hunt soon did the same. After Hunt left, he sent one letter to Mercier Vega, along with his latest novel, expressing feelings of nostalgia for "all of the correspondence and all the maneuvering and the rest of it which occupied us during those years when we were making the changes in Latin America." When Mercier Vega received that letter, he was dealing with an ever-shrinking budget, and he replied with a touch of pique: "At ILARI, everything is working and developing. But you can easily imagine that, besides the continual problems that come up all of the time, the most important one remains the mediocrity of our financial means that stop us from occupying the space that should come back to us. But that is one situation that you understand well." If Mercier was coming to understand that his cherished projects had been made possible only by the support of the CIA, he never gave any other indication of this.[9]

In the summer of 1967 the CCF sought to distance itself from its past by changing its name to the International Association for Cultural Freedom (IACF). Shepard Stone, a former Ford Foundation employee who had been instrumental in securing the Ford bailout for the CCF, became its new president. Mercier Vega's ILARI petitioned for and received inclusion within the IACF umbrella, which meant that its budget was provided by the IACF. The Ford Foundation's grant, though politically convenient, contained a poison pill: in an attempt to goad IACF operations into self-sufficiency, the amount of the foundation's subsidy decreased every year. This placed the IACF (and, consequently, ILARI) in a perpetual budget crisis, and only the most important programs were retained. Even as affiliates began to report that activities were returning to normal after the CIA disclosures, budgetary constraints put an end to the Latin American press service of the CCF and eliminated nearly all funding to the perennially embattled Mexican representative. With the reduction of the Colombian committee to a single correspondent, and expansion in Bolivia, ILARI in 1967 was left with functioning centers in Rio de Janeiro, Montevideo, Asunción, Buenos Aires, Santiago de Chile, Lima, and La Paz.[10]

The most valuable commodity that ILARI had was *Mundo Nuevo,* and although the CIA scandal did not destroy the magazine immediately, it took its toll in indirect ways. Ironically, its demise came about in part because of conflict between Emir Rodríguez Monegal and Luis Mercier Vega, two of the people associated with the CCF in Latin America with the least interest in defending U.S. politics and policies. Emir Rodríguez Monegal responded to the CIA revelations by seeking to sever his relationship with ILARI. Shepard Stone did not object, but Luis Mercier Vega thought that *Mundo Nuevo* provided ILARI with needed prestige and decided to intervene in the negotiations. He asked Ignacio Iglesias, a member of the Spanish Partido Obrero de Unificación Marxista in exile who had worked as editor in chief of *Cuadernos* and who also worked in that capacity for *Mundo Nuevo,* to prepare a report on the present state of Rodríguez Monegal's magazine. Mercier then sent that report on to Shepard Stone, bypassing Rodríguez Monegal. The results were surprising: *Mundo Nuevo,* for all its supposed influence and its undeniable quality, sold and circulated even fewer copies than had *Cuadernos.* Iglesias and Mercier Vega concluded that *Mundo Nuevo* was too "literary," targeting a narrow audience likely to be hostile to the CCF in any case. The magazine, they argued, needed to extricate itself from the small circle of authors who dominated its pages and work to engage with the general problems of the times. Other than Rodríguez Monegal, no one at the IACF or the Ford Foundation appreciated how important that small circle of literary names in fact was.[11]

The intervention of Mercier and Iglesias hurt Rodríguez Monegal a great deal when he learned of it, and he announced his intention to resign a few months later, in March 1968. Publicly, he stated that the reason was that the Ford Foundation had recommended that a magazine for Latin America should be published in Latin America, while he continued to believe that Paris was the right home for *Mundo Nuevo*. He denied rumors that he was being thrown out for being a "leftist," or that anyone with ILARI had ever interfered with the magazine. Privately, he wrote that "the problem can be reduced to this: it was no longer possible for me to continue making the magazine as we had planned so long ago." On its own, the Ford Foundation's desire to move the magazine might not have pushed him to leave. He felt, however, that "it was not going to be possible to make the move with sufficient calm and on a sufficiently solid base," and the power struggles within ILARI contributed to this.[12]

But the second generation of *Mundo Nuevo* made no impression. The responsibility for the magazine was turned over to Horacio Daniel Rodríguez in Buenos Aires. Rodríguez, the former editor of a small CCF publication titled *Informes de China,* coordinated a team of representatives responsible for obtaining geographically diverse submissions. In order to avoid the problems of censorship it would encounter in Argentina, the magazine continued to be printed in Paris. Since Mercier Vega and Rodríguez thought that the problem with Rodríguez Monegal's *Mundo Nuevo* was that it had become too narrow, they sought to make the new *Mundo Nuevo* a magazine that once again dealt with aspects of sociology and political economy. But Daniel Cosío Villegas, Mexico's liberal historian who had joined the board of directors of the IACF, thought that the new turn was a disaster. When Rodríguez solicited his opinion on the problems of the old magazine, Cosío Villegas was left with the impression that he was an "ignorant, inexperienced youngster" whose appointment was "most unfortunate . . . [He] cannot compare by any standard with Rodríguez Monegal." Shepard Stone met repeatedly with Horacio Daniel Rodríguez, concerned that he did not know how to put together the sort of magazine that the Ford Foundation wanted, and that he harbored a personal ambition to become *Mundo Nuevo*'s sole editor. Then, during one of their meetings, Stone said plainly: "You understand that this has to be a magazine of the Left, that's what we've decided. I don't know if you will know how to make a magazine of the Left." Horacio Daniel Rodríguez burst out laughing because, he wrote, "there was no possibility of a rational response to such stupidity." Rodríguez kept the job, however, and explained to his readers that the new *Mundo Nuevo* "will be a magazine of themes more than of [individual] authors." That was what it had to be, for the famous authors who had contributed to it under Rodríguez

Monegal abandoned it in droves and never contributed to it again. Emir Rodríguez Monegal, bitter but no doubt sincere, thought the new *Mundo Nuevo* "a blunder that not even its proofreaders will read."[13]

Rodríguez Monegal was right: his era of *Mundo Nuevo* had managed to be, however briefly, the cosmopolitan voice of the boom in Latin American letters. The second era of *Mundo Nuevo* had few readers and fewer consequences. Rodríguez Monegal had indeed relied on a small circle of friends and acquaintances to find contributors to his magazine, but it proved a remarkably propitious group of friends. And if the CCF had made that possible, it also brought it to an end.

When the CIA revelations had necessitated a public response in 1967, Rodríguez Monegal's essay intimated that independent intellectual "sharp-shooters" like himself had been hired into CIA projects specifically so that they would subsequently be discredited. This was a fantasy, and perhaps he did not even believe it himself, but on the consequences he was not far wrong. Because of the timing of the CIA revelations and his visibility in launching and defending his magazine, Rodríguez Monegal's reputation would suffer more because of his affiliation with the CCF than anyone else's. The engaged, open debate with Cuba he had sought could not and would not occur.

Rodríguez Monegal had been trapped. On the one hand, his idea of the role of the independent intellectual had made him a good choice when the CCF had been looking for a way to reach out to the Left in a way that still demonstrated the intransigence of Cuba's official cultural institutions. But his experience also showed the near impossibility of having a project with democratic socialist values funded by the U.S. government, or even by the Ford Foundation, over the long term. In the pages of *Mundo Nuevo*, Rodríguez Monegal had championed the cause of Juan Bosch, the Dominican writer and politician who had been part of the Democratic Left. Elected with covert CIA support, he was overthrown by the Dominican military in 1963 after only a few months in office. By 1965 his return to office was blocked by U.S. military intervention and by covert support for his opponent during the election the following year. Bosch wrote of his experience, "I have always seen that you cannot have democracy here without the U.S., but now I learn that you cannot have democracy here with the U.S." *Mundo Nuevo* was the cultural analogue to his experience: a symbol of the difficulty of building a social democratic Left that would depend on U.S. sympathy and support in the context of Cold War Latin America.[14]

Like Rodríguez Monegal, Luis Mercier Vega was not interested in defending U.S. policy or in serving as an agent. As an anarchist, Mercier Vega mistrusted state power and worried about attempts to manipulate the masses by both socialist and populist governments, but he retained his sympathy for the poor and his dislike of authoritarianism. Because the size of the Ford Foundation's grant to the IACF decreased annually, he was left defending a constantly diminishing operation. In 1969 ILARI closed operations in Chile and Uruguay and was left with only Argentina, Bolivia, Brazil, Paraguay, and Peru; Mercier Vega also created a special center in Paraguay to coordinate social science research. (On one of his many trips to Latin America in that period, the Marxist historian Eric Hobsbawm was pleased to find that he was known as the author of *Primitive Rebels* to the director of a publication whose very existence tickled him: the *Revista Paraguaya de Sociología*. He might or might not have been further amused to learn that the magazine existed only because of support from ILARI.) *Aportes,* Mercier Vega's quarterly journal, printed long, analytical articles, primarily by European and Latin American academics. His anarchism made him particularly interested in the struggle for control of the state. He saw capture of the state as the mechanism by which a secure livelihood could be obtained in Latin America, but the multiple paths to power were not equally legitimate. He saw universities—which he called the "factor[ies] that [produce] the middle class"—primarily as a means for passing privilege from one generation to the next rather than as centers of research. Similarly, he argued that the armed forces had entered into politics by forming alliances with political parties. Most distressingly for an anarchist, he found this also true of grassroots and workers' groups, which he described as being mobilized by populist governments and demagogues for demonstration effect.[15]

Mercier Vega's editorial hand at *Aportes* was light, and he was interested in projects that explored the condition of poor and marginalized populations, generally carried out by left-wing scholars. What he could not abide were ideas that he regarded as simplifying ideologies, by which he meant principally Marxism and Che Guevara's *"foco"* theory (meaning "focal point" or "ground zero") that a small group of armed guerrillas could create the conditions for revolution. In his analysis, the guerrilla enterprise, however romantic, was the provenance of disaffected middle- and upper-class youth for whom taking to the mountains was the best career choice they could imagine. His frequent insistence that the sociopolitical situation of each Latin American country be analyzed on its own terms constituted an implicit critique of Guevarist ideology. Mercier Vega intended his apparently apolitical calls for an analysis of concrete national situations to upset the slogans and clichés he observed among simple partisans of Marx or Guevara.[16]

But, equally, Mercier Vega was not at all confident that the United States was a reliable ally. He found the sloganistic analysis of the American Federation of Labor–Congress of Industrial Organizations' labor ambassador Serafino Romualdi to be as empty as that of Marxist politicians. For related reasons, he criticized the prescriptions of North American and European economists and even the technocratic modernization theory that had been part of the CCF tradition. "One would hope," he wrote, "that at least the Europeans and North Americans who are so prodigal in recipes they have not tried out would be prudent in their offer of magic solutions, even if they are afraid of being overtaken by a revolution [in Latin America]. Too much emphasis on economic indices and figures which measure economic expansion frequently leads experts and planners to forget what human suffering is. Without suspecting it, they form part of a technocratic tradition." One essay in Aportes argued explicitly against the major assumption of modernization theory that the terminal point of development would resemble the United States. "The United States is not a model" for Latin American development, the essay argued, and the most useful thing that it could do would be to stop trying to implant its bourgeois norms around the world. Aportes impartially hosted an extended debate between Aldo Solari and Orlando Fals Borda on the merits of "value-free sociology" in Latin America, which was a proxy for differences in approach between liberal and radical scholars. ILARI, which increasingly had to deal with censorship of its publications, especially in Argentina and Brazil, even sponsored an event in New York titled "The Role of the Intellectual in Authoritarian Countries" with the participation of a spectrum of thinkers from the United States and Latin America that included genuinely radical voices such as Noam Chomsky.[17]

When Aportes published its last issue in October 1972, Mercier's farewell emphasized the pride he felt in having taken the politicized centers of the past and creating groups of nonconformist intellectuals. He lashed out at the Ford Foundation for its decision not to renew support, implying without evidence that it had abandoned its liberal tradition and bowed to U.S. government pressure. ILARI had fulfilled its role, he thought, as a "sower of unease." Mercier promised to return to journalism. Shepard Stone, who had headed the IACF since 1967, left it in 1973; the IACF itself operated at a minimal level until 1977, when it closed its doors completely. Mercier, two years after leaving ILARI, founded a new magazine, Interrogations, dedicated to the exploration of contemporary anarchist thought. He edited the magazine for two years and then helped oversee its transfer to new management. In November 1977, as so many other Cold Warriors of his generation had done, he committed suicide.[18]

———————————

With the organized liberal project in disarray after the CIA revelations, Cuba's Casa de las Américas might have been in an enviable position. Indeed, the mid-1960s were heady days for Cuba. The Tricontinental Conference took place in 1966, leading to the establishment of anti-imperialist solidarity organizations in 1967. In January 1968 Havana hosted a major cultural congress, where many participants argued that revolutionary intellectual practice should be dedicated to the creation of new selves, liberated from the concepts and categories of imperialism. The recently killed Che Guevara had written of the need to develop an "ideological-cultural mechanism" that created the "New Man" under socialism but also permitted free inquiry, and many of the Cuban authors at the meeting insisted that their militancy did not require the suppression of diverse forms of art or literature in Cuba and that artistic individuality could be maintained even as they worked to end selfish individualism. "Art is not a luxury, it is a necessity," argued the Chilean painter Roberto Matta: "I expect . . . that we may discuss to what extent the triumph of our internal guerrillas will depend upon the success of our [creative] effort; and that an integral man, a poet, a new man, may become reality." At the closing session, Fidel Castro declared to cheers from the audience that Yankee imperialists were the enemies of humanity, and that "perhaps [the imperialists] will say that this [Congress] is a Vietnam in the field of culture; they will say that guer rillas have begun to appear among intellectual workers." The closing resolution declared that it was the "sacred duty of every honest intellectual to join this general movement of unrelenting struggle against the Yankee imperialists, to awaken the consciousness of the peoples to denounce and strongly condemn the Yankee crimes."[19]

But it would be harder than they hoped. Even the Third Worldist spirit of independence from major powers could not be reflected in official policy, as was seen when Castro endorsed the Soviet Union's military invasion of Czechoslovakia in 1968 to put an end to the Prague Spring. The figure who incarnated the problematic relationship between artistic freedom and revolutionary commitment was the poet Heberto Padilla. In 1968 he won Cuba's Julián del Casal Poetry Prize for his collection *Fuera del juego,* which contained poems that somewhat elliptically suggested a lack of revolutionary fellow feeling. "Cuban poets no longer dream (not even in the night)," he wrote in one; they were made to witness the horrors of the world. Prizewinning works were typically published by the

Cuban government, the only possible publisher in the country, but *Fuera del juego* was granted that treatment only after extended debate within the writers' union and the addition of a critical introduction representing the view of the authorities. It was then published but impossible to find. To the authorities, the work was "ideologically contrary to [the Cuban] Revolution." *Fuera del juego,* it was asserted, was a "defense of individualism against the needs of a society constructing the future . . . mechanically transplanting the typical skeptical attitude of a liberal intellectual under capitalism." Roberto Fernández Retamar announced in 1969 that the position of Camus, Fuentes, or Rodríguez Monegal of the "permanent insurrection" of the writer was "counterrevolutionary because the work of the intellectual within socialist society is not to criticize but to reinforce the political system."[20]

The possibility of tolerance was lessened further by the difficult years of the early 1970s. Castro announced a goal for a sugar harvest of ten million tons in 1970; a record was set. But it fell short of the desired total. Because so many other parts of the economy had been sacrificed to try to reach the ten million tons, the effort was seen as a great failure. Cuba had become more equal since the revolution, but early hopes that material abundance could be achieved in a few short years were painfully far from being realized; Cuba had not ceased to be poor. The years were a bad time for critics and even for friends. The anthropologist Oscar Lewis thought that he would find that his famous "culture of poverty," which theorized that the habits and behaviors associated with poverty were passed down from one generation to the next, did not exist in a socialist state, but he arrived with a Ford Foundation grant to carry out his study and, although initially welcomed, ended up being accused of espionage, had many of his files seized, and was expelled. The French agronomist René Dumont, who also considered himself a friend of the revolution, observed that militarization of the labor force was happening because of low productivity brought about by poor economic planning. Castro's dominant and capricious decision making alienated technicians and workers alike, and there was a deep lack of democratic control. Dumont too found himself designated as a CIA agent and an enemy of the revolution. Citizens who had once filled the plazas to hear Castro speak out of enthusiasm increasingly did so out of a sense of obligation.[21]

In such an environment, filled with the whispers of secret police, Heberto Padilla began to anticipate his own suppression. In March 1971 it arrived. Padilla was arrested, accused of promoting a negative view of the Cuban Revolution, and subjected to bizarre treatment in prison. He appeared in public to recite a Soviet-style self-criticism, partially written by the police—which he, having spent time in Moscow, sardonically insisted would be a "classic of the genre"—naming names of friends who also harbored counterrevolutionary thoughts and declaring his errors. "Under the disguise of the writer in revolt," he confessed, "I had opposed the Revolution ... Among my most serious mistakes ... [was] to think that I, a Cuban, could live a double life: on the one hand vegetate like a parasite in the shadow of the Revolution, while on the other cultivate my literary popularity abroad at the cost of the Revolution and helped by its enemies." Padilla's actions were so extreme and degrading that they constituted an invitation to read between the lines and recognize the ill treatment that had produced them. A group of international writers—including Jean-Paul Sartre, Mario Vargas Llosa, and Carlos Fuentes, all of whom had been defenders of Cuba's revolutionary government—protested Padilla's treatment in an open letter, expressing concern that Padilla's self-criticism recalled "the most sordid moments of ... Stalinism" and calling for the Cuban Revolution to return to what they said "made us consider it as a model in the realm of socialism." Castro responded to the criticism by saying that Cuba did not need the support of "pseudo-revolutionary intellectuals" from Paris literary salons and of "bourgeois intrigue-mongers." Pluralistic socialists or liberals—"bourgeois liberals," as Castro called them—were given a clear message about where they stood with the Cuban Revolution.[22]

Casa de las Américas devoted a special issue to the Padilla affair, full of reaffirmations of socialist values. Uruguayan poet Mario Benedetti, in his contribution, told the story of Che Guevara deciding, in one combat situation, that he could carry only medical supplies or a box of bullets and opting for the bullets. "I am not proposing that every writer put down the pen and pick up a submachine gun," Benedetti wrote, "although sometimes that has happened and it might happen again. The priority refers here to attitudes, perspectives, points of view, but also to risks ... The (revolutionary?) writers of Paris and Barcelona, facing that dilemma, seem to have opted for literature. They did not react like revolutionaries legitimately preoccupied by a difficult moment within the revolution, but simply as offended littérateurs, like jealous guardians of a fiefdom they considered to have been invaded." Padilla's self-criticism was a minor affair, Benedetti argued, and he more than once reminded his readers of the great sin of the bourgeois socialists who had condemned Padilla's treatment: their participation in the CIA-sponsored CCF.[23]

For Roberto Fernández Retamar, the CCF also served as the reference that demonstrated the short distance between criticism and betrayal. In his essay for *Casa de las Américas,* titled "Calibán," Fernández Retamar

Issue no. 68 of *Casa de las Américas*, the September–October 1971 edition, was devoted to the topic "Culture and Revolution in Latin America." It made a kind of official response to the Padilla affair and was illustrated by scenes of colonial violence, including this one. Some of the woodcuts used were those of the sixteenth-century artist Theodor de Bry, whose work had long been used to illustrate Bartolomé de Las Casas's account of Spanish cruelty during the conquest of the Americas. The reproductions worked by analogy to situate that issue's printed arguments, defensive responses to international criticism of Padilla's treatment, in the context of a colonized people menaced by a long history of imperialism. *Source: Casa de las Américas*, no. 68 (September–October 1971).

reached back to José Enrique Rodó, whose essay *Ariel* had made the sprightly Ariel of Shakespeare's *The Tempest* a symbol of spiritual Latin America and the hulking Caliban stand in for the industrial United States. Reinterpreting the play, Fernández Retamar revised Rodó's allegory, arguing that Prospero represented "civilizing" colonialism, while both Ariel and Caliban were his slaves. The situation of the writer in Latin America was a colonial one, he argued, and most resembled not Ariel but Caliban, who said to Prospero, "You taught me language, and my profit on't / Is, I know how to curse. The red plague rid you / For learning me your language!" But Fernández Retamar's "Calibán" was not merely a meditation on the writer in a "colonial" setting; he also made it an explicit attack on those writers who he said rejected the problematic nature of writing in the "Latin American" setting. He singled out Jorge Luis Borges and Carlos Fuentes, whom he respectively called the right-wing spokesman for a powerless class and the representative of the decadent "Mexican literary mafia," "taking advantage of the wild vociferation occasioned by a Cuban writer's month in jail [to] break obstreperously with Cuba." For Fernández Retamar, the problem of the moment was not Padilla's treatment but the criticism of it. Those who rejected Cuba in 1961 because it declared itself Marxist-Leninist were more obviously reactionary, he argued, but those who were doing so in 1971 represented merely a "changing of the guard with an identical attitude." True Cuban and Latin American culture would be revolutionary culture, born from the rejection of colonialism. Fuentes's participation in a magazine associated with the CCF proved that he did not belong.[24]

In a retrospective essay looking back on the writing of "Calibán" many years later, Fernández Retamar again foregrounded the role that the CCF had played in creating the environment in which his essay was written:

At the very outset of the cold war, before the Third World had . . . entered the ring with such intensity, the United States organized, among other operations, the Congress for Cultural Freedom, in which the crude anti-Communism of practical politicians was adorned with intellectual sighs and breast-beating. In Spanish, the Congress's journal was called *Cuadernos;* its form was so sclerotic that it was unable to ride the rising tide of the sixties, and thus, it capsized ingloriously on its one hundredth issue. Shortly thereafter, the substitution of *Mundo Nuevo* for *Cuadernos* was planned and accomplished.

The debate that raged around this review permeated the atmosphere in which "Caliban" was conceived. In the mid-sixties, when the imminent publication in Paris of the new review became known, a group of writers, myself included, called attention to the fact that *Mundo Nuevo* could do nothing more than put a better face on its predecessor and that, in essence, it would have a similar purpose . . . The project was clear: to challenge, from Europe and with a modern look, the hegemony of the revolutionary outlook in Latin-American intellectual work.

Each of Fernández Retamar's statements is perfectly correct, and his description of the fate of *Cuadernos* is elegant. Yet the attention he gives to the CCF is also revealing, for by the time he was writing "Calibán," the contentious debate over *Mundo Nuevo* and the revelations of CIA involvement in the CCF had taken place five years earlier. Invoking the CIA, a frequent practice in militant Cuban publications, served to remind the reader that the issue was not the domestic repression of a poet but an international conflict, full of spies and treachery, over the survival of the Cuban Revolution. Opposition to the revolution, to this way of thinking, did not stem from domestic discontent but was fomented by corrupt agents of a foreign empire.[25]

The "issue" of the CCF, more than the organization itself, provided a wedge between "revolutionary" and (bourgeois) "leftist" intellectuals, making it possible for the former to understand opposition to directed culture as nothing more than acquiescence to imperialism. The story of the CCF and the CIA survived not only because it was true, but also because it was useful. Fernández Retamar would go on referencing it into the next millennium. And if Fernández Retamar had a greater ability to predict the course that the CCF would take, Emir Rodríguez Monegal had a better sense of what lay in store for Cuba. The years that followed the Padilla affair were the darkest period for Cuban culture, colored in the gray hues of self-censorship and official repression. Even some of the island's defenders, like Ángel Rama, began, often obliquely, to voice their discontent. Like Russian historians in the Soviet era who wrote histories of earlier centuries to comment on the present, Rama's posthumously published account of Latin American intellectuals in the service of the Spanish empire, *The Lettered City,* can be read as a warning that the continent's intellectuals did not play only the progressive roles that the revolution would assign to them.[26]

It was part of the complex legacy of the CCF to have contributed, in different ways and at different times, to the justification of both revolutionary and counterrevolutionary violence. Its exposure as a CIA front had made networks of cultural imperialism visible while at the same time failing to convince anyone that its power was modest. The product of both U.S. national security interests and the community of thinkers that struggled to define an anti-Communist Left that might in turn influence the United States, it survived, like other front organizations of the Cold War, as a projection of both its own actions and the imaginations of its critics. But if *Mundo Nuevo*'s fate showed how difficult it would be for a democratic socialism to emerge from even a convoluted alliance with the United States, the Padilla affair and *Casa*'s reaction showed, similarly, that no such thing would be forthcoming from Cuba.

The World Peace Council had lacked significant cultural influence since the death of Stalin in 1953, and the CCF never really recovered from the revelations of its relationship with the CIA. The Padilla affair broke the spine of Cuban cultural leadership, and it too would never again regain its former appeal. Prominent supporters remained: Gabriel García Márquez, most notably, kept his criticisms of Cuban developments private, believing that doing so gave him more influence and the ability to assist occasionally in securing the release of political prisoners. But the taboo of criticizing Cuba from the Left had been broken, and with it came the final splintering of intellectual life. All the major Latin American cultural projects representing Cold War interests had been shattered. Their fragments could still be sharp and dangerous, but they would assuredly be smaller. Nonetheless, their patterns—including the sorting of intellectuals into mutually antagonistic and mutually exclusive antitotalitarian and anti-imperialist camps—would persist. Each great hope of the Left to emerge in the next years would be refracted through those lenses.[27]

The troubles of the Cold War fronts revealed problems with each of their visions of a just society, which all would have described as a democratic socialism while meaning different things by that phrase. The Chile of Salvador Allende (1970–1973) was aligned with none of these three tendencies, but it was, in many ways, a perfect synecdoche for the end of democratic socialist hopes in the region and the world. Allende, a medical doctor and member of his country's Socialist Party, had run many times for president before winning a narrow plurality of the vote in 1970. (He joked that his tombstone would read "Here lies Salvador Allende, future president of the Republic.") His version of democratic socialism had points of contact with each of the three major strands of the Latin American Left: the democratic, the orthodox Communist, and the Cuban. As recently as 1960 he had attended the international conference of the Inter-American Association for Democracy and Freedom of the Democratic Left, although he eventually broke off his friendship with Rómulo Betancourt because of their diverging views on Cuba. He was a close friend of Pablo Neruda, and Allende's Socialist Party was part of an electoral alliance with Chile's orthodox Communist Party, which favored building socialism through electoral politics instead of armed revolution. The Chilean Left also included supporters of rapid, Cuba-style transformation; Allende himself had traveled to the Tricontinental Conference in 1966, and he valued Fidel Castro's counsel.[28]

After the election of 1970, it immediately became clear that Chile's right wing would do what it could to bring down Latin America's first elected Marxist. Similarly, before Allende even took office, the Nixon administration cast about for ways to avoid his presidency. The CIA tried scheming with the center-left Christian Democratic Party, with which it had long enjoyed close contacts, to prevent Allende from taking office, but failed. Other regional anti-Communist powers, like the dictatorship of Brazil, also worked to undermine his government. The staunch refusal of the Christian Democratic representatives of the Democratic Left to work with Chile's democratically elected Socialist president over the course of his term in office was one of the factors that led to government crisis and downfall.[29]

Allende's first steps at reestablishing relations with Cuba also went poorly. He sent the left-wing writer Jorge Edwards—long a friend and aide to Pablo Neruda and a guest in Havana for the Cultural Congress of 1968—to make the first contacts. But Edwards's status as a writer and his friendship with Heberto Padilla caused him to be viewed with suspicion and placed under near-constant surveillance. His trip ended a few months later when he was expelled from the country. Edwards began writing a book that he hoped would be a warning that Chile should not follow Cuba's example, but even if it had come soon enough, few would have listened.

Allende had to deal with many leftist groups who thought that his legal, constitutional path to socialism was timid and inappropriate—some even welcomed a military coup, thinking that it would hasten a continental revolution. Armed confrontations between left- and right-wing groups grew in frequency. Workers organized themselves, and some took over factories and farms without the legal authority to do so, betting that Allende would not dare to confront them. They were right, but the situation and the economy spiraled out of control. After one of Allende's semiregular consultations with Neruda in 1972, Neruda wrote to Jorge Edwards that Allende did not even agree with his own officials who recommended that he refuse to negotiate with the North American companies whose copper interests had been nationalized. "What to think!" wrote Neruda, who agreed with Allende and was increasingly concerned that the situation was growing hopeless; "There are days in which I don't know what is happening to me."[30]

The division on the left, coupled with hostility from the Right, the armed forces, the regional dictatorships, and the United States, culminated in the coup of 11 September 1973. Allende, defending himself in the presidential palace as it was bombed, ended his life by committing suicide with a gun that had been a gift from Fidel Castro. Pablo Neruda, sick with both cancer and heartbreak, died less than two weeks later. The hopes of a socialism that came to power by election, worked by constitutional procedure, and had never resorted to suppression of its opponents had ended in violence. Thousands were tortured and murdered by the military government of Augusto Pinochet, who tried to remake Chile as a utopian model of capitalist productivity.

The book that Jorge Edwards had been writing about his experiences in Cuba, *Persona non grata a Cuba,* was completed in 1973. Many considered it the first book by a solidly left-wing intellectual to openly criticize the Cuban model for its dictatorial characteristics, and the resulting disagreement reinforced the intellectual divides in the Left. Like Serge and Gide in the 1930s, Edwards was accused of criticizing a model society at a time of vulnerability for the Left, with Pinochet and other right-wing dictators in power. But others, like Mario Vargas Llosa and Emir Rodríguez Monegal, defended the work. The point was not to defeat one dictatorship with another, they argued; it was to end the repression of them all. For that group of thinkers, Cuba had betrayed its ideals by joining the "McCarthyites of the Left" after all.

The message of opposition to dictatorship, whether of the Left or of the Right, sounded as if it could have come from the CCF, but now it came from independent sources. Octavio Paz, at one time taught by Victor Serge and Julián Gorkin, and who shared many of the CCF's causes and tastes, had nonetheless always declined to participate in it. Like Neruda, he was a poet of both love and politics and had spent a number of years in diplomatic service. He resigned his position as the ambassador to India after the Mexican government's massacre of students in 1968, calling it a ritual sacrifice. Paz came to see a common problem across much of Latin America: Mexico, Cuba, and the dictatorships of the Southern Cone all featured concentrated state power and a lack of democratic competition and control.

Paz, together with Carlos Fuentes and the Spanish poet Juan Goytisolo, sought a new magazine that would replicate the task of *Mundo Nuevo* without the complications of its patron. Their short-lived *Libre* failed as *Mundo Nuevo* had. Its attempt at dialogue with Cuba immediately ran aground when the first issue was devoted to the Padilla affair. Its alternative to CIA funding was to accept the support of the marginally less problematic left-wing granddaughter of a Bolivian tin magnate. With more caution, after *Libre,* Paz launched a monthly cultural magazine called *Plural* that ran from 1971 to 1976. *Plural* largely avoided discussing either Cuba or the United States. Paz wrote there against both the violence of the state and the violence of left-wing guerrilla movements. Although neither Paz nor his magazine ever had anything to do with the CCF, it featured some of the CCF's authors and the organization's central preoccupation: how the name of socialism in the twentieth century had been usurped by Soviet Communism. *Plural* was not antisocialist: Paz insisted that socialism was the "only rational solution" to the problems of the century. For him, the question was how to restore to it a respect for democracy and liberty. After the Mexican government engineered to have the leaders of the independent newspaper that published *Plural* replaced, Paz continued the project anew with *Vuelta* in late 1976. Its frequent contributors included Carlos Fuentes, Elena Poniatowska, Gabriel Zaid, Jorge Ibargüengoitia, Isaiah Berlin, Mario Vargas Llosa, and Leszek Kolakowski. It might as well have been Mexico's version of *Encounter.*[31]

Relationships between the antitotalitarian *Vuelta* and the insurrectionary Left were bound to be strained. By the late 1970s and early 1980s the greatest point of conflict was Central America, the latest hope of the Latin American Left. *Vuelta* was not impressed with the politics or the composition of the Marxist guerrilla groups fighting in the region. In 1980 Gabriel Zaid, a poet and essayist of great depth who had trained as an engineer, wrote a disillusioned portrait of the Salvadoran guerrillas, noting that their leaders were drawn from the same elite they were fighting. One of the highest leaders of the guerillas, aided in Mexico by the solidarity organization known as the Roque Dalton Cultural Brigade, after the revolutionary Salvadoran poet, was in fact the man who had killed Dalton in 1975, executing him after a staged trial justified with the hackneyed accusation that he was a CIA agent. But the Salvadoran guerillas only fought the U.S.-backed army to a stalemate; in nearby Nicaragua the guerrillas triumphed.[32]

Nicaragua's revolution succeeded in 1979 when it overthrew the decades-long dictatorship of the Somoza family. Nicaragua's Sandinistas triumphed on the Cuban model: boosted by the broad-based multiclass opposition of the actual Cuban Revolution, not of the myth of the guerrilla *foco.* Like the postrevolutionary states of Mexico and Cuba before it, Nicaragua's leadership considered cultural change an integral part of the revolutionary process. Its efforts prompted familiar worries from the antitotalitarian camp that their efforts would be nothing more than an attempt to turn culture into dogma.

"Culture must be democratized," insisted the radical priest Ernesto Cardenal, who became the revolutionary government's minister of culture, "so that our people will not only be consumers of culture [. . .] but also producers of culture." Before the Sandinista victory Cardenal had been the leader of an artists' collective on the island of Solentiname that had taught primitivist painting and poetry to peasants. The Somoza dictatorship had destroyed the Solentiname community, but it became a kind of model for cultural diffusion after Cardenal became minister of culture. Centers were set up throughout the country to teach poetry. Nicaragua's revolution was dubbed a "revolution of poets." Even Daniel Ortega, its most powerful political leader, had published verse, and he told the visiting Salman Rushdie in 1986 that "in Nicaragua, everybody is considered to be a poet until he proves to the contrary."[33]

Rushdie, however, found that his admiration for what was taking place in Nicaragua was constantly checked by concern. The state newspaper, *Barricada,* was the worst he had seen. "It disturbed me that a government of writers had turned into a government of censors," Rushdie wrote. *Barricada* published "rules for poetry" drawn up by Cardenal, who called for free verse and concrete poetry of things rather than ideas. In painting, he favored the primitivist style that had been taught at Solentiname. At a speech in Finland, Cardenal was proud to say that Nicaragua was the "first nation on earth to have nationalized poetry." But whatever role the state was playing in directing and encouraging cultural output, it was hardly totalitarian. Public debates about attempts of the state to mechanically impose artistic language were frequent. There had been no publishers in the entire country during the Somoza dictatorship; under the Sandinistas the state publisher released even the works of the only major poet to oppose the revolution. Yet as the semicovert war mounted by the Reagan administration escalated, and the anti-Sandinista forces known as the Contras imposed warlike conditions, budgetary austerity shifted the focus from popular production of art to its popular consumption in forms such as muralism.[34]

At the same time, although censorship of the press was considered a wartime necessity, the government went beyond what was required. The opposition paper *La Prensa,* which had been a pillar of opposition to the dictatorship of Somoza, was sometimes occupied by Sandinista forces and shut down. It was accused, naturally, of working for the CIA; it responded that its foreign funding came from the National Endowment for Democracy, a quasi-governmental body established by the United States in 1983 to do, with a greater measure of transparency, precisely the sort of thing that the CIA had once done: support newspapers, unions, and the other institutions of civil society, especially in states that the United States judged dictatorial and unfriendly. The Sandinistas lost elections in 1990 to the publisher of *La Prensa,* Violeta Barrios de Chamorro, and looted as they left office. "They had acted," Rushdie concluded, "*simultaneously,* like people committed to democracy and also like harsh censors of free expression."[35]

More moderate than Cuba, Nicaragua had tried to preserve a mixed economy, had held elections, and had treated dissidents less harshly. Even so, it had not solved the problems of democratic socialism; its government's many mistakes frequently stemmed from the cultivation of a worldview that treated disagreement as illegitimate, and its leaders had a hard time trusting its citizens when they described the problems its policies had created. When Octavio Paz criticized both U.S. policy toward Nicaragua and the Sandinista alliance with the Soviet Union and its attitude toward democracy, he was burned in effigy by the Mexican Left. Many of the intellectuals and writers who had been members of the Sandinista front, including its vice president, experienced growing doubts about the party and distanced themselves from it over time.[36]

The greater moderation of Nicaragua when compared with its Cuban predecessor granted it no further latitude from the United States during the Reagan years; the Cold War instead provided a justification for the illegal war waged by the United States and its allies against Nicaragua's government. Yet by 1990, the year the Sandinistas were defeated at the ballot box, the Cold War was closer to its final end than anyone realized at the time. Opposition political movements in Soviet-bloc Eastern Europe were putting pressure on their governments to move toward more open political and civil societies. The Berlin Wall had fallen. Within a year the Soviet Union would crack apart, bringing a symbolic end to the struggle between Communism and anti-Communism that had provided the most obvious way to divide up the world for at least half a century. In Mexico City an antitotalitarian group of intellectuals, led by Octavio Paz, gathered to discuss global developments. They called their conference "El Siglo XX: La Experiencia de la Libertad" (The twentieth century: The experience of freedom) and hardly needed to explain that by freedom they meant anti-Communism.

Most of the conference's participants had begun their professional lives on the political Left, but they had come to see the power of state tyranny and the constraints that it placed on the free exercise of personhood as the great obstacle that had to be overcome. Some, like Mario Vargas Llosa, fresh from his defeat in the Peruvian presidential elections, now happily identified with the political Right. (Vargas Llosa produced the most memorable moment of the conference when he impolitely declared Mexico's government a "perfect dictatorship" because it replaced its president every six years without giving up political control.) Others, like Paz, still wanted an anti-Marxist socialism that embraced the historical contribution of liberalism to social justice. American sociologist Daniel Bell, one of the many foreign visitors at this Mexican conference, told the press in interviews that he was "socialist in economics, liberal in politics and conservative in culture." Insofar as they identified with the political Left—which certainly no longer identified with them—it was because they thought that the Left needed to be remade with new values.[37]

The central lesson that the group gathered in Mexico City took away from the history of the twentieth century was the justness of antitotalitarianism. Yet this certitude left them curiously unequipped to think about the great transformation then under way in Latin American economies: the privatization of state-owned assets and deregulation known as "neoliberalism." What had once been associated with the Pinochet dictatorship was implemented, in an era of budget crises and austerity, by virtually everyone in power. Vargas Llosa had lost his election in Peru after trying to convince its poor and unemployed of the merits of flexible labor markets and the evils of job security. In Brazil, the former socialist dependency theorist Fernando Henrique Cardoso was elected president at the head of Brazil's Social Democratic Party and implemented a neoliberal agenda in most areas of economic policy. Although there were many reasons that neoliberal strategies were adopted in the 1980s and 1990s, the antitotalitarian tradition's fear of state power made it possible rhetorically to imbue the "market" with a moral energy that still used the language of the Left. The failings of the revolutionary Left could still occupy the attention of intellectuals at a time when, outside Cuba, they had become almost totally irrelevant. Meanwhile, what passed for social democracy was increasingly concerned with making capitalism effective, not with transforming it.[38]

The Mexico City conference was, in a way, its own sign of the unfolding change. A meeting that might have received CIA support a few decades earlier was instead sponsored primarily by the television conglomerate Televisa: a sign that intellectual life too, like so many other state assets, would be increasingly privatized. After the Cold War, intellectuals were faced with two primary possibilities: relegation to low-stakes academic disputes or lives as overeducated media entertainers. But to be culture warriors for a moral ideal, supported by a state advancing claims about universal justice, was no longer an option. The "century of the intellectual" was at an end. It had been a time during which competing visions of achieving modernity had been expressed in political and cultural language, and so the actions of the arbiters of public morality—intellectuals—seemed to have something to contribute. The sin of Cold War intellectuals—their voluntary or quasi-voluntary allegiance to powerful empires—was possible only because states saw them as repositories of moral authority. The shame and the glory of the intellectuals in the twentieth century were fibers woven into the same fabric, which turned out to be, for everyone, dirty laundry.[39]

Three major routes to achieving a humane socialism had been advanced and given shape by the Cold War. The Cuban variety depended on violence to make an authentically transformative revolution. Military discipline and concentrated power were difficult to transform into political democracy. Popular participation in government was frequently cosmetic. Cultural freedoms and the right to dissent had to exist within channels declared by the revolution, and prisoners of conscience multiplied. Cuba had become more equal and had broken from the humiliations of a compromised national sovereignty that depended on the permission of the United States. But freedom from imperialism, a collective freedom rather than an individual one, was not really achieved in Cuba, both because of the dependence on the USSR that it invited and because Cuba's hostile relationship with the United States continued to structure Cuban life in important ways. The many young intellectuals who wanted to be like Che often marched, like him, to tragic deaths with backpacks full of books.

The orthodox Communist alternative was beset by other problems. Its political and cultural force in Latin America waxed and waned with decisions about alliances and strategy that were often made many thousands of miles away in Moscow. The cultural project of "peace" had been dismissive of the value of liberty. Like its Cuban cousin, it adopted a language of opposition to the injustices of capitalism, which were very real. But its alternative was, in the early 1950s, a blind faith in Stalin that, especially when voluntarily adhered to rather than imposed, did not suggest good judgment. Some of Latin America's Communist parties, like those of Chile and eventually Mexico, moved toward embracing an electoral strategy for achieving power, accepting that democracy was something more than a bourgeois fiction. But in doing so, they had to confront their status as small minorities within pluralistic societies, as well as the fact that U.S. hostility toward them would not automatically lessen simply because they sought democratic paths to power. Their Soviet model was no example of a humane socialism, but as a leftist opposition in a democratic system, they could sometimes be sharp critics of democracy's inadequacies.

But if these two Marxist Lefts offered unlikely paths toward a humane socialism, the anti-Communist Left was a dubious alternative in the Latin American setting. It offered a strategy for surviving on the left without incurring the direct hostility of the United States, but it required repressing local Communism, frequently with force, in ways that were inimical to the personal freedoms that ostensibly distinguished it from its Marxist alternatives. Liberal ideologies did not always produce liberal results. They required constant compromise and slow transformation. They required, as the intellectuals who endorsed this path discovered, becoming a part of the U.S. system for managing geopolitical risk in the region. Costa Rica, the country that dealt best with all these challenges and held on to a social democratic welfare state without cultural repression, found itself being used as a staging ground for anti-Marxist actions against its neighbors in the 1980s. Its idea of moderate, left-wing transformation that produced sustained reductions in poverty and inequality, with the U.S. government as an ally but with those further to the left excluded, was in some ways as utopian an idea as any offered by Cuba or the Soviet Union.

The Cultural Cold War had offered three visions of a progressive democratic socialism. All of them contained deep problems that were reflected in the contradictions of the organizations—the Casa de las Américas, the World Peace Council, and the Congress for Cultural Freedom—that had once underwritten them. Each had offered a vision of political and cultural life that it considered just, but each had silenced discussion of the problems of its patron. What could not be discussed, in every case, was deeply detrimental to its cause.

The utopias and counterutopias of the generation of the Cultural Cold War were dramatic and intense, but they would eventually be left behind. By the end of the 1990s the intellectuals who had come of age during the first decades of the Cold War were well advanced in years. The debates that had been central to the Cultural Cold War—of anti-imperialism and antitotalitarianism—were perhaps no less morally urgent but were, in practice, less necessary. In the years after the end of the Cold War, prominent voices called for a "democratization" of the values and culture of the Latin American Left. But outside intellectual spheres it had in many places happened already.[40]

This was perhaps most obvious in Chile, where great mistrust had existed between Christian Democrats and Allende, whose programmatic differences had been exaggerated by the differing Cold War stances that they had taken. During the long dictatorship of Pinochet, both sides reconsidered some of their earlier disagreements. The intellectuals of the Christian Democratic Party, including Eduardo Frei and Jaime Castillo Velasco, both of whom had once also been associated with the CCF, became voices for coalition politics to end the dictatorship. The brutality exercised by the dictatorships in their "dirty war" against the Left caused many who had rejected individual human rights as merely "bourgeois" to rethink their value. The mainstream of the Socialist Party came to see electoral democracy as a way to guarantee respect for human rights.

Just as in the 1930s, Mexico in the 1970s again became a haven for many refugees from dictatorship. Institutions like the Ford Foundation that had been anathema to the radical Left helped too, establishing research centers that protected intellectuals from state repression. Their analysis, in turn, helped shape popular movements for the restoration of democracy. The Cold War—including the Cultural Cold War—had kept these parties apart. Widespread violations of human rights were divisive for the Left when they took place in Cuba, but were unifying when they were practiced by the dictatorships. This created the conditions under which the Cold War could thaw, and in which a center-left and a Left could see each other as allies rather than obstacles, with democracy as a common goal. In Mexico, where there had never been a formal dictatorship, anti–Partido Revolucionario Institucional (PRI) intellectuals of both the Left and the Right collaborated with popular movements to force the PRI to acknowledge opposition victories at the state and local levels, making possible gradual movements toward democracy at the level of federal elections. The "pink" tide of Left and center-left governments that swept across the region in the late 1990s and early years of the twenty-first century, touching nearly every country except Mexico and Colombia, was, for the most part, democratic and capitalist, with a role reserved for state welfare programs to alleviate poverty.[41]

Intellectually, Octavio Paz and other antitotalitarians had been written out of the Left. But in practice, the liberal values they had hoped would be part of the Left's program had triumphed. Even the debate between neoliberals and social democrats was, to a degree, set aside; for example, the type of program put in place by the "neoliberal" Fernando Henrique Cardoso in Brazil in the 1990s, to give cash benefits to the poor in exchange for children's school attendance, was, by the beginning of the twenty-first century, part of the agenda of the "social democratic" government of Luiz Inácio Lula da Silva. Brazil, and other governments across the region as well, saw sustained economic growth along with meaningful reductions in inequality in the first decade of the new millennium, something that many of the previous generation would have assumed was impossible.

To be sure, differences remained. Some analysis divided the "pink tide" into two Lefts that resembled Cold War divisions: one democratic and modern, the other outdated and authoritarian. To this way of thinking, Hugo Chávez of Venezuela represented the latter. Especially after he was briefly removed from power in a coup in 2002, he pledged his government to "twenty-first-century" socialism. Echoing the anti-imperialist Left of the Cold War, he made CIA and other conspiracies part of the language of the government, frustrating an opposition that could not mount a credible challenge to him. Not all of his programs to benefit the poor were effective, but high oil prices did sustain reductions in poverty and inequality, for as many times as Chávez paid homage to Cuba and Castro, his government did not stop selling oil to the United States. And as closed as he was to criticism and as much as he demonized the opposition, he was repeatedly elected, and there were no camps for opponents: his Venezuela seemed more like the child of Juan Domingo Perón and Mexico's PRI than a repeat of twentieth-century totalitarianism. With the major totalitarian power gone, and the imperial power of the United States transformed into a less obviously interventionist form, at least in Latin America, neither antitotalitarianism nor anti-imperialism had the purchase it had once had.[42]

The new democracies, like all others, were deeply flawed. Corruption and violence plagued much of the region, cutting across ideological boundaries. Inequality, even when reduced, remained appallingly high, and opportunities and rights for the poor were limited. Privatized state assets often made enormous fortunes for the well connected, and tax systems were barely redistributive. The problems of operating democratic systems in such unequal societies remained to be thought through or at least acted on. Both those in the generally neoliberal camp and those opposed to it required self-criticism and a look back to the ways in which their problems echoed those of their Cold War predecessors if they were to build a broad and deep democratic Left.

But the romantic view of themselves that intellectuals had once had, that it was they who would have to speak for a civil society that could not speak for itself, seemed less and less applicable. Vigorous social movements sprang up across the region to defend different visions of justice. The Cold War had given intellectuals clear roles to play. It had given the Russian poet Anna Akhmatova, for example, the opportunity at the height of Stalinism to promise to bear witness to the sufferings of her society. In Latin America, where the bulk of the repression was justified on anti-Communist grounds, it had allowed the Chilean Nicanor Parra to perform what he described as a "Censored Poem" during the dictatorship of Pinochet by standing, saying nothing, and retiring to applause. What gave intellectuals their power in the twentieth century was their relationship with powerful states, either as subjects of repression or as adjuncts of state power. The new democracies, however flawed, did not find them as useful. Nor did they find it necessary to repress them. This was less a sign that intellectuals had lost their grandeur or their way than it was a sign of social progress. The Cultural Cold War had offered intense dreams but no way to fulfill them. The post–Cold War world offered fewer dreams, only lowered expectations and the long, hard work of making life, slowly and unevenly, a bit less grim. Progress would be earned through the interaction of social movements, ideas, electoral politics, and economic growth. The new politics could hardly promise an end to injustice, but at least it sometimes offered the possibility that democracy itself could be made better. As always, there was much to do.

Conclusion

Hundreds of years before the Cultural Cold War, propaganda played a central part in another struggle between empires. Competition between Spain and England in the sixteenth, seventeenth, and eighteenth centuries gave rise to the Black Legend of Spanish colonialism, which described Spaniards as exceptionally brutal imperialists. This notion was based partially on the writings of the sixteenth-century Dominican friar Bartolomé de Las Casas, who had argued that the savagery of conquest and the depraved actions of Spanish soldiers made it difficult to save the souls of the "Indians." Although his documentation of murder and abuse led to reforms within the empire, his harrowing account became the touchstone of the Black Legend. English-language publication of Las Casas's work spiked in moments of intense imperial rivalry, when England used evidence of Spanish barbarism both to discredit Spain's claims to territory and to justify its own violent colonial interventions. Beyond the truth or falsity of the legend, its persistence was not an accident but an organized part of imperial competition. Critiques of one empire's cruelty served to justify the cruelty of another.[1]

Although the technology of propaganda had changed by the twentieth century, during the Cold War competition between the United States and the USSR, accounts of one empire's transgressions were similarly used to the advantage of the other. The front groups of the Cold War both generated propaganda and were its targets, and their legacies and meanings have remained politically charged. The black legends that were attached to the World Peace Council (WPC) and the Congress for Cultural Freedom (CCF)—assertions that the former was a front for Stalinist aggression and the latter a CIA ploy to extend U.S. domination—were used to justify repression. But the legends overstate the power of the WPC and the CCF and understate their unintended consequences.

The black legend of the WPC was promulgated by the U.S. government and anti-Communist entrepreneurs, who argued that the WPC's language of peace masked aggressive intent, papering over Stalinist repression to dupe the well-intentioned into affiliation. But, like any black legend, that of the WPC was meant to discredit it and bolster opposing political interests, not to capture the nuances of its position and function. The WPC's connections to Communist politics were real enough, but they were more a liability than an asset. Its rhetoric, such as that of anticosmopolitanism, was designed to criticize the culture of the West but inadvertently revealed the falsity of the Soviet Union's claims to have eliminated ethnic strife. Affiliated artists, from Pablo Neruda to Diego Rivera, tried to write and paint in ways that accorded with socialist realism, but most found it to be an artistic and ideological dead end.

The level of control that the Soviet empire exercised over the WPC was also frequently exaggerated. It paid most of the bills for the WPC at the global level, but many local initiatives were self-financed. WPC participants were culpably naïve—perhaps deliberately so—about the Soviet Union, but they rationalized their naïveté by arguing that it was not the Soviet Union but the United States that was responsible for the greatest suffering in their home countries. And in Latin America, at least, they had a point. Anti-Communist suppression of peace initiatives likely did more to damage democracy in the early years of the Cold War than the persistence of peace activities would have.

Furthermore, even though the WPC was a Communist front group, it sometimes fostered organizations that were not Communist at all. The Movimiento de Liberación Nacional that operated for a few years in Mexico in the 1960s adopted and adapted much of the language of the peace campaigns and incorporated its personnel. But, at Lázaro Cárdenas's insistence, it maintained financial and programmatic independence from the WPC, and it advocated for civil liberties in a manner characteristic of anti-Communist struggles against Communist hegemony. In a region of anti-Communist domination, Marxists and their allies could defend essential democratic rights.

The WPC's antagonist and counterpart, the CCF, has also been the subject of a black legend: that it was an accessory of U.S. power and part of the CIA's strategy to ensure capitalist hegemony around the globe. Its function, as this story has it, was to divide the Left and elicit consent to U.S. power among artists and intellectuals by focusing their attention on Communist offenses, thereby conditioning a part of the Left not to automatically reject the United States and its political and cultural leadership. As with the black legend of the WPC, this view is not entirely inaccurate, but it likewise does not attend to the failures, unintended consequences, and ironies generated by the CCF's activities.

The CCF was not only the creation of the CIA; it was also the work of dedicated anti-Stalinist activists whose work long predated the Cold War. Their commitment to "cultural freedom" was the logical extension of their experience of trying to work with Communist groups in the decades before the Cold War began. Nor did the CIA create the Left's divisions. These too had their roots in pre–Cold War differences of ideas and practices between Communists and groups that could be loosely described as social democratic. Even in the art world, as in its attempts to promote alternatives to Marxist painters like Diego Rivera and David Álfaro Siqueiros in Mexico in the 1950s, the CCF was more a trend follower than a trendsetter.

Still, the CIA unquestionably played an important role in the organization of the CCF, and many affiliates knew something about the connection. The argument for the "disinterested CIA" made by some defenders of the CCF is not credible. But its opposite, the breezy assumption that just about everyone, on some level, knew what was going on, also does not stand up to scrutiny. Although the Latin American operation can in no way stand in for the CCF as a whole, it was by the mid-1960s the most important regional operation within the CCF, and its history shows how limited knowledge of its CIA connections was. Even important members, including Luis Mercier Vega and Keith Botsford, may not have had direct knowledge of the CIA's relationship to the CCF; more remote affiliates probably knew even less. Although some micromanagement by agency officials took place, the principal way in which the CIA intervened in the CCF was by hiring the people who it thought would do the best job of making the CCF an effective organization. The CIA was naturally interested in the outcomes, but it did not always speak with one voice: John Hunt and Michael Josselson were both directly employed by the CIA but took opposing views on major issues, such as the usefulness of *Cuadernos*. And local affiliates, such as those in Brazil around the time of the coup in 1964, did not always obey the requests of the CIA employees in the CCF.

Insofar as the CCF was an instrument of U.S. hegemony, it was a complicated one. It was not really the case that the CCF was ever intentionally counterhegemonic in the sense of opposing U.S. power. It did criticize the United States, but generally from the point of view of the anti-Communist Left, arguing that the United States should be a more resolute supporter of left-wing reform in order to avoid left-wing revolution. The historian Frank Tannenbaum, writing about U.S. policy toward Latin America in *Cuadernos* in 1961, argued that "Our anti-Communist policy [meaning that of the United States] would have caused other feelings if it had been combined with a positive support for democracy . . . Nevertheless, unfortunately, we [the United States] have been opposed to Communism, but we have not visibly supported democracy." Criticism of the United States in CCF publications generally expressed disappointment in the mistakes of the United States, whereas the Soviet Union was condemned outright. The Latin American projects sponsored by the CCF that were most critical of the United States were those of Luis Mercier Vega's *Aportes* and Emir Rodríguez Monegal's *Mundo Nuevo;* both were simultaneously critical of the United States and of Cuban cultural politics and Marxist analysis. But Emir Rodríguez Monegal's belief that the role of the intellectual lay in independent criticism, for example, was useful in some ways to U.S. interests, not opposed to them. He fully intended that criticism would be directed toward the United States. But in the left-wing communities who were the intended audience for his message, his idea of the intellectual was also a potentially helpful one for the United States since it challenged the propriety of unconditional support for Cuba among left-wing intellectuals.[2]

The dark view of the CIA as the master manipulator of Latin American politics in no way should be replaced with a sunny picture of the CIA as a friend of the Left so long as the Left was anti-Communist. The case of the CCF does show, however, the limits of the CIA's power to shape the course of events in the absence of local allies. The United States was the strongest imperial power in Latin America in the twentieth century, and it got what it wanted often enough, frequently with tragic results. Still, it was not omnipotent. Moreover, the United States, rather than oscillating between liberal and authoritarian foreign policies, pursued both simultaneously. The CCF was part of a liberal current within the CIA that tried to encourage social reform in Latin America in a way that would also serve the ends of anti-Communism. It was, in a Gramscian sense, part of plans to build consent for U.S. hegemony in the region. But there is more than one possible form for hegemony to take, and Latin America might have experienced a somewhat more tolerable hegemony if the liberals had succeeded more often in creating the conditions for stable alliances between the United States and Latin America's anti-Communist Left.

Just as the black legend of the WPC justified anti-Communist repression throughout the region, the black legend of the CCF was used by Casa de las Américas to justify repression within Communist Cuba. By the late 1960s both Casa and the CCF had suppressed how much they had once had in common. They had erased the participation of CCF personnel in Cuba's government and in Casa de las Américas itself in 1959. They had forgotten the work done by parts of the CCF for Fidel Castro during the struggle against Batista, especially in the critical area of public relations. Supporting Castro was probably the most important political action taken by the members of the CCF in Latin America, and it was, entirely by accident, surely the most counterhegemonic action it ever took. That the CCF's most important political success was to help Fidel Castro to power is only one piece of evidence that the role of Cold War fronts in constructing hegemony can best be understood within a framework of ironic Gramscianism. By its work, it had discredited Communism; by its existence and exposure as a CIA front, it discredited anti-Communism.[3]

At the inaugural meeting of the CCF in 1950, Sidney Hook had argued that "the fundamental distinction of our time must be drawn . . . not in terms of a free market in goods or a closed market but only in terms of a free market in ideas." Since Hook knew that the CCF was a CIA-sponsored project that was presumably distorting the "free market in ideas," his statement might serve as a reminder of the hypocrisies that anti-Communists were willing to tolerate in the name of liberal values. But more important, the existence of the CCF strongly suggested that a free, competitive market in ideas was not a good model for thinking through the transmission of thought during the Cold War. The market in ideas was not free at all; it was full of subsidized firms producing many substandard goods and occasionally, in spite of everything, something of real quality. A world without the CCF would hardly have been one without foreign intervention in the arts and culture; indeed, intervention was so ubiquitous that it could be difficult to identify the line between what was authentic and what was imposed.

In one of the classics of Latin American left-wing cultural criticism, 1971's *How to Read Donald Duck*, its authors write that "the world of Disney is the world of the interests of the bourgeoisie without its dislocations." In their analysis, Disney cartoons' treatment of money, of violence, and of "primitive" regions and peoples all reflected imperial privilege without ever seeing the problems in the value system they depicted. But the statement could be modified to apply to the front groups of the Cultural Cold War as well. The work of the CCF represented the interests of the anti-Communist Left without its dislocations; the WPC, those of the Communist world; Casa de las Américas, those of Cuban revolutionaries. Each represented political fantasy. But the dislocations were inescapable, and each of the front groups experienced discredit because of its affiliations. All the groups advocated democratic practices in some contexts while excusing authoritarian ones in others. But in the end, neither the organized forces who claimed peace nor those who claimed freedom could escape the consequences of having been part of imperial projects. The politically engaged artists and intellectuals who participated in the Cultural Cold War had been defenders of both liberation and oppression simultaneously, regardless of the side that they chose. They enjoyed neither peace nor freedom as they worked to produce art and ideas, and they obtained neither through the roles they played in the Cold War.[4]

Abbreviations and Archival Sources

Abbreviations

AEAA	Asociación de Escritores y Artistas Americanos
AFL	American Federation of Labor
APRA	Alianza Popular Revolucionaria Americana
CCC	Continental Cultural Congress
CCF	Congress for Cultural Freedom
CIA	Central Intelligence Agency
CME	Centro Mexicano de Escritores
CTAL	Confederación de Trabajadores de América Latina
CTC	Confederación de Trabajadores de Cuba
CTM	Confederación de Trabajadores de México
FCMAR	Frente Cívico Mexicano de Afirmación Revolucionaria
FRD	Frente Revolucionario Democrático
FTUC	Free Trade Union Committee
IACF	International Association for Cultural Freedom
IADF	Inter-American Association for Democracy and Freedom
ICFTU	International Confederation of Free Trade Unions
ILARI	Instituto Latinoamericano de Relaciones Internacionales
LEAR	Liga de Escritores y Artistas Revolucionarios
MLN	Movimiento de Liberación Nacional
ORIT	Organización Regional Interamericana de Trabajadores
PCB	Partido Comunista do Brasil
PCM	Partido Comunista Mexicano
PNR	Partido Nacional Revolucionario (1929–1938)
POUM	Partido Obrero de Unificación Marxista
PP	Partido Popular (after 1960: Partido Popular Socialista, PPS)
PRI	Partido Revolucionario Institucional (1946–present)
PRM	Partido de la Revolución Mexicana (1938–1946)
WFTU	World Federation of Trade Unions
WPC	World Peace Council

Archival Sources

- Archibald S. Alexander Library, Rutgers University, New Brunswick, N.J.
  - *—Robert J. Alexander Papers*
  - *—Frances Grant Papers*
- Archivo del Colegio de México, Mexico City, Mexico
  - *—Daniel Cosío Villegas Papers*
- Archivo General de la Nación (AGN), Mexico City, Mexico
  - *—Gallery 1—Dirección Federal de Seguridad (DFS)*
  - *—Gallery 2—Dirección General de Investigaciones Políticas y Sociales (DGIPS)*
  - *—Gallery 3—Presidentes*
    - *· Lázaro Cárdenas del Río (LCR) Records*
    - *· Manuel Ávila Camacho (MAC) Records*
    - *· Miguel Alemán Valdés (MAV) Records*
    - *· Adolfo Ruiz Cortines Records*
  - *—Gallery 7—Archivos Particulares*
    - *· Clementina Batalla de Bassols Papers*
  - *—Mapoteca y Micropelícula*
    - *· Lázaro Cárdenas Papers*
- Archivo Histórico de la Universidad Nacional Autónoma de México (AHUNAM), Mexico City, Mexico
  - *—Heriberto Jara Papers*
- Beinecke Rare Book and Manuscripts Library, Yale University, New Haven, Conn.
  - *—Keith Botsford Papers*
  - *—Victor Serge Papers*
- Biblioteca Ernesto de la Torre Villar, Instituto José María Luis Mora, Mexico City
  - *—Archivo de la Palabra*
- Capilla Alfonsina, Mexico City, Mexico
  - *—Alfonso Reyes Papers*
- Centro de Documentación e Investigación de la Cultura de Izquierdas en Argentina. Buenos Aires, Argentina
  - *—Juan Antonio Solari Papers*
- Centro de Estudios del Movimiento Obrero y Socialista (CEMOS), Mexico City, Mexico
  - *—Partido Comunista Mexicano (PCM) Papers*

- Columbia University Rare Book and Manuscript Library, New York, N.Y.
  —*Frank Tannenbaum Papers*

- Federal Bureau of Investigation, Washington, D.C., files released to author through Freedom of Information Act
  —*Julián Gorkin File*
  —*Vicente Lombardo Toledano (VLT) File*
  —*Victor Serge File*

- Firestone Library, Princeton University, Princeton, N.J.
  —*Carlos Fuentes Papers*
  —*María Rosa Oliver (MRO) Papers*
  —*Emir Rodríguez Monegal (ERM) Papers*
  —*Mario Vargas Llosa Papers*

- Ford Foundation Archives (FFA), New York, N.Y.

- George Meany Memorial Archives (GMMA). Silver Spring, Md.
  —*Record Group 18–001: International Affairs Department*
  —*Record Group 18–004: Irving Brown Papers*
  —*Record Group 18–009: Serafino Romualdi Papers*

- Harry Ransom Center, University of Texas, Austin
  —*Nicholas Nabokov Papers*

- Hoover Institution Archives (HIA), Stanford, Calif.
  —*James Burnham Papers*
    Theodore Draper Papers
  —*Georgie Anne Geyer Papers*
  —*Sidney Hook Papers*
  —*Hoover Institution Library Society Papers, Congress for Cultural Freedom*
  —*Jay Lovestone Papers*
  —*Joaquín Maurín Papers*

- Institut Curie, Paris, France
  —*Frédéric Joliot-Curie Papers*

- Joseph L. Regenstein Library, University of Chicago Special Collections Research Center (UC/SCRC), Chicago, Ill.
  —*International Association for Cultural Freedom Papers (IACF)*

- Kheel Center for Labor-Management Documentation and Archives, Cornell University, Ithaca, N.Y.
  —*Serafino Romualdi Papers*

- National Archives and Records Administration (NARA), College Park, Md.
  - —*CIA Records Search Tool*
  - —*Record Group 59—Records of the Department of State*
  - —*Record Group 226—Records of the Office of Strategic Services (OSS)*
- New York Public Library, New York, N.Y.
  - —*Norman Thomas Papers*
- Tamiment Library, New York University, New York, N.Y.
  - —*American Committee for Cultural Freedom Papers (ACCF)*
- University of Illinois, Urbana-Champaign, Ill.
  - —*Oscar and Ruth Lewis Papers*

Notes

Introduction

1. Cardoso is quoted in Joseph Kahl, *Three Latin American Sociologists: Gino Germani, Pablo Gonzales Casanova, Fernando Henrique Cardoso* (New Brunswick, N.J.: Transaction Books, 1988), 179. Fuentes is quoted in Jorge G. Castañeda, *Utopia Unarmed: The Latin American Left after the Cold War* (New York: Knopf, 1993), 182. On inequality in Latin America, see Paul Gootenberg and Luis Reygadas, eds., *Indelible Inequalities in Latin America: Insights from History, Politics, and Culture* (Durham, N.C.: Duke University Press, 2010); and Kelly Hoffman and Miguel Angel Centeno, "The Lopsided Continent: Inequality in Latin America," *Annual Review of Sociology* 29 (2003): 363–390.

2. Albert Camus, *The Rebel: An Essay on Man in Revolt* (New York: Knopf, 1961), 249. Nicola Miller has also argued that the "national redeemer" idea of intellectuals was a myth, invented by Spanish American intellectuals in the early twentieth century in a bid to recover lost status. Nicola Miller, *In the Shadow of the State: Intellectuals and the Quest for National Identity in Twentieth-Century Spanish America* (London: Verso, 1999), 246.

3. E. P. Thompson, *Beyond the Cold War: A New Approach to the Arms Race and Nuclear Annihilation,* 1st U.S. ed. (New York: Pantheon Books, 1982), 158; "World Congress of Culture in Defense of Peace," *For a Lasting Peace, for a People's Democracy,* 1 September 1948, 1; Thomas W. Braden, "I'm Glad the CIA Is 'Immoral,'" *Saturday Evening Post,* 20 May 1967, 12.

4. Ronald Aronson, *Camus and Sartre: The Story of a Friendship and the Quarrel That Ended It* (Chicago: University of Chicago Press, 2004), 128.

5. Camus, *Rebel,* 4; Irving Howe, *A Margin of Hope: An Intellectual Autobiography* (San Diego: Harcourt Brace Jovanovich, 1982), 132.

6. Sartre's major work from this era is Jean-Paul Sartre, *The Communists and Peace,* trans. Martha H. Fletcher (New York: George Braziller, 1968). Sartre broke from this position following the Soviet invasion of Hungary in 1956: Jean-Paul Sartre, "La Fantôme de Staline," *Les Temps Modernes* 12, nos. 129–130–131 (November 1956–January 1957): 577–696.

7. The "public relations" quote is from Jacobo Timerman, *Cuba: A Journey,* trans. Toby Talbot (New York: Alfred A. Knopf, 1990), 32. There were personal elements to the antagonism of García Márquez and Vargas Llosa in addition to their political differences. The "famous punch" quote is from Gerald Martin, *Gabriel García Márquez: A Life,* 1st U.S. ed. (New York: Alfred A. Knopf, 2009), 375–376. On Vargas Llosa and Camus, see Efraín Kristal, *Temptation of the Word: The Novels of Mario Vargas Llosa* (Nashville: Vanderbilt University Press, 1998), 25, 100; and Mario Vargas Llosa, *Contra viento y marea, 1962–1982* (Barcelona: Seix Barral, 1983), 72–74, 231–252. On the general subject of García Márquez's friendship with Castro, see also Ángel Esteban and Stéphanie Panichelli, *Fidel and Gabo: A Portrait of the Legendary Friendship,* trans. Diane Stockwell (New York: Pegasus Books, 2009).

8. Contrary to his reputation, Benda was not in fact opposed to all political participation by intellectuals and was writing largely against France's nationalist Right, who, in his view, let politics determine morality. Julien Benda, *The Treason of the Intellectuals (La trahison des clercs),* trans. Richard Aldington (New York: Norton, 1969); Tony Judt, *Reappraisals* (New York: Penguin Press, 2008), 12–13; Mark Lilla, *The Reckless Mind: Intellectuals in Politics* (New York: New York Review Books, 2001), 197–198.

9. Antonio Gramsci, *The Gramsci Reader: Selected Writings, 1916–1935,* trans. David Forgacs (New York: New York University Press, 2000), 300–311. Although the term "organic" is commonly used to designate any progressive intellectual aligned with oppressed classes, in Gramsci an "organic" intellectual is simply a class-identified one, regardless of that class. A useful guide to the large literature on the various types of intellectual classifications scholars produced during the twentieth century is Charles Kurzman and Lynn Owens, "The Sociology of Intellectuals," *Annual Review of Sociology* 28 (2002): 63–90.

10. Christopher Lasch, *The Agony of the American Left* (New York: Vintage Books, 1969), 111. The most apologetic history of the CCF is by a former participant, Peter Coleman, *The Liberal Conspiracy: The Congress for Cultural Freedom and the Struggle for the Mind of Postwar Europe* (New York: Free Press, 1989). The critical literature includes Frances Stonor Saunders, *The Cultural Cold War: The CIA and the World of Arts and Letters* (New York: New Press, 2000); Andrew Rubin, *Archives of Authority: Empire, Culture, and the Cold War* (Princeton, N.J.: Princeton University Press, 2012); and Inderjeet Parmar, *Foundations of the American Century: The Ford, Carnegie, and Rockefeller Foundations in the Rise of American Power* (New York: Columbia University Press, 2012). It is Giles Scott-Smith who most explicitly uses Gramscian language, although his scholarship emphasizes the plural nature of the construction of the anti-Communist organizations. Giles Scott-Smith, *The Politics of Apolitical Culture: The Congress for Cultural Freedom, the CIA, and Post-war American Hegemony* (London: Routledge, 2002), 138.

11. The major examples of this line of scholarship include Hugh Wilford, *The CIA, the British Left, and the Cold War: Calling the Tune?* (London: Frank

Cass, 2003); Hugh Wilford, *The Mighty Wurlitzer: How the CIA Played America* (Cambridge, Mass.: Harvard University Press, 2008); Luc van Dongen, Stéphanie Roulin, and Giles Scott-Smith, eds., *Transnational Anti-Communism and the Cold War: Agents, Activities, and Networks* (New York: Palgrave Macmillan, 2014); Nathan Suhr-Sytsma, "Ibadan Modernism: Poetry and the Literary Present in Mid-century Nigeria," *Journal of Commonwealth Literature* 48, no. 1 (2013): 41–59; and Eric D. Pullin, "'Money Does Not Make Any Difference to the Opinions That We Hold': India, the CIA, and the Congress for Cultural Freedom, 1951–58," *Intelligence and National Security* 26, nos. 2–3 (June 2011): 377–398. See also Greg Barnhisel, *Cold War Modernists: Art, Literature, and American Cultural Diplomacy* (New York: Columbia University Press, 2015), 8–9, 136–178.

12. Almost all histories of the Cultural Cold War focus on one side over the other. A major exception is David Caute, *The Dancer Defects: The Struggle for Cultural Supremacy during the Cold War* (Oxford: Oxford University Press, 2003).

13. Democratic, that is, in the sense of Elizabeth S. Anderson, "What Is the Point of Equality?," *Ethics* 109, no. 2 (January 1999): 287–337. The literacy statistics are in Kenneth Sokoloff and Stanley Engerman, "Institutions, Factor Endowments, and Paths of Development in the New World," *Journal of Economic Perspectives* 14, no. 3 (Summer 2000): 229.

14. Roque Dalton, *Taberna y otros lugares* (Havana: Casa de las Américas, 1969), 7; Castañeda, *Utopia Unarmed*, 196.

15. Ángel Rama, *The Lettered City,* trans. John Charles Chasteen (Durham, N.C.: Duke University Press, 1996). Rama's short, posthumously published essay is necessarily an oversimplification with many omissions. For more details that incorporate differences between different national settings, see Carlos Altamirano, ed., *Historia de los intelectuales en América Latina,* 2 vols. (Buenos Aires: Katz, 2008); Oscar Terán, ed., *Ideas en el siglo: Intelectuales y cultura en el siglo XX latinoamericano* (Buenos Aires: Siglo XXI, 2004); Tulio Halperín Donghi, *Letrados y pensadores: El perfilamiento del intelectual hispanoamericano en el siglo XIX* (Buenos Aires: Emecé, 2013); and Mabel Moraña and Bret Gustafson, eds., *Rethinking Intellectuals in Latin America* (Madrid: Iberoamericana Vervuert, 2010).

16. Altamirano, *Historia de los intelectuales en América Latina,* 1:21. The word "intellectual" entered into public use during the Dreyfus affair in France. Captain Alfred Dreyfus, who was Jewish, was falsely imprisoned for treason against the French army in 1894; the novelist Émile Zola was the most prominent of the "intellectuals" who demanded the truth about the case. Anti-Dreyfusards insisted that the legitimacy of pillars of society, such as the army and the church, required that Dreyfus remain guilty. Hundreds of books have been written about the Dreyfus affair; few are more useful than Michael Burns, *France and the Dreyfus Affair: A Documentary History* (Boston: Bedford, 1999). Some recent scholarship has qualified the qualities associated with the Dreyfusards and anti-Dreyfusards: Ruth Harris, *Dreyfus: Politics, Emotion and the Scandal of the Century* (New York: Metropolitan Books, 2010).

Tony Judt cogently observes that in the sense of being committed to "higher truths" rather than the basic truthfulness of facts, the anti-Dreyfusards in many ways had more in common with the typical twentieth-century intellectual than did the Dreyfusards. Tony Judt and Timothy Snyder, *Thinking the Twentieth Century* (New York: Penguin Press, 2012), 287. And although the term "intellectual" does date to the Dreyfus affair, the type emerged in eighteenth-century Europe; Didier Masseau, *L'invention de l'intellectuel dans l'Europe du XVIIIe siècle* (Paris: Presses Universitaires de France, 1994), 6.

17. The relationship of intellectuals to the state has been a major preoccupation of several historiographies of the region. With a broad lens, Nicola Miller has argued that the influence of intellectuals in Spanish America has been exaggerated, but she makes an exception for Brazil; Miller, *In the Shadow of the State,* 82. Because of its focus on the construction of national identity, Miller's lucid book does not really engage with Cold War intellectuals' international work. Because of the high degree of perceived co-optation, scholars of and from Mexico have produced a great deal of writing trying to specify the origins of different categories of intellectuals in that country, as well as their influence or lack of it. Among the most important are Charles A. Hale, *The Transformation of Liberalism in Late Nineteenth-Century Mexico* (Princeton, N.J.: Princeton University Press, 1989); Ignacio M. Sánchez Prado, *Naciones intelectuales: Las fundaciones de la modernidad literaria mexicana, 1917–1959* (West Lafayette, Ind.: Purdue University Press, 2009); Roderic Camp, Charles A. Hale, and Josefina Zoraida Vázquez, eds., *Los intelectuales y el poder en México: Memorias de la VI Conferencia de Historiadores Mexicanos y Estadounidenses* (Mexico City: El Colegio de México, 1991); Roderic Camp, *Intellectuals and the State in Twentieth-Century Mexico* (Austin: University of Texas Press, 1985); and Gabriel Zaid, *De los libros al poder* (Mexico City: Oceano, 1998). There are parallel literatures in other countries, where currents, institutions, and political movements differed. The point is not to settle on a single definition of an intellectual, but rather to note that intellectuals' self-concept was shaped by their historical circumstances, and that those who saw themselves not just as Mexican, or Argentine, or Dominican intellectuals but rather as "Latin American" intellectuals expanded with the Cold War because they conceived of problems as "Latin American" in scope.

18. Paco Ignacio Taibo, *Guevara, Also Known as Che,* trans. Martin Michael Roberts (New York: St. Martin's Press, 1997), 300; Régis Debray, *Prison Writings,* trans. Rosemary Sheed (London: Allen Lane, 1973), 190–191.

19. The argument of Latin America as laboratory is that of Greg Grandin, *Empire's Workshop: Latin America, the United States and the Rise of the New Imperialism* (New York: Metropolitan Books, 2006), 2–5. The "racketeer" was Smedley Darlington Butler, "America's Armed Forces," *Common Sense* 6, no. 11 (November 1935): 8. For careful examinations of how U.S. occupations tried to foster political democracy on the U.S. model but left dictatorships instead, see Michel Gobat, *Confronting the American Dream: Nicaragua under U.S. Imperial Rule* (Durham, N.C.: Duke University Press, 2005); and

Alan McPherson, *The Invaded: How Latin Americans and Their Allies Fought and Ended U.S. Occupations* (Oxford: Oxford University Press, 2014). In some cases, Butler's self-criticism seems largely warranted; in others, such as U.S. intervention in the Mexican Revolution, he oversimplifies U.S. motivations for intervention. Friedrich Katz, *The Secret War in Mexico: Europe, the United States, and the Mexican Revolution* (Chicago: University of Chicago Press, 1981), 156–167, 196–199. On the assumptions of U.S. liberal empire and cultural relations that emerged from them, see especially Emily Rosenberg, *Spreading the American Dream: American Economic and Cultural Expansion, 1890–1945* (New York: Hill & Wang, 1982); and G. M. Joseph, Catherine LeGrand, and Ricardo Donato Salvatore, *Close Encounters of Empire: Writing the Cultural History of U.S.–Latin American Relations* (Durham, N.C.: Duke University Press, 1998).

20. Justin Hart, *Empire of Ideas: The Origins of Public Diplomacy and the Transformation of U.S. Foreign Policy* (Oxford: Oxford University Press, 2012); Frank A. Ninkovich, *The Diplomacy of Ideas: U.S. Foreign Policy and Cultural Relations, 1938–1950* (Cambridge: Cambridge University Press, 1981); J. Manuel Espinosa, *Inter-American Beginnings of U.S. Cultural Diplomacy, 1936–1948* (Washington, D.C.: Bureau of Educational and Cultural Affairs, U.S. Dept. of State, 1977); Gisela Cramer and Ursula Prutsch, eds., *¡Américas unidas! Nelson A. Rockefeller's Office of Inter-American Affairs* (Madrid: Iberoamericana Vervuert, 2012); Antônio Pedro Tota, *O imperialismo sedutor: A americanização do Brasil na época da Segunda Guerra* (São Paulo, Brazil: Companhia das Letras, 2000). Julie Prieto locates the creation of U.S. public diplomacy as a response to the Mexican Revolution. Julie Prieto, "The Borders of Culture: Public Diplomacy in United States–Mexico Relations, 1920–1945" (Ph.D. diss., Stanford University, 2013). European states, and even the Soviet Union, began the process somewhat earlier. Jessica C. E. Gienow-Hecht and Mark C. Donfried, eds., *Searching for a Cultural Diplomacy* (New York: Berghahn Books, 2010), 18; Jean-François Fayet, "VOKS: The Third Dimension of Soviet Foreign Policy," in Gienow-Hecht and Donfried, *Searching for a Cultural Diplomacy,* 33–49. Cultural diplomacy—though not yet its "public" variant, aimed at ordinary people—was not the province only of European powers. Mexico, for example, made a calculated show of its bid for modernity at late nineteenth-century world's fairs by, ironically, looking back hundreds of years to the civilizations that had occupied its lands before the arrival of Spanish colonialism in an attempt to claim the inheritance of a great nation. Mauricio Tenorio Trillo, *Mexico at the World's Fairs: Crafting a Modern Nation* (Berkeley: University of California Press, 1996).

21. On U.S. cultural diplomacy and its contradictions after the war, see Laura Belmonte, *Selling the American Way: U.S. Propaganda and the Cold War* (Philadelphia: University of Pennsylvania Press, 2008); Walter L. Hixson, *Parting the Curtain: Propaganda, Culture, and the Cold War, 1945–1961* (New York: St. Martin's Press, 1997); Scott Lucas, *Freedom's War: The American Crusade against the Soviet Union* (New York: New York University

Press, 1999); Robert H. Haddow, *Pavilions of Plenty: Exhibiting American Culture Abroad in the 1950s* (Washington, D.C.: Smithsonian Institution Press, 1997); Penny M. Von Eschen, *Satchmo Blows Up the World: Jazz Ambassadors Play the Cold War* (Cambridge, Mass.: Harvard University Press, 2004); Kenneth Osgood, *Total Cold War: Eisenhower's Secret Propaganda Battle at Home and Abroad* (Lawrence: University Press of Kansas, 2006); and Nicholas J. Cull, *The Cold War and the United States Information Agency: American Propaganda and Public Diplomacy, 1945–1989* (Cambridge: Cambridge University Press, 2008).

22. On the collapse of the Good Neighbor Policy, see Bryce Wood, *The Dismantling of the Good Neighbor Policy* (Austin: University of Texas Press, 1985); Steven Schwartzberg, *Democracy and U.S. Policy in Latin America during the Truman Years* (Gainesville: University Press of Florida, 2003); and Leslie Bethell and Ian Roxborough, eds., *Latin America between the Second World War and the Cold War, 1944–1948* (Cambridge: Cambridge University Press, 1992). On U.S. cultural propaganda in Latin America during the early Cold War, see Seth Fein, "New Empire into Old: Making Mexican Newsreels the Cold War Way," *Diplomatic History* 28, no. 5 (November 2004): 703–748; and Warren Dean, "The USIA Book Program: How Translations of 'Politically Correct' Books Are (Secretly?) Subsidized for Sale in Latin America," *Point of Contact* 3 (October 1976): 4–14.

23. President Kennedy is quoted in Arthur Meier Schlesinger, *A Thousand Days: John F. Kennedy in the White House* (Boston: Houghton Mifflin, 1965), 769. The dictatorship in question was Rafael Trujillo's Dominican Republic, perhaps the most totalitarian government in the Western Hemisphere during the twentieth century. Greg Grandin, *The Last Colonial Massacre: Latin America in the Cold War* (Chicago: University of Chicago Press, 2004), xii; John Coatsworth, "The Cold War in Central America, 1975–1991," in *The Cambridge History of the Cold War,* ed. Melvyn P. Leffler and Odd Arne Westad, vol. 3 (Cambridge: Cambridge University Press, 2010), 221; Kathryn Sikkink, *Mixed Signals: U.S. Human Rights Policy and Latin America* (Ithaca, N.Y.: Cornell University Press, 2004). Recent transnational scholarship has emphasized the multilayered nature of Latin America's Cold War, showing that it had local, national, and international dimensions. Hal Brands, *Latin America's Cold War* (Cambridge, Mass.: Harvard University Press, 2010); Tanya Harmer, *Allende's Chile and the Inter-American Cold War* (Chapel Hill: University of North Carolina Press, 2011). Consideration of the region's Cultural Cold War supports that interpretation.

24. For example, Octavio Paz, *El ogro filantrópico: Historia y política, 1971–1978* (Mexico City: Círculo de lectores, 1979), 380.

25. Some books that take the prehistory of the Cold War seriously are Irene Rostagno, *Searching for Recognition: The Promotion of Latin American Literature in the United States* (Westport, Conn.: Greenwood Press, 1997); Jean Franco, *The Decline and Fall of the Lettered City: Latin America in the Cold War* (Cambridge, Mass.: Harvard University Press, 2002); Germán Alburquerque, *La trinchera letrada: Intelectuales latinoamericanos y Guerra Fría* (Santiago,

Chile: Ariadna Ediciones, 2011); Olga Glondys, *La guerra fría cultural y el exilio republicano español: Cuadernos del Congreso por la Libertad de la Cultura (1953–1965)* (Madrid: Consejo Superior de Investigaciones Científicas, 2012); and Claire Fox, *Making Art Panamerican: Cultural Policy and the Cold War* (Minneapolis: University of Minnesota Press, 2013). The strength of Glondys's book is its analysis of the Spanish exile community rather than Latin American politics. The book that does the most to situate *Mundo Nuevo* as part of U.S. policies is María Eugenia Mudrovcic, Mundo Nuevo: *Cultura y guerra fría en la década del 60* (Rosario, Argentina: Beatriz Viterbo Editora, 1997). Works that emphasize its counterhegemonic potential include Russell Cobb, "Promoting Literature in the Most Dangerous Area in the World: The Cold War, the Boom, and *Mundo Nuevo*," in *Pressing the Fight: Print, Propaganda, and the Cold War,* ed. Greg Barnhisel and Catherine Turner (Amherst: University of Massachusetts Press, 2010), 248; Russell Cobb, "The Politics of Literary Prestige: Promoting the Latin American 'Boom' in the Pages of *Mundo Nuevo*," *A Contracorriente* 5, no. 3 (Spring 2008): 75–94; and Deborah Cohn, *The Latin American Literary Boom and U.S. Nationalism during the Cold War* (Nashville: Vanderbilt University Press, 2012), 23. Other insightful works on intellectuals in the 1960s include Diana Sorensen, *A Turbulent Decade Remembered: Scenes from the Latin American Sixties* (Stanford, Calif.: Stanford University Press, 2007); Idalia Morejón Arnaiz, *Política y polémica en América Latina: Las revistas* Casa de las Américas *y* Mundo Nuevo (Mexico City: Educación y Cultura, 2010); and Claudia Gilman, *Entre la pluma y el fusil: Debates y dilemas del escritor revolucionario en América Latina* (Buenos Aires: Siglo Veintiuno Editores Argentina, 2003). Gilman's exploration of intellectual debate is especially detailed, though she focuses more the intra-Latin American issues than the global Cold War.

26. These questions each represent schools of historical analysis of Latin America's Cold War. Jorge Castañeda has criticized the Left for its Marxist-inspired abandonment of the liberal institutions of democracy: Castañeda, *Utopia Unarmed.* The "two devils" argument is made at the local and regional levels, respectively, by David Stoll, *Between Two Armies in the Ixil Towns of Guatemala* (New York: Columbia University Press, 1993); and Brands, *Latin America's Cold War.* Accounts that emphasize the power of U.S.-led reaction while allowing that it is not a full explanation include Grandin, *Last Colonial Massacre;* and Stephen Rabe, *The Killing Zone: The United States Wages Cold War in Latin America* (New York: Oxford University Press, 2012). For a formulation of the problem, see Gil Joseph, "What We Now Know and Should Know: Bringing Latin America More Meaningfully into Cold War Studies," in *In from the Cold: Latin America's New Encounter with the Cold War,* ed. Gil Joseph and Daniela Spenser (Durham, N.C.: Duke University Press, 2008), 28.

1. Exile and Dissent in the Making of the Cultural Cold War

1. Victor Serge, Julián Gorkin, and Marceau Pivert to ciudadanos de México y Presidente de los Estados Unidos Mexicanos, 16 January 1942, gallery 3, Manuel Ávila Camacho (MAC), box 824bis, folder 550/9, Archivo General de la Nación (AGN), Mexico City.

2. Susan Weissman, *Victor Serge: The Course Is Set on Hope* (London: Verso, 2001), 178–179; Gustav Regler, *The Owl of Minerva: The Autobiography of Gustav Regler* (New York: Farrar, Straus and Cudahy, 1959), 167–171; Isabelle Tombs, "Erlich and Alter, 'The Sacco and Vanzetti of the USSR': An Episode in the Wartime History of International Socialism," *Journal of Contemporary History* 23, no. 4 (October 1988): 531–549; Nunzio Pernicone, *Carlo Tresca: Portrait of a Rebel* (New York: Palgrave Macmillan, 2005); Dorothy Gallagher, *All the Right Enemies: The Life and Murder of Carlo Tresca* (New Brunswick, N.J.: Rutgers University Press, 1988). Gorkin's suspicions are in Director, FBI to Commissioner, Immigration and Naturalization Service, 19 March 1950, Julián Gorkin FBI file. Like many other Soviet cultural operatives, Otto Katz was eventually murdered by the governments he served. In the postwar Slánský trial in Czechoslovakia, Katz was forced to make a false confession of having been a spy for Britain, France, and the United States during the war, a Trotskyite since the 1920s, a conspirator against the people, and a bourgeois idealist. He was put to death in 1952. Eugen Loebl, *Sentenced and Tried: The Stalinist Purges in Czechoslovakia* (London: Elek, 1969), 151–158.

3. The man protecting Serge's daughter, Jeannine, was Enrique Gironella, another member of Gorkin's POUM. Susan Weissman, *The Ideas of Victor Serge: A Life as a Work of Art* (Glasgow: Critique Books, 1997), 12–13; "Escandalosa trifulca en el Centro Cultural Ibero Mexicano por un atraco comunista," *La Prensa,* 2 April 1943, 23; "Fueron 73 los detenidos en el incidente comunista," *El Universal Gráfico,* 2 April 1943, 3.

4. Greg Grandin, *The Last Colonial Massacre: Latin America in the Cold War* (Chicago: University of Chicago Press, 2004), 17; E. J. Hobsbawm, *The Age of Extremes: The Short Twentieth Century, 1914–1991* (New York: Vintage, 1994); Anders Stephanson, *Manifest Destiny: American Expansionism and the Empire of Right* (New York: Hill & Wang, 1995), 122; Odd Arne Westad, *The Global Cold War: Third World Interventions and the Making of Our Times* (Cambridge: Cambridge University Press, 2005); Melvyn P. Leffler and Odd Arne Westad, eds., *The Cambridge History of the Cold War,* vol. 1, *Origins* (Cambridge: Cambridge University Press, 2010). For opposite views of a "centered" versus a "decentered" Cold War, see the contributions of Stephanson and Westad to Joel Isaac and Duncan Bell, eds., *Uncertain Empire: American History and the Idea of the Cold War* (New York: Oxford University Press, 2012). For the case for a "long" Cold War in Latin America, see Greg Grandin and Gilbert M. Joseph, eds., *A Century of Revolution: Insurgent and Counterinsurgent Violence during Latin America's Long Cold War* (Durham, N.C.: Duke University Press, 2010).

5. Jean Van Heijenoort, *With Trotsky in Exile: From Prinkipo to Coyoacán* (Cambridge, Mass.: Harvard University Press, 1978), 103. Mexico's asylum policy coexisted with an immigration policy that, like those of other nations, was based on cultural prejudices. Immigration permits were not granted to minority groups, including Jews, who were considered difficult to assimilate. Daniela Gleizer Salzman, *México frente a la inmigración de refugiados judíos, 1934–1940* (Mexico City: CONACULTA-INAH, Fundación Cultura Eduardo Cohen, 2000), 76, 183–184.

6. Mauricio Tenorio Trillo, *I Speak of the City: Mexico City at the Turn of the Twentieth Century* (Chicago: University of Chicago Press, 2012), 94; Mauricio Tenorio Trillo, "Stereophonic Scientific Modernisms: Social Science between Mexico and the United States, 1880s–1930s," *Journal of American History* 86, no. 3 (December 1999): 1156–1187; José Antonio Aguilar Rivera, *The Shadow of Ulysses: Public Intellectual Exchange across the U.S.-Mexican Border* (Lanham, Md.: Lexington Books, 2000), 4–6; John Reed, *Insurgent Mexico* (New York: D. Appleton and Company, 1914).

7. José Enrique Rodó, *Ariel* (Austin: University of Texas Press, 1988), 87–88; Irene Rostagno, *Searching for Recognition: The Promotion of Latin American Literature in the United States* (Westport, Conn.: Greenwood Press, 1997), 1–30; James Burkhart Gilbert, *Writers and Partisans: A History of Literary Radicalism in America* (New York: Wiley, 1968).

8. Helen Delpar, *The Enormous Vogue of Things Mexican: Cultural Relations between the United States and Mexico, 1920–1935* (Tuscaloosa: University of Alabama Press, 1992), 20–52; Gilbert M. Joseph, *Revolution from Without: Yucatán, Mexico, and the United States, 1880–1924* (Cambridge: Cambridge University Press, 1982), 221–222.

9. Robin Adèle Greeley, "Muralism and the State in Post-revolution Mexico, 1920–1970," in *Mexican Muralism: A Critical History*, ed. Alejandro Anreus, Robin Adèle Greeley, and Leonard Folgarait (Berkeley: University of California Press, 2012), 18.

10. *El Machete* became the official newspaper of the PCM in late 1924. Barry Carr, *Marxism and Communism in Twentieth-Century Mexico* (Lincoln: University of Nebraska Press, 1992), 36; Anita Brenner, *Idols behind Altars* (New York: Payson & Clarke, 1929), 244–259; Philip Stein, *Siqueiros: His Life and Works* (New York: International Publishers, 1994), 54. On the origins of Communism in Mexico, see Daniela Spenser, "Emissaries of the Communist International in Mexico," *American Communist History* 6, no. 2 (2007): 151–170; Daniela Spenser, *Los primeros tropiezos de la Internacional Comunista en México* (Mexico City: CIESAS, 2009); Arnoldo Martínez Verdugo, *Historia del comunismo en México* (Mexico City: Grijalbo, 1985), 15–57; Daniela Spenser and Rina Ortiz Peralta, *La Internacional Comunista en Mexico: Los primeros tropiezos, documentos, 1919–1922* (Mexico City: Instituto Nacional de Estudios Históricos de las Revoluciones de México, 2006); Charles Shipman, *It Had to Be Revolution: Memoirs of an American Radical* (Ithaca, N.Y.: Cornell University Press, 1993); and Carr, *Marxism and Communism in Twentieth-Century Mexico*, 20–27.

11. Brenner, *Idols behind Altars*, 255. Siqueiros and the French artist Jean Charlot had drafted similar statements earlier. Alicia Azuela de la Cueva, *Arte y poder: Renacimiento artístico y revolución social; México, 1910–1945* (Zamora, Michoacán: El Colegio de Michoacán, 2005), 159.

12. Ione Robinson, quoted in Leonard Folgarait, *Seeing Mexico Photographed: The Work of Horne, Casasola, Modotti, and Álvarez Bravo* (New Haven, Conn.: Yale University Press, 2008), 107; Patricia Albers, *Shadows, Fire, Snow: The Life of Tina Modotti* (New York: Clarkson Potter, 1999), 145–146. On Modotti, see also Margaret Hooks, *Tina Modotti: Photographer and Revolutionary* (London: Pandora, 1993); Pino Cacucci, *Tina Modotti: A Life* (New York: St. Martin's Press, 1999); Letizia Argenteri, *Tina Modotti: Between Art and Revolution* (New Haven, Conn.: Yale University Press, 2003); and Mildred Constantine, *Tina Modotti: A Fragile Life* (London: Paddington Press, 1975).

13. Hooks, *Tina Modotti*, 162–163; Christine Hatzky, *Julio Antonio Mella (1903–1929): Eine Biografie* (Frankfurt am Main: Vervuert, 2004); Raquel Tibol, *Julio Antonio Mella en* El Machete: *Antología parcial de un luchador y su momento histórico* (Mexico City: Fondo de Cultura Popular, 1968); Lazar Jeifets, Victor Jeifets, and Peter Huber, *La Internacional comunista y América Latina, 1919–1943: Diccionario biográfico* (Moscow: Instituto de Latinoamérica de la Academia de las Ciencias, 2004); Vittorio Vidali, *Comandante Carlos*, trans. Cristina Cámpora (Mexico City: Ediciones de Cultura Popular, 1986).

14. The evidence of the Cuban's government's involvement is solid; the theories that allege Mexican government collaboration or Communist participation cannot be supported by any available evidence. Hatzky, *Julio Antonio Mella*, 300–328.

15. Heather Fowler-Salamini, *Agrarian Radicalism in Veracruz, 1920–38* (Lincoln: University of Nebraska Press, 1978), 61–64.

16. Leon Trotsky, *The Revolution Betrayed: What Is the Soviet Union and Where Is It Going?*, trans. Max Eastman (New York: Pioneer Publishers, 1945), 183–184.

17. Leon Trotsky, *Literature and Revolution* (Ann Arbor: University of Michigan Press, 1960), 14, 219–221. Many scholars are skeptical that Trotsky fully deserves his reputation as a kind of "anti-Stalin." Robert Service, *Trotsky: A Biography* (Cambridge, Mass.: Belknap Press of Harvard University Press, 2009), 3–6; Leszek Kolakowski, *Main Currents of Marxism*, vol. 3, *The Breakdown* (Oxford: Clarendon Press, 1978), 183–219.

18. Orlando Figes, *Natasha's Dance: A Cultural History of Russia* (New York: Metropolitan Books, 2002), 447–474; Nigel Gould-Davies, "The Logic of Soviet Cultural Diplomacy," *Diplomatic History* 27, no. 2 (April 2003): 193–214; Abram Tertz (Andrei Donatevich Siniavskii), *The Trial Begins and On Socialist Realism* (New York: Vintage Books, 1965); Herbert R. Lottman, *The Left Bank: Writers, Artists, and Politics from the Popular Front to the Cold War* (Boston: Houghton Mifflin, 1982), 62–67; Regler, *Owl of Minerva*, 203–216; Andrei Zhdanov, Maxim Gorky, Nikolai Bukharin, Karl Radek, and

A. Stetsky, *Problems of Soviet Literature: Reports and Speeches at the First Soviet Writers' Congress* (New York: International Publishers, 1935).

19. Guillermo Sheridan, *Poeta con paisaje: Ensayos sobre la vida de Octavio Paz* (Mexico City: Ediciones Era, 2004), 241. Breton's speech and his account of the congress can be found in André Breton, *Manifestoes of Surrealism* (Ann Arbor: University of Michigan Press, 1969), 234–253. Aragon's rejoinder is in Manuel Aznar Soler, *I Congreso Internacional de Escritores para la Defensa de la Cultura, París 1935* (Valencia: Generalitat Valenciana Conselleria de Cultura, Educació i Ciencia, 1987), 433–441.

20. Only 50 of the 700 attendees of the First Soviet Writers' Congress in 1934 survived to the Second Congress in 1954. Figes, *Natasha's Dance,* 482.

21. Julián Gorkin, *El revolucionario profesional: Testimonio de un hombre de acción* (Barcelona: Aymá, 1975); Pepe Gutiérrez-Álvarez, *Retratos poumistas* (Seville: Espuela de Plata, 2006), 169.

22. On Popular Front culture in the United States, see Michael Denning, *The Cultural Front: The Laboring of American Culture in the Twentieth Century* (London: Verso, 1998).

23. Jorge Basurto, *Cárdenas y el poder sindical* (Mexico City: Era, 1983), 19, 118, 159.

24. Lázaro Cárdenas, *Apuntes, 1913–1940* (Mexico City: Universidad Nacional Autónoma de México, 1972), 334; Lázaro Cárdenas, *Apuntes, 1957–1966* (Mexico City: Universidad Nacional Autónoma de México, 1973), 104; Guadalupe Pacheco Méndez, Arturo Anguiano, and Rogelio Vizcaíno A., *Cárdenas y la izquierda mexicana: Ensayo, testimonios, documentos de Guadalupe Pacheco Méndez, Arturo Anguiano Orozco y Rogelio Vizcaíno A.* (Mexico City: J. Pablos Editor, 1975), 125; Basurto, *Cárdenas y el poder sindical,* 82–98.

25. Cárdenas, *Apuntes, 1913–1940,* 368; "What Does the CTAL Mean?," pamphlet, 1944, Vicente Lombardo Toledano FBI file. On the foreign policy objectives of the CTAL, see Amelia Kiddle, "La Política del Buen Amigo: Mexican-Latin American Relations during the Presidency of Lázaro Cárdenas, 1934–1940" (Ph.D. diss., University of Arizona, 2010), 217–220.

26. Daniela Spenser, *Unidad a toda costa: La Tercera Internacional en México durante la presidencia de Lázaro Cárdenas* (Mexico City: CIESAS, 2007), 260.

27. On Trotskyism and the LEAR, see Jean Freville, "El marxismo y la literatura," *Frente a frente,* no. 5 (August 1936): 8; Mary K. Coffey, *How a Revolutionary Art Became Official Culture: Murals, Museums, and the Mexican State* (Durham, N.C.: Duke University Press, 2012), 29; and Sheridan, *Poeta con paisaje,* 177–179. On the muralists, see Alejandro Anreus, "Los Tres Grandes: Ideologies and Styles," in Anreus, Greeley, and Folgarait, *Mexican Muralism,* 49. On the Taller de Gráfica Popular, see Helga Prignitz, *El Taller de Gráfica Popular en México,* trans. Elizabeth Siefer (Mexico City: Instituto Nacional de Bellas Artes, 1992). On the Argentine analogue to the LEAR, which lasted somewhat longer, see James Cane, "'Unity for the Defense of Culture': The AIAPE and the Cultural Politics of Argentine Antifascism, 1935–1943," *Hispanic American Historical Review* 77, no. 3 (August 1997): 443–482.

28. Franklin D. Roosevelt, after initially following a policy of nonintervention, likely pursued both legal and illegal means to aid the Republican side. Dominic Tierney, *FDR and the Spanish Civil War: Neutrality and Commitment in the Struggle That Divided America* (Durham, N.C.: Duke University Press, 2007); Pavel Sudoplatov, Anatoli Sudoplatov, Jerrold Schecter, Leona Schecter, and Robert Conquest, *Special Tasks: The Memoirs of an Unwanted Witness, a Soviet Spymaster* (Boston: Little, Brown, 1994), 30.

29. Estimates vary between 14,000 and 40,000 refugees. *El exilio Español en México, 1939–1982* (Mexico City: Fondo de Cultura Económica, 1982), 101. On Mexico in the Spanish Civil War, see Mario Ojeda Revah, *México y la Guerra Civil Española* (Madrid: Turner, 2004); José Antonio Matesanz, *Las raíces del exilio: México ante la Guerra Civil Española, 1936–1939* (Mexico City: El Colegio de México: Universidad Nacional Autónoma de México, 1999); and T. G. Powell, *Mexico and the Spanish Civil War* (Albuquerque: University of New Mexico Press, 1980). There is evidence that the Soviet Union overcharged Spain for weapons it provided, although without them the Republic would surely have fallen sooner. Gerald Howson, *Arms for Spain: The Untold Story of the Spanish Civil War* (London: J. Murray, 1998).

30. The "smoking gun" document often purported to show Communist premeditation of the attack on the anarchist-held *Telefónica,* which began the May Days fighting, in fact shows only that Communists thought that a government crisis would be to their advantage. Ronald Radosh, Mary R. Habeck, and Grigory Sevostianov, eds., *Spain Betrayed: The Soviet Union in the Spanish Civil War* (New Haven, Conn.: Yale University Press, 2001), 174, 184–195. For years there was uncertainty about the precise circumstances of Nin's death. The most widely accepted version, which asserted that he had been tortured and killed in Alcalá de Henares, northeast of Madrid, was confirmed by Spanish documentary filmmakers using KGB files after the collapse of the Soviet Union. Antonio Elorza and Marta Bizcarrondo, *Queridos camaradas: La Internacional Comunista y España, 1919–1939* (Barcelona: Planeta, 1999), 376–377. Burnett Bolloten, *The Spanish Civil War: Revolution and Counterrevolution* (Chapel Hill: University of North Carolina Press, 1991), 520; Wilebaldo Solano, *El POUM en la historia: Andreu Nin y la revolución española,* 2nd ed. (Madrid: Libros de la Catarata, 2000), 31.

31. Pablo Neruda, *Memoirs: Confieso que he vivido* (New York: Farrar, Straus and Giroux, 1977), 130–135; Ojeda Revah, *México y la Guerra Civil Española,* 186. On Republican propaganda abroad, see Hugo García, *The Truth about Spain! Mobilizing British Public Opinion, 1936–1939* (Brighton: Sussex Academic Press, 2010).

32. André Gide, *Back from the U.S.S.R.,* 3rd ed., trans. Dorothy Bussy (London: Secker and Warburg, 1937); André Gide, *Afterthoughts, a Sequel to "Back from the U.S.S.R.,"* 2nd ed. (London: Secker and Warburg, 1937), 67, 71; Robert S. Thornberry, "Writers Take Sides, Stalinists Take Control: The Second International Congress for the Defense of Culture (Spain 1937)," *Historian* 62, no. 3 (Spring 2000): 589–605; Manuel Aznar Soler, *Pensamiento literario y compromiso antifascista de la inteligencia española republicana* (Barcelona:

Laia, 1978); Manuel Aznar Soler and Luis Mario Schneider, *Ponencias, documentos, testimonios* (Barcelona: Laia, 1979); Luis Mario Schneider, *Inteligencia y guerra civil en España* (Barcelona: Laia, 1978); Alberto Ruy Sánchez, *Tristeza de la verdad: André Gide regresa de Rusia* (Mexico City: Joaquín Mortiz, 1991).

33. Adam Feinstein, *Pablo Neruda: A Passion for Life* (New York: Bloomsbury, 2004), 115–129; Neruda, *Memoirs*, 136.

34. Sheridan, *Poeta con paisaje*, 306; Octavio Paz, *Itinerario* (Mexico City: Fondo de Cultura Económica, 1993), 66–67. An example of Paz's continued work on behalf of Popular Front causes is the essay that he published in Vicente Lombardo Toledano's "Stalinist" magazine, *Futuro* (although there is nothing either Stalinist or anti-Stalinist about the essay): "Americanidad de España," *Futuro*, no. 35 (January 1939), 18–19. See also John King, *The Role of Mexico's* Plural *in Latin American Literary and Political Culture: From Tlatelolco to the "Philanthropic Ogre"* (New York: Palgrave Macmillan, 2007), 17–18. Paz wrote his first openly anti-Stalinist essay after reading David Rousset's 1949 work *L'univers concentrationnaire*, about the system of forced labor camps critical to the Soviet economy. Paz, *Itinerario*, 75–76; Sheridan, *Poeta con paisaje*, 314–315, 403–411; Enrique Krauze, *Redeemers: Ideas and Power in Latin America*, trans. Hank Heifetz and Natasha Wimmer (New York: Harper, 2011), 173.

35. Leon Trotsky, John Dewey, and Albert Manning Glotzer, *The Case of Leon Trotsky*, 1st paperback ed. (New York: Pathfinder Press, 2006), 491–494; John Dewey, Benjamin Stolberg, and Suzanne La Follette, *Not Guilty: Report of the Commission of Inquiry into the Charges Made against Leon Trotsky in the Moscow Trials*, 2nd ed. (New York: Monad Press, 1972). The tacit support of Cárdenas is clear because two of the members of the committee, Benjamin Stolberg and Suzanne La Follette, were experiencing visa troubles. When Dewey cabled Cárdenas to ask him to intervene so that Stolberg and La Follette would encounter no difficulties at the U.S.-Mexico border, Cárdenas acted immediately to ensure that they could cross into Mexico. John Dewey to Lázaro Cárdenas, 3 April 1937; and Cárdenas to Secretaría de Gobernación, 4 April 1937, Gallery 3—Lázaro Cárdenas del Río (LCR), folder 546.6/77, AGN.

36. Jay Martin, *The Education of John Dewey: A Biography* (New York: Columbia University Press, 2002), 418–421; Van Heijenoort, *With Trotsky in Exile*, 110.

37. Leon Trotsky and André Breton, "Manifesto: Towards a Free Revolutionary Art," *Partisan Review* 6, no. 1 (Fall 1938): 49–53. As in other places, this version of the manifesto, translated by Dwight Macdonald, strategically lists the authors of the manifesto as Breton and Diego Rivera and omits Trotsky.

38. Sidney Hook, *Out of Step: An Unquiet Life in the 20th Century* (New York: Harper & Row, 1987), 248–274. Signers of Hook's manifesto included, among others, Sherwood Anderson, George S. Counts, Merle Curti, John Dewey, John Dos Passos, Max Eastman, Suzanne La Follette, Sol Levitas, Eugene Lyons, James Rorty, Arthur M. Schlesinger, Norman Thomas, and Carlo Tresca. The

"fascists and their allies" quote is from "To All Active Supporters of Democracy and Peace," *The Nation* 149, no. 9 (26 August 1939): 228. The signers of the League for Cultural Freedom and Socialism manifesto included James Burnham, James T. Farrell, Clement Greenberg, Melvin J. Lasky, Dwight Macdonald, George Novack, Philip Rahv, James Rorty, Delmore Schwartz, and Bertram Wolfe. "Statement of the L.C.F.S.," *Partisan Review* 6, no. 4 (Summer 1939): 125–127. Most of the U.S. personnel of the future Congress for Cultural Freedom signed one of these two manifestos (or, in the case of James Rorty, both).

39. Betty Kirk, *Covering the Mexican Front: The Battle of Europe versus America* (Norman: University of Oklahoma Press, 1942), 88.

40. On U.S. fear of Nazism in the Americas, see Max Paul Friedman, *Nazis and Good Neighbors: The United States Campaign against the Germans of Latin America in World War II* (Cambridge: Cambridge University Press, 2003).

41. Ted Morgan, *Reds: McCarthyism in Twentieth-Century America* (New York: Random House, 2003), 184–222.

42. Isaac Deutscher, *The Prophet Outcast: Trotsky, 1929–1940* (London: Verso, 2003), 390–391; David Álfaro Siqueiros, *Me llamaban el Coronelazo: Memorias* (Mexico City: Grijalbo, 1977), 363–364. Neruda would sometimes later maintain that he did not know Siqueiros and was acting out of solidarity with someone who had fought in the Spanish Civil War. This was not true; Neruda had in fact met Siqueiros at least in 1939, although it was true that Neruda arrived in Mexico to work as Chilean consul after Siqueiros's attempt to assassinate Trotsky. Jorge Edwards, *Adios, poeta . . . : Memorias* (Barcelona: Tusquets Editores, 1990), 277–280.

43. Pete Hamill, *Diego Rivera* (New York: Harry N. Abrams, 1999), 192–194; Patrick Marnham, *Dreaming with His Eyes Open: A Life of Diego Rivera* (Berkeley: University of California Press, 2000), 288. Hamill and Marnham's references are based on unpublished research, now decades old, by William Chase of the University of Pittsburgh. The information on Gorkin comes from Report on Julián Gómez García, 16 December 1944, Julián Gorkin FBI file.

44. Luis-Martín Lozano, Juan Coronel Rivera, and Benedikt Taschen, eds., *Diego Rivera: The Complete Murals* (Hong Kong: Taschen, 2008), 398; Marnham, *Dreaming with His Eyes Open,* 292. Trotsky's final days are vividly described in Bertrand Patenaude, *Trotsky: Downfall of a Revolutionary* (New York: HarperCollins, 2009).

45. Ferdinand Lundberg to Hook, n.d. [Summer 1941], Sidney Hook Papers, folder 7, box 117, Hoover Institution Archives (HIA), Stanford, Calif. The law that the Trotskyists were charged with violating was the Smith Act, which would be used against the leadership of the Communist Party of the United States of America (CPUSA) in 1949. Although it was aware of the dangerous precedent being set, the CPUSA supported the prosecution in 1941. Maurice Isserman, *Which Side Were You On? The American Communist Party during the Second World War* (Urbana: University of Illinois Press, 1993), 123–124.

46. "Repercusiones en México de la ruptura entre nazis y soviets: Mensaje a las centrales y organismos obreros miembros de la CTAL," *La Prensa,* 24 June

1941. Communist parties got their new instructions after a meeting of Soviet agents in Mexico and Central America in Guatemala in July 1941. "Instructions from Moscow to Communist Organizations of Mexico," 30 July 1941, Record Group 226—files of the Office of Strategic Services (OSS), Research and Analysis Branch, report 10386, National Archives and Records Administration (NARA), College Park, Md.; "Activities and Public Utterances of Vicente Lombardo Toledano in Chile," 30 October 1942, OSS, report 24797, NARA; "Resolutions Approved at the Havana Meeting of the Executive Council of the Confederation of Latin American Labor (CTAL)," 31 July 1943, Jay Lovestone Papers, box 247, folder 6, HIA. The CTAL also warned that it expected democratic powers to refrain from interfering in the internal affairs of countries and to allow them to choose their own form of government at the end of the war, rejecting the "New Christian Order," superimperialism, and the Trotskyist permanent revolution.

47. Igor Damaskin and Geoffrey Elliott, *Kitty Harris: The Spy with Seventeen Names* (London: St Ermin's Press, 2001), 210–218; John Earl Haynes and Harvey Klehr, *Venona: Decoding Soviet Espionage in America* (New Haven, Conn.: Yale University Press, 1999), 283–285.

48. Monica Rankin, *¡México, la patria! Propaganda and Production during World War II* (Lincoln: University of Nebraska Press, 2009).

49. Gorkin had been charged with indiscipline in 1931 as a member of a Spanish Trotskyist group. Pelai Pagès, *El movimiento trotskista en España (1930–1935): La Izquierda Comunista de España y las disidencias comunistas durante la Segunda República* (Barcelona: Ediciones Península, 1977), 41; Claude Lévi-Strauss, *Tristes tropiques* (New York: Atheneum, 1970), 26. The magazines were *Análisis* and *Mundo*. Weissman, *Victor Serge,* 264; Olga Glondys, *La guerra fría cultural y el exilio republicano español: Cuadernos del Congreso por la Libertad de la Cultura (1953–1965)* (Madrid: Consejo Superior de Investigaciones Científicas, 2012), 33–36. President Cárdenas granted Serge asylum in the final days of his term as president, having received a decisive petition from his friend, the historian Frank Tannenbaum. Tannenbaum to Lázaro Cárdenas, 21 October 1940, LCR, folder 546.6/295, AGN.

50. Having obtained a shipment of arms, Costa Amic remained in Mexico, where he became an associate of the exiled Trotsky. Carlos Zapata Vela, *Conversaciones con Heriberto Jara* (Mexico City: Costa-Amic Editores, 1992), 90. He can be seen in photos with Trotsky in Alain Dugrand, James T. Farrell, and Pierre Broué, *Trotsky, Mexico, 1937–1940* (Paris: Editions Payot, 1988), 53–54. On Nazi starvation strategies, see Timothy Snyder, *Bloodlands: Europe between Hitler and Stalin* (New York: Basic Books, 2010), 416–417. Weissman, *Victor Serge,* 262; Victor Serge, *Mémoires* (Paris: Club des Éditeurs, Le Seuil, 1957), 379; *Exilio Español en Mexico, 1939–1982,* 618–619; Victor Serge, *Hitler contra Stalin: La fase decisiva de la Guerra Mundial* (Mexico City: Ediciones Quetzal, 1941); Julián Gorkin, *Caníbales políticos: Hitler y Stalin en España* (Mexico City: Ediciones Quetzal, 1941).

51. Owen Roche, "Mexico Trotzkyites Peril Rail Transport: Incite Wildcat Strikes to Block Vital Shipments to U.S.," *Worker,* 21 May 1944. The clipping, from

Victor Serge's FBI file, appears without any identification of its source. Its source is identified in Director, FBI to The Commissioner, Immigration and Naturalization Service, 19 March 1950, Julián Gorkin FBI file. The pamphlet quote is from Marceau Pivert, Gustav Regler, Victor Serge, and Julián Gorkin, "La G.P.U. prepara un nuevo crímen," 1942, Dirección General de Investigaciones Políticas y Sociales (DGIPS), box 121, binding 46, AGN.

52. Weissman, *Victor Serge,* 178. George S. Counts of Workers Defense League to Manual Ávila Camacho, 9 February 1942, Victor Serge Papers (Gen Mss 238), box 13, folder 509, Beinecke Rare Book and Manuscript Library, Yale University, New Haven, Connecticut; George S. Counts to Manuel Ávila Camacho, 27 February 1942, MAC, box 824bis, folder 550/9, AGN; "160 Leading Americans Protest to Avila Camacho Communist Attempts to Deport Anti-fascist Refugees," *New Leader,* 14 February 1942, 1; "CP Uses 'Mexican Labor News' for New Attack on Anti-Fascist Refugees," *New Leader,* 7 March 1942, 1. Paz, *Itinerario,* 74–76; George Orwell, *Homage to Catalonia* (New York: Harcourt Brace, 1952), 121–179. On the "New York intellectuals," see especially Alan M. Wald, *The New York Intellectuals: The Rise and Decline of the Anti-Stalinist Left from the 1930s to the 1980s* (Chapel Hill: University of North Carolina Press, 1987); Richard H. Pells, *The Liberal Mind in a Conservative Age: American Intellectuals in the 1940s and 1950s* (New York: Harper & Row, 1985); and Hugh Wilford, *The New York Intellectuals: From Vanguard to Institution* (Manchester: Manchester University Press, 1995).

53. "Incidente provocado por unos conocidos Trotskistas," *El Popular,* 2 April 1943; Victor Serge, "Gorkin Stabbed as Mexican CP Wrecks Erlich, Tresca Meeting," *New Leader,* 17 April 1943, 1. Serge's daughter, Jeannine, in attendance at the meeting, remembers being covered in blood when the man shielding her, the Spaniard Enrique Gironella, was injured by a thrown knife. Weissman, *Ideas of Victor Serge,* 12–13. Serge was unhurt in the attack. Contemporary newspaper accounts state that three, including Gorkin but not Gironella (although he was indeed injured), were taken to the hospital. "Escandalosa trifulca en el Centro Cultural Ibero Mexicano por un atraco comunista," *La Prensa,* 2 April 1943, 23; "Fueron 73 los detenidos en el incidente comunista," *El Universal Gráfico,* 2 April 1943, 3. Gorkin was struck in the same location where he had damaged himself on a rock as a child. The dramatic scarring, however, does not appear in photos of Gorkin before this event. Gorkin, *Revolucionario profesional,* 17. Other accounts of the attack can be found in Weissman, *Victor Serge,* 180–181; and Gallagher, *All the Right Enemies,* 242–243. These accounts differ in some details: whether the thugs broke in while the meeting was taking place or before it had started, the number of people who had arrived for the meeting (30 versus 300), and the number of attackers (100 versus 200). One of the few relatively impartial accounts, based on the police report of the incident, is "Fueron 73 los detenidos en el incidente comunista," *El Universal Gráfico,* 2 April 1943, 3, 5.

54. Victor Serge, "Gorkin Stabbed as Mexican CP Wrecks Erlich, Tresca Meeting," *New Leader,* 17 April 1943, 1; Alianza de Obreros y Empleados Compañía

de Tranvías de México to Manuel Ávila Camacho, 2 April 1943, MAC, folder 541.1/56, AGN, and other letters in the same location.

55. "Deciden los comunistas en México apelar al terror: Se denuncian las actividades de agentes de la GPU en este país," *Excélsior,* 4 April 1943, 1, 11, 15. According to the FBI, Gorkin went to the Secretaría de Gobernación on April 8. He went again on August 8, again accusing Vidali of being responsible for the attack as well as Carlo Tresca's murder. Gorkin said that he had received a letter from Tresca twenty days before his death stating that Tresca had been having a violent debate with Vidali. Director, FBI to Commissioner, Immigration and Naturalization Service, 19 March 1950, Julián Gorkin FBI file. Accusing Vidali of secret police crimes had begun with Trotsky when he was alive. Trotsky may have confused one Carlos Contreras (a name Vidali used as a pseudonym) with another. Carr, *Marxism and Communism in Twentieth-Century Mexico,* 346. Vidali, *Comandante Carlos,* 115–116. Vidali blames Gorkin in an interview with Concepción Ruiz-Funes, 1 May 1979, in Trieste, Italy, p. 143, PHO/10/36, Archivo de la Palabra del Instituto de Investigaciones Dr. José Ma. Luis Mora, Mexico City. Vidali claims that he requested regularization of his immigration status in order to compensate him for his suffering in solitary confinement. His letter of request, however, avoids mention of his detention. Carlos J. Contreras [Vidali] to Manuel Ávila Camacho, 14 April 1941, MAC, folder 546.6/50, AGN.

56. The account of embassy pressure comes from Gorkin, who described it in an appendix to the 1957 French edition of Serge's *Memoirs.* Serge, *Mémoires,* 381–382; Victor Serge, *Memoirs of a Revolutionary, 1901–1941* (London: Oxford University Press, 1963), xvii. The newsmagazine was *Así,* a forerunner to *Siempre!* Gorkin and Serge wrote there frequently in 1943 about the war and their hopes for a socialist Europe after the end of the war, but both disappear as contributors in early 1944. For example, see Victor Serge, "El eje perdido en África," *Así,* no. 114 (16 January 1943): 14–15; and Julián Gorkin, "44, año de la invasión," *Así,* no. 167 (22 January 1944): 11. The documents relating to Pivert and Serge are located in "Marceau Pivert Aujard y Otros," July 1944, DGIPS, box 121, folder 46, AGN. Gorkin's documents are in "Trotzkysmo [*sic*]," July 1944, DGIPS, box 127, folder 1, tome 4, AGN.

57. Serge, *Memoirs of a Revolutionary,* xvii; Victor Serge, *The Case of Comrade Tulayev* (New York: New York Review Books, 2004). The other novel he wrote during that period was not published until 1971: Victor Serge, *The Unforgiving Years* (New York: New York Review Books, 2008). Some have argued that Serge was poisoned. Both Serge and Tina Modotti, who had become Vidali's lover, died in taxis in Mexico City, and the union of taxi drivers was Communist controlled. Cacucci, *Tina Modotti,* 205. However, both Serge and Modotti were very ill before their deaths and likely passed away because of natural causes.

2. Making Peace with Repression, Making Repression with Peace

1. Andrew Barnard, "Chile," in *Latin America between the Second World War and the Cold War, 1944–1948,* ed. Leslie Bethell and Ian Roxborough (Cambridge: Cambridge University Press, 1992), 85–86; Andrew Barnard, "Chilean Communists, Radical Presidents and Chilean Relations with the United States, 1940–1947," *Journal of Latin American Studies* 13, no. 2 (November 1981): 363–374.

2. "Yo acuso," 6 January 1948, in Pablo Neruda, *Obras completas,* vol. 4 (Barcelona: Galaxia Gútenberg: Círculo de Lectores, 1999), 730; Adam Feinstein, *Pablo Neruda: A Passion for Life* (New York: Bloomsbury, 2004), 202–235.

3. Ilya Ehrenburg, *Post-war Years, 1945–1954* (London: MacGibben & Kee, 1966), 144; Patrick O'Brian, *Picasso: Pablo Ruiz Picasso; A Biography* (New York: Putnam, 1976), 396; Pierre Daix, *Picasso: Life and Art* (New York: Icon Editions, 1993), 301.

4. Clive Rose, *The Soviet Propaganda Network: A Directory of Organisations Serving Soviet Foreign Policy* (London: Pinter, 1988), 57–108; Tony Judt, *Postwar: A History of Europe since 1945* (New York: Penguin Press, 2005), 221–222; Annie Kriegel, "'Lutte pour la Paix' et 'Mouvement pour la Paix' dans la stratégie et la structure du mouvement Communiste international," in *L'Union Soviétique dans les relations internationales,* ed. Francis Conte and Jean-Louis Martres (Paris: Economica, 1982), 223–241; Donald H. McLachlan, "The Partisans of Peace," *International Affairs* 27, no. 1 (January 1951): 10–17; Fernando Claudin, *The Communist Movement: From Comintern to Cominform* (Harmondsworth: Penguin, 1975), 582; Daix, *Picasso,* 301; Herbert R. Lottman, *The Left Bank: Writers, Artists, and Politics from the Popular Front to the Cold War* (Boston: Houghton Mifflin, 1982), 272; Jo Langer, *Convictions: Memories of a Life Shared with a Good Communist* (London: A. Deutsch, 1979), 161.

5. Lawrence S. Wittner, *One World or None: A History of the World Nuclear Disarmament Movement through 1953* (Stanford, Calif.: Stanford University Press, 1993); Lawrence S. Wittner, *Resisting the Bomb: A History of the World Nuclear Disarmament Movement, 1954–1970* (Stanford, Calif.: Stanford University Press, 1997); Lawrence S. Wittner, *Toward Nuclear Abolition: A History of the World Nuclear Disarmament Movement, 1971 to the Present* (Stanford, Calif.: Stanford University Press, 2003); Robbie Lieberman, *The Strangest Dream: Communism, Anticommunism and the U.S. Peace Movement, 1945–1963* (Syracuse, N.Y.: Syracuse University Press, 2000); Alessandro Brogi, *Confronting America: The Cold War between the United States and the Communists in France and Italy* (Chapel Hill: University of North Carolina Press, 2011), 122–156.

6. Outside biographies of major figures like Neruda, there is virtually no scholarship on the World Peace Council in Latin America. (A few exceptions, discussed in Chapter 5, concern the 1960s and generally express confusion about whether the WPC was or was not a Soviet front.) Part of the problem is that the records of the WPC have probably been destroyed. Robert Prince, "The

Last of the WPC Mohicans . . . or, Ghost Ship of Lonnrotinkatu, Part 3," 1 August 2011, http://robertjprince.wordpress.com/2011/08/01/the-last-of -the-wpc-mohicans-or-ghost-ship-of-lonnrotinkatu-part-3/. Additionally, in nearly all personal collections I have consulted, whether in Europe, the United States, or Latin America, the sections on peace participation appear to have been culled. Here and in Chapter 5 I have tried to make judicious use of intelligence files and the collections of involved individuals and Communist parties to give as full a picture as possible of the movement.

7. Jadwiga E. Pieper Mooney, "Fighting Fascism and Forging New Political Activism: The Women's International Democratic Federation (WIDF) in the Cold War," in *De-centering Cold War History: Local and Global Change*, ed. Jadwiga E. Pieper Mooney and Fabio Lanza (London: Routledge, 2012), 52–72; Denis McShane, *International Labour and the Origins of the Cold War* (Oxford: Oxford University Press, 1992), 2.

8. On this conjuncture in Latin American politics, see especially Bethell and Roxborough, *Latin America between the Second World War and the Cold War;* Greg Grandin, "The Liberal Traditions in the Americas: Rights, Sovereignty, and the Origins of Liberal Multilateralism," *American Historical Review* 117, no. 1 (February 2012): 68–91; and Peter H. Smith, *Democracy in Latin America: Political Change in Comparative Perspective* (New York: Oxford University Press, 2005), 27–28.

9. George Orwell, *The Collected Essays, Journalism, and Letters of George Orwell*, ed. Sonia Orwell and Ian Angus, vol. 4, *In Front of Your Nose: 1945–1950* (New York: Harcourt, Brace & World, 1968): 9. From the large pool of scholarship on the origins of the Cold War, this paragraph draws especially from Melvyn P. Leffler, *The Specter of Communism: The United States and the Origins of the Cold War, 1917–1953* (New York: Hill & Wang, 1994), 36–63; and V. M. Zubok and Konstantin Pleshakov, *Inside the Kremlin's Cold War: From Stalin to Khrushchev* (Cambridge, Mass.: Harvard University Press, 1996), 36–54.

10. Lovestone to Brown, 21 June 1949, box 29, folder 7; and Lovestone to Brown, 4 April 1951, box 29, folder 11, record group 18–004, Irving Brown Papers, George Meany Memorial Archives (GMMA), Silver Spring, Md. Ted Morgan, *A Covert Life: Jay Lovestone, Communist, Anti-Communist, and Spymaster* (New York: Random House, 1999); Henry W. Berger, "Union Diplomacy: America's Labor Foreign Policy in Latin America" (Ph.D. diss., University of Wisconsin, 1966), 271; Ben Rathbun, *The Point Man: Irving Brown and the Deadly Post-1945 Struggle for Europe and Africa* (Montreux: Minerva Press, 1996); Ted Morgan, *Reds: McCarthyism in Twentieth-Century America* (New York: Random House, 2003), 214–217; Anthony Carew, "The American Labor Movement in Fizzland: The Free Trade Union Committee and the CIA," *Labor History* 39, no. 1 (February 1998): 30–31.

11. Latin America as laboratory is one of the major arguments of Greg Grandin, *Empire's Workshop: Latin America, the United States and the Rise of the New Imperialism* (New York: Metropolitan Books, 2006), 15–16. On the differing but overlapping strategies of State Department liberals and conservatives, see

Steven Schwartzberg, *Democracy and U.S. Policy in Latin America during the Truman years* (Gainesville: University Press of Florida, 2003).

12. Serafino Romualdi, *Presidents and Peons: Recollections of a Labor Ambassador in Latin America* (New York: Funk & Wagnalls, 1967), vi. On Soviet funding for the WFTU, see Patrick Iber, "Managing Mexico's Cold War: Vicente Lombardo Toledano and the Uses of Political Intelligence," in "Spy Reports: Content, Methodology, and Historiography in Mexico's Secret Police Archives," ed. Tanalís Padilla and Louise E. Walker, special issue, *Journal of Iberian and Latin American Research* 19, no. 1 (July 2013): 11–19.

13. Kees Boterbloem, *The Life and Times of Andrei Zhdanov, 1896–1948* (Montréal: McGill–Queen's University Press, 2004), 281.

14. Teresa Toranska, *"Them": Stalin's Polish Puppets*, trans. Agnieszka Kolakowska (New York: Harper & Row, 1987), 314–318.

15. "Americanism," *For a Lasting Peace, for a People's Democracy*, no. 18 (15 September 1949): 4.

16. Address by Juan Marinello, 7 September 1949, gallery 3, Miguel Alemán Valdés (MAV) Records, box 324, folder 433/503, Archivo General de la Nación (AGN), Mexico City; Georges Coginot, "Cosmopolitanism—Weapon of Predatory U.S. Imperialism," *For a Lasting Peace, for a People's Democracy*, no. 34 (25 August 1950): 3.

17. Full transcripts of the speeches at the Wrocław congress are found in Dispatch no. 618 from American Embassy, Warsaw, Poland, 8 September 1948, 800.00B/4–848, National Archives and Records Administration (NARA), College Park, Md. Sartre, who would later be an ally of the peace movement, was at this time considered hostile because of articles he had written questioning whether the writer's work was compatible with Stalinist politics. Gertje Utley, *Picasso: The Communist Years* (New Haven, Conn.: Yale University Press, 2000), 107.

18. Crocker to Secretary of State, 27 August 1948 and 31 August 1948, 800.00B/8–2748 and 800.00B/8–3148, NARA; Dominique Desanti, *Les Staliniens, 1944–1956: Une expérience politique* (Paris: Fayard, 1975), 115–116.

19. Desanti, *Staliniens*, 113–115; Toranska, *"Them,"* 290–291. Hovde is quoted in Enclosure no. 10 to Dispatch no. 618, 8 September 1948, 800.00B/4–848; Huxley in Dispatch no. 596, 1 September 1948, 800.00B/9–148, NARA.

20. "Preparations for World Congress of Intellectuals," 18 August 1948, 800.00B/8–1848, NARA; Jorge Amado, *Navegação de cabotagem: Apontamentos para um livro de memórias que jamais escreverei* (Rio de Janeiro: Editora Record, 1992), 27–29. Amado's speech is in Embassy Dispatch no. 618, 8 September 1948, 800.00B/9–848, NARA.

21. Daix, *Picasso*, 299.

22. Sheila Fitzpatrick, *The Cultural Front: Power and Culture in Revolutionary Russia* (Ithaca, N.Y.: Cornell University Press, 1992), 248.

23. Charles Grutzner, "'Cultural' Visas Denied to British," *New York Times*, 22 March 1949, 1; "Department Explains: Unofficial Delegates Excluded Simply as Communists," *New York Times*, 22 March 1949, 16.

24. "Report on Recent Cultural and Scientific Conference for World Peace," 21 July 1949, pp. 103–109, 800.00B/7–2149, NARA. Dmitri Shostakovich and Isaak Glikman, *Story of a Friendship: The Letters of Dmitry Shostakovich to Isaak Glikman, 1941–1975* (Ithaca, N.Y.: Cornell University Press, 2001), 213, 31; Phillip Deery, "Shostakovich, the Waldorf Conference and the Cold War," *American Communist History* 11, no. 2 (2012): 161–180. As a result of Shostakovich's visit, censors unfroze his works, as well as those of Sergei Prokofiev, Aram Khachaturian, Vissarion Shebalin, Nikolai Myaskovsky, and others. Solomon Volkov, *Shostakovich and Stalin: The Extraordinary Relationship between the Great Composer and the Brutal Dictator* (New York: Knopf, 2004), 233–234.

25. Dmitri Shostakovich and Solomon Volkov, *Testimony: The Memoirs of Dmitri Shostakovich*, 25th anniversary ed. (New York: Limelight Editions, 2004), xlii–xliii; Volkov, *Shostakovich and Stalin*, 238–240; Deery, "Shostakovich, the Waldorf Conference and the Cold War," 175–176.

26. On Rousset's trial, see Lottman, *Left Bank*, 273–274; and John V. Fleming, *The Anti-Communist Manifestos: Four Books That Shaped the Cold War* (New York: Norton, 2009), 244–262. Rousset became an important member of the Congress for Cultural Freedom. Sidney Hook, *Out of Step: An Unquiet Life in the 20th Century* (New York: Harper & Row, 1987), 382–396; Frances Stonor Saunders, *The Cultural Cold War: The CIA and the World of Arts and Letters* (New York: New Press, 2000), 54–55; Michael Warner, *Hearts and Minds: Three Case Studies of the CIA's Covert Support of American Anti-Communist Groups in the Cold War, 1949–1967* (Washington, D.C.: Central Intelligence Agency, 1999), 13; Michael Warner, "Origins of the Congress for Cultural Freedom, 1949–50," *Studies in Intelligence* 38, no. 5 (1995): 89–98; Hugh Wilford, *The Mighty Wurlitzer: How the CIA Played America* (Cambridge, Mass.: Harvard University Press, 2008), 70–98.

27. Claudin, *Communist Movement*, 577; Milovan Djilas, *Conversations with Stalin*, trans. Michael B. Petrovich (New York: Harcourt, Brace & World, 1962), 129; Michel Pinault, *Frédéric Joliot-Curie* (Paris: O. Jacob, 2000), 440–445.

28. Lieberman, *Strangest Dream*, 89; Jorge Amado, *O mundo da paz: União Soviética e democracias populares*, 4th ed. (Rio de Janeiro: Editorial Vitória, 1953), 40, 55; Andrew Brown, *J. D. Bernal: The Sage of Science* (Oxford: Oxford University Press, 2005), 328; Wittner, *One World or None*, 178–183.

29. James Burnham, "Rhetoric and Peace," *Partisan Review* 17, no. 8 (1950): 866; Wittner, *One World or None*, 180; Kriegel, "'Lutte pour la Paix' et 'Mouvement pour la Paix,'" 232. László Kürti, "'Songs for the Father, Babies for the Mother': Visual, Literary and Personal Experiences of Hungarians during the Beginning of the Cold War, 1948–1956" (paper presented at the conference "De-centering the Cold War," Tucson, Arizona, 2010).

30. "Appel de M. Frédéric Joliot-Curie, President du Conseil Mondial de la Paix Contre l'Utilisation de l'Arme Bacteriologique," *Le Bulletin du Conseil Mondial de la Paix*, no. 21 (15 March 1952), in Frédéric Joliot-Curie Papers, box

F59, folder 208, Institut Curie, Paris, France. The charges were brought to the attention of Joliot-Curie by the president of the Chinese Committee for the Defense of Peace, Kuo Mo-jo. These charges, reported by the Communist press throughout the world, remain controversial. Soviet documents that demonstrate an elaborate campaign by Chinese and North Korean authorities to deceive international inspectors have been reported: Kathryn Weathersby, "Deceiving the Deceivers: Moscow, Beijing, Pyongyang, and the Allegations of Bacteriological Weapons Use in Korea," *Cold War International History Project Bulletin*, no. 11 (Winter 1998): 176–185. On the divisions over Hungary, see, for example, "Correspondance avec M. F. Joliot-Curie," *Le Christianisme Social* 65, no. 1 (January 1957): 87–96.

31. Paz insisted that the experience of the concentration camps did not stain the reputation of socialism in general, just of the deformed version practiced in the USSR. John King, *The Role of Mexico's* Plural *in Latin American Literary and Political Culture: From Tlatelolco to the "Philanthropic Ogre"* (New York: Palgrave Macmillan, 2007), 22. On Ocampo and *Sur,* see John King, Sur: *A Study of the Argentine Literary Journal and Its Role in the Development of a Culture, 1931–1970* (Cambridge: Cambridge University Press, 1986); Doris Meyer and Victoria Ocampo, *Victoria Ocampo: Against the Wind and the Tide* (New York: G. Braziller, 1979); and Nora Pasternac, Sur: *Una revista en la tormenta* (Buenos Aires: Paradiso, 2002). On *Sur* in the broader context of Argentine liberalism, see Jorge Nállim, *Transformations and Crisis of Liberalism in Argentina, 1930–1955* (Pittsburgh: University of Pittsburgh Press, 2012), 68–73.

32. Hebe Clementi, *María Rosa Oliver* (Buenos Aires: Planeta, 1992), 168; Gabriela Mistral and Victoria Ocampo, *This America of Ours: The Letters of Gabriela Mistral and Victoria Ocampo,* ed. and trans. Elizabeth Horan and Doris Meyer (Austin: University of Texas Press, 2003), 202. Waldo Frank to Oliver, 3 August 1937, María Rosa Oliver (MRO) Papers, box 3, folder 50, Firestone Library, Princeton University, Princeton, New Jersey; María Rosa Oliver, *Mi fe es el hombre* (Buenos Aires: Ediciones C. Lohlé, 1981), 100. María Rosa Oliver to Nelson Rockefeller, 9 April 1952, MRO Papers, box 5, folder "Rockefeller, Nelson A.," Princeton.

33. Quotations are, in sequence, Ocampo to Mistral, 18 September 1951; Ocampo to Mistral, 11 July 1954; and Ocampo to Mistral, 21 February 1954, in Mistral and Ocampo, *This America of Ours,* 167–171, 222–223, 235. "Premios Literarios Argentinos: El Premio Lenin," *Sur,* no. 250 (January–February 1958): 103–104. The unsigned note about the Stalin Prize was written by Ocampo. Oliver to Ocampo, 15 February 1958; Ocampo to Oliver, 18 February 1958; and Oliver to Ocampo, 24 February 1958, MRO Papers, box 5, folder "Ocampo, Victoria," Princeton.

34. María Rosa Oliver, "La Paz," MRO Papers, box 1, folder 52, Princeton. Gabriela Mistral and Jaime Quezada, *Escritos políticos,* vol. 2 (Mexico City: Fondo de Cultura Económica, 1995), 159–161. Mistral to Ocampo, April or May 1952?, in Mistral and Ocampo, *This America of Ours,* 187–189.

35. Oliver to Nelson Rockefeller, 9 April 1952, MRO Papers, box 5, folder "Rockefeller, Nelson A.," Princeton.

36. Stanley E. Hilton, *Brazil and the Soviet Challenge, 1917–1947* (Austin: University of Texas Press, 1991); William Waack, *Camaradas: Nos arquivos de Moscou, a história secreta da Revolução Brasileira de 1935* (São Paulo: Companhia das Letras, 1993); Leslie Bethell, "Brazil," in Bethell and Roxborough, *Latin America between the Second World War and the Cold War,* 33–65.

37. Cecil M. P. Cross to Secretary of State, 25 March 1949, 800.00B/4–1849, NARA; "Seria proibido, no Rio, o Congresso Pró-Paz," *Folha da Noite,* 7 April 1949; Johnson to Secretary of State, 24 January 1952, 700.01/1–2452; and "Statement by Brazilian Minister of Justice on Communist 'Peace' Campaigns," 20 March 1952, 700.01/3–2052, NARA; "Inútilmente se trata de impedir la celebración de la Conferencia Continental por la Paz," *Paz* 1, no. 12 (March 1952): 56; Marcelo Ridenti, *Brasilidade revolucionária: Um século de cultura e política* (São Paulo: Editora UNSEP, 2010), 59, 69.

38. Adriana Petra, "Cosmopolitismo y nación: Los intelectuales comunistas argentinos en tiempos de la Guerra Fría (1946–1956)," *Contemporánea: Historia y problemas del siglo XX* 1, no. 1 (2010): 51–73; Atahualpa Yupanqui, "El folklore y el pueblo," *Cuadernos de Cultura Democrática y Popular,* no. 4 (December 1951): 101, 104; Fred Oelssner, "Acerca de nuestras tareas en la creación de un arte alemán progresista," *Cuadernos de Cultura Democrática y Popular,* no. 5 (February 1952): 47. Yupanqui left the Communist Party in 1952.

39. Adriana Petra, "Cultura comunista y Guerra Fría: Los intelectuales y el Movimiento por la Paz en la Argentina," *Cuadernos de Historia,* no. 38 (June 2013): 125–130; "Las calles de La Plata fueron sede del gran Congreso por la Paz," *Orientación,* 24 August 1949, 1; "Asamblea del Consejo Argentino por la Paz," 28 January 1951, box "Consejo Argentino por la Paz," Centro de Documentación e Investigación de la Cultura de Izquierdas en Argentina, Buenos Aires, Argentina. Varela's release in 1952 was the result of a short-lived rapprochement between Argentina's Communist Party and the government of Juan Domingo Perón.

40. Wallace W. Stuart to Department of State, "Communist Sponsored Continental Peace Conference," 27 March 1952, 700.01/3–2752, NARA; Frank J. Devine, "Meeting of Peace Conference Delegates at Agraciada and Colonia on March 15, 1952," 27 March 1952, 700.01/3–2752, NARA; Oliver to Nelson Rockefeller, 9 April 1952, MRO Papers, box 5, folder "Rockefeller, Nelson A.," Princeton. According to the Uruguayan Communist paper *Justicia,* Cuban and Mexican delegates were not granted travel documentation by their governments.

41. Elisa Servín, "Propaganda y guerra fría: La campaña anticomunista en la prensa mexicana del medio siglo," *Signos Históricos* 11 (July 2004): 9–39; Sergio Aguayo, *La charola: Una historia de los servicios de inteligencia en México* (Mexico City: Grijalbo, 2001); Aaron W. Navarro, *Political Intelligence and the Creation of Modern Mexico, 1938–1954* (University Park: Pennsylvania

State University Press, 2010). The PRI provided a monthly subsidy for the newspaper that Lombardo Toledano controlled, *El Popular* (which was technically the paper of the CTM and a legacy of the time when Lombardo Toledano headed that union). Stephen R. Niblo, *Mexico in the 1940s: Modernity, Politics, and Corruption* (Wilmington, Del.: Scholarly Resources, 1999), 279. In spite of its opportunistic reputation, in the 1960s the Partido Popular Socialista did produce antigovernment guerrilla fighters. Alexander Aviña, *Specters of Revolution: Peasant Guerrillas in the Cold War Mexican Countryside* (New York: Oxford University Press, 2014), 74.

42. "El Congreso 'de la Paz' sin la simpatía oficial," *El Universal,* 16 May 1949; "Description of Arena Mexico Where 'Peace' Congress Is to Be Held," 2 September 1949, 810.00B/9-249; Enclosure No. 1, Dispatch No. 1166, 23 September 1949, 810.00B/9-2349, NARA.

43. Memorandum, 27 July 1949, gallery 1, Dirección Federal de Seguridad (DFS), document 11-70-49, Diego Rivera Barrientos file—versión pública, AGN.

44. In fact, the Soviet Union had exploded a test nuclear bomb a few weeks earlier, but this was not yet public knowledge. At the time, the USSR lacked the capacity to deliver such a weapon to the United States. Niblo, *Mexico in the 1940s,* 201. "Informan sobre la primera sesión plenaria del Congreso Continental de la Paz," 6 September 1949; and "Informan sobre el Acto de Clausura del Congreso Americano Continental de la Paz," 12 September 1949, DGIPS, box 80, folder 1, AGN.

45. "Por Juan Marinello," MAV Records, box 324, folder 433/503, AGN. Marinello traveled to Mexico in August and September 1948 to prepare for the congress. While he was in Mexico, he sought the support of Lázaro Cárdenas and Henry Wallace. Dispatch no. 1166, "The American Continental Congress for Peace," 810.00B/9-2349, NARA. O. John Rogge, "The People Look for Peace," September 1949, MAV Records, folder 443/503, AGN. "Neutral" Rogge soon became a critic of the peace movement. Phillip Deery, "'A Divided Soul'? The Cold War Odyssey of O. John Rogge," *Cold War History* 6, no. 2 (May 2006): 177–204.

46. Embassy dispatch no. 1170, "Discurso de Pablo Neruda," 30 September 1949, 810.00B/9-3049, NARA. Amado, *O mundo da paz,* 126; David Schidlowsky, *Las furias y las penas: Pablo Neruda y su tiempo* (Berlin: Wissenschaftlicher Verlag, 1999), 696–699.

47. Jonathan Cohen, "Waldeen and the Americas: The Dance Has Many Faces," in *A Woman's Gaze: Latin American Women Artists,* ed. Marjorie Agosín (Fredonia, N.Y.: White Pine Press, 1998), 224–242; Pablo Neruda, *Canto general,* trans. Jack Schmitt (Berkeley: University of California Press, 1991), 270.

48. Neruda, *Canto general,* 266.

49. For example, Walt Whitman, "Saludo al Mundo," *Paz,* no. 4 (July 1951): 4–6; Ted Genoways, *Walt Whitman and the Civil War: America's Poet during the Lost Years of 1860–1862* (Berkeley: University of California Press, 2009).

50. Schidlowsky, *Furias y las penas,* 679–781, 1246–1252; Jaime Castillo Velasco, "El Congreso Continental de la Cultura de Santiago de Chile,"

Cuadernos, no. 2 (August 1953): 85. "Prometheus Bound," CIA-RDP78–02771R000500500004–5, CIA Records Search Tool (CREST), NARA.

51. "Fernando Santiván informa en el Congreso de la Cultura," *El Siglo,* 28 April 1953, 1; Jorge Amado and Volodia Teitelboim, "Latin American Continental Cultural Congress," *For a Lasting Peace, for a People's Democracy,* no. 25 (19 June 1953): 4.

52. Amado, *O mundo da paz,* 155.

53. *Os subterrâneos da liberdade* was published in three volumes titled *Os ásperos tempos, Agonia da noite,* and *A luz no túnel* by Martins Press in São Paulo in 1954. Neil Larsen sees in this period of Amado's writing the possibility of a Latin American literature that was neither stuck in naturalist realism nor modernist antirealism, but not even Amado saw it in those terms. Neil Larsen, *Reading North by South: On Latin American Literature, Culture, and Politics* (Minneapolis: University of Minnesota Press, 1995), 73–74; Amado, *Navegação de cabotagem,* 329.

54. On the general issue of WPC financing, see the articles by former participant Robert Prince, "The Ghost Ship of Lönnrotinkatu," *Peace Magazine* 8, no. 3 (June 1992): 16–17, 29; and Robert Prince, "Following the Money Trail at the World Peace Council," *Peace Magazine* 8, no. 6 (December 1992): 20–21, 23. The financial records that show some Mexican expenses covered by the WPC can be found in the papers of Heriberto Jara at the Archivo Histórico de la Universidad Nacional Autónoma de México, in box 36, folders 1430 through 1433. The records cover October 1949 to the end of 1951. "Informan sobre el Acto de Clausura del Congreso Americano Continental de la Paz," 12 December 1949, DGIPS, box 80, folder 1, AGN. Rivera and Siqueiros each donated money, and Siqueiros implored those in attendance to give up luxuries to help pay for the event. Some money came in via "bonds" that were collected by delegates from across Latin America. See DFS Memos, 11–84–49 and 11–71–49 of 23 August 1949 and 12 September 1949, gallery 1, Vicente Lombardo Toledano—versión pública, AGN.

55. Juan Pablo Sáinz to Ramón Danzós Palomino, 22 November 1952, Partido Comunista de México (PCM) archive, folder 6, box 24, Centro de Estudios del Movimiento Obrero y Socialista (CEMOS), Mexico City; Neruda claimed to have raised 100,000 pesos, only 20 percent of the reported deficit. "Páginas interiores del Congreso de la Cultura," *Ercilla,* no. 939 (28 April 1953): 17; "Overt Communist Activities: Continental Cultural Congress, Santiago, Chile," 398.44-SA/5–1153, NARA. It is possible that the financial relationship evolved over time; Moscow did eventually provide regular support to various Communist parties in the region. Olga Uliánova and Eugenia Fediakova, "Algunos aspectos de la ayuda financiera del Partido Comunista de la URSS al comunismo chileno durante la guerra fría," *Estudios Públicos* 72 (Spring 1998): 113–148. There were no doubt other, concealed contributions, some of which are described in Christopher M. Andrew and Vasili Mitrokhin, *The World Was Going Our Way: The KGB and the Battle for the Third World* (New York: Basic Books, 2005). Still, the period of intense peace activities does not coincide with one of financial support of Latin American Communism from Moscow.

56. Jorge Amado and Alfred Mac Adam, "From 'Sailing the Shore: Notes for Memoirs I'll Never Write,'" *Review: Latin American Literature and Arts,* no. 47 (Fall 1993): 36.

57. Amado, *O mundo da paz,* 189–191; Amado, *Navegação de cabotagem,* 35, 120; Amado and Mac Adam, "From 'Sailing the Shore: Notes for Memoirs I'll Never Write,'" 37–38.

58. Bobby J. Chamberlain, *Jorge Amado* (Boston: Twayne, 1990), 4–10; Lottman, *Left Bank,* 61–63, 247.

59. Raquel Tibol, *Diego Rivera, luces y sombras* (Barcelona: Lumen, 2007), 291–300; Bertram David Wolfe, *The Fabulous Life of Diego Rivera* (New York: Stein & Day, 1963), 385–388; Salvador Novo, *La vida en México en el periodo presidencial de Miguel Alemán* (Mexico City: Empresas Editoriales, 1967), 766–767. The Mexican government's decision not to display the mural came after pressure from the U.S. ambassador. Stephen R. Niblo, *War, Diplomacy, and Development: The United States and Mexico, 1938–1954* (Wilmington, Del.: Scholarly Resources, 1995), 286.

60. Pete Hamill, *Diego Rivera* (New York: Harry N. Abrams, 1999), 192–202; Wolfe, *Fabulous Life of Diego Rivera,* 383–389.

3. The Congress for Cultural Freedom and the Imperialism of Liberty

1. Leandro A. Sánchez Salazar and Julián Gorkin, *Ainsi fut assassiné Trotsky* (Paris: Éditions Self, 1948); Julián Gorkin, *Cómo asesinó Stalin a Trotsky* (Buenos Aires: Plaza & Janés, 1961); David Wingeate Pike, *In the Service of Stalin: The Spanish Communists in Exile, 1939–1945* (New York: Oxford University Press, 1993), 304; Olga Glondys, *La guerra fría cultural y el exilio republicano español: Cuadernos del Congreso por la Libertad de la Cultura (1953–1965)* (Madrid: Consejo Superior de Investigaciones Científicas, 2012), 33–34.

2. Gorkin to Joaquín Maurín, 14 May 1949, Joaquín Maurín Papers, box 6, folder "Gorkin," Hoover Institution Archives (HIA), Stanford, Calif.: John V. Fleming, *The Anti-Communist Manifestos: Four Books That Shaped the Cold War* (New York: Norton, 2009), 260; Herbert R. Southworth, "'The Grand Camouflage': Julián Gorkin, Burnett Bolloten and the Spanish Civil War," in *The Republic Besieged: The Civil War in Spain, 1936–1939,* ed. Paul Preston and Ann L. Mackenzie (Edinburgh: Edinburgh University Press, 1996), 264; E. Howard Hunt and Greg Aunapu, *American Spy: My Secret History in the CIA, Watergate, and Beyond* (Hoboken, N.J.: John Wiley & Sons, 2007), 56; Valentín R. González and Julián Gorkin, *El Campesino: Life and Death in Soviet Russia* (New York: G. P. Putnam's Sons, 1952).

3. Gorkin to Serafino Romualdi, 12 September 1951, Jay Lovestone Papers, box 296, folder 2, HIA.

4. Pepe Gutiérrez-Álvarez, *Retratos poumistas* (Sevilla: Espuela de Plata, 2006), 195.

5. "Imperialismo de la libertad nació en Congreso de intelectuales: Seis países preparan en Santiago una réplica al Congreso del 53; El sabio Nicolai dividió al mundo en culturas," *Ercilla,* no. 998 (15 June 1954), 13.

6. There were places in Europe, such as Spain, that used alliances with the United States to strengthen dictatorships during the 1950s. And there was one place in Latin America, Bolivia, where a nationalist revolutionary government forged good relations with the United States and used them to protect nationalizations of U.S. businesses and to take limited but important steps to improve the welfare of most Bolivians. Still, it remains the general rule that in much of Europe U.S. hegemony helped establish what many in the United States considered "socialism," while in Latin America the United States used its power to prevent a similar outcome. On Bolivian-U.S. relations, see James Siekmeier, *The Bolivian Revolution and the United States, 1952 to the Present* (University Park: Pennsylvania State University Press, 2011); and Thomas C. Field, *From Development to Dictatorship: Bolivia and the Alliance for Progress in the Kennedy Era* (Ithaca, N.Y.: Cornell University Press, 2014). European welfare states were not uniform in structure, of course, and "social democratic" here refers to a variety of welfare-state political democracies, not only the Scandinavian model. On the diversity of European welfare states, see Gøsta Esping-Andersen, *The Three Worlds of Welfare Capitalism* (Princeton, N.J.: Princeton University Press, 1990).

7. Patrick Iber, "Anti-Communist Entrepreneurs and the Origins of the Cultural Cold War in Latin America," in *De-centering Cold War History: Local and Global Change*, ed. Jadwiga E. Pieper Mooney and Fabio Lanza (London: Routledge, 2012), 167–186; Olivia Gall, *Trotsky en México y la vida política en el periodo de Cárdenas, 1937–1940* (Mexico City: Ediciones Era, 1991), 86–87.

8. "New York Operations of the Congress for Cultural Freedom," 16 August 1950, James Burnham Papers, box 11, folder 2, HIA. For Hook's knowledge of the CIA connection, see Hugh Wilford, *The Mighty Wurlitzer: How the CIA Played America* (Cambridge, Mass.: Harvard University Press, 2008), 84. Sidney Hook Address at CCF Opening Session, Hoover Institution Library Society Papers, Congress for Cultural Freedom, 2; Karl Jaspers, "On Dangers and Chances of Freedom," Congress Paper no. 17, Hoover Institution Library Society Papers, Congress for Cultural Freedom, 17. Arthur Schlesinger Jr., author of *The Vital Center*, was an enthusiastic participant in CCF events. Arthur M. Schlesinger, *The Vital Center: The Politics of Freedom* (Boston: Houghton Mifflin, 1949).

9. Michael Josselson and Diana Josselson, *The Commander: A Life of Barclay de Tolly* (Oxford: Oxford University Press, 1980). The "junior year abroad" quote is from Tim Weiner, *Legacy of Ashes: The History of the CIA* (New York: Doubleday, 2007), 36. On those who knew of the CIA relationship, see Frances Stonor Saunders, *The Cultural Cold War: The CIA and the World of Arts and Letters* (New York: New Press, 2000), 394–395. When the Ford Foundation made its deal with the CIA to work on projects of mutual interest, one of its concerns was that a refusal to do so would simply lead the CIA to place an agent in the Ford Foundation and use its money surreptitiously. Kai Bird, *The Chairman: John J. McCloy, the Making of the American Establishment* (New York: Simon & Schuster, 1992), 426–428; Volker Rolf Berghahn,

America and the Intellectual Cold Wars in Europe: Shepard Stone between Philanthropy, Academy, and Diplomacy (Princeton, N.J.: Princeton University Press, 2001), 223–240. For a diagram of the structure of the CCF, see ibid., 300.

10. Arciniegas to Daniel Cosío Villegas, 30 May 1949, Daniel Cosío Villegas Papers, box 12, folder 71, El Colegio de México, Mexico City; Arciniegas to Burnham, 20 September 1950, James Burnham Papers, box 11, folder 2, HIA.

11. On Burnham's career in the CIA, see Daniel Kelly, *James Burnham and the Struggle for the World: A Life* (Wilmington, Del.: ISI Books, 2002), 149–193. Arciniegas to Burnham, 20 September 1950; and Burnham to E. Howard Hunt, 27 September 1950, James Burnham Papers, box 11, folder 2; and Burnham to Frank Wisner and Gerald Miller, 11 December 1950, box 11, folder 3, HIA; Arciniegas to Alfonso Reyes, 23 December 1950, and Reyes to Arciniegas, 29 December 1950, Alfonso Reyes Papers, correspondence files, folder 135, Capilla Alfonsina, Mexico City.

12. Julián Gorkin, "Pour un Congrès pour la Liberté de la Culture en Amérique Latine," 30 May 1952, International Association for Cultural Freedom Papers (IACF), series II, box 204, folder 5, Joseph L. Regenstein Library, University of Chicago Special Collections Research Center (UC/SCRC), Chicago, Ill.; Julián Gorkin, "Report," 18 July 1953, IACF, series II, box 205, folder 1, UC/SCRC.

13. Romuladi to Irving Kristol and Nabokov, IACF, series II, box 204, folder 5, UC/SCRC.

14. "Continental Cultural Congress," 24 December 1952, 398.44-SA/12–2452, National Archives and Records Administration (NARA), College Park, Md.; Dialoguitos, *El Siglo,* 16 January 1953, 3; Sims to Clarence A. Canary, 3 July 1953, and Embassy Dispatch no. 1250, 12 May 1953, 398.44-SA/6–853, NARA.

15. "Sus reservas frente al Congreso de la Cultura plantean intelectuales," *La Nación,* 24 April 1953, 6. The manifesto was signed by, among others, Eduardo Anguita, Jaime Castillo Velasco, Eduardo Frei, Alejandro Magnet, Georg Nicolai, Chela Reyes, Andrés Santa Cruz, Radomiro Tomic, and Gabriel Valdés Subercaseaux. Jorge Edwards, *Adios, poeta . . . : Memorias* (Barcelona: Tusquets Editores, 1990), 46.

16. On Baráibar's reporting, see "Revista de la radio," *El Siglo,* 25 April 1953, 4; "Revista de la radio," *El Siglo,* 9 May 1953, 4; "Por la libertad de la cultura," *El Mercurio,* 23 April 1953, 3; and Julián Gorkin, "Detrás del telón de hierro se oculta la realidad de la experiencia soviética," *El Mercurio,* 29 April 1953, 1. On the formation of the committee, see Germain to Josselson, 5 October 1953; and Carlos de Baráibar to Michael Josselson, 5 July 1953, IACF, series II, box 204, folder 6, UC/SCRC.

17. Jaime Castillo, "El Congreso Continental de la Cultura de Santiago de Chile," *Cuadernos,* no. 2 (June–August 1953): 84. Delegates included Jorge Mañach and Mario Llerena from Cuba, Salvador Pineda and Rodrigo García Treviño from Mexico, Carlos Izaguirre and Mirta Rinza from Honduras, Rubem Braga from Brazil, Roberto Ibáñez and F. Ferrándiz Alborz (a Spanish exile)

from Uruguay, and J. González, Ramón Cortés, Alejandro Magnet, Jaime Castillo Velasco, and Carlos de Baráibar from Chile.

18. Nicolai to Josselson, 26 June 1954, IACF, series II, box 204, folder 8, UC/SCRC; Wolf W. Zuelzer, *The Nicolai Case: A Biography* (Detroit: Wayne State University Press, 1982).

19. Julián Gorkin to Carlos de Baráibar, 21 September 1954, IACF, series II, box 212, folder 1; and Josselson to Nicolai, 19 July 1954, IACF, series II, box 204, folder 8, UC/SCRC.

20. The United Fruit Company did subsidize the *New Leader,* which featured an anti-Communist perspective similar to that of the CCF, and also received CIA funds. The *New Leader* was not, however, affiliated with the CCF. Stephen C. Schlesinger and Stephen Kinzer, *Bitter Fruit: The Untold Story of the American Coup in Guatemala,* rev. and exp. ed. (Boston: David Rockefeller Center for Latin American Studies, 2005), 89; Saunders, *Cultural Cold War,* 163. "Imperialismo de la libertad nació en congreso de intelectuales: Seis países preparan cn Santiago una réplica al congreso del 53; El sabio Nicolai dividió al mundo en culturas," *Ercilla,* no. 998 (15 June 1954): 13; "Polémicas y derechos del hombre," *Cultura y Libertad,* no. 1 (December 1954): 18–19.

21. "Congrès pour la liberté de la culture: Comités nationaux," n.d. [1958?], IACF, series II, box 210, folder 5, UC/SCRC. For more details on the local organizations of the CCF in Latin America, see Karina Jannello, "Los intelectuales de la Guerra Fría: Una cartografía latinoamericana (1953–1962)," *Políticas de la Memoria,* no. 14 (Summer 2013/2014): 79–101.

22. Robert J. Alexander and Victor Raúl Haya de la Torre, *Aprismo: The Ideas and Doctrines of Victor Raúl Haya de la Torre* (Kent, Ohio: Kent State University Press, 1973); Felipe Cossío del Pomar, *Víctor Raúl: Biografía de Haya de la Torre* (Mexico City: Editorial Cultura, 1961); Harry Kantor, *The Ideology and Program of the Peruvian Aprista Movement* (New York: Octagon Books, 1966); Robert J. Alexander, *Rómulo Betancourt and the Transformation of Venezuela* (New Brunswick, N.J.: Transaction Books, 1982); Rómulo Betancourt and Manuel Caballero, *Rómulo Betancourt: Leninismo, revolución y reforma* (Mexico City: Fondo de Cultura Económica, 1997); Manuel Caballero, *Rómulo Betancourt, político de nación* (Caracas, Venezuela: Alfadil, 2004); Alejandro Gómez, *Rómulo Betancourt y el Partido Comunista de Costa Rica (1931–1935)* (San José: Editorial Costa Rica, 1994).

23. Charles D. Ameringer, *The Caribbean Legion: Patriots, Politicians, Soldiers of Fortune, 1946–1950* (University Park: Pennsylvania State University Press, 1996); Fabrice E. Lehoucq and Iván Molina, *Stuffing the Ballot Box: Fraud, Electoral Reform, and Democratization in Costa Rica* (New York: Cambridge University Press, 2002), 210–225.

24. Cossío del Pomar, *Víctor Raúl,* 228.

25. Truman administration officials preferred Acción Democrática in Venezuela but did virtually nothing to support it when it was overthrown in 1948. Figueres in Costa Rica got tacit support from the United States during his civil war but later had to deal with hostility. Juan Bosch of the Dominican Republic also received covert U.S. support at some points during his career, but his

restoration to office was blocked by the U.S. military in 1965. Steven Schwartzberg, "Rómulo Betancourt: From a Communist Anti-imperialist to a Social Democrat with US Support," *Journal of Latin American Studies* 29, no. 3 (October 1997): 661; Kyle Longley, "Peaceful Costa Rica, the First Battleground: The United States and the Costa Rican Revolution of 1948," *Americas* 50, no. 2 (October 1993): 150–151; Charles D. Ameringer, *Don Pepe: A Political Biography of José Figueres of Costa Rica* (Albuquerque: University of New Mexico Press, 1978); Patrick Iber, "'Who Will Impose Democracy?' Sacha Volman and the Contradictions of CIA Support for the Anti-Communist Left in Latin America," *Diplomatic History* 37, no. 5 (November 2013): 995–1028. On the anti-Communist Left more broadly, see Charles D. Ameringer, *The Democratic Left in Exile: The Antidictatorial Struggle in the Caribbean, 1945–1959* (Coral Gables, Fla.: University of Miami Press, 1974).

26. Paul W. Drake, *Socialism and Populism in Chile, 1932–52* (Urbana: University of Illinois Press, 1978), 255; Alexander, *Rómulo Betancourt*, 155. The president of Cuba in 1950 was Carlos Prío, who will be discussed in Chapter 4. Caballero, *Rómulo Betancourt*, 280.

27. "Report on the American Federation of Labor Delegation to the Inter-American Conference for Democracy and Freedom," n.d., Record group 18–009, Serafino Romualdi Papers, box 10, folder 5, George Meany Memorial Archives (GMMA), Silver Spring, Md.

28. "Inter-American Association for Democracy and Freedom," n.d., Record Group 18–009, Serafino Romualdi Papers, box 10, folder 5, GMMA. On Grant, see David Mark Carletta, "Frances R. Grant's Pan American Activities, 1929–1949" (Ph.D. diss., Michigan State University, 2009).

29. Van Gosse, *Where the Boys Are: Cuba, Cold War America and the Making of a New Left* (London: Verso, 1993), 23–24, 77; Inter-American Association for Democracy and Freedom, *Report of the Second Inter-American Congress: Maracay, Venezuela, April 22 to 26, 1960* (New York: Inter-American Association for Democracy and Freedom, 1961), 44–76. The IADF received small contributions from groups associated with the CIA, like the Free Trade Union Committee, but they were a small part of the budget. The IADF, in other words, was not a CIA front. The financial records are in the Frances Grant Papers, box 28, folders 1–19, Archibald S. Alexander Library, Rutgers University, New Brunswick, N.J.

30. On the "bourgeois law," see Nick Cullather, *Secret History: The CIA's Classified Account of Its Operations in Guatemala, 1952–1954* (Stanford, Calif.: Stanford University Press, 1999), 22; and Daniel Wilkinson, *Silence on the Mountain: Stories of Terror, Betrayal, and Forgetting in Guatemala* (Boston: Houghton Mifflin, 2002), 165. On the CTAL and peace movement connections, see Ronald M. Schneider, *Communism in Guatemala, 1944–1954* (New York: Praeger, 1958), 153. On the reasons that the Eisenhower administration chose hostility to the revolutionary government in Guatemala but accommodation in Bolivia, see Kenneth Lehman, "Revolutions and Attributions:

Making Sense of the Eisenhower Administration Policies in Bolivia and Guatemala," *Diplomatic History* 21, no. 2 (Spring 1997): 185–213.

31. Bryce Wood, *The Dismantling of the Good Neighbor Policy* (Austin: University of Texas Press, 1985), xiv. Arguing the case for the United Fruit Company's influence in the decision to depose Arbenz, the major work is Schlesinger and Kinzer, *Bitter Fruit*. Those who emphasize political factors include Piero Gleijeses, *Shattered Hope: The Guatemalan Revolution and the United States, 1944–1954* (Princeton, N.J.: Princeton University Press, 1991); and Cullather, *Secret History*. See also Richard H. Immerman, *The CIA in Guatemala: The Foreign Policy of Intervention* (Austin: University of Texas Press, 1982). On the isolation of Guatemalan Communism from the Soviet Union, see especially Gleijeses, *Shattered Hope,* 184–188. Arbenz, three years after he was deposed, did join the Communist Party.

32. Cullather, *Secret History,* 67; Gleijeses, *Shattered Hope,* 317–318. Culturcongress to Gorkin, 10 June 1954, IACF, series II, box 204, folder 10; and "Información sur La Reunion de Santiago du Chili," 1954, box 204, folder 11, UC/SCRC.

33. Gorkin to Carlos de Baráibar, 21 December 1954, IACF, series II, box 212, folder 1, box 212, UC/SCRC; Juan José Arévalo to Basili Pyakubovsky, 18 March 1945, IACF, series II, box 51, folder 6, UC/SCRC. Both the Soviet embassy in Mexico and the U.S. embassy in Guatemala were aware that the letter was a forgery. Juan José Arévalo and Oscar de León Castillo, *Despacho presidencial: Obra póstuma* (Guatemala City: Editorial Oscar de León Palacios, 1998), 164–166. Gorkin may have first seen the letter when it was published by a Mexican tabloid in 1946 amid photographs of car crashes and anti-Red propaganda. The letter, in facsimile, is identical to the one found among Gorkin's papers in the IACF archive. "México, Sede de un Vasto Complot Rojo," *Prensa Gráfica,* 13 July 1946, 3.

34. Julián Gorkin, "La experiencia de Guatemala: Por una política de la libertad en Latinoamérica," *Cuadernos,* no. 9 (November–December 1954): 92–93.

35. Raymond Aron first broached the subject of the "end of ideology" at the conference; in their original formulations, both Aron and Shils posed the "end of ideology" as a question. Daniel Bell, also in attendance in Milan, published an expanded exploration of the "end of ideology" thesis in 1960 (without the question mark), arguing that Marxism had lost its capacity to appeal to intellectuals. Daniel Bell, *The End of Ideology: On the Exhaustion of Political Ideas in the Fifties; With "The Resumption of History in the New Century,"* 40th anniversary ed. (Cambridge, Mass.: Harvard University Press, 2000).

36. Nor did liberal-socialist consensus extend to Friedrich von Hayek, in attendance in Milan, who thought that the welfare state led inexorably to totalitarian serfdom. Ignoring this form of right-wing ideology was one of the more significant errors of the "end of ideology" thesis.

37. Edward Shils, "The End of Ideology?," *Encounter* 5, no. 5 (November 1955): 57. "Meeting between the North and South American Delegates at the Milan Conference," September 1955, American Committee for Cultural Freedom

(ACCF) Papers, box 2, folder 3, Tamiment Library, New York University, New York.

38. "Censuras y loas de culturólogos a Estados Unidos," *Excélsior,* 22 September 1956, 11.

39. Pedro de Alba's remarks are in "Hoy se inaugura la Asamblea pro Cultura Libre," *Excélsior,* 18 September 1956, 4. On government relations, see "Publicidad por radio y televisión a la conferencia interamericana del Congreso por la Libertad de la Cultura," n.d., IACF, series II, box 229, folder 7, UC/SCRC. When it had formed, the Asociación Mexicana had sent a letter to President Adolfo Ruiz Cortines, expressing complete agreement with his policies and pledging to cooperate as much as possible with his government. Asociación Mexicana por la Libertad de la Cultura to Adolfo Ruiz Cortínes, 3 March 1954, Gallery 3—Adolfo Ruiz Cortines, box 472, folder 437.1/133, Archivo General de la Nación (AGN), Mexico City. Rodrigo García Treviño reported that Serafino Romualdi and Arturo Jáuregui of ORIT had assured him that they could ask Fidel Velázquez to fill seats if necessary. García Treviño to Gorkin, 12 April 1956, IACF, series II, box 228, folder 11, UC/SCRC.

40. "Discurso de Luis Alberto Sánchez" and "Discurso de Ricardo Montilla," both in IACF, series II, box 229, folder 1, UC/SCRC.

41. "Todos los esfuerzos de los pensadores de América y España, pro libertad de prensa," *Excélsior,* 20 September 1956, 11.

42. "Intervención del Sr. Mario Monteforte Toledo," IACF, series II, box 229, folder 2, UC/SCRC. Mario Monteforte Toledo, *Guatemala, monografía sociológica,* vol. 1 (Mexico City: Instituto de Investigaciones Sociales, Universidad Nacional Autónoma de México, 1959); Mario Monteforte Toledo, *La revolución de Guatemala, 1944–1954* (Guatemala City: Editorial Universitaria, 1974); Luis Cardoza y Aragón, Enrique Muñoz Meany, Jorge Luis Arriola, Arturo Taracena Arriola, Arely Mendoza Deleón, and Julio César Pinto Soria, *El placer de corresponder: Correspondencia entre Cardoza y Aragón, Muñoz Meany y Arriola* (Guatemala City: Editorial Universitaria Universidad de San Carlos de Guatemala, 2004), 268; Arévalo and León Castillo, *Despacho presidencial,* 68–89, 94, 289, 364, 401, 502; Seymour Menton, *Historia crítica de la novela guatemalteca,* 2nd ed. (Guatemala City: Editorial Universitaria de Guatemala, 1985), 311.

43. "Intervención del Sr. Madariaga para hacer algunas aclaraciones sobre lo que está hablando el Sr. Monteforte," IACF, series II, box 229, folder 2, UC/SCRC.

44. Arthur Whitaker, for example, argued that Eduardo Santos was incorrect in arguing that the United States had done nothing to protest the actions that the Argentine government of Juan Domingo Perón had taken against the press of that country. "Intervención del Sr. Arthur Whitaker" and "Intervención del Sr. José Luis Romero," both in IACF, series II, box 229, folder 2, UC/SCRC. Monge's remarks are in "Censuras y loas de culturólogos a Estados Unidos," *Excélsior,* 22 September 1956, 11.

45. "Minutes of October 1, 1956 meeting," ACCF Papers, box 7, folder 3, Tamiment Library; Norman Thomas to Michael Josselson, 5 October 1956, IACF, series II, box 229, folder 8; and Roger Baldwin to Nicholas Nabokov,

1 November 1956, IACF, series II, box 42, folder 12; Josselson to Michael Polanyi, 30 October 1958, IACF, series II, box 267, folder 2, UC/SCRC.

46. Baráibar to Gorkin, 21 July 1955 and 13 October 1955, IACF, series II, folder 9, box 51, UC/SCRC. Baráibar reported that after the Youth Congress was banned in Chile, it was rescheduled for Brazil, but the head of the youth section of the CCF in Chile took the CCF propaganda to Brazil, and the government banned the gathering there as well. Baráibar interview with Robert J. Alexander, 23 July 1956, in Santiago, folder 23, box 6, Robert J. Alexander Interview Collection, Archibald S. Alexander Library, Rutgers University, New Brunswick, N.J. On the National Student Association and its relationship with the CCF in Chile, see Karen Paget, *Patriotic Betrayal* (New Haven, Conn.: Yale University Press, 2015), 164–169. For praise from Frei, see Baráibar to Gorkin, 24 August 1955, IACF, series II, folder 9, box 51, UC/SCRC. After Neruda's Continental Cultural Congress in 1953, Argentine Communists tried to hold an Argentine Congress of Culture but were blocked, as usual, by government harassment. Jorge Nállim, *Transformations and Crisis of Liberalism in Argentina, 1930–1955* (Pittsburgh: University of Pittsburgh Press, 2012), 179–180. For a detailed account of the Chilean operations of the CCF, see Karina Jannello, "El Congreso por la Libertad de la Cultura: El caso chileno y las 'ideas fuerza' de la Guerra Fría," *Revista Izquierdas,* no. 14 (December 2012): 14–52. On its operations in Argentina, see Karina Jannello, "Redes intelectuales y Guerra Fría: La agenda argentina del Congreso por la Libertad de la Cultura," *Revista de la Red Intercátedras de Historia de América Latina Contemporánea* 1, no. 1 (June 2014): 60–85; and Jorge Nállim, "Local Struggles, Transnational Connections: Latin American Intellectuals and the Congress for Cultural Freedom," in *The Material of World History*, ed. Tina Mai Chen and David S. Churchill (New York: Routledge, 2015), 106–131.

47. John M. Crewdson and Joseph B. Treaster, "Worldwide Propaganda Network Built by the C.I.A.," *New York Times,* 26 December 1977, 37; Josselson to Praeger, 19 December 1957, IACF, series II, box 267, folder 11, UC/SCRC. The book was brought out as Milovan Djilas, *La nueva clase: Análisis del régimen comunista* (Buenos Aires: Editorial Sudamericana, 1957).

48. Schlesinger and Kinzer, *Bitter Fruit,* 230. In Schlesinger and Kinzer's book, the quote is anonymous. However, the speaker is described as the publisher of some of the works of Guatemalan Communist double agent Carlos Manuel Pellecer, and that was almost certainly Costa Amic; Carlos Manuel Pellecer, *Renuncia al Comunismo,* 4th ed. (Mexico City: Costa-Amic, 1965). On the CCF's publishing relationships in Argentina, see Karina Jannello, "Las políticas culturales del socialismo argentino bajo la Guerra Fría: Las redes editoriales socialistas y el Congreso por la Libertad de la Cultura," *Papeles de Trabajo* 7, no. 12 (Spring 2013): 212–247.

49. Glondys, *Guerra fría cultural y el exilio republicano español,* 88–89; Jean Franco, *The Decline and Fall of the Lettered City: Latin America in the Cold War* (Cambridge, Mass.: Harvard University Press, 2002), 35.

50. For an example of how Gallegos was seen by anti-Communists, see Raúl Roa, "Rómulo Gallegos, novelista con novela," in *Retorno a la alborada,* vol. 1,

3rd ed. (Havana: Editorial de Ciencias Sociales, 1977), 689–697. Gerald
Martin, *Gabriel García Márquez: A Life,* 1st U.S. ed. (New York: Alfred A.
Knopf, 2009), 311.

51. "Así Veían a Stalin," IACF, series II, box 204, folder 1, UC/SCRC; "SECh
cambió a Pablo Neruda por otro poeta: Julio Barrenechea," *El Mercurio,*
21 April 1959; "Las mentiras del Señor Baráibar," *El Siglo,* 23 April 1959;
"¿Qué pasó en la Sociedad de Escritores?," *Las Últimas Noticias,* 18 April
1959. Baráibar wanted to help Barrenechea financially and in terms of prestige by sending him on a CCF-sponsored lecture tour and publishing his books
in the United States. Baráibar to Gorkin, IACF, series II, box 208, folder 7,
UC/SCRC. Juan Ramón Jiménez, *Españoles de tres mundos* (Buenos Aires:
Editorial Losada, 1942), 122–125. See also Arturo Torres Rioseco, "Neruda
y sus detractores"; Ricardo Paseyro, "Neruda: Vuelta y fin"; and Juan Ramón
Jiménez, "Un gran mal poeta," in *Cuadernos,* no. 30 (May–June 1958): 49–
59. Ricardo Paseyro, *Mito y verdad de Pablo Nerudo* (Mexico City: Aso-
ciación Mexicana por la Libertad de la Cultura, 1958); Pablo Neruda and
Jorge Edwards, *Correspondencia entre Pablo Neruda y Jorge Edwards: Cartas
que romperemos de inmediato y recordaremos siempre,* ed. Abraham Quezada
Vergara (Santiago, Chile: Alfaguara, 2008), 96–97. For more on the anti-
Neruda campaigns, see Chapter 6.

52. Robin Adèle Greeley, "Muralism and the State in Post-revolution Mexico,
1920–1970," in *Mexican Muralism: A Critical History,* ed. Alejandro Anreus,
Robin Adèle Greeley, and Leonard Folgarait (Berkeley: University of California
Press, 2012), 29.

53. "No hay más ruta que la nuestra," published in 1945, is now extremely rare.
Selections can be found in David Álfaro Siqueiros and Raquel Tibol, *Palabras
de Siqueiros* (Mexico City: Fondo de Cultura Económica, 1996), 238–257.
The painters' debate in the late 1940s is well covered in Rafael Loyola Díaz,
Una mirada a México: El Nacional, 1940–1952 (Mexico City: Instituto de
Investigaciones Sociales, Universidad Nacional Autónoma de México, 1996),
114–120.

54. Luis Suárez, *Confesiones de Diego Rivera* (Mexico City: Ediciones Era, 1962),
160. Toward the end of his life, Rivera reversed some of his criticisms of
Tamayo. Raquel Tibol, *Diego Rivera, luces y sombras* (Barcelona: Lumen,
2007), 174.

55. Suárez, *Confesiones de Diego Rivera,* 156–157. The debate about abstract expressionism and the Cold War has been substantial. Among the works that
see it as a tool of U.S. propaganda are Eva Cockcroft, "Abstract Expressionism,
Weapon of the Cold War," *Artforum* 12, no. 10 (June 1974): 39–41; and Serge
Guilbaut, *How New York Stole the Idea of Modern Art: Abstract Expressionism, Freedom, and the Cold War* (Chicago: University of Chicago Press,
1983). Those who include other, more complex causes in the rise of abstract
expressionism include Annette Cox, *Art-as-Politics: The Abstract Expres-
sionist Avant-Garde and Society* (Ann Arbor: UMI Research Press, 1982);
and Diana Crane, *The Transformation of the Avant-Garde: The New York
Art World, 1940–1985* (Chicago: University of Chicago Press, 1987). On the

shifting meaning of modernist culture in the Cold War, see Greg Barnhisel, *Cold War Modernists: Art, Literature, and American Cultural Diplomacy* (New York: Columbia University Press, 2015).

56. "Mexico," n.d. [1955], IACF, series II, box 52, folder 4, UC/SCRC. The Mexican Association for Cultural Freedom claimed Paz as a member, but there is no evidence that this was so. Although he spoke at this event, he never appeared on letterhead as one of the many members of the Mexican Association. When approached directly about joining the CCF in the 1960s, Paz declined. F. Cossio del Pomar, "Exposición de 'La Jovén Pintura' en México," *Cuadernos*, no. 34 (January–February 1959): 100.

57. Víctor Alba, "Coloquio con Rufino Tamayo," *Cuadernos*, no. 22 (January–February 1957): 98; Elena Poniatowska, "Artes plásticas: Juan Soriano," *Universidad de México* 12, no. 10 (June 1958): 22–24.

58. The original plan had been to invite Rufino Tamayo, Manuel Rodríguez Lozano, Federico Cantú, Antonio Ruiz, Agustín Lazo, Leonora Carrington, Dr. Atl, Juan Soriano, José Luis Cuevas, Vlady, Harold Winslow, and several other painters. The styles of these painters ranged from abstraction to surrealism to "classic" Mexican muralism. García Treviño to Gorkin, 25 February 1957, IACF, series II, box 206, folder 5, UC/SCRC. Manuel Rodríguez Lozano criticized Rufino Tamayo in an interview in *El Universal*. García Treviño blamed the political pressure on Rivera, Siqueiros, and Lázaro Cárdenas, but there is probably no way to evaluate this claim. García Treviño to Gorkin, 22 March 1957, IACF, series II, box 206, folder 5, UC/SCRC. The exhibition ran from 12 August to 5 September 1957. Manuel Rodríguez Lozano, Alberto Gironella, Bridget Bate Tichenor, Margarita Michelena, Margarita Nelken, and Rodrigo García Treviño were among those who attended the opening. "Exposición colectiva en Galerías Excélsior," *Excélsior*, 14 August 1957, 3B. Rafael Anzures, "Exposición de 'La Joven Pintura,'" *Examen*, no. 3 (November–December 1958): 79–81. Enrique F. Gual, "Las difíciles novedades," *Excélsior* (supplement *Diorama de la Cultura*), 12 October 1958. On Sicre, see Claire F. Fox, "The PAU Visual Arts Section and the Hemispheric Circulation of Latin American Art during the Cold War," *Getty Research Journal*, no. 2 (2010): 83–106; and Claire Fox, *Making Art Panamerican: Cultural Policy and the Cold War* (Minneapolis: University of Minnesota Press, 2013).

59. Nicanor Parra, *Poemas para combatir la calvicie: Muestra de antipoesía* (Mexico City: Fondo de Cultura Económica, 1993), 178.

4. The Anti-Communist Left and the Cuban Revolution

1. Lillian Guerra, *Visions of Power in Cuba: Revolution, Redemption, and Resistance, 1959–1971* (Chapel Hill: University of North Carolina Press, 2012), 59; Van Gosse, *Where the Boys Are: Cuba, Cold War America and the Making of a New Left* (London: Verso, 1993), 108.

2. Rafael Rojas, "México, las dictaduras caribeñas y los orígenes de la Guerra Fría, 1934–1959," in *Los diplomáticos mexicanos y la Guerra Fría: Memoria e historia, 1947–1989,* ed. Leticia Bobadilla González (Morelia,

Michoacán: Universidad Michoacana de San Nicolás de Hidalgo, 2009), 234–235.

3. Mario Llerena, "Manifiesto ideológico del Movimiento 26 de Julio," *Humanismo* 6, no. 44 (July–August 1957): 88–103. The special issue, number 47, was from January–February 1958. Fidel Castro Ruz, "Figueres," *Humanismo* 8, nos. 55–56 (May–August 1959): 71–75. For the change of sponsorship, see nos. 58–59 (November 1959–February 1960): 8. The magazine disappeared after issue nos. 60–61. On the puppy story, see Jon Lee Anderson, *Che Guevara: A Revolutionary Life* (New York: Grove Press, 1997), 458.

4. The best treatment of the sensitive matter of Communist influence over the course of the revolution is Guerra, *Visions of Power in Cuba.*

5. Quoted in Lars Schoultz, *That Infernal Little Cuban Republic: The United States and the Cuban Revolution* (Chapel Hill: University of North Carolina Press, 2009), 24. On the close cultural relationship between the United States and Cuba, see especially Louis A. Pérez Jr., *On Becoming Cuban: Identity, Nationality, and Culture* (Chapel Hill: University of North Carolina Press, 1999).

6. Hugh Thomas, *Cuba: The Pursuit of Freedom* (New York: Harper & Row, 1971), 591–594; Calixto Masó, *Historia de Cuba: La lucha de un pueblo por cumplir su destino histórico y su vocación de libertad,* 2nd ed. (Miami, Fla.: Ediciones Universal, 1976), 538–540. Masó was a member of the CCF.

7. Marifeli Pérez-Stable, *The Cuban Revolution: Origins, Course, and Legacy,* 2nd ed. (New York: Oxford University Press, 1999), 41; Louis A. Pérez Jr., *Cuba: Between Reform and Revolution,* 3rd ed. (New York: Oxford University Press, 2006), 203–209.

8. Rafael E. Tarragó, "'Rights Are Taken, Not Pleaded': José Martí and the Cult of the Recourse to Violence in Cuba," in *The Cuban Republic and José Martí: Reception and Use of a National Symbol,* ed. Mauricio A. Font and Alfonso W. Quiroz (Lanham, Md.: Lexington Books, 2006), 59; Charles D. Ameringer, *The Cuban Democratic Experience: The Auténtico Years, 1944–1952* (Gainesville: University Press of Florida, 2000), 14.

9. Message of Fulgencio Batista y Zaldívar, 2 September 1949, Miguel Alemán Valdés 433/503, Gallery 3, Archivo General de la Nación (AGN), Mexico City.

10. The ratio of congressional laws passed to executive decrees issued under Batista was 1:57; under Grau, 1:70, and under Grau's successor, Carlos Prío, 1:26. Pérez-Stable, *Cuban Revolution,* 45. The danger of the university is in Fidel Castro, Rolando E. Bonachea, and Nelson P. Valdés, *Revolutionary Struggle, 1947–1958* (Cambridge, Mass.: MIT Press, 1972), 16. On the acquisition of arms, see Ameringer, *Cuban Democratic Experience,* 73; and Charles D. Ameringer, *The Caribbean Legion: Patriots, Politicians, Soldiers of Fortune, 1946–1950* (University Park: Pennsylvania State University Press, 1996), 36–37. Juan Bosch to Theodore Draper, 5 February 1964, Theodore Draper Papers, box 24, envelope "Misc. Correspondence," Hoover Institution Archives (HIA), Stanford, Calif.

11. The Ministry of Education was one of the principal vehicles for the distribution of the spoils of corruption. Ameringer, *Cuban Democratic Experience,* 74–75, 88; Pérez-Stable, *Cuban Revolution,* 50; Pérez, *Cuba,* 217.

12. Rojas, "México, las dictaduras caribeñas y los orígenes de la Guerra Fría," 229; Ameringer, *Cuban Democratic Experience*, 90–91; Carlos Zapata Vela, *Conversaciones con Heriberto Jara* (Mexico City: Costa-Amic Editores, 1992), 157–159; Thomas, *Cuba*, 765. A photo of Lombardo in the Cuban prison appears in Vicente Lombardo Toledano, "Carta abierta a Carlos Prío Socarrás," *Siempre!*, no. 429 (13 September 1961). Julián Gorkin, *El revolucionario profesional: Testimonio de un hombre de acción* (Barcelona: Aymá, 1975), photo plates; Herbert R. Southworth, "'The Grand Camouflage': Julián Gorkin, Burnett Bolloten and the Spanish Civil War," in *The Republic Besieged: The Civil War in Spain, 1936–1939*, ed. Paul Preston and Ann L. Mackenzie (Edinburgh: Edinburgh University Press, 1996), 264; Charles D. Ameringer, *Don Pepe: A Political Biography of José Figueres of Costa Rica* (Albuquerque: University of New Mexico Press, 1978), 165; Jesús Arboleya, *The Cuban Counterrevolution* (Athens: Ohio University Center for International Studies, 2000), 69.

13. Romualdi to George Meany, Matthew Woll, and David Dubinsky, 18 February 1946, Serafino Romualdi Papers, box 4, folder 1, Kheel Center, Ithaca, N.Y.; Cornell University; Thomas, *Cuba*, 748–753; Ameringer, *Cuban Democratic Experience*, 45–49. From 1 January to 30 November 1951, for example, the AFL contributed $30,150 to ORIT, the Congress of Industrial Organizations contributed $25,500, the United Mine Workers $12,000, and the CTC $12.916.66. No other Latin American federation contributed more than $100. "Organización Regional Interamericana de Trabajadores, estado de situación," 30 November 1951, Serafino Romualdi Papers, box 7, folder 13, George Meany Memorial Archives (GMMA), Silver Spring, Md. Even after the Mexican CTM joined ORIT in 1953, the CTC still contributed more financially.

14. James Dunkerley, *Political Suicide in Latin America, and Other Essays* (London: Verso, 1992), 35–37; Luis Conte Agüero, *Eduardo Chibás, el adalid de Cuba* (Miami: La Moderna Poesía, 1987), 718–785; Tad Szulc, *Fidel: A Critical Portrait* (New York: Avon, 1986), 212.

15. Robert J. Alexander, "Confidential Report to Executive Council of the American Federation of Labor: On Cuban Labor Situation after Batista Revolt," Jay Lovestone Papers, box 286, folder 12, HIA; Lovestone to Romualdi, 20 March 1952, Serafino Romualdi Papers, folder 2, box 4, Kheel. In 1958 the CTC defeated a motion advanced by Luis Alberto Monge to label Batista's government a dictatorship. Report, 3 February 1958, Serafino Romualdi Papers, box 4, folder 4, Kheel; CTC in exile to Bill Kemsley, 18 July 1957, Serafino Romualdi Papers, box 4, folder 3, Kheel; Thomas, *Cuba*, 1177–1179.

16. Schoultz, *That Infernal Little Cuban Republic*, 47, 61.

17. On the mythologizing of the Cuban Revolution, see Julia Sweig, *Inside the Cuban Revolution: Fidel Castro and the Urban Underground* (Cambridge, Mass.: Harvard University Press, 2002), 1–5.

18. Carlos Franqui, *Family Portrait with Fidel: A Memoir* (New York: Random House, 1984), xiii; Antonio Rafael de la Cova, *The Moncada Attack: Birth of the Cuban Revolution* (Columbia: University of South Carolina Press,

2007), 236; Fidel Castro, *The Prison Letters of Fidel Castro*, ed. Ann Louise Bardach and Luis Conte Agüero (New York: Nation Books, 2007); Thomas, *Cuba*, 1273.

19. Interview with Alberto Bayo Hijo, 12 February 1986, Georgie Anne Geyer Papers, box 7, folder 31, HIA; "Cuba: Hairbreadth Escape," *Time*, 7 June 1954, 42; Thomas, *Cuba*, 854–862.

20. Alfred Padula, "Financing Castro's Revolution, 1956–1958," *Revista/Review Interamericana* 8, no. 2 (Summer 1978): 234.

21. Ameringer, *Cuban Democratic Experience*, 91.

22. Lázaro Cárdenas, "México contra la guerra," *América* 1, no. 1 (January 1939): 5–10; and Cordell Hull, "En pro del acercamiento intelectual," *América* 1, no. 1 (January 1939): 10–12. The AEAA was created in 1934 and given status as an autonomous international organization for the public good in 1936.

23. Membership on the board of directors of the AEAA was extensive and, in overlap with the CCF, included most of the writers in the Cuban Association of the CCF, among them Jorge Mañach, Francisco Ichaso, Pastor del Río, and Luis A. Baralt. Pedro Vicente Aja to Gorkin, 31 July 1957, International Association for Cultural Freedom Papers (IACF), series II, box 206, folder 4, Joseph L. Regenstein Library, University of Chicago Special Collections Research Center (UC/SCRC), Chicago; "Por la libertad de la cultura," *América* 47, nos. 1, 2, and 3 (January, February, and March 1956): photo plates; Idalia Morejón Arnaiz, *Política y polémica en América Latina: Las revistas* Casa de las Américas y Mundo Nuevo (Mexico City: Educación y Cultura, 2010), 61.

24. Mario Llerena, *The Unsuspected Revolution: The Birth and Rise of Castroism* (Ithaca, N.Y.: Cornell University Press, 1978); Thomas, *Cuba*, 910.

25. Enrique de la Osa, *Visión y pasión de Raúl Roa* (Havana: Editorial de Ciencias Sociales, 1987), 9; Llerena, *Unsuspected Revolution*, 82–91. After Llerena left for Mexico, his salary was passed on to his wife (who remained in Cuba) for the business of the association. Given the danger of continued operation, the Cuban Association of the CCF was shut down at the end of 1957. When it became clear to Gorkin that Llerena was operating in an executive capacity with the Cuban Association for Cultural Freedom and the 26th of July Movement, he asked Llerena to step down as an officer of the Cuban Association for Cultural Freedom. Llerena remained a member, and Gorkin continued to assist him in New York. Gorkin to Llerena, 17 June 1957; Gorkin to Llerena, 29 November 1957, IACF, series II, box 206, folder 4, UC/SCRC.

26. In Mexico, Llerena was hosted by Rodrigo García Treviño. Llerena to Gorkin, 8 May 1957; Gorkin to Llerena, 17 May 1957; Llerena to Gorkin, 31 October 1957, IACF, series II, box 206, folder 4, UC/SCRC. On Mañach's beating, see Carlos Franqui, *Diary of the Cuban Revolution* (New York: Viking Press, 1980), 44–45. "Las dictaduras contra 'Cuadernos,'" *Cuadernos*, no. 33 (November–December 1958): 113; and Jorge Mañach, "El drama de Cuba," *Cuadernos*, no. 30 (May–June 1958): 63–76. The manifesto in the supplement was signed in Cuba by Roberto Agramonte, Manuel Bisbé, Roberto Esquenazi Mayo, Mario Llerena for the 26th of July Movement, Salvador Massip, Felipe Pazos, and Manuel Urrutia. It was also signed by, among others,

Jorge Luis Borges. On Llerena's press work in the United States, see Llerena, *Unsuspected Revolution*, 121, 148–149; and Gosse, *Where the Boys Are*, 77.

27. Guevara is quoted in Thomas, *Cuba*, 1038–1039. Fulgencio Batista y Zaldívar, *Cuba Betrayed* (New York: Vantage Press, 1962), 52. Anthony DePalma, *The Man Who Invented Fidel: Cuba, Castro, and Herbert L. Matthews of the New York Times* (New York: Public Affairs, 2006), 100–101, 116–117.

28. On the *Granma*, see Padula, "Financing Castro's Revolution," 236; Castro, Bonachea, and Valdés, *Revolutionary Struggle*, 82. Interview with Alberto Bayo Jr., 12 February 1986, Georgie Anne Geyer Papers, box 7, folder 31, HIA. On Figueres, see Fernando Salazar Navarette in conversation with Robert J. Alexander, 1 July 1967, Robert J. Alexander Interview Collection, reel 6, frame 420, Archibald S. Alexander Library, Rutgers University, New Brunswick, N.J.; Castro, Bonachea, and Valdés, *Revolutionary Struggle*, 80; and Huber Matos, *Cómo llegó la noche* (Barcelona: Tusquets Editores, 2002), 76–81. Figueres also financed another invasion by Aureliano Sánchez Arango that arrived in Cuba after the rebel victory in 1959 and turned over its arms to the new government. Interview with José Figueres, 27 May 1985, Georgie Anne Geyer Papers, box 9, folder 5, HIA. On U.S. relations with Castro before his victory, see Vanni Pettinà, *Cuba y Estados Unidos, 1933–1959: Del compromiso nacionalista al conflicto* (Madrid: Libros de la Catarata, 2011), 150–161, 211–271; Sweig, *Inside the Cuban Revolution*, 29, 92, 178; Thomas G. Paterson, *Contesting Castro: The United States and the Triumph of the Cuban Revolution* (New York: Oxford University Press, 1994), 63–64, 105–106, 112–117, 218–223; and Anderson, *Che Guevara*, 271–273.

29. Gosse, *Where the Boys Are*, 77; Sheldon Liss, *Roots of Revolution: Radical Thought in Cuba* (Lincoln: University of Nebraska Press, 1987), 121.

30. Pedro Vicente Aja to Gorkin, 13 January 1959, box 208, folder 9; Llerena to Gorkin, 18 August 1958, box 208, folder 1; García Treviño to Gorkin, n.d., box 208, folder 10; Gorkin to Aja, 20 January 1959, box 208, folder 9; all in IACF, series II, UC/SCRC.

31. Betsy Maclean, *Haydée Santamaría* (Melbourne: Ocean Press, 2003). From the perspective of the Cuban government, Casa de las Américas began more as a rival to the Fondo de Cultura Económica, the publishing house that operated with Mexican government support and was seen by Cuba to represent a more ossified revolutionary tradition. Judith A. Weiss, *Casa de las Américas: An Intellectual Review in the Cuban Revolution* (Chapel Hill, N.C.: Estudios de Hispanófila, 1977), 42–43.

32. The crowd was dispersed by Camilo Cienfuegos, one of the heroes of the guerrilla struggle. Interview of Julio Amoedo by Keith Botsford, n.d., Julio Amoedo Papers, HIA. On the withdrawal from ORIT, see Alfonso Sánchez Madariaga to William F. Schnitzler, 11 September 1959, Serafino Romualdi Papers, folder 6, box 4, Kheel; Thomas, *Cuba*, 1250–1251; and Guerra, *Visions of Power in Cuba*, 126–127. "Lázaro Peña habla de la nueva ley de organización sindical," *Verde Olivo*, 27 August 1961, 47–49; Serafino Romualdi, *Presidents and Peons: Recollections of a Labor Ambassador in Latin America* (New York: Funk & Wagnalls, 1967), 213–214.

33. On Castro's secret meeting with the CIA, see William LeoGrande and Peter Kornbluh, *Back Channel to Cuba: The Hidden History of Negotiations between Washington and Havana* (Chapel Hill: University of North Carolina Press, 2014), 18–21. On anti-anti-Communism, see Thomas, *Cuba*, 1214.

34. Sergio López Rivero, *El viejo traje de la Revolución: Identidad colectiva, mito y hegemonía política en Cuba* (València: Universitat de València, 2007), 250; Anderson, *Che Guevara*, 499; Piero Gleijeses, *Conflicting Missions: Havana, Washington, and Africa, 1959–1976* (Chapel Hill: University of North Carolina Press, 2002), 23; Ameringer, *Don Pepe*, 154–156.

35. Matos, *Cómo llegó la noche*, 78; Guerra, *Visions of Power in Cuba*, 77. In July, Air Force Chief Pedro Luis Díaz Lanz had defected to the United States and accused Castro of Communism in testimony before the U.S. Senate. His case had been more compelling to U.S. conservatives than to liberals.

36. Franqui, *Diary of the Cuban Revolution*, 243; Franqui, *Family Portrait with Fidel*, 79–81. Many Cuban newspapers, including even *Prensa Libre*, had been subsidized by Batista. Guerra, *Visions of Power in Cuba*, 40. On Mañach's views, see "La situación de la intelectualidad cubana," IACF, series II, folder 8, box 209, UC/SCRC. On the origins of *coletillas*, see Guerra, *Visions of Power in Cuba*, 121–125; and Thomas, *Cuba*, 1261.

37. Mario Llerena, "El imagen en el espejo," *Prensa Libre*, [date unknown, early 1960], IACF, series II, box 217, folder 8, UC/SCRC; Mario Llerena, "Reflexiones ociosas," *Prensa Libre*, 27 March 1960, IACF, series II, box 217, folder 8, UC/SCRC.

38. Quoted in Manuel Urrutia Lleó, *Fidel Castro & Company, Inc.: Communist Tyranny in Cuba* (New York: Praeger, 1964), 89.

39. Guerra, *Visions of Power in Cuba*, 123–125; Patrick Symmes, *The Boys from Dolores: Fidel Castro and His Generation—From Revolution to Exile* (London: Robinson, 2007), 244–245; Peter Kornbluh, *Bay of Pigs Declassified: The Secret CIA Report on the Invasion of Cuba* (New York: New Press, 1998), 107.

40. Invitations were extended by multiple parties, not only Betancourt, so there were some pro-Castro delegates in attendance and even some Communists. The bulk of the delegates, however, came from Christian Democratic parties and the traditional Democratic Left. Robert J. Alexander, *Rómulo Betancourt and the Transformation of Venezuela* (New Brunswick, N.J.: Transaction Books, 1982), 550–551; Enrique Ros, *Playa Girón: La verdadera historia* (Miami, Fla.: Ediciones Universal, 1994), 17–19.

41. Llerena's comment is in Gorkin to Carlos de Baráibar, 30 May 1960, IACF, series II, box 209, folder 6, UC/SCRC. On involuntary exile, see Gorkin to Ferrándiz Alborz, 22 September 1960, IACF, series II, box 210, folder 2, UC/SCRC. Rosario Rexach de León, March 14, 1961, Robert J. Alexander Interview Collection, reel 6, frame 572.

42. Jaime Benítez, "Jorge Mañach en la Universidad de Puerto Rico," 35–40, in Jorge Mañach, *Jorge Mañach (1898–1961): Homenaje de la nación cubana* (Río Piedras, P.R.: Editorial San Juan, 1972). Before his suicide, Aja was serving as an instructor at the Universidad de Puerto Rico and was worried

about his reappointment. Additionally, he had fallen and broken some ribs. It is not clear whether the failure of the Bay of Pigs invasion contributed to his decision to commit suicide. Botsford to Josselson, 20 July 1961, IACF, series II, box 46, folder 3, UC/SCRC. On the silencing of Mañach, see Rafael Rojas, *Tumbas sin sosiego: Revolución, disidencia y exilio del intelectual cubano* (Barcelona: Editorial Anagrama, 2006), 16.

43. Ros, *Playa Girón*, 71; Don Bohning, *The Castro Obsession: U.S. Covert Operations against Cuba, 1959–1965* (Washington, D.C.: Potomac Books, 2005), 136.

44. Roa is quoted in Thomas, *Cuba*, 1225–1226. His time with the CCF is omitted from later revolutionary hagiographies and from anthologies of his writing: Osa, *Visión y pasión de Raúl Roa*; Raúl Roa, *Raúl Roa, el canciller de la dignidad* (Mexico City: Editorial Nuestro Tiempo, 1985). Roa did, however, meet Che while he was in Mexico, and that may have been the key for the later transfer of *Humanismo* to Cuban hands. Anderson, *Che Guevara*, 168. "Material to Discredit Cuban Foreign Minister Raúl Roa," 10 January 1962, Lot file—Arturo Morales Carrión Papers, box 9, folder 6, National Archives and Records Administration (NARA), College Park, Md. The "piece-of-shit thief" is "Un caco que jamás trascendió la categoría de caca." Raúl Roa, *Retorno a la alborada,* vol. 1, 3rd ed. (Havana: Editorial de Ciencias Sociales, 1977), 800–801.

45. Llerena, *Unsuspected Revolution,* 97. Javier Pazos, for example, had been recruited by Llerena and was a director of the 26th of July underground. Pazos was the son of economist Felipe Pazos, who served as head of the National Bank under both Prío and Castro before resigning in October 1959 over the treatment of Huber Matos. He left for exile in August 1960. Felipe Pazos was replaced by Che Guevara as head of the National Bank, according to an apocryphal anecdote, because Che misheard Fidel's request for an "economist" as for a "Communist." Jorge G. Castañeda, *Compañero: The Life and Death of Che Guevara* (New York: Vintage Books, 1998), 167–168. Javier Pazos remained in the Ministry of Economics until September 1960, when he made his own break. Javier Pazos, "The Revolution," *Cambridge Opinion,* no. 32 (February 1963): 18–27.

46. Kepa Artaraz, *Cuba and Western Intellectuals since 1959* (New York: Palgrave Macmillan, 2009), 34–35. "¿Por qué me gusta y no me gusta *Lunes?,*" *Lunes de Revolución,* no. 52 (28 May 1960): 2–3.

47. Sabá Cabrera, Guillermo's brother, was one of the directors of *P.M.* Liliana Martínez Pérez, *Los hijos de Saturno: Intelectuales y revolución en Cuba* (Mexico City: FLASCO, 2006), 34–35.

48. Gosse, *Where the Boys Are,* 214. Theodore Draper, "Castro's Cuba," *Encounter* 16, no. 3 (March 1961): 12, 23; Arthur M. Schlesinger to President Kennedy, 14 March 1961, http://www.jfklibrary.org/Asset-Viewer/Archives /JFKPOF-115–008.aspx; Theodore Draper, "Cuba y la política norteamericana," *Cuadernos,* no. 51 (August 1961): 14; Kornbluh, *Bay of Pigs Declassified,* 2; Theodore Draper, *Castro's Revolution: Myths and Realities* (New York: Praeger, 1962), 59; Anderson, *Che Guevara,* 519.

49. Julio García Luis, *Cuban Revolution Reader: A Documentary History of 40 Key Moments of the Cuban Revolution* (Melbourne: Ocean Press, 2001), 76–82.

50. On state control of newspapers, see Symmes, *Boys from Dolores,* 284–291. Guillén is quoted in Anderson, *Che Guevara,* 483. His Stalin anecdote is in Martínez Pérez, *Hijos de Saturno,* 55.

51. David Craven, *Art and Revolution in Latin America, 1910–1990* (New Haven, Conn.: Yale University Press, 2002), 75–116. For the impact of the Cuban Revolution on the New Left, see Artaraz, *Cuba and Western Intellectuals since 1959;* and Gosse, *Where the Boys Are.*

52. Cortázar to Eduardo Jonquières, 22 January 1963, in Julio Cortázar, *Cartas a los Jonquières,* eds. Aurora Bernárdez and Carles Álvarez Garriga (Buenos Aires: Alfaguara, 2010), 411.

53. On Rayuela, see Craven, *Art and Revolution in Latin America,* 133.

5. Peace and National Liberation in the Mexican 1960s

1. Che Guevara, *Guerrilla Warfare: A Method* (New York: Monthly Review Press, 1961); Régis Debray, *Revolution in the Revolution? Armed Struggle and Political Struggle in Latin America,* trans. Bobbye Ortiz (New York: Monthly Review Press, 1967). Guevara was not the only author responsible for the myth; see also, for example, Carlos Franqui, *El libro de los doce* (Havana: Guairas, 1967). Enthusiasm for sponsoring revolutionaries abroad did wax and wane with results. On the complicated relationship between Cuba and the Soviet Union over the issue of armed insurrection, see Daniela Spenser, "The Caribbean Crisis: Catalyst for Soviet Projection in Latin America," in *In from the Cold: Latin America's New Encounter with the Cold War,* ed. Gil Joseph and Daniela Spenser (Durham, N.C.: Duke University Press, 2008), 77–111; Piero Gleijeses, *Conflicting Missions: Havana, Washington, and Africa, 1959–1976* (Chapel Hill: University of North Carolina Press, 2002); and Tanya Harmer, "Two, Three, Many Revolutions? Cuba and the Prospects for Revolutionary Change in Latin America, 1967–1975," *Journal of Latin American Studies* 45, no. 1 (February 2013): 61–89.

2. John Dinges, *The Condor Years: How Pinochet and His Allies Brought Terrorism to Three Continents* (New York: New Press, 2004), 2.

3. The number of the "disappeared" in Mexico is given in Sergio Aguayo, *La charola: Una historia de los servicios de inteligencia en México* (Mexico City: Grijalbo, 2001), 190. The peak year for counterinsurgent violence was 1974, with 180 disappearances. This is much less than in Chile or Argentina but probably more than in the entirety of Brazil's Dirty War. Forcefully arguing for including Mexico within the dirty-war framework is Alexander Aviña, *Specters of Revolution: Peasant Guerrillas in the Cold War Mexican Countryside* (New York: Oxford University Press, 2014). Kate Doyle, "After the Revolution: Lázaro Cárdenas and the Movimiento de Liberación Nacional," *National Security Archive Electronic Briefing Book,* 31 May 2004, http://www

.gwu.edu/~nsarchiv/NSAEBB/NSAEBB124/index.htm; Renata Keller, "A Foreign Policy for Domestic Consumption: Mexico's Lukewarm Defense of Castro, 1959–1969," *Latin American Research Review* 47, no. 2 (Summer 2012): 100–119. On the "secret deal," see William LeoGrande and Peter Kornbluh, *Back Channel to Cuba: The Hidden History of Negotiations between Washington and Havana* (Chapel Hill: University of North Carolina Press, 2014), 100. For an account of a Mexican guerrilla fighter who was denied training in Cuba, see Alberto Ulloa Bornemann, *Surviving Mexico's Dirty War: A Political Prisoner's Memoir*, trans. Arthur Schmidt and Aurora Camacho de Schmidt (Philadelphia: Temple University Press, 2007), 101–117.

4. Emilio Portes Gil, "El cuarto informe presidencial," *El Universal*, 14 September 1962; Lázaro Cárdenas, "El Movimiento de Liberación Nacional no depende de ninguna potencia," *El Día*, 22 September 1962.

5. On continuity between the MLN and the PRD, see Cuauhtémoc Cárdenas Solórzano, *Sobre mis pasos* (Mexico City: Aguilar, 2010); and Carlos B. Gil, ed., *Hope and Frustration: Interviews with Leaders of Mexico's Political Opposition* (Wilmington, Del.: SR Books, 1992), 63, 150, 254.

6. Lázaro Cárdenas, *Apuntes, 1957–1966* (Mexico City: Universidad Nacional Autónoma de México, 1973), 212.

7. "Por un millón de firmas," *Paz* 1, no. 9 (December 1951): 57; Heriberto Saucedo (Secretario de Finanzas del PCM), "Apliquemos nuestra política justa de finanzas," 27–30 May 1950, PCM archive, box 22, folder 3, Centro de Estudios del Movimiento Obrero y Socialista (CEMOS), Mexico City; "Se informa el resultado de las investigaciones practicidades por este dependencia en relación con el Comité Mexicano por la Paz," 8 September 1950, Dirección Federal de Seguridad (DFS), Diego Rivera Barrientos file—versión pública, document 11–71–50, Archivo General de la Nación (AGN), Mexico City.

8. Letter from Juan Pablo Sainz Aguilar, 1951 or 1952, PCM archive, box 24, folder 1, CEMOS. The party confronted the problem of control versus assembling a broad front in other organizations as well, such as the Unión Democrática de Mujeres Mexicanas, the national women's affiliate. Dionisio Encina and J. Encarnación Valdés, "Instructivo para los Comités Estatales y Comisión Organizadoras para Ayudar a Organizar la U.D.M.M.," 27 February 1951, PCM archive, box 23, folder 1, CEMOS.

9. *The Iron Heel* detail comes from Carlos Zapata Vela, *Conversaciones con Heriberto Jara* (Mexico City: Costa-Amic Editores, 1992), 20. On the Constitutional Assembly, see Jorge Sayeg Helú, *El constitucionalismo social mexicano: La integración constitucional de México* (Mexico City: Cultura y Ciencia Política, 1972), 95–96, 244–248, 314–315. On Jara's political career, see John Lear, *Workers, Neighbors, and Citizens: The Revolution in Mexico City* (Lincoln: University of Nebraska Press, 2001), 172, 220–221, 250; Heather Fowler-Salamini, *Agrarian Radicalism in Veracruz, 1920–38* (Lincoln: University of Nebraska Press, 1978), 55–57; and Rodolfo Lara Ponte and Heriberto Jara Corona, *Heriberto Jara: Vigencia de un ideal* (Mexico City: Fondo de Cultura Económica, 2000), 39–40.

10. "Campeones de la lucha por la paz: El General Heriberto Jara, Premio Stalin de la Paz," *Paz* 1, no. 2 (May 1951): 13; Zapata Vela, *Conversaciones con Heriberto Jara,* 143. The PRI awarded Jara the Belisario Domínguez Prize in 1959. Lara Ponte and Jara Corona, *Heriberto Jara,* 53.

11. Heriberto Jara, "Europa lucha por la paz," published by Comité Mexicano por la Paz, 1950, gallery 3—Miguel Alemán Valdés Records, box 1152, folder 050/22301, AGN, 14, 38, 46–47; Zapata Vela, *Conversaciones con Heriberto Jara,* 123–124.

12. The WPC experienced structural changes that reflected its new posture. Its headquarters were moved from Prague to Vienna, and it increased efforts to combine forces with Christian peace groups. Austria, worried about WPC activities on its soil, requested that it leave in 1957; it dissolved and re-formed at the same address as the International Institute for Peace. Clive Rose, *The Soviet Propaganda Network: A Directory of Organisations Serving Soviet Foreign Policy* (London: Pinter, 1988), 108–110. In 1968 WPC headquarters were reestablished in Finland. On Khrushchev, see Andrew Brown, *J. D. Bernal: The Sage of Science* (Oxford: Oxford University Press, 2005), 415. On the Soviet Union and the Third World, see Michael E. Latham, "The Cold War in the Third World, 1963–1975," in *The Cambridge History of the Cold War,* ed. Melvyn P. Leffler and Odd Arne Westad, vol. 2 (Cambridge: Cambridge University Press, 2010), 264; and Roy Allison, *The Soviet Union and the Strategy of Non-alignment in the Third World* (Cambridge: Cambridge University Press, 1988). On Bernal, see Brenda Swann and Francis Aprahamian, *J. D. Bernal: A Life in Science and Politics* (London: Verso, 1999), ix–xx, 212–234.

13. Lázaro Cárdenas, *Apuntes, 1941–1956* (Mexico City: Universidad Nacional Autónoma de México, 1973), 182, 220, 223, 235.

14. Raquel Tibol, *Frida Kahlo: An Open Life* (Albuquerque: University of New Mexico Press, 1993), 79; Frida Kahlo, Carlos Fuentes, and Sarah M. Lowe, *The Diary of Frida Kahlo: An Intimate Self-Portrait* (New York: H. N. Abrams, 1995), 257; Isolda Pinedo Kahlo, *Intimate Frida* (Bogotá, Colombia: Cangrejo, 2006), 192. Elena Vázquez Gómez has been identified as code names "Elena" and "Seda" in the Venona decrypts. Mexico City to Moscow, 15 and 21 January 1944, http://www.nsa.gov/public_info/_files/venona/1944/15jan_kgb_personality_elena.pdf and http://www.nsa.gov/public_info/_files/venona/1944/21jan_info_about_kgb.pdf.

15. Proenza to Jara, 13 February 1952, Heriberto Jara Papers, folder 1433, box 36, Archivo Histórico de la Universidad Nacional Autónoma de México (AHUNAM), Mexico City. On the poetry and politics of Huerta, see Frank Dauster, *The Double Strand: Five Contemporary Mexican Poets* (Lexington: University Press of Kentucky, 1987), 59–84. Jara to Palamede Borsari (Budapest), 21 June 1953, Heriberto Jara Papers, folder 1434, box 36, AHUNAM.

16. Barry Carr, *Marxism and Communism in Twentieth-Century Mexico* (Lincoln: University of Nebraska Press, 1992), 189; Aaron W. Navarro, *Political Intelligence and the Creation of Modern Mexico, 1938–1954* (University Park: Pennsylvania State University Press, 2010); Aguayo, *Charola.*

17. "Se informa en relación con los estudiantes universitarios," 22 June 1954, document 63–1–54, Cuauhtémoc Cárdenas Solorzano file—versión pública, gallery 1, AGN; Cárdenas Solórzano, *Sobre mis pasos*, 23–32; Cárdenas, *Apuntes, 1941–1956*, 573. "La independencia de los pueblos de la América Latina y el mantenimiento de la paz," 20 May 1955, PCM archive, box 27, folder 5, CEMOS. On the general subject of student politics in Mexico's 1950s and 1960s, see Jaime Pensado, *Rebel Mexico: Student Unrest and Authoritarian Political Culture during the Long Sixties* (Stanford, Calif.: Stanford University Press, 2013).

18. Selden Rodman, *Mexican Journal* (New York: Devin-Adair Co., 1958), 259. Tannenbaum to Lázaro Cárdenas, 24 February 1956, Frank Tannenbaum Papers, folder "Cárdenas," box 1, Columbia University Rare Books and Manuscripts Library, New York. I thank Carlos Bravo Regidor for making his copies of these materials available to me.

19. Lázaro Cárdenas to Tannenbaum, 11 March 1956, Frank Tannenbaum Papers, folder "Cárdenas," box 1, Columbia University; "Discurso de entrega por el Prof. Grigori Alexandrov, a nombre del 'Comité Adjudicador de los Premios Internacionales Stalin,'" Heribero Jara Papers, box 36, folder 1428, AHUNAM; Eric Zolov, "Between Bohemianism and a Revolutionary Rebirth: Che Guevara in Mexico," in *Che's Travels: The Making of a Revolutionary in 1950s Latin America*, ed. Paulo Drinot (Durham, N.C.: Duke University Press, 2010), 270–271. "Discurso del General Lázaro Cárdenas," Heriberto Jara Papers, folder 1428, box 36, AHUNAM.

20. Heriberto Jara to Lázaro Cárdenas, May 1957, Lázaro Cárdenas del Río (LCR) Papers, microfilm roll 23, AGN; Bernal to Cárdenas, 31 July 1959, Cárdenas to Bernal, 7 October 1959, LCR Papers, section "Consejo Mundial de la Paz—I, 1949–1960," roll 23, AGN.

21. Valentín Campa, *Mi testimonio: Memorias de un comunista mexicano*, 2nd ed. (Mexico City: Ediciones de Cultura Popular, 1985), 239–268; Carr, *Marxism and Communism in Twentieth-Century Mexico*, 16–19. "Se informa en relación con el Partido Popular," 30 April 1959, Vicente Lombardo Toledano—versión pública, volume 5, gallery 1, AGN; "Poder ejecutivo: secretaria de gobernación," *Diario Oficial* 129, no. 12 (14 November 1941), 1–2.

22. "Se informa en relación con las actividades del Lic. Narciso Bassols e Ing. Jorge L. Tamayo," 22 July 1959; and "Se informa en relación con el Círculo de Estudios Mexicanos," 20 August 1959, VLT—versión pública, volume 5, gallery 1, AGN; Jorge L. Tamayo and Narciso Bassols to Heriberto Jara, 26 June 1959, Heriberto Jara Papers, box 38, folder 1443, AHUNAM; Jorge L. Tamayo to Jara, 5 May 1960, Heriberto Jara Papers, box 38, folder 1444, AHUNAM.

23. Remarkably, Cárdenas's only prior trip outside Mexico was a day visit to Los Angeles in 1957. The only other time he would leave his country would be to travel to Cuba later in 1959. Cárdenas Solórzano, *Sobre mis pasos*, 63. The diary entry mentioning China is in Cárdenas, *Apuntes, 1941–1956*, 88. The one defining the Mexican Revolution is from 1961 and is in Cárdenas, *Apuntes, 1957–1966*, 210. The comparative mildness of Mexico's revolutionary

experience is put in stark relief by Friedrich Katz, "Violence and Terror in the Mexican and Russian Revolutions," in *A Century of Revolution: Insurgent and Counterinsurgent Violence during Latin America's Long Cold War,* ed. Greg Grandin and Gilbert M. Joseph (Durham, N.C.: Duke University Press, 2010), 45–61. On the hopes of Cárdenas for Cuba, see Cárdenas, *Apuntes, 1941–1956,* 91.

24. The meeting took place on 2 August 1956. Cárdenas, *Apuntes, 1941–1956,* 646–647.

25. "Se informa en relación con las actividades del Ing. Jorge L. Tamayo," 11 June 1960, Lázaro Cárdenas del Río—versión pública, binder 2, gallery 1, AGN.

26. Víctor Flores Olea, "Cuba, una democracia concreta," *Política* 1, no. 2 (15 May 1960): 10–11; Castro is quoted in Carlos Fuentes, "Primero de mayo en la Habana," *Política* 1, no. 2 (15 May 1960): 46–47.

27. "El preso 46788/60," *Política* 1, no. 9 (1 September 1960): 5–20; "La sentencia de David Álfaro Siqueiros y Filomeno Mata, se finca en informes policiacos, en opiniones y noticias periodistas, relacionado esto con las finalidades y principales del Partido Comunista Mexicano," Heriberto Jara Papers, box 47, folder 1530, AHUNAM; Julio Scherer García, *La piel y la entraña (Siqueiros)* (Mexico City: Era, 1965), 12.

28. The foreign delegates were Domingo Vellasco of Brazil, Tomás Alberto Casella of Argentina, and Olga Poblete of Chile, all members of their respective national peace organizations. Lázaro Cárdenas, Domingo Vellasco, and Alberto T. Casella, "Convocatoria," 17 January 1961, PCM archive, box 40, folder 20, CEMOS.

29. Memo, 5 March 1961, DFS archive, file 11–6–1961, gallery 1, AGN.

30. "Conferencia Latinoamericana por la Soberanía Nacional, la Emancipación Económica y la Paz: Documentos," 1961, 3–4, PCM archive, box 40, folder 86, CEMOS.

31. Carlos Fuentes, "Siete días con Lázaro Cárdenas," *Política* 1, no. 23 (1 April 1961): 16, 22.

32. The executive and coordinating committee consisted of Alonso Aguilar Monteverde, Narciso Bassols Batalla, Enrique Cabrera, Cuauhtémoc Cárdenas, Enrique González Pedrero, Braulio Maldonado, and Manuel Terrazas. "Movimiento de Liberación Nacional, bases generales de organización aprobadas por unanimidad en la asamblea nacional celebrada en la ciudad de México, D.F., los días 4 y 5 de agosto de 1961," Heriberto Jara Papers, box 47, folder 1523, AHUNAM; Memo, 30 October 1961, DFS archive, file 11–6–61, gallery 1, AGN; "Llamamiento al pueblo mexicano del Movimiento de Liberación Nacional," *Siempre!,* no. 429 (13 September 1961): 132–133.

33. Cárdenas, *Apuntes, 1957–1966,* 213–216; Doyle, "After the Revolution"; Olga Pellicer de Brody, *México y la revolución cubana* (Mexico City: El Colegio de México, 1972), 91. Cárdenas rejected taking a salary for the Balsas River position. Cárdenas, *Apuntes, 1957–1966,* 270.

34. Rodrigo García Treviño, "Cárdenas y la conferencia comunista," *Examen,* no. 20 (April 1961): 12; Cárdenas, *Apuntes, 1957–1966,* 192.

35. "Se informa en relación con el Partido Popular Socialista," 20 December 1960, VLT—versión pública, volume 5, gallery 1, AGN; "Lista de personas, agrupaciones, comités de auspicio, municipios, etc. que cooperaron para los trabajos de la Conferencia Latinoamericana por la Soberanía Nacional, la Emancipación Económica, y la Paz," April 1961, Clementina Batalla de Bassols Papers, box 3, folder 10, gallery 7, AGN; Jorge L. Tamayo to Victor Chkhikvadze, 20 January 1961, LCR Papers, section "Consejo Mundial de la Paz—II: Enero a Diciembre de 1961," roll 23, AGN; Memorandum, 14 March 1961, document 11–6–61, Cuauhtémoc Cárdenas Solorzano file—versión pública, gallery 1, AGN. The Argentine journalist was Sara Goldenberg, editor of the Argentine Peace Council's magazine, *Queremos Vivir;* Argentine police had raided her apartment. "Informe sobre Sara Goldenberg," 27 February 1961, file 11–6–61, gallery 1, AGN.
36. "Movimiento de Liberación Nacional," 25 October 1961, DFS archive, Cuauhtémoc Cárdenas—versión pública, volume 1, AGN; Keller, "Foreign Policy for Domestic Consumption," 114–115.
37. On the nature of the Mexican press in that era, see Chappell Lawson, *Building the Fourth Estate: Democratization and the Rise of a Free Press in Mexico* (Berkeley: University of California Press, 2002); Richard Ray Cole, *The Mass Media of Mexico: Ownership and Control* (Ann Arbor, Mich.: Xerox University Microfilms, 1972); and Rafael Rodríguez Castañeda, *Prensa vendida: Los periodistas y los presidentes; 40 años de relaciones* (Mexico City: Grijalbo, 1993). *Excélsior* and *Novedades* had declined to run paid advertisements for the event in January. Daniel Ramos Nava, "Nada perjudica tanto a la libertad de prensa como el uso irresponsable: Coinciden el juicio de López Mateos y el de la SIP," *Novedades,* 12 March 1961, 1; Cárdenas, *Apuntes, 1957–1966,* 186; Cárdenas Solórzano, *Sobre mis pasos,* 50–51.
38. Rodríguez Castañeda, *Prensa vendida,* 80–83; Lawson, *Building the Fourth Estate,* 90.
39. On Pagés Llergo, see María Emilia Paz Salinas, *Strategy, Security, and Spies: Mexico and the U.S. as Allies in World War II* (University Park: Pennsylvania State University Press, 1997), 29–30; John Mraz, "Today, Tomorrow, and Always: The Golden Age of Illustrated Magazines in Mexico, 1937–1960," in *Fragments of a Golden Age: The Politics of Culture in Mexico since 1940,* ed. Gil Joseph, Anne Rubenstein, and Eric Zolov (Durham, N.C.: Duke University Press, 2001), 121, 156. At *Novedades* the supplement had been known as *México en la Cultura;* the director of *Novedades* was a de facto member of the anti-MLN group discussed later in this chapter, the Frente Cívico Mexicano de Afirmación Revolucionaria.
40. *Problemas Agrícolas e Industriales de México* began publication in the summer of 1946 as *Problemas Económico-Agrícolas de México* and changed its name in 1949. It ceased publication in 1959. Many of its contributors, include Marcué Pardiñas, Alonso Aguilar, Elí de Gortari, Vicente Lombardo Toledano, Manuel Mesa, Enrique Ramírez y Ramírez, and Carlos Sánchez Cárdenas, went on to active militancy in the MLN. Juan Rafael Reynaga

Mejía, *La revolución cubana en México a través de la revista* Política: *Construcción imaginaria de un discurso para América Latina* (Toluca, Mexico; Universidad Autónoma del Estado de México, 2007), 33–34.

41. "Actividades del Ing. Manuel Marcué Pardiñas," 12 October 1961, Cuauhtémoc Cárdenas—versión pública, gallery 1, AGN. The document that claims Soviet and Cuban support dates from 1965, and the timing of this possible dependence is not well understood. By 1965 and 1966 the Mexican government's monitoring of Manuel Marcué Pardiñas and his personal and financial problems allowed it to exert substantial power over *Política,* which led to its eventual dissolution at the end of 1967. Jacinto Rodríguez Munguía, *La otra guerra secreta: Los archivos prohibidos de la prensa y el poder* (Mexico City: Random House Mondadori, 2007), 197–207.

42. Narciso Bassols and Jesús Silva Herzog were instrumental in the creation of PIPSA. Jesús Silva Herzog, *Una vida en la vida de México* (Mexico City: Siglo Veintiuno Editores, 1972), 157–158. "A nuestros lectores," *Política* 1, no. 11 (1 October 1960): unnumbered page facing page 1; "Intervención contra 'Política,'" *Política* 1, no. 12 (15 October 1960): unnumbered page facing page 1; "La maniobra continúa," *Política* 1, no. 13 (1 November 1960): unnumbered page facing page 1.

43. Memo, 23 August 1961, DFS archive, file 48–59–61, gallery 1, AGN; Rodrigo García Treviño and Benjamín Tobón to Serafino Romualdi, 11 July 1949, International Affairs Department, box 22, folder 21, George Meany Memorial Archives (GMMA), Silver Spring, Md.; "Revolucionarios amillonados," *Política* 2, no. 33 (1 September 1961): 5. On the functions of the FCMAR, see Robert J. Alexander interview with Horacio Porres, president of section six of the FCMAR, 24 August 1963, Robert J. Alexander Interview Collection, reel 10, frame 370, Archibald S. Alexander Library, Rutgers University, New Brunswick, N.J.; Doyle, "After the Revolution"; and José Agustín, *Tragicomedia mexicana,* vol. 1 (Mexico City: Planeta, 1991), 195. Cárdenas, *Apuntes, 1957–1966,* 241.

44. Carr, *Marxism and Communism in Twentieth-Century Mexico,* 227–228; Doyle, "After the Revolution."

45. Heriberto Jara to Hugo Cuesta Jara, 24 October 1961, Heriberto Jara Papers, box 47, folder 1522, AHUNAM; "Delegación Mexicana a la Conferencia de los Pueblos Latinoamericanos en La Habana, Cuba," 23 January 1962, file 11–6–62, gallery 1, AGN; Lázaro Cárdenas to Vicente Lombardo Toledano, 9 July 1962, Lázaro Cárdenas Papers, section "Comité Mexicano por la paz, 1955–1963," roll 23, AGN. Carlos Maciel, *El Movimiento de Liberación Nacional: Vicisitudes y aspiraciones* (Mexico City: Universidad Autónoma de Sinaloa, 1990), 143. "Declaraciones del Movimiento de Liberación Nacional sobre las posiciones del Partido Popular Socialista," 18 June 1962, Heriberto Jara Papers, box 47, folder 1523, AHUNAM.

46. Circular, 9 May 1963, Heriberto Jara Papers, box 47, folder 1523, AHUNAM; "El PCM ha hecho y seguirá haciendo sus mejores esfuerzos para vigorizar el MLN," n.d. [October 1963], PCM archive, box 48, folder 3, CEMOS; "El MLN reafirma su posición unitaria y denuncia la conducta provocadora de

líderes del PC y del FEP," n.d. [October 1963], *El Día*, in PCM archive, box 49, folder 56, CEMOS. Cárdenas Solórzano, *Sobre mis pasos*, 61–63; Arnoldo Martínez Verdugo, *Historia del comunismo en México* (Mexico City: Grijalbo, 1985), 294–295. Memo, 14 August 1964, DFS archive, Cuauhtémoc Cárdenas Solórzano—versión pública, volume 3, AGN. The best guide to the MLN's internal fissures, precisely because it is a partisan text, is Maciel, *Movimiento de Liberación Nacional.*

47. Jon Lee Anderson, *Che Guevara: A Revolutionary Life* (New York: Grove Press, 1997), 457. Lázaro Cárdenas to Olga Poblete, 6 March 1962, LCR Papers, section "Conferencia Latinoamericana y Tricontinental—I," roll 24, AGN; Lázaro Cárdenas to Fidel Castro, 25 September 1962, LCR Papers, section "Cuba—III," roll 25; and Olga Poblete to Lázaro Cárdenas, 26 November 1962, and J. D. Bernal to Lázaro Cárdenas, 14 December 1962, LCR Papers, section "Consejo Mundial de la Paz—III," roll 23, AGN; "Notas informativas sobre el Congreso Mundial por el Desarme General y la Paz," 1 August 1962, LCR Papers, section "Conferencia Latinoamericana y Tricontinental—II," roll 25, AGN; "The Hemisphere: Where Did Everybody Go?," *Time*, 5 April 1963, 30.

48. "Comité del pueblo chino por la defensa de la paz mundial," 21 February 1962, LCR Papers, section "China," roll 26, AGN; Lázaro Cárdenas to Kuo Mo-jo, 5 September 1963, and "Puntos principles enunciados en el artículo titulado 'El origen y el desarrollo de las diferencias entre la dirección del P.C. de la URSS y nosotros,'" 6 September 1963, LCR Papers, section "China," roll 26, AGN.

49. Guevara had been considered pro-China since 1963, but in fact, he was not satisfied with the behavior of either the USSR or China. Jorge G. Castañeda, *Compañero: The Life and Death of Che Guevara* (New York: Vintage Books, 1998), 285–292; U.S. Senate, Subcommittee to Investigate the Administration of the Internal Security Act and Other Internal Security Laws of the Committee on the Judiciary, *The Tricontinental Conference of African, Asian, and Latin American Peoples* (Washington, D.C.: USGPO, 1966), 96; Anderson, *Che Guevara,* 682–686; Tad Szulc, *Fidel: A Critical Portrait* (New York: Avon, 1986), 672–673; Jorge I. Domínguez, *To Make a World Safe for Revolution: Cuba's Foreign Policy* (Cambridge, Mass.: Harvard University Press, 1989), 69–72.

50. Kate Doyle, "El pacto secreto: México-EU-Cuba, 1964," *Proceso*, no. 1374 (2 March 2003): 37–43; Jefferson Morley, *Our Man in Mexico: Winston Scott and the Hidden History of the CIA* (Lawrence: University Press of Kansas, 2008).

6. Modernizing Cultural Freedom

1. This trend toward "experts" was in some ways global, although it was more pronounced in certain places than in others. On the shift in Argentina, see Federico Neiburg and Mariano Ben Plotkin, *Intelectuales y expertos: La constitución del conocimiento social en la Argentina* (Buenos Aires: Paidós, 2004). Carlos Carranza to Juan Antonio Solari, 13 June 1961, Juan Antonio

Solari Papers, binder 3, Centro de Documentación e Investigación de la Cultura de Izquierdas en Argentina, Buenos Aires, Argentina; Luis Mercier Vega to Millares Reyes, 31 March 1963, International Association for Cultural Freedom Papers (IACF), series VI, box 2, folder 13, Joseph L. Regenstein Library, University of Chicago Special Collections Research Center (UC/SCRC), Chicago.

2. On the contributions of politicians from Latin America to the construction of the Alliance for Progress, see Christopher Darnton, "Asymmetry and Agenda-Setting in U.S.–Latin American Relations: Rethinking the Origins of the Alliance for Progress," *Journal of Cold War Studies* 14, no. 4 (Fall 2012): 57–58. On the way in which it functioned in practice, see Jeffrey F. Taffet, *Foreign Aid as Foreign Policy: The Alliance for Progress in Latin America* (New York: Routledge, 2007).

3. W. W. Rostow, *The Stages of Economic Growth: A Non-Communist Manifesto* (Cambridge: Cambridge University Press, 1960); Arthur Meier Schlesinger, *A Thousand Days: John F. Kennedy in the White House* (Boston: Houghton Mifflin, 1965), 589.

4. Fernández Retamar is quoted in Irwin Silber, ed., *Voices of National Liberation: The Revolutionary Ideology of the "Third World" Expressed by Intellectuals and Artists at the Cultural Congress of Havana, January 1968* (Brooklyn, N.Y.: Central Book Company, 1970), 179; Fernando Henrique Cardoso and Enzo Faletto, *Dependency and Development in Latin America* (Berkeley: University of California Press, 1979), xxiv.

5. Irving Louis Horowitz, *The Rise and Fall of Project Camelot: Studies in the Relationship between Social Science and Practical Politics* (Cambridge, Mass.: M.I.T. Press, 1967), 7–8.

6. Frances Stonor Saunders, *The Cultural Cold War: The CIA and the World of Arts and Letters* (New York: New Press, 2000), 234–251.

7. Josep Alemany, "Entrevista con Louis Mercier Vega," *Interrogations,* no. 13 (January 1978): 23–39; "Luis Mercier Vega—Curriculum Vitae," IACF, series VI, box 23, folder 5, UC/SCRC; Botsford to Colleagues [Hunt and Josselson], 12 March 1963, Keith Botsford Papers, box "Botsford Letters A–G," folder "Botsford to CCF, 1963," Beinecke Rare Book and Manuscripts Library, Yale University, New Haven, Conn.; "Datos acerca del Centro de Documentación Social y Político del Centro Argentino del I.L.A.R.I.," n.d., IACF, series VI, box 15, folder 5, UC/SCRC; when Mercier Vega took over, Gorkin remained editor of *Cuadernos.* Gorkin to Pedro Vicente Aja, 16 October 1961, IACF, series II, box 210, folder 8, UC/SCRC.

8. Mercier to Guillermo de Torre, 13 February 1964, IACF, series VI, box 3, folder 11, UC/SCRC; Luis Mercier Vega, "Rapport sur Le Congrès pour la Liberté de la Culture en Amérique Latine," 2 June 1953, IACF, series II, box 204, folder 7, UC/SCRC.

9. "Case Study: Uruguayan National Representative," IACF, series VI, box 8, folder 6, UC/SCRC; Aldo E. Solari, *El tercerismo en el Uruguay* (Montevideo: Editorial Alfa, 1965). Milla eventually left his son, Leonardo, in charge of Alfa and moved to Venezuela, where he founded Monte Ávila Editores, which

later distributed one of Mercier Vega's monographs. On Milla and the publishing situation in Uruguay as a precursor to *Mundo Nuevo,* see Karina Jannello, "El *boom* Latinoamericano y la Guerra Fría cultural: Nuevas aportaciones a la gestación de la revista *Mundo Nuevo,*" *Ipotesi* 47, no. 2 (July–December 2013): 115–133.

10. Mercier to Arciniegas, 29 May 1963, IACF, series VI, box 3, folder 3, UC/SCRC. *Sur's* finances had been severely strained during the presidency of Juan Domingo Perón, and the magazine's relationship with the CCF helped stabilize its precarious financial situation; the CCF paid for *Sur* to publish a series of monographs in a collection under the Tercer Mundo label. Baráibar to Hunt, 10 Jan 1964, IACF, series VI, box 3, folder 14, UC/SCRC.

11. Hunt to Botsford, 10 October 1961, IACF, series II, box 46, folder 3, UC/SCRC.

12. "Badge of honor": e-mail from Keith Botsford to the author, 30 September 2006. Botsford did work in U.S. Army Counterintelligence in Europe during 1946 and 1947. Botsford Curriculum Vitae, attached to Botsford to Hunt, 13 August 1961, IACF, series II, box 46, folder 3, box 46, UC/SCRC. Saul Bellow, *Humboldt's Gift* (New York: Viking, 1973), 75. Bellow and Botsford worked on the short-lived magazine *The Noble Savage* together, which was published between 1960 and 1962; Botsford to Congress, n.d. [mid-1962], Keith Botsford Papers, box "Botsford Letters A–G," folder "Congress," Yale.

13. Stefan Baciu, *Juan Bosch, un hombre solo* (Madrid: Benzal, 1967), 11–16; Peter Burke and Maria Lúcia G. Pallares-Burke, *Gilberto Freyre: Social Theory in the Tropics,* 2nd ed. (New York: Peter Lang, 2008), 115–123.

14. John Crowe Ransom, *The New Criticism* (Norfolk, Conn.: New Directions, 1941); Afrânio Coutinho, *Da crítica e da nova crítica* (Rio de Janeiro: Civiliação Brasileira, 1975); Saunders, *Cultural Cold War,* 240–244.

15. Nabokov to Baciu, 2 April 1962, IACF, series VI, box 2, folder 6, UC/SCRC; Baciu to Mercier, 14 August 1962, IACF, series VI, box 2, folder 5, box 2, UC/SCRC.

16. Riordan Roett argues that disagreements stemming from different visions for SUDENE (Furtado in social and economic terms, the U.S. Agency for International Development in national security terms) contributed to the agency's failure. Riordan Roett, *The Politics of Foreign Aid in the Brazilian Northeast* (Nashville: Vanderbilt University Press, 1972), 92.

17. Kristine Vanden Berghe, *Intelectuales y anticomunismo: La revista* Cadernos Brasileiros *(1959–1970)* (Leuven, Belgium: Leuven University Press, 1997), 59. Botsford's comments on Lowell are quoted in Ian Hamilton, *Robert Lowell: A Biography* (New York: Random House, 1982), 300–302. Botsford to Hunt and Josselson, 10 September 1962, Keith Botsford Papers, box "Botsford Letters A–G," folder "Congress," Yale.

18. Thomas E. Skidmore, *Politics in Brazil, 1930–1964: An Experiment in Democracy* (New York: Oxford University Press, 1967), 218, 234–239. The gallery was known as the Goeldi Gallery, named after Oswaldo Goeldi, a Brazilian artist who had died in 1961. Coutinho to Hunt, 3 April 1964, IACF, series II, box 47, folder 4, UC/SCRC.

19. The United States had planned to move an aircraft carrier and several destroyers into place to support the military in case of civil war, but this plan was never carried out. How consequential U.S. actions were for developments in Brazil remains a subject of debate. The anti-Goulart views of the United States were certainly known; it was also certainly much less involved in creating the conditions for the coup than it had been in Guatemala in 1954, for example. James Naylor Green, *We Cannot Remain Silent: Opposition to the Brazilian Military Dictatorship in the United States* (Durham, N.C.: Duke University Press, 2010), 18–48; U.S. Department of State, *Foreign Relations of the United States, 1964–1968: South and Central America; Mexico,* ed. David C. Geyer, David H. Herschler, and Edward C. Keefer (Washington, D.C.: USGPO, 2004), 398–544; Phyllis R. Parker, *Brazil and the Quiet Intervention, 1964* (Austin: University of Texas Press, 1979); Jan Knippers Black, *United States Penetration of Brazil* (Philadelphia: University of Pennsylvania Press, 1977); Ruth Leacock, *Requiem for Revolution: The United States and Brazil, 1961–1969* (Kent, Ohio: Kent State University Press, 1990).

20. John Hunt to Afrânio Coutinho, 21 April 1964, IACF, series II, box 47, folder 4, UC/SCRC. Hunt's was also the position of the U.S. ambassador to Brazil, Lincoln Gordon, who had approved and arranged for covert support to antigovernment groups but warned Castelo Branco of the negative effect on international opinion of withdrawing the rights of Furtado. United States Department of State, *Foreign Relations of the United States,* 464.

21. Coutinho to Hunt, 3 April 1964, and Coutinho to Hunt, 30 April 1964, IACF, series II, box 47, folder 4, UC/SCRC.

22. To write the report, the CCF sent Peruvian mining engineer Mario Samamé Boggio, a democracy and education activist, to conduct the investigation. The science arm of the CCF was run by Edward Shils, who edited the magazine *Minerva* for the CCF. The funding for Samamé Boggio's trip came from the *Minerva* account. Robert J. Oppenheimer and Edward Shils to Samamé Boggio, 27 August 1964, Nicholas Nabokov Papers, box 5, folder 1, Harry Ransom Center, University of Texas Libraries, Austin; Raúl-Estuardo Cornejo, *Mario Samamé Boggio* (Lima: Consejo Nacional de Ciencia y Tecnología, 1990); Mario Samamé Boggio, *La revolución por la educación* (Lima: Editorial Gráfica Labor, 1969). Vicente Barreto to Hunt, 11 March 1965, IACF, series II, folder 5, box 47, UC/SCRC. By 1966 *Cadernos Brasileiros* was clearly in the opposition camp. Vanden Berghe, *Intelectuales y anticomunismo,* 200, 46. Compare the ambivalent "Direto à heresia," *Cadernos Brasileiros* 6, no. 3 (May–June 1964): 4, with the increasingly critical Wilson Figueiredo, "Doze mêses depois," *Cadernos Brasileiros* 7, no. 28 (March–April 1965): 5–13, and the clearly oppositional Vicente Barreto, "O perfil do reacionarismo," *Cadernos Brasileiros* 8, no. 37 (September–October 1966): 3–6.

23. Keith Botsford, "Report on Mexico," September 1964, p. 25, IACF, series VI, box 4, folder 1, UC/SCRC; Mercier to Hunt, 30 November 1961, IACF, series VI, box 1, folder 14, UC/SCRC. *Examen*'s issue 28, from February 1962, was the first number to bear no imprint of the CCF; no. 30, from April 1962, was the final issue. On García Treviño, see Robert J. Alexander in

conversation with Pedro Pagès and Sra. de Pagès, August 20, 1963, Robert J. Alexander Interview Collection, reel 10, frames 38, 256, Archibald S. Alexander Library, Rutgers University, New Brunswick, N.J.

24. Mercier to García Treviño, 2 November 1961, IACF, series VI, box 1, folder 14, UC/SCRC.

25. Botsford to Hunt and Josselson, IACF, series II, box 46, folder 6, UC/SCRC; Botsford, "Report on Mexico," September 1964, p. 25, IACF, series VI, box 4, folder 1, UC/SCRC.

26. Botsford had to push a bit to ensure that Pablo Neruda's (nonpolitical) poetry would be included, but he said that it would be absurd to do an anthology of Latin American poetry without the continent's best poet. Neruda, like other poets who were to be included, was selecting fifty of his poems for inclusion, from which the editorial board could choose to include some or none. Botsford to Hunt, n.d. [likely 1963], Keith Botsford Papers, box "Botsford Letters H–R," folder "John Hunt," Yale. The social science review was to have been edited by the Ph.D. student John Womack Jr., then in Mexico researching his dissertation on Emiliano Zapata. Before he joined the CIA, Hunt had been a teacher at a secondary school in Missouri, and Womack had been one of his students. In addition to Rulfo and Fuentes, other writers of note who received grants from the CME included Juan José Arreola, Alí Chumacero, Rosario Castellanos, Carlos Monsiváis, José Agustín, Gustavo Sainz, Vicente Leñero, Luisa Josefina Hernández, Emilio Carbaillido, Inés Arredondo, Ricardo Garibay, Jorge Ibargüengoitia, Marco Antonio Montes de Oca, and Elena Poniatowska. Martha Domínguez Cuevas, *Los becarios del Centro Mexicano de Escritores (1952–1997)* (Mexico City: Editorial Aldus, 1999). Margaret Shedd, "I Hate You, Cruz Rivera," *Encounter* 19, no. 4 (October 1962): 11–15; Margaret Shedd, "The Everlasting Witness," *Encounter* 21, no. 2 (August 1963): 48–53; Juan Rulfo, "They Gave Us the Land," trans. Jean Franco, *Encounter* 25, no. 3 (September 1965): 11–15.

27. Hunt to Botsford, 27 June 1962, Keith Botsford Papers, box "Letters to Botsford D–I," folder "Hunt, John," Yale; Shedd to Botsford, 15 December 1963, IACF, series II, box 46, folder 6, UC/SCRC. In a forthcoming work I will describe the organizational history of the CME and its funding sources in detail.

28. "Talón de Aquiles," *Revista Mexicana de Literatura*, no. 1 (Septenber–October 1955): 90–95; "Talón de Aquiles," *Revista Mexicana de Literatura*, no. 2 (November–December 1955): 192–193; M.A.R., "La región más transparente," *Examen*, no. 1 (July–August 1958): 92–101; Botsford to Hunt, 25 May 1964, Keith Botsford Papers, box "Botsford Letters H–R," folder "John Hunt," Yale; Botsford to Hunt, 25 May 1964, IACF, series II, box 46, folder 7, UC/SCRC. Botsford to Fuentes, 19 October 1964, Carlos Fuentes Papers, box 89, folder 29, Firestone Library, Princeton University, Princeton, N.J.

29. Jorge Ibargüengoitia, "Os relâmpagos de agôsto," *Cadernos Brasileiros* 5, no. 6 (November–December 1963): 45–48; Jorge Ibargüengoitia, "En primera persona: Hijo de Bloomsbury," *El Porvenir,* 28 November 1983.

30. Jorge Ibargüengoitia, *Los relámpagos de agosto: La ley de Herodes* (Mexico City: Promexa Editores, 1979), 235.
31. Keith Botsford, "Yanqui Gringo," *Encounter* 25, no. 3 (September 1965): 27–28. The CCF or Farfield paid for travel to Bled for Julio Cortázar, João Guimarães Rosa, David Rousset, Heinrich Böll, P. Hartling, Stephen Spender, M. Hayward, Nicola Chiaromonte, Ignazio Silone, G. Herling, Carlos Fuentes, Emir Rodríguez Monegal, and possibly Wole Soyinka. The CCF also paid for René Tavernier, Pierre Emmanuel, Kot Jelenski, and Manès Sperber to attend. Tim Foote to Botsford, 2 July 1964, IACF, series II, box 46, folder 9, UC/SCRC.
32. Luis Mercier Vega and Keith Botsford, "Draft Memorandum on Latin American Intellectuals," 14 May 1963, IACF, series VI, box 2, folder 18, p. 24, UC/SCRC; Botsford to Hunt and Josselson, 11 February 1962, Keith Botsford Papers, box "Botsford Letters A–G," folder "Congress," Yale; Arciniegas to Botsford, 11 May 1964, Keith Botsford Papers, box "Letters to Keith Botsford A–C," folder "Arciniegas," Yale. Arciniegas argued that Alejo Carpentier, for example, was an agent of the Cuban government to such a degree that he no longer wrote literature. Arciniegas thought that the only thing to be done was to work with the "free" Cubans.
33. Horacio Daniel Rodríguez to Mercier, 20 September 1963, IACF, series VI, box 2, folder 10, UC/SCRC; Murena to Mercier, 30 May 1964, IACF, series VI, box 3, folder 11, UC/SCRC.
34. Mercier to Rodríguez Monegal, 8 January 1965, IACF, series VI, box 5, folder 17, UC/SCRC. Germán Arciniegas and Antonio Cacua Prada, *Germán Arciniegas: Cien años de vida para contar* (Santafé de Bogotá: Fundacion Universidad Central, 1999), 474. Arciniegas to Josselson, 19 August 1965, IACF, series II, box 34, folder 6, UC/SCRC.
35. The campaign has been described in Saunders, *Cultural Cold War,* 349–351. The evidence is found in letters and memos between Gorkin, Hunt, and René Tavernier from 1963 in IACF, series II, box 300, folder 9, and box 301, folder 2, UC/SCRC. The focus on Neruda during 1963 began after Ernesto Dethorey, who was the Spanish Republic's representative in Sweden and an anti-Communist, wrote to Luis Mercier Vega suggesting that the CCF take actions to counter those of Artur Lundkvist and other fellow travelers who were lobbying for him. Mercier Vega to Hunt, 22 November 1962, IACF, series II, box 227, folder 4, UC/SCRC.
36. The European popularity of Borges had already begun to expand after he shared the International Publishers' Prize in 1961 with Samuel Beckett. María Esther Vázquez, *Borges: Esplendor y derrota* (Barcelona: Tusquets Editores, 1996), 236–247; Edwin Williamson, *Borges: A Life* (New York: Viking, 2004), 345–347. Hunt to Luis Mercier Vega, 10 December 1962, IACF, series VI, box 22, folder 9, UC/SCRC. For Borges's 1963 trip, mostly to the United Kingdom, the CCF paid his plane fare and that of his mother, while the British Council bore the rest of the expenses. Scott Charles to Evelyn Best, 8 January 1963, IACF, series IV, box 5, folder 6, UC/SCRC. For his European trip of 1964, he came as the guest of the CCF. Williamson, *Borges,* 355.

37. Luis Mercier Vega to John Hunt, 19 December 1962, IACF, series VI, box 3, folder 4, UC/SCRC. Adam Feinstein, *Pablo Neruda: A Passion for Life* (New York: Bloomsbury, 2004), 333–335; Jorge Amado, *Navegação de cabotagem: Apontamentos para um livro de memórias que jamais escreverei* (Rio de Janeiro: Editora Record, 1992), 105–107; Williamson, *Borges,* 426.

38. Ana Alejandra Germani, *Gino Germani: Antifascism and Sociology* (New Brunswick, N.J.: Transaction Publishers, 2008), 27; Joseph Kahl, *Three Latin American Sociologists: Gino Germani, Pablo Gonzales Casanova, Fernando Henrique Cardoso* (New Brunswick, N.J.: Transaction Books, 1988); Alejandro Blanco, *Razón y modernidad: Gino Germani y la sociología en la Argentina* (Buenos Aires: Siglo Veintiuno Editores, 2006).

39. Nils Gilman, *Mandarins of the Future: Modernization Theory in Cold War America* (Baltimore: Johns Hopkins University Press, 2003), 3. On modernization theory's use as Cold War ideology, see Michael E. Latham, *Modernization as Ideology: American Social Science and "Nation Building" in the Kennedy Era* (Chapel Hill: University of North Carolina Press, 2000).

40. Mariano Ben Plotkin, *Mañana es San Perón: A Cultural History of Perón's Argentina,* trans. Keith Zahniser (Wilmington, Del.: SR Books, 2003), x; Joseph Kahl, "Gino Germani, 1911–1979," *Latin American Research Review* 16, no. 2 (1981): 188; Germani, *Gino Germani,* 113; Federico Neiburg, *Los intelectuales y la invención del peronismo: Estados de antropología social y cultural* (Madrid: Alianza Editorial, 1988), 119; Silvia Sigal, *Intelectuales y poder en Argentina: La década del sesenta* (Buenos Aires: Siglo Veintiuno, 2002), 84–90.

41. Rostow, *Stages of Economic Growth,* 144.

42. Seymour Martin Lipset and Aldo E. Solari, *Elites in Latin America* (New York: Oxford University Press, 1967), viii.

43. Ángel Rama, "Las Condiciones del Diálogo," *Marcha,* no. 1258 (11 June 1965): 29.

44. Aldo Solari to Director of *Marcha, Marcha,* no. 1303 (13 May 1966): 28.

45. Ángel Rama, "Los intelectuales en la época desarrollista," *Marcha,* no. 1305 (27 May 1966): 31; Rama, "Nota de Redacción," *Marcha,* no. 1303 (13 May 1966): 29; Rama, "Las fachadas culturales," *Marcha,* no. 1306 (3 June 1966): 31; Emir Rodríguez Monegal to Vicente Barreto, Emir Rodríguez Monegal (ERM) Papers, box 4, folder 6, Princeton.

46. Volker Rolf Berghahn, *America and the Intellectual Cold Wars in Europe: Shepard Stone between Philanthropy, Academy, and Diplomacy* (Princeton, N.J.: Princeton University Press, 2001), 214–249. "Patman Attacks 'Secret' C.I.A. Link," *New York Times,* 1 September 1964, 1, 19; Foster Hailey, "Kaplan Fund, Cited as C.I.A. 'Conduit,' Lists Unexplained $395,000 Grant," *New York Times,* 3 September 1964, 1, 10; Patrick Iber, "'Who Will Impose Democracy?': Sacha Volman and the Contradictions of CIA Support for the Anti-Communist Left in Latin America," *Diplomatic History* 37, no. 5 (November 2013): 995–1028. Sol Stern, "NSA and the CIA," *Ramparts* 5, no. 9 (March 1967): 30–31; "C.I.A. Issue Dropped," *New York Times,* 1 September 1964, 19; Peter Coleman, *The Liberal Conspiracy: The Congress for Cultural*

Freedom and the Struggle for the Mind of Postwar Europe (New York: Free Press, 1989), 220.

47. "Organizational Conference of the Instituto Latinoamericano de Relaciones Internacionales—Lima, Peru; 29 November–3 December 1965," IACF, series VI, box 8, folder 2, UC/SCRC; Cosío Villegas to Mercier, 18 January 1966, IACF, series VI, box 8, folder 3, UC/SCRC. Octavio Paz's note, declining the invitation, can be found in Paz to Mercier, 14 January 1966, IACF, series VI, box 8, folder 4, UC/SCRC; Mercier to Cosío Villegas, 7 November 1966, IACF, series VI, box 8, folder 3, UC/SCRC; "Functions and Programs of the Instituto Latinoamericano de Relaciones Internacionales," IACF, series VI, box 20, folder 11, UC/SCRC. On the arts scene in Argentina in the 1960s and its attempts to achieve international recognition through cultural "modernization," see John King, *El Di Tella y el desarrollo cultural argentino en la década del sesenta* (Buenos Aires: Ediciones de Arte Gaglianone, 1985), and Andrea Giunta, *Vanguardia, internacionalismo y política: Arte argentino en los años sesenta* (Buenos Aires: Paidós, 2001).

48. "Functions and Programs of the Instituto Latinoamericano de Relaciones Internacionales," IACF, series VI, box 20, folder 11, UC/SCRC.

49. José Donoso, *Historia personal del "boom"* (Santiago, Chile: Alfaguara, 1998), 122. Gabriel García Márquez, "Cien años de soledad," *Mundo Nuevo*, no. 2 (August 1966): 5–11. The chapters were passed to Rodríguez Monegal by Carlos Fuentes. Gerald Martin, *Gabriel García Márquez: A Life*, 1st U.S. ed. (New York: Alfred A. Knopf, 2009), 298. José Donoso, "El obsceno pájaro de la noche," *Mundo Nuevo*, no. 13 (July 1967): 14–22. Sarduy and Cabrera Infante's contributions were numerous. Rodríguez Monegal negotiated with publishers to support Sarduy and Cabrera Infante; his lobbying led to the publication of Cabrera Infante's *Tres tristes tigres* by Seix Barral, establishing it as one of the key experimental novels of the boom. María Eugenia Mudrovcic, Mundo Nuevo: *Cultura y guerra fría en la década del 60* (Rosario, Argentina: Beatriz Viterbo Editora, 1997), 100–102. John King, Sur: *A Study of the Argentine Literary Journal and Its Role in the Development of a Culture, 1931–1970* (Cambridge: Cambridge University Press, 1986), 185.

50. Founded in Montevideo in 1939 by Carlos Quijano and headed by him until its close in 1974, *Marcha* in the 1960s was a combative cultural, literary, and political magazine oriented toward the emerging politics of *tercerismo*. On the history of *Marcha*, see Emir Rodríguez Monegal, *Literatura uruguaya del medio siglo* (Montevideo: Alfa, 1966), 22–46; Luisa Peirano Basso, Marcha *de Montevideo y la formación de la conciencia latinoamericana a través de sus cuadernos* (Buenos Aires: Javier Vergara Editor, 2001); Pablo Rocca, *35 años en* Marcha: *Crítica y literatura en* Marcha *y en el Uruguay, 1939–1974* (Montevideo: División Cultura, Intendencia Municipal de Montevideo, 1992); and Mabel Moraña and Horacio Machín, eds., Marcha *y América Latina* (Pittsburgh, Penn.: Instituto Internacional de Literatura Iberoamericana, 2003). Salvador de Madariaga suggested the name *Mundo Nuevo* to Rodríguez Monegal. Emir Rodríguez Monegal to Luis Guillermo Piazza, 31 January 1966, ERM Papers, box 12, folder 13, Princeton.

51. Alfred Mac Adam and Emir Rodríguez Monegal, "The Boom: A Retrospective," *Review: Latin American Literature and Arts,* no. 33 (September–December 1984): 31. Hunt to Mercier, 2 October 1964, IACF, series VI, box 4, folder 10, UC/SCRC; Mudrovcic, Mundo Nuevo, 11–12.

52. Miller had met Neruda at the PEN Conference in Bled and had promised to help him obtain a visa. Since typically this sort of active campaign was necessary to overcome State Department resistance, Miller's lobbying was responsible for securing permission for Neruda to attend. Feinstein, *Pablo Neruda,* 341–343.

53. Carlos Fuentes, "'El P.E.N.: Entierro de la Guerra Fría en la literatura,'" *Life en Español* 28, no. 3 (1 August 1966): 54–59. Deborah Cohn, "PEN and the Sword: U.S. Latin American Cultural Diplomacy and the 1966 PEN Club Congress," in *Hemispheric American Studies,* ed. Caroline F. Levander and Robert S. Levine (New Brunswick, N.J.: Rutgers University Press, 2008), 206–222.

54. Judith A. Weiss, Casa de las Américas: *An Intellectual Review in the Cuban Revolution* (Chapel Hill, N.C.: Estudios de Hispanófila, 1977), 48; King, Sur, 185; Van Gosse, *Where the Boys Are: Cuba, Cold War America and the Making of a New Left* (London: Verso, 1993), 151; Jorge Edwards, *Adiós, poeta . . . : Memorias* (Barcelona: Tusquets Editores, 1990), 92.

55. Carlos Fuentes and Emir Rodríguez Monegal, "Situación del escritor en América Latina," *Mundo Nuevo* 1, no. 1 (July 1966): 21. For more on how *Mundo Nuevo* used aesthetic experimentation to shift the definition of commitment toward that of the "independent" intellectual, see Russell Cobb, "The Politics of Literary Prestige: Promoting the Latin American 'Boom' in the Pages of *Mundo Nuevo*," *A Contracorriente* 5, no. 3 (Spring 2008): 84.

56. On anti-intellectualism in Cuba and the pro-Cuban left, see Claudia Gilman, *Entre la pluma y el fusil: Debates y dilemas del escritor revolucionario en América Latina* (Buenos Aires: Siglo Veintiuno, 2003), 151–187.

57. Roberto Fernández Retamar, "Los dichos y los hechos: Cartas vistas," *Marcha,* no. 1295 (11 March 1966): 29.

58. Emir Rodríguez Monegal, "Los dichos y los hechos: Cartas vistas," *Marcha,* no. 1296 (18 March 1966): 29. Draper's criticism was that the Dominican invasion was a betrayal of the Latin American Democratic Left. Its expanded version was published as Theodore Draper, *The Dominican Revolt: A Case Study in American Policy* (New York: Commentary Reports, 1968). Roberto Fernández Retamar, "Los dichos y los hechos: Cartas vistas," *Marcha,* no. 1296 (18 March 1966): 29. Fernández Retamar was referring to Theodore Draper, *Castro's Revolution: Myths and Realities* (New York: Praeger, 1962). Emir Rodríguez Monegal, "Cartas vistas (III)," *Marcha,* no. 1302 (6 May 1966): 29; "La CIA: ¿Cerebro Político o Chivo Emisario?," *Marcha,* no. 1302 (6 May 1966): 16–18.

59. "Electronic Prying Grows," *New York Times,* 27 April 1966, 28; Luis Mercier Vega, "Carta circular No. 24," 29 April 1966, IACF, series VI, box 8, folder 12, UC/SCRC; Murena to Mercier, 23 May 1966, IACF, series VI, box 7, folder 1, box 7, UC/SCRC; Benito Milla to Mercier, 28 June 1966, IACF, series VI, box 7, folder 12, UC/SCRC.

60. Jean Franco, *The Decline and Fall of the Lettered City: Latin America in the Cold War* (Cambridge, Mass.: Harvard University Press, 2002), 45; Mac Adam and Rodríguez Monegal, "Boom," 30–36.

61. Rita Guibert, "Neruda: 'Adoro a Nueva York, aunque yo no viviría en ella,'" *Life en Español* 28, no. 3 (1 August 1966): 60–61; Pablo Neruda, *Memoirs: Confieso que he vivido* (New York: Farrar, Straus and Giroux, 1977), 325; Jorge Edwards, *Persona Non Grata: A Memoir of Disenchantment with the Cuban Revolution,* trans. Andrew Hurley (New York: Nation Books, 2004), 36; Edwards, *Adios, poeta,* 148–150. The letter is excerpted in Silber, *Voices of National Liberation,* 44.

62. Edwards to Neruda, 8 July 1966 and Neruda to Edwards, 3 August 1966, in Pablo Neruda and Jorge Edwards, *Correspondencia entre Pablo Neruda y Jorge Edwards: Cartas que romperemos de inmediato y recordaremos siempre,* ed. Abraham Quezada Vergara (Santiago, Chile: Alfaguara, 2008), 79–83. Pablo Neruda, "La Barcarola (fragmentos)," *Mundo Nuevo,* no. 4 (October 1966): 19–22.

63. Roberto Fernández Retamar to María Rosa Oliver, 19 May 1966, and Fernández Retamar to Oliver, 6 October 1966, María Rosa Oliver Papers, box 2, folder 59, Princeton.

64. "Presentación," *Mundo Nuevo* 1, no. 1 (July 1966): 4.

65. Quoted in Mudrovcic, Mundo Nuevo, 47; Max Aub, *Diarios,* ed. Manuel Aznar Soler, vol. 3 (Mexico City: CONACULTA, 2000), 47.

66. Emir Rodríguez Monegal to Homero Alsina Thevenet, 7 March 1967 and 21 March 1967, IACF, series VI, box 26, folder 10, UC/SCRC.

67. Michael Warner, "Sophisticated Spies: CIA's Links to Liberal Anti-Communists, 1949–1967," *International Journal of Intelligence and Counterintelligence* 9, no. 4 (Winter 1996): 426. See also Rhodri Jeffreys-Jones, *The CIA and American Democracy,* 3rd ed. (New Haven, Conn.: Yale University Press, 2003), 153–164; and Cord Meyer, *Facing Reality: From World Federalism to the CIA* (Washington, D.C.: University Press of America, 1982), 93. Thomas W. Braden, "I'm Glad the CIA Is 'Immoral,' " *Saturday Evening Post,* 20 May 1967, 10. Other Cold War liberals, like William Bundy, similarly argued that funding had to be covert because right-wingers in the U.S. Congress would oppose funding to foreign social democrats. Kai Bird, *The Color of Truth: McGeorge Bundy and William Bundy, Brothers in Arms; A Biography* (New York: Simon & Schuster, 1998), 160.

68. Peter Coleman, *The Liberal Conspiracy: The Congress for Cultural Freedom and the Struggle for the Mind of Postwar Europe* (New York: Free Press, 1989), 276. Luis Mercier Vega to Horacio Daniel Rodríguez, 11 December 1967, IACF, series VI, box 8, folder 15, UC/SCRC; Emir Rodríguez Monegal, "Diario del P.E.N. Club," *Mundo Nuevo,* no. 4 (October 1966): 51.

69. Emir Rodríguez Monegal, "La CIA y los intelectuales," *Mundo Nuevo,* no. 14 (August 1967): 19.

70. Emir Rodríguez Monegal to Pierre Emmanuel, 2 July 1967, IACF, series VI, box 11, folder 5, UC/SCRC; "El proceso de la corrupción," *Marcha,* no. 1344 (10 March 1967): 16–21; Gerard Sandoz, "Más revelaciones sobre la CIA,"

Marcha, no. 1354 (27 May 1967): 23; quoted, for consistency, from the English translation in Roberto Fernández Retamar, *Caliban, and Other Essays* (Minneapolis: University of Minnesota Press, 1989), 49. Mario Vargas Llosa, "Epitafio para un imperio cultural," *Marcha,* no. 1354 (27 May 1967): 31.

7. Disenchantment and the End of the Cultural Cold War

1. Haydée Santamaría to Mario Vargas Llosa, 14 May 1971, Mario Vargas Llosa Papers, box 6, section IIIA, folder 6, Firestone Library, Princeton University, Princeton, N.J.
2. Mario Vargas Llosa, *Contra viento y marea, 1962–1982* (Barcelona: Seix Barral, 1983), 134–135.
3. Emir Rodríguez Monegal to Homero Alsina Thevenet, 5 October 1967, Emir Rodríguez Monegal (ERM) Papers, box 1, folder 10, Firestone Library, Princeton.
4. Diana Sorensen, *A Turbulent Decade Remembered: Scenes from the Latin American Sixties* (Stanford, Calif.: Stanford University Press, 2007), 3; Efraín Kristal, *Temptation of the Word: The Novels of Mario Vargas Llosa* (Nashville: Vanderbilt University Press, 1998), 70; Max Weber, *From Max Weber: Essays in Sociology,* ed. and trans. H. H. Gerth and C. Wright Mills (New York: Oxford University Press, 1946), 139.
5. Bell to Botsford, 24 May 1967, ERM Papers, box 2, folder 23, Princeton. There were persistent questions about a 1958 essay by Dwight Macdonald titled "America! America!" that had been accepted and then rejected under pressure at *Encounter.* The essay was later published in other CCF magazines, as well in the unaffiliated *Dissent.* But there were also other examples of editorial intervention, well chronicled in Frances Stonor Saunders, *The Cultural Cold War: The CIA and the World of Arts and Letters* (New York: New Press, 2000), 314–326.
6. Botsford to Bell, 26 May 1967, ERM Papers, box 2, folder 23, Princeton; Botsford to Emir Rodríguez Monegal, 25 May 1967, ERM Papers, folder 23, box 2, Princeton. The full context was: "Mr. [Thomas W.] Braden [in "I'm Glad the CIA Is 'Immoral' "] mentioned two people he had planted in the Congress. I am certain that the other one is not John Hunt, whom I have known the better part of my life and whom I believe incapable of lying to me with such cold consistency. I brought the subject to him many times on a purely personal basis and have been assured that it is not the case." He, like many others, thought that Melvin Lasky was the other person to whom Braden referred. On the other hand, in his letter to Bell, composed the next day, he wrote in the margin: "I have some 'direct' evidence of John's longstanding links with the CIA—from the one agent in London I know personally," showing that Botsford investigated Hunt when he could and was aware of intelligence interest in the CCF but was not sure how to deal with what he learned.
7. Luis Mercier Vega, "Carta circular no. 46," 21 February 1967, International Association for Cultural Freedom Papers (IACF), series VI, box 10, folder 3, Joseph L. Regenstein Library, University of Chicago Special Collections

Research Center (UC/SCRC), Chicago; Horacio Daniel Rodríguez to Mercier, 24 February 1967, IACF, series VI, box 8, folder 17, UC/SCRC; Hunt to Mercier, 8 March 1967, IACF, series VI, box 10, folder 3, UC/SCRC; Mercier to Horacio Daniel Rodríguez, 1 March 1967, IACF, series VI, box 8, folder 17, UC/SCRC.

8. Milla to Mercier, 2 May 1967, IACF, series VI, box 9, folder 8, UC/SCRC; Rodrigo García Treviño, "La C.I.A. et Le Congrès pour la Liberté de la Culture," n.d., IACF, series VI, box 9, folder 10, UC/SCRC.

9. Hunt to Mercier, 9 October 1968, IACF, series VI, box 10, folder 16, UC/SCRC; Mercier to Hunt, 15 October 1968, IACF, series VI, box 10, folder 16, UC/SCRC.

10. Mercier to Luis Guillermo Piazza, 28 October 1966, IACF, series VI, box 7, folder 8, UC/SCRC.

11. Mercier to Stone, 18 October 1967, IACF, series VI, box 10, folder 13, UC/. SCRC; Ignacio Iglesias, Report on "Mundo Nuevo," 15 November 1967, IACF, series VI, box 10, folder 13, UC/SCRC. Iglesias gives circulation figures of 8,900 for *Cuadernos* under Gorkin, 5,000 for *Cuadernos* under Arciniegas, and 5,000 for *Mundo Nuevo* (including 1,000 subscriptions "inherited" from *Cuadernos*).

12. Emir Rodríguez Monegal, "A propósito de 'Mundo Nuevo,'" *Mundo Nuevo*, no. 25 (July 1968): 93; Rodríguez Monegal to Homero Alsina Thenevet, 30 May 1968, IACF, series VI, box 26, folder 10, UC/SCRC.

13. Daniel Cosío Villegas to Shepard Stone, 13 May 1968, IACF, series VI, box 11, folder 8, UC/SCRC; Rodríguez to Mercier Vega, 26 June 1968, IACF, series VI, box 11, folder 4, UC/SCRC; Horacio Daniel Rodríguez, "Una nueva etapa," *Mundo Nuevo*, nos. 26–27 (August/September 1968): 1; Cosío Villegas is quoted in María Eugenia Mudrovcic, *"Mundo Nuevo": Cultura y guerra fría en la década del 60* (Rosario, Argentina: Beatriz Viterbo Editora, 1997), 110.

14. Fred Goff, ed., "Commission on Free Elections in the Dominican Republic report," April [?] 1966, Norman Thomas Papers, reel 67, frame 350, New York Public Library; Juan Bosch, "El porvenir de América Latina," *Mundo Nuevo*, no. 13 (July 1967): 57–61.

15. The grant allotted $1.5 million for 1967, $1.3 million for 1968, $1.1 million in 1969 and 1970, and $1 million in 1971 and 1972. Volker Rolf Berghahn, *America and the Intellectual Cold Wars in Europe: Shepard Stone between Philanthropy, Academy, and Diplomacy* (Princeton, N.J.: Princeton University Press, 2001), 240. These quantities were reduced to $900,000 for 1970, $750,000 for 1971, and $600,000 for 1972. Fiscal years began in November, so the payment for 1967, for instance, was disbursed in late 1966. ILARI received $320,000 in 1967, $250,000 in 1968, and $200,000 in 1969 and 1970. Mercier to Shepard Stone, 3 January 1969, IACF, series VI, box 13, folder 2, UC/SCRC. Money for *Aportes* and *Cadernos Brasileiros* was allocated separately, as it was for *Mundo Nuevo*. *Mundo Nuevo* was given a three-year, $225,000 grant in 1968. Howard R. Dressner to Shepard Stone, 22 April 1968, PA68–335, Ford Foundation Archives (FFA), New York. E. J.

Hobsbawm, *Interesting Times: A Twentieth-Century Life* (London: Allen Lane, 2002), 369; Louis Mercier Vega, *Roads to Power in Latin America* (New York: Praeger, 1969), 24–25.

16. Luis Mercier Vega, "The Myth of the Guerrilla," *Dissent,* May–June 1968, 20–21. Mercier Vega's analysis holds up well for the "first generation" of guerrillas in Latin America but not so well for the second. Timothy P. Wickham-Crowley, *Guerrillas and Revolution in Latin America: A Comparative Study of Insurgents and Regimes since 1956* (Princeton, N.J.: Princeton University Press, 1992), 26–28.

17. Mercier Vega, *Roads to Power in Latin America,* 3, 200. In the anarchist tradition, the "United States is not a model" essay argued that Latin American development required coparticipation and self-government, free from the intervention of the state. Fernando Guillén Martínez, "Los Estados Unidos y América Latina," *Aportes,* no. 7 (January 1968): 4–28; Orlando Fals Borda, "Ciencia y compromiso: Problemas metodológicos del libro 'La subversión en Colombia,'" *Aportes,* no. 8 (April 1968): 117–128; Aldo Solari, "Algunas reflexiones sobre el problema de los valores, la objetividad y el compromiso en las ciencias sociales," *Aportes,* no. 13 (July 1969): 6–24; Orlando Fals Borda, "La crisis social y la orientación sociológica: Una réplica," *Aportes,* no. 15 (January 1970): 62–76; Aldo Solari, "Usos y abusos de la sociología: Una dúplica," *Aportes,* no. 19 (January 1971): 42–53. Narrative report on International Association for Cultural Freedom for 1970, 15 March 1971, p. 18, PA57–395, FFA. Other participants included Edward Shils, S. N. Eisenstadt, Kalman Silvert, Richard Morse, Oscar Lewis, Paul Goodman, Florestan Fernandes, Fernando Henrique Cardoso, Celso Furtado, Domingo Rivarola, and Aldo Solari.

18. Kalman Silvert to Luis Mercier Vega, 26 February 1971, PA68–335, FFA; Luis Mercier Vega, "Desaparición del ILARI," *Aportes,* no. 26 (October 1972): 4; "Obituary," *Interrogations,* no. 13 (January 1978): 4. Mercier Vega's suicide was probably spurred by the natural death of his unmarried partner, Eliane Casserini, who had assisted with much of his work with the CCF. Roselyne Chenu, interview by the author, Chicago, Ill., 2 November 2006.

19. Irwin Silber, *Voices of National Liberation: The Revolutionary Ideology of the "Third World" Expressed by Intellectuals and Artists at the Cultural Congress of Havana, January 1968* (Brooklyn, N.Y.: Central Book Company, 1970), 124, 267, 325; David Craven, *Art and Revolution in Latin America, 1910–1990* (New Haven, Conn.: Yale University Press, 2002), 75.

20. Heberto Padilla, *Fuera del juego* (Lima: Ecoma, 1968), 5, 8–9. Some of the poems in *Fuera del juego* had been published earlier, even in *Casa de las Américas* and other official magazines, without incident. Part of the reason for the sudden reproach seems to have been that Padilla had defended Guillermo Cabrera Infante's work *Tres tristes tigres* in the pages of *El Caimán Barbudo,* and Cabrera Infante had been declared a traitor to the revolution. Fernández Retamar is quoted in Kristal, *Temptation of the Word,* 71.

21. René Dumont, *Is Cuba Socialist?* (London: Deutsch, 1974); Jorge Edwards, *Persona Non Grata: A Memoir of Disenchantment with the Cuban Revolution,*

trans. Andrew Hurley (New York: Nation Books, 2004), 17. Oscar Lewis to Carleton Beals, 14 September 1961, Oscar Lewis Papers, box 55, folder "Beals," University of Illinois, Urbana-Champaign; John Womack, "An American in Cuba," *New York Review of Books,* 4 August 1977, 25–29; Oscar Lewis, Ruth M. Lewis, and Susan M. Rigdon, *Four Men: Living the Revolution; An Oral History of Contemporary Cuba* (Urbana: University of Illinois Press, 1977).

22. Heberto Padilla and Carlos Verdecia, *La mala memoria: Conversación con Heberto Padilla* (Buenos Aires: Kosmos, 1992), 81–89; "Havana Discloses Arrest of Writer," *New York Times,* 2 May 1971, 9; "Text of the Statement," *New York Times,* 22 May 1971, 8; " 'Confessions' of a Cuban Poet," *New York Times,* 26 May 1971, 43; the full text of Padilla's self-criticism was published in *Casa de las Américas* 11, nos. 65–66 (March–June 1971): 191–203.

23. Mario Benedetti, "Las prioridades del escritor," *Casa de las Américas* 12, no. 68 (September–October 1971): 75.

24. Roberto Fernández Retamar, "Calibán," *Casa de las Américas* 12, no. 68 (September–October 1971): 124–151. Roberto Fernández Retamar, *Caliban, and Other Essays* (Minneapolis: University of Minnesota Press, 1989), 30.

25. Criticism of Padilla had first appeared in the Cuban army magazine *Verde Olivo,* which frequently described Guillermo Cabrera Infante as a CIA agent. For example, Leopoldo Avila, "Las respuestas de Caín," *Verde Olivo,* 3 November 1968, 17–18. Fernández Retamar, *Caliban, and Other Essays,* 48–49.

26. Roberto Fernández Retamar, *Cuba defendida* (Buenos Aires: Nuestra América, 2004), 313–320. The period from 1971 to 1976 was known as the *quinquenio gris.* Elzbieta Sklodowska and Ben A. Heller, eds., *Roberto Fernández Retamar y los estudios latinoamericanos* (Pittsburgh, Penn.: Instituto Internacional de Literatura Iberoamericana, Universidad de Pittsburgh, 2000), 156–157. It is difficult to maintain repressive conditions indefinitely, and the environment for artists did improve in the late 1970s. See John M. Kirk and Leonardo Padura Fuentes, *Culture and the Cuban Revolution: Conversations in Havana* (Gainsville: University Press of Florida, 2001). Ángel Rama, *The Lettered City,* trans. John Charles Chasteen (Durham, N.C.: Duke University Press, 1996).

27. On García Márquez and Cuban political prisoners, see Reinol González, *Y Fidel creó el punto X* (Miami: Saeta Ediciones, 1987), 17–30. A few, like the Argentine crime writer Rodolfo Walsh, were radicalized in favor of Cuba by the Padilla affair. He reasoned that if Padilla had been a peasant, no one would have complained. Michael McCaughan, *True Crimes: Rodolfo Walsh* (London: Latin America Bureau, 2002), 164–167.

28. Tanya Harmer, *Allende's Chile and the Inter-American Cold War* (Chapel Hill: University of North Carolina Press, 2011), 36; Robert J. Alexander, *The Tragedy of Chile* (Westport, Conn.: Greenwood Press, 1978), 140–141. As there was CIA support to defeat Allende, so Moscow sent money to Allende directly and to the Chilean Communist Party to support him in 1970. But the

Soviet Union backed away from support of his government. Christopher M. Andrew and Vasili Mitrokhin, *The World Was Going Our Way: The KGB and the Battle for the Third World* (New York: Basic Books, 2005), 71–79; Olga Uliánova, "La Unidad Popular y el golpe militar en Chile: Percepciones y análisis soviéticos," *Estudios Públicos,* no. 79 (Winter 2000): 83–171.

29. The CIA's actions are documented in Peter Kornbluh, *The Pinochet File: A Declassified Dossier on Atrocity and Accountability* (New York: New Press, 2004). How much effect they had will perhaps forever remain a matter of debate; many historians believe that the United States was relatively impotent to influence the course of events. See, for example, Joaquín Fermandois, *Mundo y fin de mundo: Chile en la política mundial, 1900–2004* (Santiago: Ediciones Universidad Católica de Chile, 2005), 333; and Paul E. Sigmund, *The United States and Democracy in Chile* (Baltimore: Johns Hopkins University Press, 1993), 201–212. On Brazil's role, see Tanya Harmer, "Brazil's Cold War in the Southern Cone, 1970–1975," *Cold War History* 12, no. 4 (2012): 659–681. Responsibility for the fall of Allende's government is surely one of the most litigated of historical cases. The ideological rather than pragmatic character of Chile's "centrists" has been identified as an important factor: Arturo Valenzuela, *The Breakdown of Democratic Regimes, Chile* (Baltimore: Johns Hopkins University Press, 1978), 34.

30. The classic case study of the Yarur factory, the first to be seized, is Peter Winn, *Weavers of Revolution: The Yarur Workers and Chile's Road to Socialism* (Oxford: Oxford University Press, 1986). Neruda to "Georgius," 26 November 1972, in Pablo Neruda and Jorge Edwards *Correspondencia entre Pablo Neruda y Jorge Edwards: Cartas que romperemos de inmediato y recordaremos siempre,* ed. Abraham Quezada Vergara (Santiago, Chile: Alfaguara, 2008), 113; Jorge Edwards, *Adios, poeta . . . : Memorias* (Barcelona: Tusquets Editores, 1990), 257.

31. John King, *The Role of Mexico's* Plural *in Latin American Literary and Political Culture: From Tlatelolco to the "Philanthropic Ogre"* (New York: Palgrave Macmillan, 2007), 53–57, 104; Claudia Gilman, *Entre la pluma y el fusil: Debates y dilemas del escritor revolucionario en América Latina* (Buenos Aires: Siglo Veintiuno, 2003), 281–306; Enrique Krauze, *Redeemers: Ideas and Power in Latin America,* trans. Hank Heifetz and Natasha Wimmer (New York: Harper, 2011), 245.

32. Gabriel Zaid, "Enemy Colleagues," *Dissent,* Winter 1982, 17–18. The CIA was interested in trying to recruit Dalton as a double agent, and he had been apprehended and interrogated by the CIA. But there is no evidence that he was recruited. Brian Latell, *Castro's Secrets: Cuban Intelligence, the CIA, and the Assassination of John F. Kennedy* (New York: Palgrave Macmillan, 2013), 114–117.

33. Craven, *Art and Revolution in Latin America,* 117; Salman Rushdie, *The Jaguar Smile: A Nicaraguan Journey* (New York: Picador, 2003), 23.

34. Rushdie, *Jaguar Smile,* xviii; Craven, *Art and Revolution in Latin America,* 137–174.

35. Rushdie, *Jaguar Smile,* xvi. Emphasis in the original.

36. Stephen Kinzer, *Blood of Brothers: Life and War in Nicaragua* (Boston: David Rockefeller Center for Latin American Studies, 2007), 120; Claire Brewster, *Responding to Crisis in Contemporary Mexico: The Political Writings of Paz, Fuentes, Monsiváis, and Poniatowska* (Tucson: University of Arizona Press, 2005), 22. Maarten van Delden, "Polemical Paz," *Literal,* no. 7 (2006): 16–18. Sergio Ramírez, *Adiós muchachos: Una memoria de la revolución sandinista* (San José, Costa Rica: Aguilar, 1999), 288–289; Gioconda Belli, *The Country under My Skin: A Memoir of Love and War* (New York: Anchor Books, 2003), 277.

37. "Coinciden destacados priistas: Imprudentes y torpes las declaraciones del autor de *El hablador,* Vargas Llosa," *El Día,* 1 September 1990; Arnaldo Córdova, "La difícil libertad," *Uno más uno,* 31 August 1990. Bell had laid out his position in Daniel Bell, *The Cultural Contradictions of Capitalism* (New York: Basic Books, 1976). On the trajectory and values of *Vuelta* and its eventual transformation into *Letras Libres* after the death of Paz in 1998, see Ignacio Sánchez Prado, "Claiming Liberalism: Enrique Krauze, *Vuelta, Letras Libres,* and the Reconfiguration of the Mexican Intellectual Class," *Mexican Studies / Estudios Mexicanos* 26, no. 1 (Winter 2010): 47–78.

38. Alma Guillermoprieto, *Looking for History: Dispatches from Latin America* (New York: Pantheon Books, 2001), 166; Mario Vargas Llosa, *A Fish in the Water: A Memoir,* trans. Helen Lane (London: Faber and Faber, 1994), 41–44. In some areas, such as the fight against HIV, Cardoso recognized the limits the markets placed on securing just outcomes. Fernando Henrique Cardoso and Brian Winter, *The Accidental President of Brazil: A Memoir* (New York: PublicAffairs, 2006), 216. On Paz and the Siglo XX conference, see Rafael Lemus, "Octavio Paz o las trampas del liberalismo," *Confabulario de El Universal,* 29 March 2014.

39. One of the most powerful media companies in the world, Televisa maintained a close relationship with the PRI. Celeste González de Bustamante, *"Muy buenas noches": Mexico, Television, and the Cold War* (Lincoln: University of Nebraska Press, 2012).

40. Jorge G. Castañeda, *Utopia Unarmed: The Latin American Left after the Cold War* (New York: Knopf, 1993).

41. Cardoso and Winter, *Accidental President of Brazil,* 113; Jeffrey Puryear, *Thinking Politics: Intellectuals and Democracy in Chile, 1973–1988* (Baltimore: Johns Hopkins University Press, 1994). Those who remained left-wing critics of the Ford Foundation lamented these developments, seeing in them, not incorrectly from their point of view, the creation of an antidictatorial coalition that would not challenge Western liberal market hegemony: James Petras, "The Metamorphosis of Latin America's Intellectuals," *Latin American Perspectives* 17, no. 2 (Spring 1990): 102–112. Julia Preston and Sam Dillon, *Opening Mexico: The Making of a Democracy* (New York: Farrar, Straus and Giroux, 2004), 118–147.

42. Jorge G. Castañeda, "Latin America's Left Turn," *Foreign Affairs* 85, no. 3 (May/June 2006): 28–43.

Conclusion

1. Benjamin Keen, "The Black Legend Revisited: Assumptions and Realities," *Hispanic American Historical Review* 49, no. 4 (November 1969): 717. Keen is clear that elements of the Black Legend preceded even the conquest of the Americas, and that English editions were also reissued for antipapist reasons within England, not just ones of imperial competition.
2. Frank Tannenbaum, "Estados Unidos y América Latina," *Cuadernos,* no. 53 (October 1961): 84.
3. In a rather direct analogy to the publication of Las Casas's work in England, the only foreign book about the Cultural Cold War that has been translated and published in Cuba is the one most critical of the CCF: Frances Stonor Saunders, *La CIA y la Guerra Fría Cultural,* trans. Rafael Fonte (Havana: Editorial de Ciencias Sociales, 2003).
4. Ariel Dorfman and Armand Mattelart, *Para leer al pato Donald: Comunicación de masa y colonialismo* (Buenos Aires: Siglo Veintiuno Editores, 1972), 89.

Acknowledgments

More than half a lifetime ago, as a young man who loved both literature and mathematics, I was captivated by the world Jorge Luis Borges crafted in "The Library of Babel." Borges imagined a possibly infinite library, made up of all possible books of a fixed length and given a fixed number of characters. It is populated by monk-like residents who search out meaning among the gibberish, and who frequently despair. (If all the book permutations were present in the library, the number of books he imagines would easily surpass the number of elementary particles physicists tell us exist in our universe.)

For me, the story has always captured something of the power of actual libraries. It is the simplest of tasks to surround oneself with more knowledge than it would be possible to assimilate in several lifetimes. But now I have written a book, and the entire process seems different than it should be. The monks in Borges's library look for perfect texts, but they know that most readable things they find will be flawed. Yet what would be missing from a randomly generated universal library is the thing that matters most to the production of actual human books: time. What goes between the covers of a book is not simply a collection of words and images, but years in the life of the author that could have been spent doing many things but were devoted instead to producing one very particular work. A library contains knowledge, but it also encloses time—in my case, a decade or so of life, cataloged and shelved.

So this is what I want to say: the years I have spent on this project have been hard ones, but I am happy with the choices that I have made. When this project began, I was young, unmarried, and childless. My wife, Nicole, should know that there is no one with whom I would have rather spent these past years, and my two boys, Isaiah and Julian, should know someday how much joy they have given me. I do not have the words to express how important they have been, but their continued presence has been the most important thing in my life. The care of other members of my families—including many Hammonds, Ibers, and Louies—have made progress on this book possible.

One does not build ideas alone. Among scholars and friends of more or less my own generation, I have benefited greatly from conversations with María Balandrán,

Matt Barton, Pablo Ben, Jake Betz, Ananya Chakravarti, Denali DeGraf, Stuart Easterling, Frederico Freitas, Olga Glondys, James Halliday, Amanda Hartzmark, Darryl Heller, José Ángel Hernández, Ben Johnson, James Kaltreider, Patrick Kelly, Jamie Kreiner, Sam Lebovic, Aiala Levy, Casey Lurtz, Monica Mercado, Calvin Miaw, Nicole Mottier, Raphael Murillo, Sarah Osten, Jaime Pensado, Ben Peters, Ann Schneider, Diana Schwartz, Aaron Shaw, Peter Simons, Antonio Sotomayor, Jackie Sumner, Tess Taylor, Germán Vergara, Matt Vitz, Mikael Wolfe, and Julia Young. Special thanks to Carlos Bravo Regidor, whose interests have overlapped with mine in a way that has made him an especially good interlocutor, as well as a close friend.

Academic conversation is also increasingly taking place on social media, and I am grateful for insights acquired from people whom I have never met in person. This list too could be long, but I would especially like to thank Aaron Bady, Tim Barker, L. D. Burnett, Gerry Canavan, Merlin Chowkwanyun, Paula Daccarett, Robert Greene, Andrew Hartman, Jeet Heer, Matt Hunte, Bill King, Peter Krupa, Noah McCormack, Drew McKevitt, Kurt Newman, Arissa Oh, Kristy Rawson, Linda Rodríguez, Colin Snider, Greg Weeks, Audra Wolfe, Ben Wurgaft, Richard Yeselson, and Brian Zimmerman. A chain of inquiry involving Heer and Yeselson led me to Alan Wald, then to Susan Weissman, and finally to Trotsky's grandson Esteban Volkov, who solved a mystery by identifying Antonio Hidalgo as the man standing next to Trotsky in the photo in Chapter 1.

All historians are indebted to librarians and archivists too numerous to name. I have also had the good fortune to talk to a few of the people who now inhabit these pages. Although I have preferred to rely on the documentary record and have cited these conversations little, I appreciate the time, generosity, and insights of Keith Botsford, Cuauhtémoc Cárdenas (who identified most of the people in the MLN photo in Chapter 5), Roselyne Chenu, Jorge Edwards, John Hunt, Luis B. Prieto, Rob Prince, Raquel Tibol, and Jack Womack. As I have traveled through Argentina, Chile, Mexico, and the Dominican Republic, I have been treated with unfailing courtesy by Matías Bosch, Joaquín Fermandois, Karina Jannello, Jorge Myers, Elisa Servín, Daniela Spenser, and Horacio Tarcus.

Alhough the years during which this project was completed were profession-ally challenging, they have also been rewarding. At the University of Chicago, I was part of a wonderful community of scholars who did more than anyone else to shape the historian I am today. Special thanks go to Dain Borges, Bruce Cum-ings, Emilio Kourí, and especially Mauricio Tenorio for never losing faith or pa-tience. I could not have asked for better teachers. At Stanford, I would like to thank the entire community of scholars at the Humanities Center, and the Mellon Fel-lows more specifically. Thank you to J. P. Daughton and Lanier Anderson for your confidence, and to Zephyr Frank, Jennifer Burns, and Caroline Winterer for your company. A long time ago, Jorge Ruffinelli and Sergio Missana taught a course that helped me think differently about my future. During a few different intervals at Berkeley, I have been deeply grateful for the support of Max Auff-hammer, Richard Cándida-Smith, Margaret Chowning, Brad DeLong, Nils Gilman, Rosemary Joyce, Alan Karras, and Peter Zinoman. Thanks to John Lear and Eric Zolov for their help and insight, to Mark Healey for being a stalwart friend and counselor, and to Arturo García Bustos for the honor of allowing us to use his artwork as a cover image. Thank you to George Hammond for your help with proofreading, among much else. Thank you to my future students and colleagues at the University of Texas at El Paso for the opportunity to work as a part of your community. I have been delighted to work with Harvard University Press, and especially my editor Brian Distelberg. I appreciate his trust in this project and want to thank him and the anonymous reviewers for everything they have done to make the final text as good as possible. Financially, this project could not have been completed without the support of the University of Chicago and its Center for Latin American Studies, the Mellon Foundation, the George C. Marshall Foundation, and a UC-AFT Unit 18 Professional Development grant.

There are a few people without whom the course of my life would have been different and less rewarding. My father helped me learn Spanish at a young age. Mark Mancall steered me toward history and introduced me to the set of problems that I still find fascinating. My interest in what a democratic Left would look like in Latin America has been informed by my time living in El Salvador with John Guiliano, Jon Cortina, S.J., and many other friends. And Alma Guillermoprieto has shown me, among many other things, that even the best of writers must also be a diligent editor.

Finally, the period during which I have worked on this project has been marked by the deaths of two extraordinary people. Before he passed away in 2010, I was fortunate to have known Friedrich Katz. His life intersected with my work—I once stumbled on his father's FBI file, which mentioned a teenage "Federico Katz" living in Mexico—and as we talked about what I was finding in the archives, he helped me think through many issues. He treated me with the same gallantry and respect that he afforded to everyone in his life. He had a warm sense of humor; one of his favorite jokes was the quip "Capitalism is the exploitation of man by man; in Communism, it is the other way around." Katz seems to me to have been a man whose personal and professional life was pledged to bringing about the end of exploitation, irrespective of the political system behind it, and the generous way in which he treated those around him was but one expression of that commitment. He is a constant example.

When my mother passed away unexpectedly in early 2014, it was during a visit to see her new grandson that was also supposed to help me, her son, finish this book. It has been a heartbreaking loss. She had an incredible soul. She was loving and generous, tolerant of my many faults, and supportive of the turns I have taken in my life. She read to me patiently when I was a child and listened to me as I grew up. My mother did not especially care for electoral politics, but she believed deeply in justice and, most especially, in peace. With the hope that the future may hold more of both, I dedicate this book to her memory.

Index

Cabrera Infante, Guillermo, 134, 140, 198, 205, 306n49, 312n25
Cadernos Brasileiros, 180–182, 184–185, 189
Calles, Plutarco Elías, 25–26, 31
Camus, Albert, 1, 4–5, 201, 222
Cardenal, Ernesto, 231
Cárdenas, Cuauhtémoc, 147, 154, 157, 167–168, 170
Cárdenas, Lázaro, 31–34, 40, 71–72, 127, 151; and Leon Trotsky, 36–37, 263n35; and the MLN, 147–148, 165, 167–170, 240; and the WPC, 152–158, 161–165; and the Cuban Revolution, 158–160; and the Tricontinental Conference, 171–172
Cardoso, Fernando Henrique, 1, 176, 233, 236
Caribbean Legion, 96, 99, 121, 129, 134
Carranza, Carlos, 174, 179
Casa de las Américas, 10, 14–17, 131–132, 143, 189–190, 211, 242–243; increasing militancy, 200–201; and the Padilla affair, 221–227, 289n31
Castelo Branco, Humberto, 183–184, 302n20
Castillo Armas, Carlos, 100, 104–105, 115
Castillo Velasco, Jaime, 92–93, 102, 236
Castro, Fidel, 5, 12, 111, 121, 146, 172–173, 206, 221–223, 228, 229, 237; and the anti-Communist Left, 17, 116–118, 122, 123–126, 128–135, 137–140, 243; and the CIA, 119, 129–130, 133, 137, 138–139, 141; on art in revolution, 141–142; and Lázaro Cárdenas, 148, 158–160
Central Intelligence Agency (CIA), 2, 11–12, 54, 83–84, 107, 181, 183, 211, 222, 226, 237; and the anti-Communist Left, 47, 96, 98–99, 228; and the coup in Guatemala, 99–100, 104; and book publishing, 108–109; and Fidel Castro, 119, 129–130, 133, 137, 138–139, 141, 176; and the MLN, 165. *See also* Congress for Cultural Freedom
Centro Mexicano de Escritores, 186–188, 303n26
Chávez, Hugo, 237
Chibás, Eduardo, 123
Chomsky, Noam, 220
Cominform (Communist Information Bureau), 54, 56–58, 60, 62–63, 77, 85, 185

Comintern (Communist International), 19, 22, 26, 28, 30, 36, 39, 54
Committee for Cultural Freedom, 39, 42, 61
Committee in Defense of Leon Trotsky, 37–38
Confederación de Trabajadores de América Latina, 32, 123, 154; and World War II, 42–43; and the Cold War, 55, 96, 99, 164
Confederación de Trabajadores de Cuba, 121–124, 132–133
Confederación de Trabajadores de México, 32, 42, 45–46, 52, 55, 154
Conferencia Latinoamericana por la Soberanía Nacional, la Emancipación Económica y la Paz, 161–165, 171–172
Congress for Cultural Freedom (CCF), 2–3, 13, 16–17, 62, 86–87, 145; and the CIA, 6–7, 12, 14–15, 62, 85, 87, 88–90, 93–94, 177, 178, 196–197, 200, 204–205, 207–210, 212–216, 218, 226–227, 241–242; and U.S. hegemony, 6–7, 16, 18, 85, 90, 241–243; and Spanish exiles in Latin America, 13, 86, 90–91; and antipeace campaigns, 87–92; in Mexico, 87–88, 103, 111–114, 185–190; in Chile, 92–94, 107; and the coup in Guatemala, 99–102, 104–106; and The Future of Freedom conference (Milan, 1955), 101–102; and the Inter-American Conference for Cultural Freedom (Mexico City, 1956), 102–107, 128; and book publishing, 108–109; in Argentina, 108, 179, 192–195; and the Breakaway generation, 111–114; and anti-Neruda campaigns, 111, 191–192, 304n35; and Cuba, 115, 118–119, 126–128, 130–132, 137–139, 140, 141, 180; and reforms in the 1960s, 174, 177–180, 190–191; in Brazil, 180–185; and the Formation of Elites in Latin America conference (Montevideo, 1965), 195–196; and ILARI, 197, 209, 214–217, 219, 220; and the Black Legend, 239, 240–241. See also *Mundo Nuevo*
Conte Agüero, Luis, 125
Cortázar, Julio, 143, 207
Cosío Villegas, Daniel, 197, 217
"Cosmopolitanism," 51, 56–59, 64, 70, 77, 80
Costa Amic, Bartolomeu, 43–44, 109
Coutinho, Afrânio, 181, 184–185

Argentina, 65–68, 70; and the São Paulo State Congress for Peace (São Paulo, 1949), 68–70; in Uruguay, 71; and the Continental Congress for Peace (Mexico City, 1949), 71–76, 87, 153; and socialist realism, 74–76, 77–78, 82; and the Continental Cultural Congress (Santiago, 1953), 76–77, 91–92; and the Mexican Pro-Peace Committee, 78, 149, 151, 153, 157, 169; financing, 78–79,

153–154, 275n54; and the MLN, 147–148, 156–157, 161, 163; and Guatemala, 154; and the Tricontinental Conference, 171–172; black legend of, 239–240, 243

Yupanqui, Atahualpa, 70, 273n38

Zaid, Gabriel, 230
Zhdanov, Andrei, 56, 61, 70, 78